TROUBLING TRANSPARENCY

Lovern

347-244-4120

TROUBLING TRANSPARENCY

THE HISTORY AND FUTURE OF FREEDOM OF INFORMATION

Edited by David E. Pozen
and Michael Schudson

COLUMBIA UNIVERSITY PRESS   NEW YORK

COLUMBIA UNIVERSITY PRESS
Publishers Since 1893
New York   Chichester, West Sussex
cup.columbia.edu

Library of Congress Cataloging-in-Publication Data
Names: Pozen, David E., editor. | Schudson, Michael, editor.
Title: Troubling transparency : the history and future of freedom of
    information / Edited by David Pozen and Michael Schudson.
Description: New York : Columbia University Press, 2018. | Includes index.
Identifiers: LCCN 2017061191 (print) | LCCN 2018000742 (ebook) |
    ISBN 9780231545808 (electronic) | ISBN 9780231184984 (cloth : alk. paper) |
    ISBN 9780231184991 (pbk.)
Subjects: LCSH: United States. Freedom of Information Act. |
    Government information–United States. | Public records–Law
    and legislation–United States.
Classification: LCC KF5753 (ebook) | LCC KF5753 .T76 2018 (print) |
    DDC 342.73/0662–dc23
LC record available at https://lccn.loc.gov/2017061191

Columbia University Press books are printed on permanent
and durable acid-free paper.

Printed in the United States of America
Cover design: Milenda Nan Ok Lee
Cover art: Blend Images / © Alamy

CONTENTS

Acknowledgments   vii

Introduction: Troubling Transparency   1
David E. Pozen and Michael Schudson

PART I FOIA'S HISTORICAL AND CONCEPTUAL FOUNDATIONS

1. How Administrative Opposition Shaped the Freedom
   of Information Act   13
   Sam Lebovic

2. Positive Rights, Negative Rights, and the Right to Know   34
   Frederick Schauer

3. FOIA as an Administrative Law   52
   Mark Fenster

PART II FOIA AND THE NEWS MEDIA

4. The Other FOIA Requesters   73
   Margaret B. Kwoka

5. State FOI Laws: More Journalist-Friendly, or Less?   91
   Katherine Fink

6. FOIA and Investigative Reporting: Who's Asking What, Where,
   and When—and Why It Matters   116
   James T. Hamilton

PART III THEORIZING TRANSPARENCY TACTICS

7. The Ecology of Transparency Reloaded 135
   Seth F. Kreimer

8. Monitoring the U.S. Executive Branch Inside and Out: The Freedom
   of Information Act, Inspectors General, and the Paradoxes
   of Transparency 166
   Nadia Hilliard

9. Output Transparency vs. Input Transparency 187
   Cass R. Sunstein

10. Open Data: The Future of Transparency in the Age of Big Data 206
    Beth Simone Noveck

11. Striking the Right Balance: Weighing the Public Interest in Access
    to Agency Records Under the Freedom of Information Act 226
    Katie Townsend and Adam A. Marshall

PART IV COMPARATIVE PERSPECTIVES

12. The Global Influence of the United States on Freedom
    of Information 249
    Kyu Ho Youm and Toby Mendel

13. Transparency as Leverage or Transparency as Monitoring?
    U.S. and Nordic Paradigms in Latin America 269
    Gregory Michener

14. Structural Corruption and the Democratic-Expansive Model
    of Transparency in Mexico 291
    Irma Eréndira Sandoval-Ballesteros

List of Contributors 311
Index 315

ACKNOWLEDGMENTS

THIS BOOK represents the work of many hands. Most obviously, we are indebted to the contributors who have provided fine papers and have weathered in good spirit our editorial interventions along the way.

Less apparent, we owe much to those who offered moral and financial support for the conference we organized in honor of the fiftieth anniversary of the U.S. Freedom of Information Act. Held at the Columbia Journalism School in June 2016, the two-day event was made possible by a generous gift from Columbia University President Lee Bollinger, who also supplied welcoming remarks. Both of us significantly underestimated how much a conference like this would cost; President Bollinger, fortunately, did not. Bruce Shapiro, executive director of the Dart Center for Journalism and Trauma at the Columbia Journalism School, provided us our first financial assistance and thereby helped us believe that we would indeed be able to pull together an ambitious gathering of journalists, FOIA officers, freedom of information activists, historians, media scholars, and legal scholars. We are grateful also to Dean Steve Coll of Columbia Journalism School, to the Journalism School's Dean of Academic Affairs Sheila Coronel, and to Dean Gillian Lester of Columbia Law School, all of whom endorsed our efforts.

Many other participants in the conference contributed to our own education about freedom of information laws in the United States and elsewhere. Their absence from these pages reflects only that this book is not a "conference proceedings" but rather a collection of the academic (yet nonetheless readable!) papers that were presented in early form at Columbia—along with four other papers that were not part of the event but that, in earlier incarnations, seemed so essential to our thinking about FOIA that we twisted arms to have the authors revise earlier work for presentation here.

There are a great many logistical issues that arise in the planning of an international interdisciplinary conference, and we could not have managed without the stellar assistance of Soomin Seo, then an advanced Ph.D. student in communications at Columbia, now an assistant professor in the Klein College of Media and Communication at Temple University. Kelly Boyce, assistant director of the Dart Center, also provided indispensable support. More recently, Kara Kohn-Gardner assisted with proofreading of the manuscript.

We are very grateful to our editor, Philip Leventhal, for shepherding this project to completion. He has worked wonders to make Columbia University Press a leader in journalism studies and adjacent fields. The whole staff at Columbia University Press has been a pleasure to work with.

We recognize that edited volumes do not make most publishers swoon. Nonetheless, sometimes edited volumes can become important signposts in intellectual life, and we hope that this may be one such case. Taking transparency in governmental affairs seriously, without taking it as a Holy Grail of democracy, is an ongoing scholarly and political task that we hope this book helps advance.

We dedicate this book to our families, whom we love more than we can say.

TROUBLING TRANSPARENCY

INTRODUCTION

Troubling Transparency

David E. Pozen and Michael Schudson

TRANSPARENCY IS a value in the ascendance. Across the globe, the past several decades have witnessed a spectacular explosion of legislative reforms and judicial decisions calling for greater disclosure about the workings of public institutions. Freedom of information laws have proliferated, claims of a constitutional or supra-constitutional "right to know" have become commonplace, and an international transparency lobby has emerged as a civil society powerhouse. Open government is seen today in many quarters as a foundation of, if not synonymous with, good government.

At the same time, a growing number of scholars, advocates, and regulators have begun to raise hard questions about the costs and limits of the transparency movement. Some of these commentators accept the movement's standard premises and prescriptions but worry that open government measures are not actually delivering the openness they promise due to inadequate legislative funding, bureaucratic resistance, or cramped judicial interpretations. Others wonder whether traditional open records and open meetings laws are well suited to twenty-first-century transparency challenges, or whether these laws need to be reimagined for the digital age. A third group of commentators has thrown a harsh light on transparency's political and administrative effects, emphasizing its potential to facilitate "neoliberal" agendas or to undermine deliberation, deal-making, and institutional capacity.

These different strains of skepticism are coalescing and have largely been confined to discrete discourses so far. They have not arrested transparency's ascent in the NGO community or in popular culture. But they have developed to the point where we might say that government transparency, as a democratic ideal, is contested not only in practice but also in theory.

This volume seeks to highlight the richness of these debates and to grapple with some of the complexity and ambivalence that increasingly characterize the best academic writing on transparency. It focuses on the United States Freedom of Information Act (FOIA)—both to contain what might otherwise be an unwieldy inquiry and because FOIA is an especially canonical transparency instrument, one of the ur-texts of the field. The essays collected here ask, in various ways, why FOIA and associated arrangements have come to be seen as troubling; whether that perception is warranted; and, if so, what can be done about it. In asking these questions, the essays themselves trouble the notion that we are reaching durable consensus, or indeed any widespread agreement, with regard to many aspects of open government design.

The overarching objective of this volume, accordingly, is not to advance any particular normative vision or reform program. Quite the opposite. The overarching objective is to deepen our debates about transparency by exploring a range of challenges, possibilities, and contradictions that arise when it is pursued through law. Our hope is that anyone interested in "freedom of information" practices or debates will benefit from being exposed to this diverse set of perspectives.

FOIA'S FIFTIETH AND THE ORIGINS OF THIS BOOK

After years of legislative debate, FOIA was enacted by the U.S. Congress in the summer of 1966 and took effect one year later. The Kingdom of Sweden had created the world's original freedom of information (FOI) law two centuries earlier. The U.S. statute was among the first such laws developed for the modern age of administrative government.

FOIA was, and still is, a strikingly bold piece of legislation in some respects. It allows "any person"—including both legal persons, such as corporations, and foreigners—to request any federal agency record for any reason. Agencies are required to turn over responsive records within weeks. If an agency believes a requested record or a portion thereof ought to be withheld under one of FOIA's nine exemptions, the burden is on the agency to justify that withholding, and courts are instructed to review such justifications without deference. Users of the law pay only a small fraction of the costs the government incurs in fulfilling their requests.

By 1990, a dozen-odd countries had followed the American example in adopting FOI measures of their own. By 2016, that number had mushroomed to more than one hundred. The FOIA model has been updated and refined many times over during this process of policy diffusion as countries have built on, or departed from, various components of the U.S. law in developing their own versions. Even so, virtually all of the world's FOI laws replicate FOIA's basic features, "including the focus on official records; affordance of access rights to any individual or association; reliance on private requests to trigger disclosure obligations; independent or quasi-independent review of denial decisions; and exemptions for the protection of national security, public safety, personal privacy, commercial secrets, and internal deliberations."[1] The FOIA model has become so prevalent that it is difficult to have a conversation about government transparency today without adverting to it.

This book grows out of a conference the two of us organized at Columbia University in the summer of 2016 to honor the fiftieth anniversary of FOIA's enactment. One goal we had in bringing together dozens of FOIA experts of different stripes—with scholars, journalists, advocates, and administrators all represented—was commemorative in nature. We wished to applaud FOIA's achievements and to mark an important milestone in U.S. legal and cultural history.

Also, and more important, we saw FOIA's fiftieth anniversary as an occasion for critical reflection. This anniversary, it seemed to us, created an opportunity and a responsibility to consider the ways in which the statutory regime has evolved and the extent to which it has or has not been serving its founding goals; to consider FOIA's relationship to other laws and policies within the larger "ecology of transparency," as Seth Kreimer (chapter 7) calls it; and to consider how FOIA might be improved in the years ahead. These critical aspirations are represented, in a wide range of views, by the essays gathered here, many of them presented in a preliminary form at the conference.

Interpreting FOIA's past and present is no simple matter. On some dimensions, the FOIA regime appears to be thriving. The law itself has proven highly resilient to legislative retrenchment: most of the amendments Congress has passed since 1966 have sought to make the requesting process easier or more effective. Usage rates continue to climb, with over 700,000 requests submitted to federal agencies in fiscal year 2015.[2] There is a substantial FOIA bar and an increasingly professionalized FOIA workforce, as well as a robust coalition of journalists, advocacy groups, and businesses that promote and defend the law. In the broader culture, too, FOIA has assumed a quasi-constitutional if not quasi-sacred status, becoming, in the words of President Obama, a symbol of the United States' "profound national commitment to ensuring an open Government."[3] And, as already noted, FOIA-style laws can now be found not only in all fifty U.S. states but also in most nation-states. FOIA, in short, has conquered the world, not so much through its specific details as by giving the ideal of transparency practical form and demonstrating the potential of a user-generated process for information disclosure.

Yet, on other dimensions, FOIA appears to be not flourishing but floundering, even in a state of crisis. The U.S. House of Representatives Committee on Oversight and Government Reform issued a scathing report in 2016 titled, simply, "FOIA Is Broken."[4] Echoing a set of complaints that have long dogged the act, the report found that FOIA is "systematically broken" on account of severe processing delays, overuse of exemptions, and other barriers to accessing records. To be sure, there may have been an element of partisan grandstanding to this report, which Republican representatives used to criticize the Obama administration. A 2004 report by House Democrats had accused the Bush administration of "not only sucking the spirit out of the FOIA, but shriveling its very heart."[5] "FOIA Is Broken" nevertheless tapped into a deep well of frustration, generated not just by response deadlines that are routinely missed (and in some cases patently unrealistic in light of congressionally allocated resource levels) but also by the extraordinary deference many courts seem to afford to withholding agencies, notwithstanding the statutory standard of zero deference ("de novo" review); by the law's limited reach into the national security state, where millions upon millions of classified documents reside; and by the predominance of commercial requesters and the apparent distortions of FOIA's public purposes that follow.

Without doubt, FOIA is a tremendously important statute that has done some tremendously important things in its first fifty years. It is also a markedly inefficient, adversarial, and corporate-friendly response to the postwar rise of official secrecy, and one that interacts in complicated ways with the U.S. system of governance. The Columbia conference reinforced our conviction that FOIA defies easy assessment. Students of transparency, we believe, should strive to appreciate what has been working well in this iconic transparency regime while remaining open to reconsidering, and possibly supplementing or even supplanting, parts of the FOIA model that have not been working so well. These sorts of inquiries require, in turn, that we connect our debates on FOIA to broader debates on open government law, policy, and theory, both at home and abroad.

RESPECTING AND REFLECTING ON TRANSPARENCY— WITHOUT ROMANTICIZING IT

The title of this volume suggests correctly that we do not see transparency, either in society at large or with respect to government specifically, as an unalloyed good or an overriding objective in a democracy. Certain forms of transparency may be a prerequisite for the effective exercise of human rights or the flourishing of political discourse, among other goods. But the provision of transparency also can have deleterious impacts. Free citizens require privacy and security, both of which require some amount of secrecy. A growing body of evidence suggests that effective negotiation and decision-making within political institutions requires the same.[6] The idea that transparency is nonetheless the sort of value that ought to be maximized in a liberal democracy is a piety that, at best, hinders clear thinking and, at worst, smuggles in antigovernment biases on the sly.

Has the Freedom of Information Act improved the operation of democracy in the United States? One of us has become increasingly skeptical about this. Pozen has argued in recent work that FOIA's request-and-respond model— identified by Gregory Michener (chapter 13) as an archetype of the Transparency-as-Leverage Paradigm—"empowers opponents of regulation, distributes government goods in a regressive fashion, and contributes to a culture of contempt surrounding the domestic policy bureaucracy while insulating the national security state from similar scrutiny."[7] Some of these effects, as Sam Lebovic demonstrates (chapter 1), were anticipated by agencies such as the Department of Health, Education, and Welfare in the early 1960s when the law was still being conceived in Congress. Over time, Pozen suggests, FOIA may have come "to legitimate the lion's share of government secrecy while delegitimating and debilitating government itself."[8] Even if FOIA represented a progressive breakthrough at its creation, the rise of mass communications technologies, statutory reporting requirements, whistleblower protection laws, external watchdog groups, and internal oversight mechanisms, among other developments, has changed the act's practical and normative meaning.

Schudson, on the other hand, feels more confident that FOIA has improved democracy, especially in concert with other transparency-producing mechanisms (Nadia Hilliard [chapter 9] and Beth Noveck [chapter 10] examine two others, and Kreimer [chapter 7] explores the overall transparency environment). The importance of a law is not necessarily to be measured by who uses it most (in the case of FOIA, the answer Margaret Kwoka establishes is often "corporations" [chapter 4]) but by whether its central purposes are being advanced at reasonable cost. In Schudson's estimation, FOIA's benefits in terms of public knowledge and government accountability plausibly outweigh its costs in terms of taxpayer dollars, bureaucratic hassle, and misleading messages that corruption, malfeasance, and mismanagement are especially endemic to government rather than phenomena that are just as likely—or possibly even more likely—to be found in organizations dedicated to private or partisan ends.[9]

Many transparency advocates would take Schudson's points further. Given the lack of a general "right to know" in the United States, FOIA can be seen as an achievement of constitutional magnitude (the extent to which FOIA is or is not fungible with a constitutional guarantee is explored by Mark Fenster [chapter 3] and Frederick Schauer [chapter 2]). Dating back to the earliest efforts to craft FOIA in the 1950s, some of the statute's staunchest friends have been members of the news media. In this volume, their faith in a judicially enforceable right to seek agency records may seem vindicated by Kreimer's (chapter 7) review of the disclosures about the "global war on terror" under President George W. Bush that were made possible by FOIA requests from news organizations and civil liberties groups. It is hard to ignore the important role of FOIA in enhancing public understanding of these secretive operations and the abuses they inflicted. The standard case for FOIA is likewise supported by James Hamilton's (chapter 6) innovative collection of data on the frequency with which prize-winning investigative journalism has made use of FOI requests at the state or federal level. It is further fleshed out, and complicated, in the argument advanced by Katie Townsend and Adam Marshall (chapter 11) that FOIA should be revised to encourage greater disclosure of information that falls within one of its exemptions. For Townsend and Marshall, FOIA is already an indispensable tool for journalism, but it could be made more valuable still if Congress followed the lead of countries such as Australia, Belgium, India, Ireland, Japan, Mexico, New Zealand, South Africa, and the United Kingdom in creating a "public interest" override.

Other proposals to revise FOIA could have even more far-reaching implications. Cass Sunstein (chapter 9) calls for much more aggressive and systematic disclosure concerning government "outputs," yet much more reticence about disclosure when it comes to government "inputs." Noveck (chapter 10) sketches a vision of a future in which "open data" policies, and the public-private collaborations they facilitate, are the major engine of government transparency, with FOIA transitioned into a supporting role. Kyu Ho Youm and Toby Mendel (chapter 12) highlight a number of ways in which the U.S. FOIA falls short of certain foreign counterparts as a transparency tool, and they recommend that U.S. legislators borrow "best practices" on issues such as the scope of public authorities covered (the U.S. FOIA covers only executive branch agencies and does not reach Congress, the courts, or government contractors) and the availability of independent administrative review. Writing in a more critical vein, Irma Sandoval-Ballesteros (chapter 14) offers a cautionary tale about recent experiences in Mexico—whose FOI law is often hailed as the international gold standard—and urges that FOI laws be revamped to reach powerful private entities as well as government bodies.

Despite our disagreements, the two of us draw inspiration and insight from each of these analyses. Along with their authors, we agree that the Freedom of Information Act matters enough to deserve serious scholarly attention, not just gauzy expressions of praise or exasperated anecdotes of delays and denials. Even though we resist romanticizing FOIA, we agree that there is a symbolic nobility to the law and its guarantee that "any person" can demand that the government disclose information. We agree that the tendency of some transparency commentary to pit "the people and their friends in civil society" (the good guys) versus "the government" (the presumed bad guys until proven otherwise) is the wrong way to think about a vibrant democracy. In that spirit, we agree with Sandoval-Ballesteros that transparency advocates should be concerned about a potentially debilitating "anti–public sector bias" to U.S.-style FOI laws, and with Kwoka that they should be concerned about the skew in FOIA usage toward requesters who have no public-regarding purpose. We agree that both the more radical and the more conventional reform proposals articulated in this volume merit consideration. And on all of these issues, we agree that it helps to see FOIA in light of comparable laws developed by the fifty states (as taken up by Katherine Fink [chapter 5]) and by other countries (as taken up in Sandoval-Ballesteros's assessment of Mexico, in Youm and Mendel's global survey, and in Michener's study of Latin American legislation).

We do not resolve any of these issues here, but we air them. We invite readers to examine them collectively as well as individually to see the variety of ways of thinking about open government. With the assistance of organizations such as the American Society of Access Professionals, lively discussions among journalists, media advocacy groups, and FOIA administrators have been taking place for years now. There is a much less unified discussion about transparency in the law schools and among historians and political scientists. We bring together these disparate strands of scholarship in pursuit of a broader understanding of what we have in FOIA, and what we can and should wish for in structuring the place of information in a twenty-first-century democracy.

PLAN OF THE BOOK

The volume turns first, in part I, to "FOIA's Historical and Conceptual Foundations." In his study of executive branch opposition to FOIA in the 1950s and 1960s, Lebovic draws on original archival research to illustrate how agencies did not see FOIA as a serious threat to national security but *did* see it as a threat to their ability to develop sound public policy and to their capacity to regulate the economy. These concerns, in Lebovic's telling, foreshadowed the "uneven effectiveness" of FOIA following its passage and reveal important assumptions about the relationship between the state and the public that helped shape the law's design.

The next two chapters explore another fundamental feature of FOIA's original design: that it was created by ordinary legislation rather than a constitutional amendment or judicial interpretation of the First Amendment. Schauer looks at FOIA through the lens of the theory of rights and suggests that it can be seen as "remedying" the absence of a positive right to government information in the U.S. Constitution. Fenster explains that transparency advocates have generally assumed that a constitutional right would be better. Both Schauer and Fenster put pressure on this assumption, although in different ways. Schauer gives reasons to believe that a statutory approach is in fact superior, whereas Fenster gives reasons to doubt that the constitutional/nonconstitutional distinction matters much in this area—or, indeed, that many of the goals of the freedom of information movement are attainable.

Part II considers the relationship between "FOIA and the News Media." The architects of FOIA hoped and assumed that professional journalists would be the leading acquirers and interpreters of agency records. That is not how things have turned out. Kwoka documents the remarkable scope of commercial requesting under FOIA, as well as the prevalence of "first-person" requesting by individuals seeking information about themselves. Fink documents a similar surfeit of commercial requesters at the state level. Hamilton finds that government records requests have contributed to many significant investigative stories but that the media's use of FOI laws has been declining over time, especially for local newspapers. Alarmed by these developments,

Kwoka, Fink, and Hamilton each propose reforms that might invigorate journalists' relationship to transparency law.

Part III, on "Theorizing Transparency Tactics," zooms out to consider FOIA's relationship to other disclosure policies and to emerging trends in the transparency field. Arguing against critics (including Pozen) who have questioned FOIA's democratic value, Kreimer draws on case studies from the early 2000s to highlight ways in which FOIA can support other transparency and accountability mechanisms even when a records request is denied or an appeal rejected. Hilliard complicates the place of FOIA in this ecology of transparency by looking at the paradoxical role of bureaucrats and experts in managing, interpreting, and narrating the enormous volumes of information that are generated by both FOIA and the inspector general system.

The remaining chapters in this section are more reform-minded. Sunstein draws a distinction between disclosure about government outputs (regulations, policies, findings, and the like) and government inputs (information about the deliberative process) and proposes a reorientation of transparency law to prioritize the former. Noveck reviews and extols the rise of the "open data" movement—a movement to which she has made significant contributions—as an alternative approach to transparency that is organized around problem-solving rather than accountability per se. Going forward, Noveck suggests, FOIA and open data policies ought to be harmonized much more closely than they are currently. Townsend and Marshall diagnose a problem *within* FOIA doctrine in the lack of a balancing test that would require disclosure of otherwise exempt records when the public interest in their release strongly outweighs the government's interest in withholding them. The experience of foreign FOI regimes, according to Townsend and Marshall, suggests that such a balancing test would be workable and beneficial.

Building on this discrete cross-national inquiry, part IV offers several broader "Comparative Perspectives" on FOI law. Youm and Mendel use the global Right to Information (RTI) rating system to investigate the extent to which other countries have or have not followed the U.S. FOIA's approach; they find that foreign FOI laws frequently incorporate elements that are more advantageous to requesters. After identifying competing paradigms of transparency embodied in the FOI laws of the United States and Finland, Michener applies this framework to help explain the successes and failures of FOI legislation in Latin America. Finally, Sandoval-Ballesteros offers a sobering account of FOI performance in Mexico, the world's top-ranked RTI regime. The arrival of this regime, Sandoval-Ballesteros argues, has not fundamentally curbed corruption or transformed authoritarian ways of exercising power in Mexico, which suggests that transparency law must be reconstructed in more "democratic-expansive" terms. The chapters in this concluding part vividly convey how far the FOI movement has come in recent decades—and how much work remains to be done.

NOTES

1. David E. Pozen, "Freedom of Information Beyond the Freedom of Information Act," *University of Pennsylvania Law Review* 165 (2017): 1097–1158, at 1106.
2. The Department of Justice reported that 713,168 FOIA requests were received by the federal government in FY 2015. U.S. Department of Justice, Office of Information and Privacy, "Summary of Annual FOIA Reports for Fiscal Year 2015," 2016, 2.
3. "Freedom of Information Act: Memorandum for the Heads of Executive Departments and Agencies," *Federal Register* 74 (January 21, 2009): 4683.
4. Staff of the House of Representatives Committee on Oversight and Government Reform, 114th Congress, *FOIA Is Broken: A Report*, 2016, https://oversight.house.gov/wp-content/uploads/2016/01/FINAL-FOIA-Report-January-2016.pdf.
5. Minority Staff of House of Representatives Committee on Government Reform, 108th Congress, *Secrecy in the Bush Administration*, 2004, iv, https://fas.org/sgp/library/waxman.pdf.
6. See, for example, Mark E. Warren et al., "Deliberative Negotiation," in *Political Negotiation: A Handbook*, ed. Jane Mansbridge and Cathie Jo Martin (Washington, D.C.: Brookings Institution Press, 2016), 141–96. See also Congressional Research Institute, "Transparency Citations," compiled September 19, 2016, http://www.congressionalresearch.org/citations.html [http://perma.cc/3JY3-N4VG], for a collection of sources that "address the problem of excessive . . . transparency in legislatures."
7. Pozen, "Freedom of Information Beyond the Freedom of Information Act," 1101. See also David E. Pozen, "Transparency's Ideological Drift," *Yale Law Journal* 128 (forthcoming 2018), available at https://ssrn.com/abstract=3120807.
8. Pozen, "Freedom of Information Beyond the Freedom of Information Act," 1100.
9. Schudson's views on FOIA, as well as his historical interpretation of its origins and enactment, are developed in Michael Schudson, *The Rise of the Right to Know: Politics and the Culture of Transparency, 1945–1975* (Cambridge, Mass.: Belknap Press, 2015), 28–63.

PART ONE

FOIA'S HISTORICAL AND CONCEPTUAL FOUNDATIONS

1

HOW ADMINISTRATIVE OPPOSITION SHAPED THE FREEDOM OF INFORMATION ACT

Sam Lebovic

AS THE FREEDOM OF INFORMATION ACT made its slow passage through Congress in the early 1960s, it was not popular in President Lyndon B. Johnson's administration. "We should not kid ourselves about the legislation's prospects," declared Senator Edward Long in March 1964, shortly after shepherding a FOIA bill through his subcommittee. "There is intense opposition to the bill from virtually every government agency in Washington." A year later, when twenty-seven agencies and departments offered their views on FOIA to a House subcommittee, the Civil Service Commission was the lone supporter of the bill. Behind the scenes, the Bureau of the Budget advised the White House to prevent the bill from coming to a vote in the House. LBJ apparently implored the House leadership to "scrap" it.[1]

Ultimately, of course, opposition by the agencies could not kill FOIA. By the end of 1965, it had become clear to the White House that congressional pressure to pass the act was unrelenting and that it was not politically feasible to publicly oppose a Freedom of Information bill. Republicans, particularly a young Donald Rumsfeld, were beginning to make partisan hay out of the issue, and the public was fixating on the credibility gap. Sam Archibald, chief of staff for the House Committee pushing for the bill, advised the White House that caving to administrative opposition would be "politically damaging." As he dryly put it, "the arguments against the legislation are technical ones by bureaus and agencies. . . . [T]he arguments in favor of the legislation are based on the democratic principle of the informed electorate. They also touch upon God and motherhood."[2]

Still, the administration was not willing to abandon the fight completely. Rather than be placed in what White House counsel Lee White described as the "awkward position of opposing freedom of information," the White House looked for ways to sculpt FOIA to calm the agencies.[3] The administration flirted with the idea of referring the problem to a presidential commission, and also tried, unsuccessfully, to encourage Congress to adopt a weaker version of FOIA drafted by the Justice Department.[4]

Then the White House hit upon another, rather desperate, strategy to bring the agencies on board. Congress's proposed FOIA bill would pass without amendment, but the Department of Justice (DOJ) would draft the House Report explaining the legislative intent behind the bill. To protect FOIA from potential presidential veto, the bill's champion in the House, California representative John Moss, agreed to the deal. FOIA passed quickly through Congress with a DOJ-written report designed to limit the scope of the act.[5] As the bill sat awaiting presidential signature in the early summer of 1966, the agencies were polled on their attitudes to FOIA. On July 1, LBJ was informed that "the departments and agencies have been concerned about this bill for many years, but have come around to the view that they can live with it." The language in the House Report, as well as the promise that the report would provide the template for the administrative implementation of FOIA, had sufficiently calmed the agencies.[6] Three days later, LBJ signed the bill into law.[7]

What we call the Freedom of Information Act was actually an amendment to the public information provisions of the Administrative Procedure Act of 1946. (Explaining the law in 1967, the attorney general called FOIA the "Public Information Act of 1966."[8]) The new sections made three important changes that promised to make the administrative state far more transparent. Whereas the old APA had guaranteed access to information only for persons "properly and directly concerned" with a matter, FOIA empowered anyone to request government records, without any need to show "standing." Whereas the old APA sections had allowed the agencies to withhold information for any "good cause found," FOIA created a general presumption of disclosure, allowing the withholding of information only in specific instances, outlined in nine exemptions to the act. Finally, whereas the old APA sections had provided no remedy for citizens improperly denied access to information, FOIA empowered the courts to force disclosure.[9]

Despite these laudatory changes, the meaning of FOIA was nonetheless shaped in important ways by the opposition of the agencies. In particular, the drafting of the nine exemptions to disclosure had been a difficult process, and the meaning of the exemptions was unclear. The House Report and the subsequent attorney general's manual thus played an important role in defining their substance. As John Moss commented sharply during committee debate on the bill, "the tendency in agencies is to regard these [exemptions] very narrowly when we discuss them in committee, and very broadly when they administer them."[10] In so doing, agency opposition expanded the scope of the exemptions, limiting the scope of transparency.

The opposition of the agencies also provides a unique vantage point from which to consider the broader significance of FOIA. As the administration offered testimony to Congress, drafted alternative legislation, and proposed interpretations of the act to guide the writing of the House Report and the attorney general's manual, it provided a rich documentary record of state attitudes to such important topics as national security, the regulatory process, the philosophy of good governance, and the relations of the executive branch to the public. Agency opposition to FOIA reveals an important cross-section of the intellectual and political history of the state in modern America, as well as an opportunity to reflect on the normative dimensions of transparency in democratic governance.

This chapter considers agency opposition to FOIA in four parts. First, I explore agency concerns that transparency would undermine state capacity to regulate economic activity and reflect on the significance of corporate use of FOIA since 1966. Second, I look at the lack of agency concern about the threats FOIA posed to national security and explain this lack of concern by arguing that FOIA actually consolidated the legitimacy of national security secrecy. Third, I analyze administration concerns that FOIA would make policy deliberations impossible by requiring governance in a fishbowl and show how FOIA exempted such deliberations from disclosure. The chapter concludes with an examination of the deeper assumptions about the state and the public (and the relationship between the two) that underpinned agency opposition to FOIA.

TRANSPARENTLY REGULATING THE ECONOMY

Of all the agencies that opposed FOIA, only one maintained its opposition to the bitter end. When the Bureau of the Budget surveyed the agencies and departments about FOIA in June 1966, shortly before it was signed into law, the Department of Health, Education, and Welfare (HEW) provided the longest and most detailed response, and it alone continued to believe that passage of FOIA was against the public interest. It was worried that disclosure of correspondence with local and state governments would undermine negotiations over state grant-in-aid programs. It was worried that being forced to disclose the confidential assessments of research grant applications, such as those submitted to the National Institutes of Health, would harm honest and frank evaluations. And it was concerned that revealing staff manuals and procedures for auditing social benefits claims would impede "administration of the social security programs" and "invite fraud."[11]

HEW's opposition to FOIA revealed some consistent themes in the complaints of the agencies. Many of the agencies complained that FOIA would force them to disclose forms of information that would interfere with the state's ability to interact with civil society, particularly its ability to regulate economic activity.

Some of this was concern that FOIA would undermine the state's ability to negotiate advantageous contracts. The Department of Defense (DOD), for instance, was one of several agencies worried that if its guidelines for contracts became public, revealing what DOD was willing to concede in contract negotiations, it would be impossible to negotiate more favorable terms for the government. The General Services Administration was likewise worried about revealing its guidelines for the sale of surplus government property.[12] Exempting such material raised possibilities for covering up corruption, but this pushback against FOIA also reflected a desire to protect the taxpayers' interest in cost-effective government.

Most of the anxieties of the agencies, however, centered on a different point of state-economic relations—the state's role in regulating the economy. The Department of Agriculture was worried that FOIA could make public the ballots of producers that were collected in the making of marketing orders under the Agricultural Marketing Act of 1937, which could expose some producers to "economic duress" in retaliation for their voting.[13] The Federal Reserve Board was concerned that the records of the Federal Open Market Committee would be disclosed prematurely, undermining its ability to gather confidential testimony on market conditions and thus manage monetary policy free from the gaze of speculators.[14] The Securities and Exchange Commission fretted that if it could not continue to hold "informal discussions by which business problems are resolved in a businesslike way, administration of the securities laws would be greatly impaired." The Department of Labor worried about the premature disclosure of its enforcement policies.[15]

A number of agencies also worried that their ability to conduct investigations would be impaired if their investigatory files could be requested through FOIA. The National Labor Relations Board feared that informants of labor law violations would stop coming forward if employers would be able to FOIA their names. The Federal Communications Commission had similar concerns about protecting tip-offs from employees of licensees who were engaged in misconduct.[16] The Civilian Aeronautics Board was worried about the frankness of accident reports; so was the National Aeronautics and Space Administration, which also worried about oversight reports about contractors.[17]

Such objections unsettle any easy assumptions that agency opposition to FOIA could only have been motivated by cynical self-interest, a hostility to democratic governance, or a wish to conceal abuses. If anything, the concern for protecting the confidentiality of audit and investigation processes suggests a preoccupation with guaranteeing the sanctity of internal agency processes designed to keep the agencies honest. FOIA, in this view, risked reducing government accountability, not aiding it. It is, of course, possible that these arguments were strategic, palatable rhetoric masking more selfish desires. But given that these arguments were made within the privacy of the administration as well as in public, it seems unlikely that these concerns were nothing more than posturing. Opposition to FOIA, in other words, was not necessarily antidemocratic. It could emerge from agency desires to protect the public interest.

These concerns for state efficacy molded many of the exemptions to FOIA. To begin with, FOIA acknowledged that many state functions required secrecy. The first exemption transparency advocates had written into FOIA was an exemption for any material that a statute had declared should be kept confidential. In essence, this was an accordion-like exemption that could expand to protect all sorts of government activities. In 1965, some 78 statutes included such provisions; by 2011, the list had grown to over 140 statutes.[18]

To this general exemption, Congress then added three other classes of broad exemption that helped to shield regulatory functions. Their scope was expanded substantially as a result of agency complaints, which found expression in the House Report and in Attorney General Clark's implementing memorandum. Exemption 2 covered material "related solely to the internal personnel rules and practices of any agency." The Senate had thought this would cover only matters such as parking facility rules, sick leave, and lunch hours. But the Clark memorandum followed the more expansive House Report and explained that it covered "internal rules and practices which cannot be disclosed to the public without substantial prejudice to the effective performance of a significant agency function"—such as bargaining for acquisition of lands, unannounced inspections, or spot audits. Exemption 7 covered investigatory material compiled for law enforcement purposes. Quoting from the House Report, Clark's memorandum explained that this language was used in its "broadest sense" to cover "all kinds of laws, labor and security laws as well as criminal laws." And the fourth exemption carved out all information provided in confidence to the government. It too was interpreted so broadly by Clark's memorandum that it rendered rather redundant the final two exemptions of FOIA—for information related to the "regulation or supervision of financial institutions" (Exemption 8) and for information related to oil wells (Exemption 9). As Clark explained, these forms of information fell comfortably within Exemption 4.[19]

Nevertheless, these last two exemptions suggest the fine line that the regulatory state needed to walk when handling information collected from the marketplace. The state needs information to regulate, yet it relies on the objects of regulation to provide that information. And in the competitive environment of capitalism, control over information is a key to advantage. So economic actors will offer information to the regulator only if they can be assured that the regulator will preserve their advantage. This, in any case, was the logic of the exemption for information related to oil wells, which was added late in the day to ensure that companies that had filed a discovery of an oil well with the Bureau of Land Management would not find themselves outbid on the lease by competitors who had not invested in the expensive process of finding the oil well and had, instead, relied on the existence of the government filings.

* * *

Since FOIA came into existence, it has, in fact, been used primarily by the commercial sector. The first three FOIA cases that produced lawsuits all targeted areas that had been of concern to the agencies: Shell Oil sought information about land patents in the Department of the Interior; a private practitioner FOIA'd the Defense Department's Contract Audit Manual; and a Puerto Rican shoe company sought access to National Labor Relations Board investigative files to defend itself from an unfair labor practices charge.[20] By 1971, one journalist was already lamenting the "rather ironic fact that the press has not been particularly prominent among the users of FOIA." Of one hundred early FOIA lawsuits, none had been brought by newspapers.[21]

Subsequent studies have confirmed that FOIA is used much more by commercial requesters than by the media or transparency activists. In 2005, one study found that 61 percent of FOIA requests came from commercial interests and only 6 percent from the media.[22] In 2013 and 2014, legal scholar

Margaret Kwoka analyzed the FOIA logs of seven agencies likely to be used by commercial requesters and found that a striking percentage of FOIA requests came from those commercial interests: 96 percent at the Defense Logistics Agency, 79 percent at the Environmental Protection Agency, and 75 percent at the Food and Drug Administration.[23] Commercial dominance of FOIA makes sense. FOIA has long been plagued by delays, which undermines its utility for reporters on deadline. Using FOIA takes patience and time, but for commercial requesters seeking a competitive advantage, this is a worthwhile expense.

Whether or not this is a deeply problematic state of affairs, or just a less than desirable one, is more uncertain. It certainly creates inefficiencies and inequalities. Kwoka has shown that a private industry has sprung up to resell FOIA'd information, suggesting that the government is expending considerable time and money to subsidize profit-making. Her research also suggests that relying on FOIA as a public information tool has produced an uneven method of disclosure that has created opportunities for informational arbitrage.[24]

If FOIA has been beneficial primarily to commercial interests, has it also harmed the regulatory state? Although there is a need for more research on this front, one can imagine several ways in which FOIA might have undermined the capacity and effectiveness of the regulatory state. Aggressive use of FOIA—repeated requests for vast swaths of information—adds to administrative costs and gums up the operations of the state, taking resources away from regulatory activity. The ability to FOIA government records but not corporate records also produces an inequality in public debate as the information behind government position papers is subject to greater transparency and scrutiny than private sector statements. This was the fear that led transparency groups to oppose a 1999 extension of FOIA that forced the disclosure of scientific data produced on government grants; conservative politicians and corporate interests wanted access to data on the health consequences of pollution to challenge proposed environmental regulations. (In the end, contrary to the expectations of both its proponents and opponents, this extension has hardly been used, largely due to greater affirmative disclosure of such data.[25]) At the broadest level, it seems likely that Americans' ability to FOIA the state but not the private sector contributes to a general public impression of relative state incompetence and corruption. FOIA seems to function as one more mechanism that reflects and reinforces the strong antigovernment currents in U.S. political culture.[26]

If it does turn out that FOIA has operated as an antiregulatory tool, it is important to be careful in distinguishing whether this is because of the particular circumstances and context in which it has been administered or because of a deeper tension between transparency and state capacity for regulation. Perhaps more transparency would improve matters. One could, for instance, resolve problems of informational arbitrage by expanding affirmative disclosures.[27] If excessive use of FOIA is interfering with agency functions, this is perhaps most easily fixed by expanding agency budgets. Although it may be somewhat dispiriting to discover that commercial interests are the greatest beneficiaries of FOIA, we should not too quickly assume that that is antithetical to the democratic purposes of the act insofar as FOIA is directing information into at least a portion of the public sphere.

In sum, much work remains to be done to determine exactly how FOIA has interacted with the regulatory state, but there is little doubt that FOIA has been an important tool for commercial interests. This might have surprised the journalists who championed FOIA in the 1950s, but it would not have surprised the agencies in the 1960s, who were well aware of the various forms of information they held that might appeal to economic interests. However we may feel about FOIA's impact on the regulatory state, it is telling that agencies were much more concerned about its effects on these state functions than they were about its impact on issues of national security.

THE HEGEMONY OF NATIONAL SECURITY

In the lead-up to FOIA's passage, there was remarkably little concern that FOIA would interfere with national security secrecy. At the 1965 hearings and in internal memoranda on the enrolled bill, only the departments of State, Defense, and Treasury raised objections to FOIA on these grounds. Their objections were mild, concerned less with challenging the act than with clarifying the relevant exemption to FOIA that covered matters "specifically required by executive order to be kept secret in the interest of the national defense or foreign policy." State, for instance, was worried that there were some aspects of foreign relations that were not currently classified as secret that might be improperly disclosed: memoranda of conversations with diplomatic agencies abroad or Office of Munitions Control deliberations about arms transactions.[28] Treasury was worried that exchange stabilization arrangements would be prematurely disclosed because these were not currently classified.[29]

What the three departments wanted, therefore, were assurances that the national security exemption was broad. The draft administration bill, for instance, sought to protect information related to "national security or foreign relations" rather than information about "national defense or foreign policy"—the administration favoring the more capacious term in both instances.[30] After FOIA was passed, State, DOJ, and DOD briefly flirted with the idea of revising the then-controlling classification order, Executive Order 10501, to "broaden its provisions to the full scope of national defense and foreign policy permitted by the first exemption."[31]

But little came of this, and the departments adapted instead by concluding that FOIA's national security exemption did not need revision because it could simply be interpreted broadly. State, for instance, "assumed" that the exemption was "designed to encompass at least the coverage of the present Executive Order [on classification] rather than to restrict further such coverage." And for good measure, State classified its memorandum of objection to FOIA, perhaps because it used the details of some arms deals as illustrative examples.[32]

Defenders of the national security state had little reason to fear that FOIA was going to interfere with their prerogatives; even FOIA's champions conceded the importance of secrecy in the domain of national security. In 1957, James S. Pope, a leader of the freedom of information movement, had declared that "none of us wants security information—genuine security information—revealed."[33] An exemption for national defense and foreign policy was the second exemption included in early drafts of the FOIA legislation. On the important issue of the scope of that exemption, FOI advocates were deferential to a broad notion of national security prerogatives. Discussing the exemption with a DOJ representative during hearings on the bill, John Moss made this plain: "we do not challenge that right to withhold for the national interest, because we specifically require it by executive order to be kept secret in the interest of the national defense or foreign policy. Now, that is very broad."[34]

As FOIA was implemented, it was this broad understanding of the national security exemption that took hold. As Clark's explanatory memorandum put it, "the reference in the House Report to Executive Order 10501 indicates that no great degree of specificity is contemplated in identifying matters subject to this exemption."[35] State, Treasury, and Defense need not have worried about FOIA; it institutionalized their conceptualization of the national security exemption.

* * *

Thereafter, as many legal scholars have shown, the courts were equally deferential to the national security exemption. In the early 1970s, many took at face value any citation of the exemption, refusing to consider whether the disclosure of the classified information would actually pose a threat to national security. In 1973, the Supreme Court upheld this deferential reading of the exemption, stating that Congress "has built into the Freedom of Information Act an exemption that provides no means to question an Executive decision to stamp a document 'secret,' however cynical, myopic or even corrupt that decision might have been."[36] This reasoning basically invited Congress to reform FOIA to allow for judicial review of the act of classification, and the 1974 amendments did so. But, at the last minute, Congress hedged on the issue. Fearful of a threatened presidential veto, Congress explained in its conference report that the amendments instructed future courts to "accord substantial weight" to representations about the need to keep classified information secret.[37] (President Gerald Ford vetoed even this revised bill, but his veto was overridden.[38]) Ever since, courts have remained deferential to executive claims about the need for secrecy.[39]

In fact, FOIA helped consolidate the legitimacy of the classification system. The classification system was only fifteen years old at the time of FOIA's passage, and it had been created by unilateral executive order. Congress had had no input into its design and had not previously recognized its legitimacy. But now it did. The significance of this development was immediately apparent to Professor Kenneth Culp Davis, doyen of post–World War II administrative law. FOIA "does precisely nothing to carry out the point of view of the press with respect to national defense and foreign policy," Davis noted shortly after the act passed. "Instead, it strengthens the President's hand in withholding information on these subjects. . . . Under the Act, the President may withhold information about national defense or foreign policy with the formal approval of Congress, previously lacking."[40]

That was certainly an ironic outcome of the Freedom of Information Act. It stemmed from a simple slip from theory to practice. It was one thing to say, as did James Pope and the other freedom of information activists, that one wanted to protect "genuine security information." But it was another thing entirely to presume that the particular bureaucratic process that the executive branch had created to define state secrets covered only "genuine security information." In fact, as commentators have noted since the 1950s, the classification system incentivizes the overclassification of documents. The system requires classifiers to consider potential risks to the nation when reviewing documents, but it does not require that they take into account the public's interest in knowing the information. And there are no penalties for overclassifying a document when in doubt. As a result, much of what is "classified" is not "genuine security information."[41]

The passage of FOIA might have provided a moment to revise this system. The classification system might have been placed on a statutory basis. Classifiers could have been required to consider the public interest in disclosure. An administrative organ could have been created to audit classification decisions. Even without affirmatively challenging the classification system, FOIA could have provided a stronger tool for declassification, one that balanced public rights to know against claims of national security. Instead of any of these moves, FOIA exempted national security information and deferred to the classification system. FOIA was thus more deferential to the national security state than the regulatory state, a bifurcation that raises deeper questions about the general attitudes to governance embedded in the act.

THE INCONVENIENCE OF GOVERNING IN A FISHBOWL

Prior to the passage of FOIA, many of the agencies argued that FOIA posed challenges to good governance at an elemental level. These criticisms took two main forms: concerns about the practical, bureaucratic costs of implementing the act; and concerns that creating a more transparent executive branch would interfere with the effective development of policy.

Concerns about the bureaucratic costs of FOIA were easy to understand, for the terms of the act were generous. Anyone was allowed to ask for access to vast swaths of government information, and the costs were going to fall on the agencies and departments. As Treasury expressed it, FOIA "invites demands for all sorts and kinds of documents, requiring a large expenditure of time and money to satisfy"—expenditures that would ultimately be borne by the taxpayer.[42] Twelve of the twenty-seven agencies testifying against the bill in 1965 raised such issues, and six agencies continued to protest about the burdens of FOIA just before LBJ signed it into law. HEW, for instance, worried about FOIA's "inestimable costs and manpower burden."[43] State worried that it would have to make all of its records available at all of its 290 foreign service posts.[44] NASA, perhaps thinking of space enthusiasts and UFO spotters, anticipated having to "undertake very burdensome administrative actions, solely to provide information to persons requesting it for unjustifiable or frivolous purposes."[45]

In the short term, these fears would be assuaged by the Clark memorandum, which, following the House Report, stated that the costs of FOIA requests had to be covered by the user. The head of each agency was to establish "any fee, price or charge" that they determined to be "fair and equitable" to ensure that the government wasn't out of pocket. Such fees also would serve to discourage "frivolous requests."[46] By the early 1970s, it had become clear that the elasticity of these provisions allowed for prohibitive fees that undermined FOIA's central aim. One request for Department of Agriculture information on pesticides, for instance, was met with a fee of almost $92,000.[47] In 1974, FOIA was therefore amended to require the waiver or reduction of fees when the information is being requested in the public interest. Today, although FOIA undeniably creates a bureaucratic burden and imposes large costs on the agencies—in 2013, for instance, the Food and Drug Administration devoted eighty-two full-time staff and $33.5 million to FOIA—supporters of the law consider this the necessary price of ensuring a more transparent government.[48]

Mid-1960s complaints about the bureaucratic costs of FOIA are thus primarily interesting as a by-product of a deeper sense among the agencies that transparency was not a virtue worth any price. In fact, many agencies questioned whether it was desirable at all to expose internal deliberations within the executive branch to the light of publicity. This was the second way agencies argued that FOIA undermined good governance. As the House Report put it, "agency witnesses argued that a full and frank exchange of opinions would be impossible if all internal communications were made public."[49]

Agency officials were worried, in other words, about being forced to "operate in a fishbowl." They thought that creative, efficient, and honest policy work required some protection from public scrutiny and judgment, and that FOIA would tear the cocoon too soon, allowing criticism of immature deliberations.[50] The Department of Defense captured the logic of the argument best:

> It is a well-accepted maxim that no large organization can function effectively if subject to general public scrutiny. If agency decisions by superiors are to be made with the benefit of full, frank, and open discussion, and recommendations by and between subordinates, these comments and recommendations must have the protection of privileged information. Otherwise, every memorandum would be carefully written with a view toward its possible impact on the public. The inhibiting effect of such a requirement is obvious.[51]

It was appropriate that DOD presented this argument as a form of common sense so "well-accepted" and "obvious" that it required no proof. Six other agencies made this argument in 1965, and four continued to raise it in 1966.

But some segments of the executive branch went further still, dressing these arguments about the need for confidentiality in constitutional garb. Offering congressional testimony in 1965, six agencies argued that FOIA violated the

separation of powers, and DOD and DOJ continued to worry about these constitutional issues in 1966. Their argument rested on a belief that the president
had an "executive privilege"—a right to maintain certain forms of confidentiality in the fulfillment of his constitutionally assigned functions. FOIA, these
agencies and departments argued, violated this right by unconstitutionally
providing either the judiciary or the legislature with powers that impinged on
executive decisional autonomy (opinions varied as to the precise violation of
the separation of powers).[52]

In this sense, the timing of FOIA's passage left a clear mark on its substance. Executive privilege had only begun to be thought of as a sweeping
right to confidentiality during the McCarthy era. It had been elaborated by
Truman administration efforts to protect the secrecy of its loyalty files from
anti-Communist Republicans, and it was most forcefully expressed in a 1954
letter by President Eisenhower aimed at stopping Senator Joe McCarthy's
investigations into the Army. After this remarkable rise, executive privilege was
held in high political esteem until President Nixon's abuse of the privilege
during Watergate did much to discredit it in the early 1970s.[53]

So FOIA's passage fell within a relatively short period in which claims that
internal deliberations within the executive should be confidential had real
normative and constitutional clout. Signing FOIA into law, LBJ reiterated
that the president had constitutional powers to provide for confidentiality
and that "officials within Government must be able to communicate with
one another fully and frankly without publicity."[54] These sentiments shaped
the meaning of Exemption 5, which covered "inter-agency or intra-agency
memorandums or letters" and was understood to extend to materials related
to the deliberative process.

During FOIA's long gestation, and in defiance of administration
demands, John Moss had said he would not agree to a bill that included
"any language that grants statutory recognition to executive privilege."[55]
Yet the expansive understanding of the deliberative process incorporated
into Exemption 5 essentially did so. According to the 2015 Department of
Justice Guide to the Freedom of Information Act, one of the "most frequently
invoked privileges that ha[s] been held to be incorporated into Exemption 5 [is] the deliberative process privilege (referred to by some courts
as 'executive privilege')."[56] In 2014, in the context of a general increase in
FOIA requests, a new record was set when Exemption 5 was invoked 81,752
times. (The national security exemption, by way of comparison, was cited
8,496 times that year.[57])

In 2016, when Congress amended FOIA, it placed a twenty-five-year limit on Exemption 5. The ability to access more internal documents from the past is clearly a boon to historians, but it is significant that even this reformed FOIA still seeks to shield deliberative discussions from contemporary scrutiny.[58] Its opponents took an even stronger stand to protect deliberative discussions. Cass Sunstein, recently returned to academia from his stint in the Office of Information and Regulatory Affairs, argued that the reform would "have a chilling effect on those discussions."[59]

The similarity of these arguments against transparency across a half-century is striking, and it raises an important practical issue. In both instances, administrators were concerned that internal debate was likely to be chilled by knee-jerk public reactions—by an inability of the news media, the electorate, and political opposition to see proposals in context. Rather than assessing debate coolly and calmly, and waiting to see what the final policy might be, opponents would be quick to seize on particular statements or proposals to smear or discredit policies and policy makers. However we may think about this problem moving forward, the history of Exemption 5 reflects persistent fears about "governing in a fishbowl." It also reminds us that agency opposition to FOIA reflected broader mid-century attitudes about the relationship between the state and the public.

FOIA BETWEEN STATE AND PUBLIC

More than anything else, agency opposition to FOIA revealed a persistent faith in the authority and rationality of the executive branch. From the position of the Executive, questions about information disclosure were difficult, subtle, and complex. But FOI advocates, according to the administration, didn't grasp that fact. As one Office of Legal Counsel memo explained, FOI advocates thought that

the problem is an easy one, and that protection of official information is unnecessary except in cases involving the national security and a few other areas easily defined. In fact, the responsibility of the government for the proper handling of information and records in its possession frequently involves most careful judgments. Because of the reach and complexity of modern government and the volume and variety of information which is in the [government's] possession . . . the different kinds of situations in which improvident disclosure may cause serious injury to private and public interests are infinite in number.[60]

Putting the same attitude another way, the Office of Legal Counsel also asserted that FOIA sought to "eliminate any aspect of judgment" in the decision to disclose information. Instead, FOIA naively substituted a "simple, self-executing word formula."[61] The Department of Labor likewise decried FOIA's "inherent inflexibility." Testifying to Congress, Norbert Schlei, assistant attorney general for the Office of Legal Counsel, summed up the "basic thesis" of the administration's opposition to FOIA: "there is no form of words that can protect the public interest well enough to justify substituting that form of words for 'executive judgment' and 'discretion.'"[62] In all, such advocacy of the need for administrative discretion, such trust in the judgment of agency heads, and such distrust of legislated procedures for disclosure reflected a broad faith in administrative expertise.

Agency understandings of the public were less straightforward. They were certainly more complicated than the expansive and vague notion of the "public" championed by FOI advocates and articulated by the bill. Explaining FOIA, Ramsey Clark declared that it provided that "all individuals have equal rights of access," which was true, and was a striking provision in the bill.[63] Not only did one not need to show standing, one did not need to be a citizen to use FOIA. FOIA, in this sense, embodied a militantly democratic theory of the public—any individual, acting rationally for themselves or the common good, would create public goods by freeing information from the state.

Agencies were skeptical that the "public" would live up to this role for two reasons. First, agencies argued that, in practice, it would be difficult to differentiate citizens using FOIA for the public good and citizens abusing FOIA for private benefit. Treasury, for instance, testified to Congress that it already had problems with individuals pretending to have power-of-attorney to represent taxpayers and thus gain access to personal information for business purposes.[64] In one sense, this seemed to represent a nascent critique of the ways that formally egalitarian rights could serve to benefit primarily those economic interests with the incentives and resources to take best advantage of them.

But the second, and more prevalent, reason for agency skepticism stemmed from a broader distrust of the public. When agencies and the departments spoke of the public, they imagined a parade of irresponsible troublemakers—high school children and the "mentally disturbed" (Treasury); "subversives, aliens," or "claim hunters" (Comptroller General); "intermeddlers, idle curiosity seekers, smut peddlers, persons with irrelevant prejudicial motives and others having no reasonably legitimate interest in the information" (General

Services Administration).[65] These figures were invoked primarily because they promised to create bureaucratic burdens. But insofar as the agencies also worried about governing in a fishbowl, and worried that disclosures to irresponsible individuals would then reverberate throughout the public, they also seemed to have assumed that the general public was ill-suited to calmly considering matters of public policy. The public was intrigued enough by public affairs to be mischievous and annoying in calling for transparency, yet irresponsible and skittish enough to misuse or misunderstand the information that came into their possession.

After World War II, a procedural orientation to administrative governance may have been on the rise, displacing agency discretion in favor of clear rules of operation and clear formulas for public involvement. But when it came to the disclosure of information, these trends were far from settled by the mid-1960s. In 1966, the agencies continued to distrust the public and formally egalitarian procedures and to exalt the expertise of the administrator.

* * *

By shaping the drafting and interpretation of FOIA, the opposition of the agencies left its imprint on the law and practice of transparency. The concerns of the administration foreshadowed the uneven effectiveness of FOIA in its first half-century: the act has been much more effective in producing information about the regulatory state than in producing information about the national security state; and it has been used more often by commercial interests than by journalists or those interested in public goods. At a deeper level, agency concerns reflected some important assumptions about the relationship between the state and the public in modern American democracy. Agency opposition provided something of a heat-map of "state-ness" in mid-century American democracy, revealing those areas in which the democratic state thought that it needed autonomous capacity to work effectively—particularly in the domain of national security but also, to a lesser extent, in the regulation of the economy. Agency opposition also reflected the lingering hold of ideas about administrative expertise and discretion even in the era of an increasingly proceduralist state. We still live with the FOIA shaped by the assumptions and concerns of mid-century America. As FOIA passes the fifty-year mark, it is helpful to reflect on its historical origins to better understand its present state and, perhaps, to imagine ways to reform it in the future.

NOTES

1. "Information Bill Faces Stiff Test," *Washington Post*, August 10, 1965; "White House Opposition Stalls Information Bill," August 9, 1965, clipping, box 44, folder FE 14–1, WHCF, LBJ Library; "Information Freedom Bill Backed in Senate," *Washington Post*, March 3, 1964; "Shop Talk at 30," *Editor and Publisher*, August 29, 1964; *Federal Public Records Law: Part 1: Hearings Before a Subcommittee of the Committee on Government Operations*, 89th Congress, 1965.

2. "Hill Drive on to Reduce Secrecy in Government," *Washington Post*, February 18, 1965; "Senate Again Votes a Bill on News Flow," *New York Times*, August 1, 1964; "An Information Bill Is Passed by Senate," *New York Times*, October 14, 1965; Paul Wieck, "Chill Threatens Press Bill," *Albuquerque Journal*, July 11, 1965; Sam Archibald to Bill Moyers, December 13, 1965, box 44, folder FE 14–1, WHCF, LBJ Library.

3. Lee C. White memorandum, January 15, 1966, box 25, folder FE 14–1, WHCF, LBJ Library.

4. Phillip S. Hughes to Lee White, March 19, 1965, box 44, folder LE/FE 14–1, WHCF, LBJ Library; "Background Statement" included in memo from Leon Ulman, Acting Assistant Attorney General, Office of Legal Counsel, to Bill Moyers, March 16, 1966, box 44, folder LE/FE 14–1, WHCF, LBJ Library.

5. *Freedom of Information, Executive Privilege, Secrecy in Government, Volume 2: Hearings Before the Subcommittees on Administrative Practice and Procedure*, 93rd Congress (1973), 122–26; Robert Okie Blanchard, "The Moss Committee and a Federal Public Records Law, 1955–1965" (PhD diss., Syracuse University, New York, 1966), 200–206; "Disclosure Bill Gains Approval of House Unit," *Washington Post*, April 28, 1966; Bryce Nelson, "House Votes Information Access Bill," *Washington Post*, June 21, 1966.

6. Milton Semer to LBJ on enrolled bill S.1160, July 1, 1966, box 25, folder FE 14–1, WHCF, LBJ Library.

7. "Statement by the President Upon Signing the 'Freedom of Information Act,'" July 4, 1966, *American Presidency Project*, www.presidency.ucsb.edu/ws/?pid=27700.

8. Ramsey Clark, "Attorney General's Memorandum on the Public Information Section of the Administrative Procedure Act," June 1967, www.justice.gov/oip/attorney-generals-memorandum-public-information-section-administrative-procedure-act.

9. Milton Semer to LBJ on enrolled bill S.1160, July 1, 1966, box 25, folder FE 14–1, WHCF, LBJ Library; "House Report 1497," May 9, 1966, 5; "Senate Report 813," October 1, 1965, 3, both in box 36, folder PL 89–487, S1160, Reports on Enrolled Legislation, LBJ Library.

10. *Federal Public Records Law: Part 1: Hearings*, 72.

11. John W. Gardner, Secretary of HEW, to Charles Schultze, June 23, 1966, box 36, folder PL 89–487, S1160, Reports on Enrolled Legislation, LBJ Library.

12. *Federal Public Records Law: Part 1: Hearings*, 219, 249.

13. Department of Agriculture to Charles Schultze, June 23, 1966, box 36, folder PL 89–487, S1160, Reports on Enrolled Legislation, LBJ Library.

14. J. L Robertson, Office of Vice-Chairman, Board of Governors Federal Reserve System, to Wilfred Rommel, July 1, 1966, box 36, folder PL 89–487, S1160, Reports on Enrolled Legislation, LBJ Library.

15. *Federal Public Records Law: Part 1: Hearings*, 224, 259.

16. *Federal Public Records Law: Part 1: Hearings*, 241, 257.

17. CAB chairman to Wilfred Rommel, June 22, 1966, box 36, folder PL 89–487, S1160, Reports on Enrolled Legislation, LBJ Library; Robert C. Seamans, Deputy Administrator NASA to Charles L. Schultze, n.d., box 36, folder PL 89–487, S1160, Reports on Enrolled Legislation, LBJ Library.

18. *Federal Public Records Law: Part 1: Hearings*, 20; Jennifer LaFleur, "FOIA Eyes Only: How Buried Statutes Are Keeping Information Secret," *ProPublica*, March 14, 2011; "Agencies Rely on Wide Range of Exemption 3 Statutes," September 3, 2003, www.justice.gov/oip/blog/foia-post-2003-agencies-rely-wide-range-exemption-3-statutes.

19. Senate Report 813, October 1, 1965, box 36, folder PL 89–487, S1160, Reports on Enrolled Legislation, LBJ Library; Clark, "Attorney General's Memorandum on the Public Information Section."

20. Frank M. Wozencraft, "The Freedom of Information Act—The First 36 days," *Administrative Law Review* 20 (1968): 249–61, at 253.

21. Louis M. Kohlmeier, "The Journalist's Viewpoint," *Administrative Law Review* 23 (1971): 143–45.

22. Coalition of Journalists for Open Government, "Frequent Filers: Businesses Make FOIA Their Business," July 3 2006, www.gfaf.org/resources/who_uses_foi.pdf; Michael Doyle, "Missed Information: The Reporting Tool That Reporters Don't Use," www.johnemossfoundation.org/foi/doyle.htm.

23. Margaret B. Kwoka, "FOIA, Inc.," *Duke Law Journal* 65 (2016): 1361–1437, at 1379–1414.

24. Kwoka, "FOIA, Inc.," 1415–26.

25. Jason Ross Arnold, *Secrecy in the Sunshine Era: The Promise and Failure of US Open Government Laws* (Lawrence: University Press of Kansas, 2014), 227–32; Eric A. Fischer, "Public Access to Data from Federally Funded Research: Provisions in OMB Circular A-110," *Congressional Research Service Report*, March 1, 2013.

26. David E. Pozen, "Freedom of Information Beyond the Freedom of Information Act," *University of Pennsylvania Law Review* 165 (2017): 1097–1158, at 1123–36.

27. Kwoka, "FOIA, Inc.," 1429.

28. Leonard C. Meeker to Frank Wozencraft, April 29, 1966, box 36, folder PL 89–487, S1160, Reports on Enrolled Legislation, LBJ Library.

29. *Federal Public Records Law: Part 1: Hearings*, 228–229.

30. "Background Statement"; "Explanation of the Differences Between S.1160 and the Draft Public Information Bill," March 16, 1966, box 44, folder LE/FE 14–1, WHCF, LBJ Library.

31. Ramsey Clark, Deputy AG, to Charles Schultze, Director, Bureau of the Budget, June 28, 1966; Unsigned DoD memorandum to Charles Schultze, June 28, 1966; Douglas MacArthur II to Charles Schultze, June 23, 1966; Leonard C. Meeker to Frank Wozencraft, April 29 1966, all in box 36, folder PL 89–487, S1160, Reports on Enrolled Legislation, LBJ Library.

32. Leonard C. Meeker to Frank Wozencraft, April 29 1966, box 36, folder PL 89–487, S1160, Reports on Enrolled Legislation, LBJ Library.

33. "Moss Committee Vital to Public Information," *Editor and Publisher*, January 26, 1957.

34. *Federal Public Records Law: Part 1: Hearings*, 14.

35. Clark, "Attorney General's Memorandum on the Public Information Section."

36. EPA v. Mink 410 U.S. 73 (1973).

37. "Freedom of Information Act Amendments," H.R. Rep. No. 93–1380, Conference Report, 1974.

38. Gerald R. Ford, "Veto of Freedom of Information Act Amendments," October 17, 1974, www.presidency.ucsb.edu/ws/?pid=4477.

39. David E. Pozen, "The Mosaic Theory, National Security, and the Freedom of Information Act," *Yale Law Journal* 115 (2005): 628–79, at 638–39; Robert P. Deyling, "Judicial Deference and De Novo Review in Litigation over National Security Information Under the Freedom of Information Act," *Villanova Law Review* 37 (1992): 67–112; Christina E. Wells, " 'National Security' Information and FOIA," *Administrative Law Review* 56 (2004): 1195–1221.

40. Kenneth Culp Davis, "The Information Act: A Preliminary Analysis," *University of Chicago Law Review* 34 (1967): 761–816, at 784–85.

41. Arnold, *Secrecy in the Sunshine Era*, 21–22; Committee on Classified Information, U.S. Department of Defense, "Report to the Secretary of Defense," 1957; Morton H. Halperin and Daniel N. Hoffman, *Top Secret: National Security and the Right to Know* (Washington D.C.: New Republic Books, 1977), 51–54; Mike German and Jay Stanley, "Drastic Measures Required: Congress Needs to Overhaul U.S. Secrecy Laws and Increase Oversight of the Secret Security Establishment," ACLU Report, July 2011, www.aclu.org/other/drastic-measures-required.

42. Fred B. Smith, General Counsel Treasury, June 23, 1966, box 36, folder PL 89–487, S1160, Reports on Enrolled Legislation, LBJ Library.

43. John W. Gardner, Secretary of HEW, to Charles Schultze, June 23, 1966, box 36, folder PL 89–487, S1160, Reports on Enrolled Legislation, LBJ Library.

44. Leonard C. Meeker to Frank Wozencraft, April 29, 1966, box 36, folder PL 89–487, S1160, Reports on Enrolled Legislation, LBJ Library.

45. Robert C. Seamans, Deputy Administrator, NASA, to Charles L. Schultze, box 36, folder PL 89–487, S1160, Reports on Enrolled Legislation, LBJ Library.

46. Clark, "Attorney General's Memorandum on the Public Information Section."

47. Committee on Government Operations, Administration of the Freedom of Information Act, H.R. Rep. No. 92–1419, at 8, 21–22, 73, 76; Ralph Nader, "Freedom from Information: The Act and the Agencies," *Harvard Civil Rights and Civil Liberties Review* 5 (1970): 1–15, at 5.

48. Kwoka, "FOIA, Inc.," 1417.

49. House Report 1497, 10.

50. House Report 1497, 10; Samuel J. Archibald to John Moss, January 7 1966, box 44, folder LE/FE 14–1,WHCF, LBJ Library.

51. *Federal Public Records Law: Part 1: Hearings*, 220

52. *Federal Public Records Law: Part 1: Hearings*; Unsigned DoD memorandum to Charles Schultze, June 28, 1966; Ramsey Clark, Deputy AG to Charles Schultze, Director, Bureau of the Budget, June 28, 1966, both in box 36, folder PL 89–487, S1160, Reports on Enrolled Legislation, LBJ Library.

53. See Mark J. Rozell, *Executive Privilege: Presidential Power, Secrecy and Accountability*, 3rd ed. (Kansas: University Press of Kansas, 2010); Raoul Berger, *Executive Privilege: A Constitutional Myth* (New York: Bantam Books, 1974); Arthur S. Miller, "Executive Privilege: A Political Theory Masquerading as Law," in *The Presidency and Information Policy: Center for the Study of the Presidency Proceedings*, ed. Harold C. Relyea, 4 (1981): 48–65; Robert Kramer and Herman Marcuse, "Executive Privilege: A Study of the Period 1953–1960," *George Washington Law Review* 29 (1961): 669–87; Sam Lebovic, *Free Speech and Unfree News: The Paradox of Press Freedom in America* (Cambridge Mass.: Harvard University Press, 2016), 172–74, 207–08.

54. "Statement by the President Upon Signing the 'Freedom of Information Act.'"

55. "White House Opposition Stalls Information Bill," *Washington Star*, August 9, 1965, clipping attached to Phillip S Hughes to Lee White, August 12, 1965, box 44, folder LE/FE 14–1,WHCF, LBJ Library.

56. "Exemption 5," in *Department of Justice Guide to the Freedom of Information Act*, 2014, 358, www.justice.gov/sites/default/files/oip/legacy/2014/07/23/exemption5_1.pdf.

57. Arnold, *Secrecy in the Sunshine Era*, 77; Jack Gillum and Ted Bridis, "US Cites Security More to Censor, Deny Records," *Associated Press*, March 16, 2014, www.bigstory.ap.org/article/us-cites-security-more-censor-deny-records.

58. Lee White, "New Life for FOIA," *Perspectives on History*, September 2016, 19.

59. Cass R. Sunstein, "Let Public Officials Work in Private," Bloomberg, July 9, 2014, www.bloomberg.com/view/articles/2014-07-09/let-public-officials-work-in -private. See also Cass R. Sunstein, chapter 9 in this volume.

60. "Background Statement."

61. "Background Statement."

62. *Federal Public Records Law: Part 1: Hearings*, 6, 223.

63. Clark, "Attorney General's Memorandum on the Public Information Section."

64. *Federal Public Records Law: Part 1: Hearings*, 62.

65. *Federal Public Records Law: Part 1: Hearings*, 48–49, 203, 227, 250.

2

POSITIVE RIGHTS, NEGATIVE RIGHTS, AND THE RIGHT TO KNOW

Frederick Schauer

THE FREEDOM OF INFORMATION ACT[1] creates legal rights. Specifically, it creates certain rights of access to certain federal government documents. But understanding FOIA requires understanding what kind of rights the act creates and what it is for there to be a "right to know," as the ubiquitous phrase expresses it.[2] In this chapter, I explore the right to know from the perspective of various topics in the theory of rights more generally, especially, but not exclusively, with reference to the important distinction between positive and negative rights. Understanding this distinction facilitates situating FOIA within a host of broader and deeper legal and constitutional questions. Thus, when Justice Potter Stewart, himself a noteworthy supporter of strong and sometimes special First Amendment rights for the institutional press,[3] observed that "[t]he Constitution itself is neither a Freedom of Information Act nor an Official Secrets Act,"[4] he distinguished between the First Amendment, which creates (or recognizes) rights, and the Freedom of Information Act, which also creates rights. But did Justice Stewart mean to suggest that there is no freedom of information component to the First Amendment? If so, was he right? A look at FOIA through the lens of the theory of rights may help to answer these questions.

SOME PRELIMINARIES

About a century ago, the legal theorist Wesley Hohfeld sought to clear up a cluster of confusions about the very idea of a "right."[5] Hohfeld believed that the same word—right—was used to label (at least) four different legal relationships, and his enduring analysis and taxonomy of what he called jural relations and the connections among them (he called them "opposites" and "correlatives") is a useful starting point for understanding what rights are and how they work.

In Hohfeld's taxonomy, some rights create or recognize[6] "privileges," which others have labeled "liberties."[7] These are rights to do something without interference, and most of the familiar U.S. constitutional rights are of this variety. The First Amendment right to the free exercise of religion, for example, is a right against state interference with (and restriction of) one's religious beliefs, and sometimes with religious practices.[8] Similarly, the Second Amendment right to keep and bear arms is a right not to be restricted in aspects of one's gun ownership,[9] and much of the First Amendment right to freedom of speech is a right against state interference with speaking or writing.[10] Because such rights require nothing from the state except inaction, they are understood as "negative" rights, or liberties.[11]

Negative rights need not be rights against the world. Under U.S. "state action" doctrine, for example, constitutional liberties are rights against state, but not non-state, restriction.[12] Students at government institutions such as the University of Michigan thus have (some) First Amendment rights against (some) restrictions on (some) speaking and writing, but students at a private institution, such as Columbia University, have no such rights at all. Although the *New York Times* has liberty rights protecting the *Times* from sanctions by the United States or the State of New York for what it prints, reporters for the *Times* have no such rights against the *Times* itself.

In contrast to negative rights, other rights, often described as "positive,"[13] require the entity against which the rights are claimed to *do* something rather than simply refrain from doing something. A right against my landlord to have him provide heat,[14] for example, is not merely the right to keep the landlord from interfering with my providing my own heat with my own resources but is also the right to have him take the positive act of providing that heat. In the constitutional context, the Sixth Amendment right to counsel is, since 1963,[15] not simply the negative right against the state interfering with my right to be represented by a lawyer in a criminal case against me but also the positive right to have the state take the positive action of (sometimes) providing me with a lawyer at the state's expense. But this right to counsel is a positive right only against the state, not against the world. For example, Clarence Earl Gideon had a right to have Florida provide him with a lawyer, but he did not have a right to have an individual Florida citizen do the same.

In addition to being only *against* some but not all entities, liberty rights are typically *held* by some people or entities but not by others. As the current controversy about corporate free speech and freedom of religion rights illustrates,[16] the existence of a right does not mean that every person or entity will possess or be able to enforce it.[17] Less controversial, infants are widely understood not to have free speech rights,[18] and corporations have no rights against self-incrimination.[19] An important and persistent question about both positive and negative rights is just who has and can enforce them.[20]

Just as rights are neither possessed *by* everyone nor *against* everyone, nor are they rights to *do* everything. The right of conscientious objection to conscription, for example, is a right to an exemption on the basis of religious objection to war in general but not on the basis of objection to particular wars.[21] Less controversial, the right to free speech is not a right to engage in non-speech conduct,[22] although it is more controversial whether the right includes the right to spend money on political campaigns,[23] make misleading statements in securities offerings,[24] or engage in public nude dancing for paying customers.[25]

In summary, it is important in discussing particular rights to specify (1) who has the right, (2) what the right is a right to do, (3) whom the right is a right against, and (4) what the entity against which the right is claimed is required to do or not do.

THE CHARACTER OF U.S. CONSTITUTIONAL RIGHTS

The rights provisions of the U.S. Constitution, at least as interpreted by the courts, largely protect negative and not positive rights, with the right to counsel one of very few exceptions. A woman has a constitutional right to obtain an abortion,[26] but under current doctrine she has no constitutional right to financial or other assistance from the government in obtaining it.[27] There is a right to freedom of speech but no right to the education that would make such speech effective.[28] There is a right to keep and bear arms but no right to government assistance for the citizen who cannot afford a gun, just as the right to the free exercise of religion does not create a right to government assistance in erecting houses of worship.

More generally, the U.S. Constitution has long been interpreted as not containing constitutional rights to welfare,[29] health care, housing, a minimum wage, a pension, protection against violence or mistreatment,[30] or many of the other things most Americans would think, the Constitution aside, were components of a minimally satisfactory existence. Securing such positive social rights or social welfare rights, as they are often called,[31] has generally (as a descriptive and historical matter) not been part of U.S. constitutional doctrine. Why this is so is a complex historical, philosophical, cultural, political, and economic question, but it is not irrelevant that the Constitution of the United States was drafted and gained its judicial and public acceptance long before the very notion of enforceable citizen entitlements against government, whether constitutional or otherwise, had much currency. In this respect, the U.S. Constitution differs from those constitutions whose origins coincided with or postdated twentieth-century understandings of the very idea of the welfare state.

In addition to the "exception" emerging out of *Gideon v. Wainwright*, other exceptions to the negative rights focus of U.S. constitutionalism occasionally surface. The First Amendment right of affirmative access to streets, parks, and sidewalks might be considered to be a positive right, especially insofar as it is based on the view that freedom of speech would be essentially meaningless were there no public places at which to exercise it.[32] Some state constitutions do recognize the positive right to education (and occasionally other needs) that the federal Constitution, as interpreted, appears to disclaim.[33] But the U.S. Constitution, unlike these state constitutions,[34] and unlike many constitutions around the world,[35] remains largely a protector of negative rights and not a creator, recognizer, or enforcer of positive rights.

AND SO TO THE FREEDOM OF INFORMATION

The largely negative character of the U.S. Constitution—far more "freedom from" than "freedom to" or "ability to"—has long been reflected in First Amendment doctrine. With respect to information (and, a fortiori, opinions), individuals and the press are largely free to publish and distribute the information they happen to have or happen to obtain, and, indeed, that freedom generally extends even to information originally obtained unlawfully.[36] But despite long efforts by the institutional press and its allies, there as yet exists no positive right to obtain that information in the first place. The press is free to publish *The Pentagon Papers*, but it had no constitutional right to demand that document from the government. More broadly, the publication of "leaked" documents and information is protected, but the First Amendment provides no assistance to a publisher who wishes to obtain government information without the benefits of a willing leaker.[37]

Thus, when in a series of 1970s cases the press claimed a First Amendment right of positive access to various government facilities, these efforts were overwhelmingly unsuccessful.[38] In the context of a claim to access to prisons, for example, Chief Justice Burger, writing for the plurality in *Houchins v. KQED*,[39] summarized the prevailing judicial conclusion: "[N]either the First Amendment nor the Fourteenth Amendment mandates a right of access to government information or sources of information within the government's control."[40] For complex doctrinal and historical reasons, access to criminal trials has been treated differently,[41] and even here the Supreme Court has made clear that the First Amendment right emerges largely out of historical practice specific to the openness of criminal trials. But apart from this right of public access to criminal trials, a right enjoyed by members of the press as members of the public rather than because of any special status for reporters or the press, the doctrine that has explicitly prevailed for almost half a century (and implicitly for much longer than that) is that information controlled by the government need not, as a matter of constitutional law, be disclosed directly to interested or curious members of the public. There are many circumstances in which Congress may demand information from the other branches of government,[42] information that Congress or its individual members may then reveal to the public. But from the perspective of the First Amendment specifically, and constitutionally law generally, a government agency that wishes to keep some or even all of its documents and proceedings from direct public access is constitutionally permitted to do so.[43]

"Information" is a broad concept, but in practice the lack of a general First Amendment right of access to information has two principal manifestations. One is the lack of a constitutional right of access to government facilities and government meetings. The other is the equivalent absence of a constitutional right to obtain or examine government documents. Together these two aspects of the lack of a positive First Amendment right to access to information produce the conclusion that Chief Justice Burger accurately summarized, and, of course, helped to create. Although Justice Stewart and Chief Justice Burger disagreed about the results in many of the important cases involving press access or press privileges, Justice Stewart's observation that the First Amendment is not "a Freedom of Information Act"[44] is an accurate statement of the doctrine, and he might have added as well that it is not a "sunshine" law, insofar as we understand such state and federal laws to require public and press access to government meetings of countless varieties.[45] Thus the absence of a positive freedom of information component in existing First Amendment understandings—the absence of a positive constitutional right to access to information—reflects both a First Amendment and a constitutional philosophy more generally. The rights to freedom of speech and freedom of the press are negative rights to noninterference, but they are not positive rights to obtain the information that in many aspects is necessary to make the negative right effective.[46]

THE STATUTORY SOLUTION

In light of the foregoing, one way of understanding the Freedom of Information Act is as "remedying" the absence of a positive constitutional right to government information and thus fulfilling some sort of constitutional or quasi-constitutional function.[47] But "remedying" is placed in scare quotes here for two reasons. One is that the idea of a remedy suggests some attempt to repair or compensate for that which has already occurred. The 1966 Freedom of Information Act slightly predates the Supreme Court cases on access,[48] and thus it is more accurate to understand FOIA as being part of a more or less simultaneous two-pronged effort on the part of the press and various other transparency advocates to gain an enforceable right to government information. FOIA was largely successful, whereas the attempt to have the First Amendment interpreted as providing positive rights to government information was, for the most part, unsuccessful.

In addition, the language of "remedy" implies that the constitutional approach is primary and is to be preferred, with the statutory approach being the backup. But I want to challenge this implication. Assuming that substantial citizen and press access to government documents is a good thing,[49] as a normative policy matter, is it better, holding constant the amount of access, for that access to be achieved by statute or by judicial interpretation of the First Amendment?

The arguments for the constitutional approach are familiar. One of them is that giving a right the aura of constitutional protection will make the right seem more important and will thus inculcate for the public and for officials the genuine internalization of that value. There has never been a Supreme Court case involving restriction of a religious belief or practice just because of its religious provenance, for example. One reason for this might be that the impropriety of such a course of action is by now self-evident to lawyers, judges, political figures, and to the larger community. As a result, there is little more reason to believe that a state or the federal government would prohibit the religious practice of a particular religion than that a sitting president would run for a third term in violation of the Twenty-Second Amendment, or that federal

prosecutors would attempt a treason prosecution with only one witness in violation of the two-witness requirement in Section 3 of Article III.[50] One argument
for constitutionalizing the positive right of access to some or most government
information, therefore, is that constitutionalization, even if by judicial decision
rather than by plain text as in the examples just mentioned, will have considerable value in shaping public opinion, a value not present, or less present, when
the same goal is embodied in a "mere" statutory protection.[51]

Although this argument for the effect of constitutionalization on public
and official attitudes has some surface and logical appeal, empirical evidence
supporting the argument turns out to be thin. Experimental research indicates that people rarely choose legal or constitutional values over first-order
substantive preferences when the two conflict,[52] and the same holds for the
actions of the public officials who are typically responsive to public opinion.[53]
Moreover, there is some evidence, consistent with the foregoing, that people's
institutional preferences, if any, are largely determined or dominated by their
first-order substantive preferences.[54] Other research suggests that Supreme
Court opinions recognizing various values have little positive effect on the
acceptance of those values[55] and may even, at times and on some issues,
have the reverse effect.[56] Much of the evidence is complex and contested,
and much of it does not precisely focus on the comparative effect of statutes
when compared to judicial (or Supreme Court, specifically) constitutional
decisions. At the very least, however, we can conclude that there is little evidence supporting the proposition that constitutionalizing a right of access to
government information through judicial opinions will have greater public
opinion shifting effects than simply embodying the same right in a statute.

Of course, it is, in theory, much easier to repeal or modify an "ordinary"
statute than it is to amend the Constitution. Repealing a statute requires only
a majority of the House of Representatives and of the Senate, followed by
the president's signature, but amending the Constitution requires the votes
of two-thirds of both houses followed by the usually impossible ratification
of three-quarters of the states. As a result, another argument for the constitutional approach to access to government information generally and government documents in particular is that statutes are vulnerable to the vagaries
of politics in ways that the more stable and more entrenched Constitution
and its interpretation are not. Embodying the positive right to government
information in a series of constitutional judicial decisions[57] might thus be
thought to entrench the right to access to government information in ways
that ordinary legislation cannot.

This argument is entirely consistent with the fact of constitutional supremacy, as well as being consistent with the practical difficulty of amending the document itself. Yet although the argument might have seemed plausible in the 1960s, when FOIA was in its infancy, it is far from clear that the plausibility of the view that constitutional interpretations are more stable and entrenched than statutes persists today. Assisted by the fact that FOIA has the press as its very powerful advocate—"Never argue with the fellow who buys ink by the barrel," as the old political adage has it—and assisted as well by FOIA's increasing age, it seems no more likely that the act would be repealed or that its force would be substantially blunted by legislative action than that the same could happen to the 1890 Sherman Antitrust Act, to the Civil Rights Act of 1964, to the Social Security Act of 1935, or to the National Environmental Policy Act of 1970. None of these laws has constitutional status and all could thus be repealed without constitutional objection, but as a practical political and sociological matter, all of these laws, and others, are as deeply entrenched as any Supreme Court opinion, and arguably more than most.[58]

Other arguments also weigh in favor of the statutory approach. One such argument starts with the premise that freedom of information is not free. The compliance costs of FOIA are considerable, and although some of these costs might be worth bearing, or at least so we can assume here, it is nevertheless plausible to conclude that, in a world of limited resources, the allocation of those resources in a democracy ought to be made by a representative body able to evaluate the benefits that those costs bring compared to potential alternative uses of the same resources. Congress, or a parallel state legislative body, can decide how much access to information is worth, for example, how much health care, or how much police protection, or how much education, but it is not entirely obvious that courts can or should make these decisions.[59] By treating the costly process of access to information as a subject for judicial interpretation and enforcement, the constitutional approach may risk allocating scarce government resources on the basis of who gets to the courthouse first rather than on some more systematic foundation. When a court says to Congress that it must allocate some amount to access to information because the Constitution requires it, as would be the case were positive access to information a requirement of the First Amendment, and when Congress then finds itself with fewer resources for health care or environmental protection or national defense, for example, there is a risk of winding up with an allocation process even less rational than the one we have now.

Moreover, the very process of lawmaking by litigation is slow, inefficient, and suboptimal in other ways. Courts tend to decide cases one at a time,[60] and thus they tend to decide issues one at a time.[61] Had the Supreme Court decided *Houchins v. KQED* differently, for example, and held that the press had a First Amendment right of access to prisons for the purpose of interviewing prisoners, there would then inevitably have followed litigation about whether that decision extended to documents as well as to personal physical access, and thereafter litigation about who was entitled to access and who was entitled to information, and so on and so on. The law, in common law fashion, would have developed incrementally in the context of particular controversies, and it would have developed slowly and unsystematically. There may well be advantages to regulation by litigation, or rights creation by litigation, but the process is invariably more piecemeal, much slower, and much less systematic than an initial pronouncement and specification of a large range of applications.[62] It is true that the 1966 Freedom of Information Act has been amended on numerous occasions, has been supplemented by other laws,[63] and has been explicated by literally thousands of court cases. But the right of access to federal government information, as we now know it, nevertheless is built on a framework set forth in 1966, a framework that might have taken decades to develop had the principal vehicle for developing the right been constitutional litigation rather than a single and at least somewhat, for all of its gaps and indeterminacies, comprehensive congressional enactment.

POSITIVE RIGHTS AND THE FREEDOM OF INFORMATION ACT

This volume is about FOIA and not about the idea of positive rights more generally. Nevertheless, many of the themes surrounding the positive right of access to government information have surfaced worldwide as various constitutional regimes deal with the question of positive social welfare rights and other positive constitutional rights.[64] Many of the considerations raised here about a positive right of access to information, and especially one found in the Constitution and enforced by courts as a matter of constitutional interpretation, bear some resemblance to issues raised by decisions such as those of the South African Constitutional Court recognizing the positive right to housing[65] and the positive right to antiretroviral medication,[66] of decisions in Eastern Europe dealing with judicial determination of minimum levels of pension and salary payments[67] and many others, and of issues in Ireland and India as those countries negotiate the existence of positive constitutional rights that are designated by their respective constitutions as judicially unenforceable.[68] There is undoubtedly a place for positive legal rights, and undoubtedly a place for a positive right to access to government information, but experiences elsewhere suggest that the question whether that place is in a constitution and is enforced by the normal methods of constitutional adjudication is hardly one with an easy answer.

The question of a positive right of access to government information is merely one component of larger questions about positive rights generally, and even that latter question is merely one component of still larger questions about the nature and structure of rights. As it now exists, FOIA is a statutory grant of positive rights, granted to all persons,[69] and consisting of a right against most agencies of the federal government to obtain access to many of the documents used by those agencies. Virtually every word in the previous sentence is subject to explanation and controversy, but by understanding just what kind of rights the rights created by and embedded in FOIA are, we will have made a start in understanding what the act does and what it does not, and what it can do and what it cannot.

NOTES

1. Pub. L. No. 89-487, 80 Stat. 250 (1966), *codified as amended at* 5 U.S.C. § 552 (2012).
2. See, for example, David M. O'Brien, *The Public's Right to Know: The Supreme Court and the First Amendment* (New York: Praeger, 1981); Michael Schudson, *The Rise of the Right to Know: Politics and the Culture of Transparency, 1945–1975* (Cambridge, Mass.: Belknap Press, 2015).
3. See Richmond Newspapers, Inc. v. Virginia, 448 U.S. 555, 598 (1980) (Stewart, J., concurring in the judgment); Zurcher v. Stanford Daily, 436 U.S. 547, 570 (1978) (Stewart, J., dissenting); Pittsburgh Press Co. v. Pittsburgh Commission on Human Relations, 413 U.S. 376, 400 (1973) (Stewart, J., dissenting); Branzburg v. Hayes, 408 U.S. 665, 725 (1971) (Stewart, J., dissenting); Potter Stewart, "'Or of the Press,'" *Hastings Law Journal* 26 (1975): 631–37.
4. Stewart, "'Or of the Press,'" 636.
5. Wesley Newcomb Hohfeld, *Fundamental Legal Conceptions as Applied in Judicial Reasoning*, ed. Walter Wheeler Cook (New Haven, Conn.: Yale University Press, 1919), republishing articles first published in 1913 and 1917.

6. I say "recognize" to allow for the possibility that some constitutional or legal rights recognize and enforce preexisting moral or natural rights, as perhaps with the Eighth Amendment right to be free from "cruel and unusual punishments" and the First Amendment right to the "free exercise" of religion, whereas other legal or constitutional provisions create rights that have no prelegal natural or moral status, as with the (now uniquely American) Seventh Amendment right to jury trial in civil cases. On the distinction, see Ronald Dworkin, *A Matter of Principle* (Cambridge, Mass.: Harvard University Press, 1985), 375–80.

7. See Glanville Williams, "The Concept of Legal Liberty," in *Essays in Legal Philosophy*, ed. Robert S. Summers (Oxford: Basil Blackwell, 1970), 121–45.

8. See, for example, Church of the Lukumi Babalu Aye, Inc. v. City of Hialeah, 508 U.S. 520 (1993); West Virginia State Board of Education v. Barnette, 319 U.S. 624 (1943). In practice, "pure" free exercise cases rarely arise in the United States, at least in the sense of laws singling out a religious practice for restriction because of its religious nature. Most free exercise cases involve either seemingly neutral restrictions that in reality are aimed at a particular religion, as with the prohibition on animal sacrifice in *Church of the Lukumi Babalu Aye*, or claims of exemption from laws of genuinely general application in intent and design that nevertheless incidentally turn out to restrict the religious practices of adherents of particular religions, as with the flag salute requirement in *Barnette* or the mandatory schooling requirement in *Wisconsin v. Yoder*, 406 U.S. 205 (1972), which the Supreme Court held could not constitutionally be applied to the Old Order Amish.

9. See McDonald v. City of Chicago, 561 U.S. 742 (2010); District of Columbia v. Heller, 554 U.S. 570 (2008).

10. The "pure" examples include protections against government criminal sanctions against speaking or writing because of the content of the speech or writing, as in *United States v. Alvarez*, 567 U.S. 709 (2012), which invalidated a statute prohibiting falsely claiming to have won the Medal of Honor; *Brandenburg v. Ohio*, 395 U.S. 444 (1969), which recognized the right to advocate illegality short of explicit incitement to imminent violence; and *Kingsley International Pictures Corp. v. Regents*, 360 U.S. 684 (1960), which stated that the freedom to advocate even the propriety of adultery is "at the very heart of constitutionally protected liberty" (per Stewart, J.).

11. See Charles Fried, *Right and Wrong* (Cambridge, Mass.: Harvard University Press, 1978), 110–14. The classic discussion of the distinction between positive and negative liberties is Isaiah Berlin, "Two Concepts of Liberty," in *Four Essays on Liberty*, ed. Isaiah Berlin (Oxford: Oxford University Press, 1969), 118–72.

12. See Civil Rights Cases, 109 U.S. 3, 11 (1883), announcing that "individual invasion of individual rights is not the subject-matter of the [Fourteenth]

amendment." See also Jackson v. Metropolitan Edison Company, 419 U.S. 345 (1974); Moose Lodge v. Irvis, 407 U.S. 163 (1972). Numerous Supreme Court cases have dealt with the question of what kind and amount of connection between a non-state entity and the state is sufficient to treat the actions of the non-state entity as actions of the state for constitutional purposes. See, for example, Marsh v. Alabama, 326 U.S. 501 (1946), which treated a "private" company town as the state for First Amendment purposes; Burton v. Wilmington Parking Authority, 365 U.S. 715 (1961), which found sufficient "entanglement" between a private restaurant and the state as to render the restaurant's discriminatory actions state action. But that area of constitutional doctrine is far from the principal concerns of this chapter.

13. See, for example, the sympathetic (to positive rights) discussion in Susan Bandes, "The Negative Constitution: A Critique," *Michigan Law Review* 88 (1990): 2271–2347; and the decidedly less sympathetic treatment in Frank Cross, "The Error of Positive Rights," *UCLA Law Review* 48 (2001): 857–924.

14. A moral right, to be sure, and often a legal right under state or local law.

15. Gideon v. Wainwright, 372 U.S. 335 (1963).

16. Compare Citizens United v. Federal Election Commission, 588 U.S. 310 (2010), and First National Bank of Boston v. Bellotti, 435 U.S. 765 (1978), recognizing corporations as right-holders under the First Amendment's speech and press clauses, with Robert C. Post, *Citizens Divided: Campaign Finance Reform and the Constitution* (Cambridge, Mass.: Harvard University Press, 2014), arguing that corporations have First Amendment free speech rights only as derivative from and for the benefit of natural persons. See also Frederick Schauer, "Constitutions of Hope and Fear," *Yale Law Journal* 124 (2014): 528–62. With respect to the free exercise of religion (as embodied in a statute, the Religious Freedom Restoration Act of 1993, 42 U.S.C. § 2000 (2012), and not as a matter of constitutional law), see Burwell v. Hobby Lobby Stores, Inc., 134 S. Ct. 2751 (2014).

17. See John H. Garvey, *What Are Freedoms For?* (Cambridge, Mass.: Harvard University Press, 1996).

18. I say "infants," and not "minors" or "juveniles." See Tinker v. Des Moines Independent School District, 393 U.S. 503 (1969). On the distinction, see Steven H. Shiffrin, "The First Amendment and the Socialization of Children," *Cornell Journal of Law and Public Policy* 11 (2005): 503–51.

19. Hale v. Henkel, 201 U.S. 43 (1906).

20. These are distinct questions because sometimes rights can be enforced by entities only on behalf of others. See Robert Allen Sedler, "Standing to Assert Constitutional Jus Tertii in the Supreme Court," *Yale Law Journal* 71 (1962): 599–658.

21. Gillette v. United States, 401 U.S. 437 (1971).

22. In other words, the right to freedom of speech is different from a general right to liberty. See Frederick Schauer, "On the Distinction Between Speech and Action." *Emory Law Journal* 65 (2015): 427–54.

23. Compare Buckley v. Valeo, 424 U.S. 1 (1976), with Joshua Rosenkranz, ed., *If* Buckley *Fell: The First Amendment Blueprint for Regulating Money in Politics* (New York: Century Foundation Press, 1999).

24. Compare Aleta G. Estreicher, "Securities Regulation and the First Amendment," *Georgia Law Review* 24 (1990): 223–326, with Frederick Schauer, "The Boundaries of the First Amendment: A Preliminary Exploration of Constitutional Salience," *Harvard Law Review* 117 (2004): 1765–1809.

25. See Erie v. Pap's A.M., 529 U.S. 277 (2000).

26. Roe v. Wade, 410 U.S. 113 (1973); Planned Parenthood of Southeastern Pennsylvania v. Casey, 505 U.S. 833 (1992).

27. Harris v. McRae, 448 U.S. 297 (1980); Maher v. Roe, 432 U.S. 464 (1977).

28. San Antonio Independent School District v. Rodriguez, 411 U.S. 1 (1973). The obligatory reference here is to A. J. Liebling: "Freedom of the press is guaranteed only to those who own one." A. J. Liebling, "The Wayward Press: Do You Belong in Journalism?," *New Yorker*, May 14, 1960, 105, 109.

29. See James v. Valtierra, 402 U.S. 137 (1971). Compare Frank I. Michelman, "On Protecting the Poor Through the Fourteenth Amendment," *Harvard Law Review* 83 (1969): 7–59.

30. See Deshaney v. Winnebago County Department of Social Services, 489 U.S. 189 (1989).

31. See, for example, Katharine G. Young, *Constituting Economic and Social Rights* (Oxford: Oxford University Press, 2012). Such rights are often referred to as "second-generation" rights. See Dieter Grimm, "The Protective Function of the State," in *European and US Constitutionalism*, ed. Georg Nolte (Cambridge, UK: Cambridge University Press, 2005), 137–55, at 145–46. See also T. H. Marshall's distinction among civil rights, political rights, and social rights, with social rights being both more recent and encompassing the kinds of positive rights often described as social welfare rights. T. H. Marshall, *Citizenship and Social Class, and Other Essays* (Cambridge, UK: Cambridge University Press, 1950).

32. Hague v. CIO, 307 U.S. 496 (1939). See generally, Harry Kalven, "The Concept of the Public Forum: *Cox v. Louisiana*," *Supreme Court Review* (1965): 1–38.

33. See Mila Versteeg and Emily Zackin, "American Constitutional Exceptionalism Revisited," *University of Chicago Law Review* 81 (2014): 1641–1707.

34. See Emily Zackin, *Looking for Rights in All the Wrong Places: Why State Constitutions Contain Positive Rights* (Princeton, N.J.: Princeton University Press, 2013).

35. See Courtney Jung, Ran Hirschl, and Evan Rosevear, "Economic and Social Rights in National Constitutions," *American Journal of Comparative Law* 62 (2014): 1043–92.

36. The existing cases are typically ones in which the publisher has legally obtained information from someone who has obtained or, often, stolen it illegally. The prominent example in the Supreme Court is *New York Times Co. v. United States* (the Pentagon Papers Case), 403 U.S. 713 (1971), and others are *Bartnicki v. Vopper*, 532 U.S. 14 (2001), protecting the right to publish information originally obtained by an unlawful wiretap, and *Landmark Communications, Inc. v. Virginia*, 435 U.S. 829 (1978), upholding the right of a newspaper to publish confidential court records obtained unlawfully by a court employee. In *Bartnicki* and *Landmark Communications*, the Supreme Court was careful to emphasize that the publisher played no part in the original illegality. Whether a publisher can be punished for publishing information that the publisher has obtained unlawfully, or where the publisher has been more involved with the original illegality than was the case with respect to the Pentagon Papers or the material in *Bartnicki* and *Landmark Communications*, remains an open question.

37. See generally, Rahul Sagar, *Secrets and Leaks: The Dilemma of State Secrecy* (Princeton, N.J.: Princeton University Press, 2013); David E. Pozen, "The Leaky Leviathan: Why the Government Condemns and Condones Unlawful Disclosures of Information," *Harvard Law Review* 127 (2013): 512–635. For suggestions that existing legal doctrine ought to be changed to provide First Amendment protection for the original leaker, see Heidi Kitrosser, "Leak Prosecutions and the First Amendment: New Developments and a Closer Look at the Feasibility of Protecting Leakers," *William and Mary Law Review* 56 (2015): 1221–77; Mary-Rose Papandrea, "Leaker Traitor Whistleblower Spy: National Security Leaks and the First Amendment," *Boston University Law Review* 94 (2014): 449–544.

38. See Saxbe v. Washington Post Co., 417 U.S. 843 (1974); Pell v. Procunier, 417 U.S. 817 (1974).

39. 438 U.S. 1 (1978).

40. 438 U.S. at 15 (Burger, C. J., for the plurality).

41. Richmond Newspapers, Inc. v. Virginia, 448 U.S. 555 (1980). See also Globe Newspaper Co. v. Superior Court, 457 U.S. 596 (1982); Press-Enterprise Co. v. Superior Court, 464 U.S. 501 (1984); Press-Enterprise Co. v. Superior Court, 478 U.S. 1 (1986). An earlier case, *Gannett Co. v. DePasquale*, 443 U.S. 368 (1979), had held that a right of public access (in that case to a pretrial suppression hearing) was not required by the Sixth Amendment right to a public trial. *Richmond Newspapers* did recognize a constitutional right of public access and located that right in some combination of historical practice and a First Amendment right to receive information and ideas.

42. See William P. Marshall, "The Limits on Congress's Authority to Investigate the President," *University of Illinois Law Review* (2004): 781–825.

43. A government agency cannot, as the above cases and discussion make clear, enforce this secrecy by prohibiting the publication of such information, or by sanctioning a publisher who has lawfully obtained it. But an agency that wishes to guard its documents and information with strong walls, good locks, and competent security guards is, as far as the First Amendment is concerned, fully entitled to do so.

44. Stewart, "'Or of the Press,'" 636.

45. See Kathy Bradley, "Do You Feel the Sunshine? Government in the Sunshine Act: Its Objectives, Goals, and Effect on the FCC and You," *Federal Communications Law Journal* 49 (1997): 473–89; "Report and Recommendations by the Special Committee to Review the Government in the Sunshine Act," *Administrative Law Review* 49 (1997): 421–28.

46. "The right to speak and publish does not carry with it the unrestrained right to gather information." Zemel v. Rusk, 381 U.S. 1, 17 (1965). A prominent view to the contrary is Anthony Lewis, "The First Amendment as a Sword," *Supreme Court Review* (1980): 1–34.

47. See Seth F. Kreimer, "The Freedom of Information Act and the Ecology of Transparency," *University of Pennsylvania Journal of Constitutional Law* 10 (2008): 1012–80, at 1013; David E. Pozen, "Deep Secrecy," *Stanford Law Review* 62 (2010): 257–339, at 314 n. 204. The extent to which the idea of transparency or freedom of information is small-"c" constitutional depends on one's views both of democracy and of a constitution, issues that are far too large to take on here. Still, it is worth noting the possibilities that not everything that facilitates openness in government is or ought to be considered a necessary component of democracy, and, less controversially, that not everything that is a component of democracy is or ought to be thought of as constitutional.

48. The Freedom of Information Act was itself preceded by the access to information provisions in Section 3 of the Administrative Procedure Act, Pub. L. No. 79–404, 60 Stat. 238 (1946), but those provisions were widely understood to be more concerned with ensuring secrecy than with providing increased access to information. See Norman Dorsen, Paul Bender, and Burt Neuborne, *Political and Civil Rights in the United States, Volume I*, 4th ed. (Boston, Mass.: Little, Brown, 1976), 203–04.

49. It is not quite self-evident that openness is an unqualified good. Not only do rights to information at times interfere with the right of informational privacy (as in, for example, *Florida Star v. B.J.F.*, 491 U.S. 524 (1989), where, to oversimplify, the right to public information about a trial was deemed to outweigh the privacy interests of the juvenile rape victim), but these rights also may

interfere with the efficient or otherwise optimal operation of government. The law of privileges, after all, is based on the view that immunity from compelled disclosure—secrecy, in a word—in various trial and nontrial contexts will, at times, produce more and not less candor and thus more and not less information. See Christopher B. Mueller and Laird C. Kirkpatrick, *Evidence*, 5th ed. (New York: Wolters Kluwer, 2012), § 5.1, at 294–95. Perhaps ironically to some, therefore, the quest by the press for more information is, in the press's view, sometimes facilitated by laws ensuring access and sometimes by privileges—shield laws, most obviously—that limit access to information. Not only will transparency—access to information—sometimes produce less information, at times it also may produce less sound decisions. See Frederick Schauer, "Transparency in Three Dimensions," *University of Illinois Law Review* (2011): 1339–57. For the view in another but related context that more information may produce worse judgments, see Omri Ben-Shahar and Carl E. Schneider, *More Than You Wanted to Know: The Failure of Mandated Disclosure* (Princeton, N.J.: Princeton University Press, 2014).

50. "No Person shall be convicted of Treason unless on the Testimony of two Witnesses to the same overt Act, or on Confession in open Court." U.S. Constitution, Art. III, § 3, cl. 1.

51. Despite the qualifications regarding openness provided in note 49, here I assume that both openness and public acceptance of it are valuable. With this assumption in hand, I focus only on the question whether these goals are better served by constitutionalization or by statute.

52. Much of the primary evidence is cited and summarized in Frederick Schauer, *The Force of Law* (Cambridge, Mass.: Harvard University Press, 2015), 57–74, 197–205.

53. Schauer, *The Force of Law*, 75–92, 205–11. See also Frederick Schauer, "Official Obedience and the Politics of Defining 'Law,'" *Southern California Law Review* 58 (2013): 1165–94; "The Political Risks (If Any) of Breaking the Law," *Journal of Legal Analysis* 4 (2012): 83–101; "Is Legality Political?," *William and Mary Law Review* 53 (2011): 481–506; and "How and When (If at All) Does Law Constrain Official Action?," *Georgia Law Review* 44 (2010): 769–801.

54. See David Fontana and Donald Braman, "Judicial Backlash or Just Backlash? Evidence from a National Experiment," *Columbia Law Review* 112 (2012): 731–99.

55. This is the conclusion, drawing on and summarizing much of the primary research at the time, in Gerald N. Rosenberg, *The Hollow Hope: Can Courts Bring About Social Change?*, 2nd ed. (Chicago, Ill.: University of Chicago Press, 2008), 25–36. Rosenberg's conclusions have been highly controversial, and there is evidence that in some areas judicial constitutional decisions may,

even if through an indirect causal mechanism, produce attitudinal change. See, for example, Thomas M. Keck, "Beyond Backlash: Assessing the Impact of Judicial Decisions on LGBT Rights," *Law and Society Review* 43 (2009): 151–86; Scott L. Cummings, "Empirical Studies of Law and Social Change: What Is the Field? What Are the Questions?," *Wisconsin Law Review* (2013): 171–204. A good broader overview of research on law and attitudinal and behavioral change is Kenworthey Bilz and Janice Nadler, "Law, Moral Attitudes, and Behavioral Change," in *Oxford Handbook of Behavioral Law and Economics*, ed. Eyal Zamir and Doron Teichman (New York: Oxford University Press, 2014), 241–67. Like much of the post-Rosenberg research in the field, however, it does not distinguish the attitudinal influence of constitutional judicial decisions from the attitudinal influence of law generally. But if the question is whether to achieve some goal by constitutional judicial decisions as opposed to statutes, this is precisely the distinction that is important.

56. See Michael J. Klarman, *From the Closet to the Altar: Courts, Backlash, and the Struggle for Same-Sex Marriage* (New York: Oxford University Press, 2012).

57. Assuming, plausibly, that a constitutional amendment to this effect is beyond the realm of realistic possibility.

58. See William N. Eskridge Jr. and John Ferejohn, *A Republic of Statutes: The New American Constitution* (New Haven, Conn.: Yale University Press, 2010); William N. Eskridge Jr. and John Ferejohn, "Super-Statutes," *Duke Law Journal* 50 (2001): 1215–76; Kathryn E. Kovacs, "Superstatute Theory and Administrative Common Law," *Indiana Law Journal* 90 (2015): 1207–60.

59. See Ronald Dworkin, *Law's Empire* (Cambridge, Mass.: Harvard University Press, 1986), 178–84, arguing that "checkerboard" policies requiring allocation of resources across competing claims of policy (but not of principle) should be made by legislatures and not by courts. In the context of FOIA, however, there is little evidence that Congress actually carefully considered these allocative questions, however desirable it might have been had Congress done so. As a result, application of FOIA might at times be more arbitrary than is optimal, as is argued in David E. Pozen, "Freedom of Information Beyond the Freedom of Information Act," *University of Pennsylvania Law Review* 165 (2017): 1097–1158. The issue is complex because at times the unintended consequences of congressional action may have useful dimensions. Consider, for example, the sometimes lamented (see Margaret B. Kwoka, "FOIA, Inc.," *Duke Law Journal* 65 [2016]: 1361–1437) domination of FOIA requests by self-interested corporations as opposed to journalists and members of the public. Given that the vast majority of federal administrative regulation involves the regulation of corporations, FOIA, even as so used, might serve a valuable even if unintended due process function—giving access to information about regulation to those who are most directly affected by the regulation.

60. See Cass R. Sunstein, *One Case at a Time: Judicial Minimalism on the Supreme Court* (Cambridge, Mass.: Harvard University Press, 1999), which both describes and endorses this approach.

61. Some of us wish it were otherwise, and that courts, especially the Supreme Court, would acknowledge their law-making function and thus be more willing to set out general rules for the guidance of lower courts and primary politi-cal and policy actors. See Frederick Schauer, "Our Informationally Disabled Courts," *Daedalus* 143 (2014): 105–14; "Abandoning the Guidance Function: *Morse v. Frederick*," *Supreme Court Review* (2007): 316–48; and "Opinions as Rules," *University of Chicago Law Review* 62 (1995): 1455–75.

62. For various perspectives on exactly this question, see Daniel P. Kessler, ed., *Regulation vs. Litigation: Perspectives from Economics and Law* (Chicago, Ill.: University of Chicago Press, 2011). See also Frederick Schauer, "Do Cases Make Bad Law?," *University of Chicago Law Review* 73 (2006): 883–918.

63. For example, the Federal Advisory Committee Act, Pub. L. 92–463, 86 Stat. 770 (1972), regulates federal advisory bodies in numerous ways, one of which is to grant public access to advisory committee proceedings and documents and another of which is to prohibit secret advisory committee deliberations.

64. See Young, *Constituting Economic and Social Rights.*

65. Government of the Republic of South Africa v. Grootboom, 2001 (1) SA 46 (CC).

66. Minister of Health v. Treatment Action Campaign, 2002 (5) SA 721 (CC).

67. See Julia Szalaï, "Fragmented Social Rights in Hungary's Postcommunist Welfare State," in *Policy and Citizenship: The Changing Landscape*, ed. Adalbert Evers and Anne-Marie Guillemard (Oxford: Oxford University Press, 2012), chap. 12; Andras Sajo, "Implementing Welfare in Eastern Europe After Communism," in *Economic, Social and Cultural Rights in Practice: The Role of Judges in Implementing Economic, Social and Cultural Rights*, ed. Yash Ghai and Jill Cottrell (London: InterRights, 2004), 50–57.

68. See P. M. Bakshi, *The Constitution of India*, 10th ed. (New Delhi: Universal Law, 2010), 84–92; Michael Forde and David Leonard, *Constitutional Law of Ireland*, 3rd ed. (Dublin: Bloomsbury, 2013): 285–304.

69. In a comprehensive recent study, Kwoka, "FOIA, Inc.," documents the extent to which the vast majority of claimants under FOIA at certain agencies are corporations and neither individual citizens nor individual journalists. Kwoka views this state of affairs with alarm, but it is not so clear why it should be thought of as alarming. It should be no surprise that the subjects of regulation would be disproportionately interested in obtaining the information relevant to the regulation of their activities. Indeed, we might think of FOIA as embody-ing, in part, something of a due process interest insofar as it provides the kind of information to regulatory subjects that the subjects might desire in order to comply with, resist, or seek to change the regulation.

3

FOIA AS AN ADMINISTRATIVE LAW

Mark Fenster

IN ONE TELLING—the conventional wisdom among transparency advocates and the press—the Freedom of Information Act's history is a sad, disappointing story of a second-best, not very good alternative.

Enacted in 1966 as an amendment to the Administrative Procedure Act, FOIA is neither a freestanding constitutional right to access government information nor recognized as part of the First Amendment prerogatives of the press. As a result, U.S. law largely limits the "right to know" to FOIA's statutory terms. These terms appear unobjectionable: requiring executive branch agencies to make certain information generally available; allowing individuals to request information through a standardized process; and enabling individuals to seek judicial review if they are dissatisfied by the government's denial of their requests. But FOIA frustrates in practice. Despite congressional and executive branch efforts to make the process more easily navigable, FOIA advocates and many users regularly complain about unchecked bureaucratic resistance to FOIA's letter and spirit.

Viewed this way, FOIA constitutes more of a symbolic commitment to the free flow of government information than an effective means to regulate secrecy. It may be better than nothing, but no reasonable observer would argue that FOIA's fifty-odd years of existence have seen the end of excessive state secrecy. Quite the opposite in fact: FOIA may not have caused the increased expansion of state secrecy (although one could imagine an argument otherwise), but the government holds more secrets today than fifty years ago, and the public seems at least as disconnected to and ignorant of the state's actions as it was in 1966. We were promised freed information, an open government, and a truly democratic state; all we have received in the decades since are political scandal, an ever-expanding classification system, and a means to file a records request and await full or partial denial. Viewed this way, FOIA deserves and needs greater status and stricter enforcement. A robust freedom of information right enshrined in the Constitution and vigorously enforced by the courts can cure the ills from which FOIA has suffered since its inception.

In this chapter, I consider two issues that derive from the gulf between FOIA's symbolic role as the preeminent means of democratically controlling secrecy and its relative lack of efficacy. First, does FOIA's character as an administrative rule rather than a constitutional mandate help explain the limits of its effects? Upon reviewing the history of advocacy in the area, my answer is a "very qualified yes." *Yes*, because advocates are right to maintain that transparency is still viewed as a secondary value, notwithstanding rhetoric suggesting otherwise, not just in spite of but because of FOIA; and *yes*, because a constitutional right would at least extend further into the federal and state and local governments than FOIA; but a *very qualified yes*, because I'm not sure it matters. The administrative rule/constitutional right issue is, in fact, less important than the second issue: is secrecy (and its cure, transparency) a cause or a symptom of the failure of democracy to meet its promise in the contemporary administrative state? I take on the second issue by way of questioning whether the choice of constitutional or statutory right matters to any significant degree.

TRANSPARENCY ADVOCACY: BETTER A CONSTITUTIONAL RIGHT THAN A STATUTORY ONE (BUT BETTER A STATUTORY ONE THAN NONE AT ALL)

The preference for constitutionalizing transparency is not new; debates about secrecy and transparency in the United States during the post–World War II era have operated in the distance between claims grounded in transcendent legal rights on one hand and responses found in workaday administrative rules on the other. These positions date from transparency advocacy's earliest days when press organizations fought the expansion of government secrecy in the decades following World War II. The American Society of Newspaper Editors (ASNE) and prominent publishers and press executives used the bully pulpit of their pages and their relationships with legislators to push for creation of a legal means to obtain access to government information. The initial campaign for freedom of information legislation took more than a decade, and Congress passed FOIA over the Johnson administration's resistance.

As Sam Lebovic explains in *Free Speech and Unfree News*, his intellectual history of the relationship between the media and theories of the First Amendment, this campaign emerged in the shadow of the Cold War and followed a mostly successful effort by the same advocates and their predecessors to establish the Press Clause of the First Amendment as a shield against government interference in their output and their business.[1] Equally significant, it followed a campaign to export American journalistic ideals abroad as part of the broader pre- and postwar campaign to transmit U.S. political, economic, and cultural ideals to Europe. Advocates developed the terms "right to know" and "freedom of information" during this period as part of a classical liberal conception of the press as a check on the state, with legal rights and freedoms serving as a means by which the public would benefit from the free flow of information presented to it by a privately held press free from state interference.[2]

The campaign resulted in one historically important scholarly monograph, a fairly dull book titled *The People's Right to Know*, by retired media attorney and media law professor Harold Cross at the Columbia School of Journalism. Cross had worked with ASNE, which had commissioned the book, from the early stages of its campaign against state secrecy. His vast knowledge and talent in understanding and synthesizing existing legal doctrine gave him considerable influence over the press—the interest group most interested in addressing government secrecy and most capable of using its political influence to accomplish its goal. James Pope, the chair of ASNE's Freedom of Information Committee, recruited Cross to serve as legal advisor and gushed in his foreword to *The People's Right to Know* that Cross had become "our leader" in a movement in which the press would serve as an "agent of the people" to enforce the right of access to information.[3] It was not the sole book on the subject. James Russell Wiggins, a former ASNE FOI Committee chair, published *Freedom or Secrecy* in 1956 and joined Cross in advocating on behalf of an enforceable right to know.[4]

The People's Right to Know would prove, along with its author, to be the most influential legal authority in the campaign for government transparency. Cross's book compiled the existing (as of 1953) state and federal laws on information access across federal and state governments. He documented in some detail the conditions under which government entities and officials kept information secret: the "world trends," officials' "habits of secrecy and censorship" and their desire for greater privilege in handling information, the expansion of a right to privacy about which Cross was skeptical, and a lack of faith among progressives and the press in the importance of advocating for greater transparency. To counter these adverse trends, Cross offered an extensive legal brief that sought to implant the rights concept into intellectual and legal opinion. A series of opening declarations emphasized the most prominent terms from the earlier free press campaign: "Public business is the public's business. The people have the right to know. Freedom of information is their just heritage. Without that the citizens of a democracy have but changed their kings." "Rights" against the state, along with the ideal of "freedom" from state barriers to access, served as the logical way for a legal advocate such as Cross to champion transparency. But the prevailing law of access to government information, Cross complained, was a mess. It existed only "where you find it," in a "welter of varying statutes, conflicting court opinions and wordy departmental regulations [that] present the problem as a veritable Chinese puzzle."[5]

The resulting information access law could not confront and control the expansion of Cold War secrecy. Access to information was "a neglected constitutional right," Cross noted. Citing a range of historical and contemporary figures for support, he argued that it ought to be encompassed within First Amendment protections.[6] Cross lamented what he presciently viewed as the dim prospects of that right's judicial recognition. Setting aside his preference for a constitutional right as a stronger, universal means to gain public access to government information, Cross instead advocated federal legislation as an alternative to the elusive enshrinement of a federal constitutional right to know.

In the decade prior to World War II, Congress and lobbyists on behalf of regulated parties had sought to establish a uniform set of legal procedures that would rein in an increasingly active federal bureaucracy. Their efforts led to the Administrative Procedure Act of 1946, whose existing information access provisions were vague and riddled with exceptions.[7] Although the APA imposes some requirements that force agencies to create and disclose information regarding the regulatory process, it was not the sweeping law that would encompass the full range of government information for which Cross and others advocated. Specifically, it established no judicially enforceable public right to information in the event of a government entity's refusal to disclose information. Cross urged Congress to "begin exercising effectually its function to legislate freedom of information for itself, the public, and the press" by creating a legal right to know.[8]

Soon after the publication of Cross's book, the ASNE committee finally found in California Representative John Moss an effective legislative partner for establishing the legal rights that Cross described.[9] In November 1954, a new Democratic majority had wrestled control of the U.S. House of Representatives back from a small Republican majority that had ridden Dwight Eisenhower's coattails in his 1952 election to a first presidential term. Although Eisenhower's moderate conservatism held at arm's length both Senator Joseph McCarthy (whose prominence was fast receding by 1954) and Vice President Richard Nixon, politics was ultimately partisan, and Democrats resented having lost the presidency for the first time since Franklin Roosevelt's initial election in 1932. Moreover, the executive branch's expansion during the New Deal and the president's administrative prerogative over executive branch secrets following the end of World War II constituted a source of political conflict. Even with a war hero and political moderate in the White House and a common enemy in the Soviet Union, Congress viewed its role both as a principled, institutional source of opposition to the presidency and the branch he controlled and as a source of political opposition to a Republican electoral foe.

To that end, the House of Representatives' Government Operations Committee, chaired by Democratic Representative William Dawson of Illinois, established a Special Subcommittee on Government Information, with Moss as chair, to investigate executive branch secrecy. ASNE leaders and prominent newspaper editors played key roles in spurring the Subcommittee on Government Information (referred to popularly as "the Moss Committee") into action. The press provided personnel, with former journalists dominating the committee's staff and prominent editors helping devise its aggressive strategy of investigating federal agencies that kept information secret from the press and the public.[10] ASNE introduced Cross to Moss and his subcommittee, and Cross played a key role as the committee's legal advisor until his death in 1959. The press also provided publicity, with newspapers around the country promoting the subcommittee's work and especially its hearings and investigations.[11] The press helped frame the issue as one of insufficiently recognized and enforced legal rights. In James Pope's words, when he testified at the Moss Committee's first hearing, "freedom of information is not a political issue. . . . The right to know is the right of the people."[12] Tellingly, Harold Cross's argument in favor of imposing legal obligations through the creation of privately exercised statutory rights proved to be the only satisfactory legislative solution to secrecy.

After an amendment to existing law failed to change bureaucratic norms, the Freedom of Information Act—a statute whose title was apparently appropriated from the title of ASNE member Herbert Brucker's 1949 book and was not mentioned in the *Congressional Record* as the act's original title—finally gained sufficient legislative support in 1966, cleared the procedural hurdles in Congress, and was enacted despite President Johnson's expressed ambivalence and unexpressed hostility.[13] According to Bill Moyers, his press secretary at the time, Johnson "had to be dragged kicking and screaming to the signing ceremony. He hated the very idea of the Freedom of Information Act; hated the thought of journalists rummaging in government closets; hated them challenging the official view of reality."[14] It is no wonder that Johnson disliked the act so much; it represented a significant incursion into what had long been executive and bureaucratic prerogative. FOIA enacted a version of a "right to know" and pledged to protect the "freedom" of information that first had been conceptualized and developed in the early postwar and Cold War effort to instill Western democratic values abroad through the ideal of a free, independent press. It was also, from a president's perspective, a pain in the ass.

Cross's book is largely unreadable today because of the success enjoyed by those who initially relied on Cross to advocate against secrecy. It collects and restates a set of common law and early statutory doctrines that it helped make obsolete via modern statutes and, in some instances, state constitutions. The book remains interesting for two reasons, however: first, for rehearsing a set of general claims and theoretical proclamations about the necessity of information access for a democratic political system, claims that have proven robust and long-lived; and, second, for Cross's strategic decision ultimately not to strongly pursue a constitutional basis for access to information.

It is not that Cross ignored the possibility or value of a constitutional right to know. After all, he strongly advocated a constitutional right of access under a broadly interpreted First Amendment. But at least regarding the federal administrative state, the bulk of his book was instead an argument for a lesser, second-best solution—amendment of the APA. He closed *The People's Right to Know* with the argument that "the time is ripe for an end to ineffectual sputtering about executive refusals of access to official records and for Congress to begin exercising effectually its function to legislate freedom of information for itself, the public, and the press. The powers of Congress to that end are not unlimited but they are extensive."[15]

Cross did not explain the distinction he saw between a constitutional right to information and a statutory obligation on the state to disclose, nor did he suggest whether he or his press collaborators should prefer one to the other. They were alternatives to the same goal, and he considered the statutory path the more likely one to succeed. Cross no doubt found this worthy of a lament, but he clearly did not view it as a reason to stop his advocacy.

The distinction between statutory and constitutional rights seemed to make a greater difference to the next generation of legal advocates, when leading First Amendment scholar Thomas Emerson took up the same issue in 1976.[16] A civil libertarian and theorist of civil and political rights, Emerson hoped to place the right to know within the First Amendment and alongside his own preferred theory of the amendment as protecting the right of the speaker to self-fulfillment through self-expression, a theory he had previously developed across a series of articles and books.[17] The right to know, he argued, could plug the holes left by the First Amendment's primary purpose of protecting speech and the press. Among other things, it could protect a right to read, listen, or see others' communications that the state attempts to block, to restrict the state's ability to shape the information it communicates, and in some limited contexts (specifically broadcasting) to allow the state to regulate content to expand available viewpoints.[18]

More important for present purposes, however, Emerson viewed the concept as including "a constitutional right in the public to obtain information from government sources necessary or proper for the citizen to perform his function as ultimate sovereign." The right would flow directly from the First Amendment, as an element of enabling democracy "to work," or enabling the people to maintain their "ultimate decision-making authority" as a "fourth branch of government." Although not the "sole purpose" of the broad First Amendment right, Emerson argued, access to government information "is surely a main element of that provision and should be recognized as such." This right would extend, "as a starting point, to all information in the possession of the government." And he meant his sweeping statement to be taken literally, as access to *all* information by *everyone*—because, he asserted, "it is hard to conceive of any government issue that would not be relevant to the concerns of the citizen and taxpayer."[19]

But "all" did not in fact mean all. Emerson immediately backslid, readily conceding "exceptions" to this right that included the president's "right to executive privilege," "sensitive national security data," trade secrets, and so on. Privacy, too, needed protection. Given his classical liberal orientation to the state, Emerson found the relationship between the right of privacy, which secures the individual's autonomy against the state's intrusion, and the right to information, which protects the citizen's political authority, particularly vexing. Each is a paramount right of private citizens, and yet they come into conflict when the state holds information about an individual. Emerson saw no easy answers in reconciling the conflict because he did not trust the government to resolve the issue by determining the relative values of the rights in particular instances, nor did he trust courts to properly "balance" the rights in individual cases. To resolve the conflict, he proposed a rule in which the right of privacy trumps the right to information, thereby privileging individual autonomy over the citizen's right of political participation. Having conceded the obvious point that the privacy right has no clear definition or boundary, he preferred a clear rule protecting privacy to a standard that would invite courts to balance privacy against information access.[20] Judicial authority might be paramount, but courts could not be trusted to weigh rights against each other.

To summarize, Emerson viewed the right to information as an essential element of the First Amendment's broad scope. It could bend to the state's legitimate needs, although he deferred comment on the issue of how and to what extent this bending would occur. But the right must give way, at a minimum, when in conflict with the individual's right to privacy.

How is Emerson's constitutional right distinct from the federal FOIA? The easy partial answer is that the former would apply to everything—to Congress and the judiciary, and to every state and local unit of government. But FOIA had already existed for a decade by the time Emerson's article was published, and it provided a good case study for how well or how poorly a right to information might operate. Curiously, Emerson barely mentioned the statute, and only after he had offered his constitutional scheme. He noted that FOIA "adopts much of the basic pattern just outlined"—a peculiar construction regarding a statute that had come before his basic pattern. He complained in passing that some of the statute's exceptions are "excessively broad," but he praised its mechanisms for judicial review and concluded by stating that "acceptance of the constitutional right would provide a firm foundation for further development and close gaps in the legislative structure," gaps that he did not describe in any detail.[21]

Indeed, the article's absences and utter lack of grounded realism and institutional detail are extraordinary, especially in contrast to Cross's work. Emerson ignored the case law that had already built up around FOIA, as well as the 1974 amendments intended to strengthen the statute in the wake of that case law and frustrations with the statute's enforcement and reach. Nor did he demonstrate any interest in imagining how an abstract constitutional right would avoid FOIA's shortcomings. Nor did he foresee the waning of the

Supreme Court's interest in expanding civil rights and civil liberties or how his abstract right might survive an increasingly conservative judiciary and self-protective executive branch. Emerson merely assumed that a broadly understood constitutional right would surely provide broader protection than a statutory right with explicit obligations. Unlike Cross, who correctly foresaw little chance that courts, much less Congress, would find or create such a right, Emerson assumed that, at least as an academic matter, the right was not only necessary but obvious and, really, *already existed* without acknowledgment.

Cross correctly recognized the best path for achievable legal reform, whereas Emerson argued his case poorly and failed to contemplate the potential shortcomings of his approach. I contrast Emerson with Cross to highlight the point that Emerson's desire to wish away the difficult questions FOIA has faced since its inception is symptomatic of a widely held desire to solve the administrative and bureaucratic problem of the state's information asymmetries through the judicial application of constitutional rights. The notion that the right legal mechanism can fix secrecy has permeated the assumptions of generations of transparency advocates and has been abandoned only in the present by those who privilege data, markets, or WikiLeaks-style hacking over the law's menu of solutions.[22] It continues to influence some constitutional law scholars who view information access as part of a broad reading of the First Amendment's protection of the right to self-government and free speech.[23] As the example of Emerson suggests, this has sometimes led to the view that if only the right of access were constitutional rather than statutory the state wouldn't hold as many secrets and we would have a more democratic, accountable government, one more thoroughly protected against antiliberal and anticonstitutional forces.[24]

CONSTITUTIONAL LAW, ADMINISTRATIVE LAW, AND THE SEARCH FOR A LEGAL FIX

Emerson's explicit argument and Cross's preference for a constitutional solution over an administrative one suggest that there is something special about constitutional law, and it is clearly true that the constitutionalization of information access rights could have expansive doctrinal effects. A constitutional right could not be overridden by statutory repeal or undercut by statutory amendment, and it would cover more institutions and more ground than limited statutes such as FOIA, which affect only parts of the federal executive branch and leave untouched the federal judiciary, the legislature, and the entirety of all subfederal units. In that regard, as a matter of formal doctrine, Emerson and Cross quite reasonably preferred a constitutional right of access.

But their preference reflected a more profound set of concerns and aspirations. It assumed that constitutional guarantees not only would cover more territory but also would be more vigorously enforced and broadly respected—that the Constitution has more gravitas and carries more weight than the federal code as a source of power and as a symbol. This would be true, not just with courts but with other branches and levels of government as well. Government officials might skirt an ordinary law, but they would be loath to violate the Constitution. If only we fought secrecy with the Constitution in our hands, the thinking goes, we could more readily contain it than with the U.S. code and the Code of Federal Regulations. And if the judiciary did as Emerson had advocated—establishing clear rules rather than balancing opposed interests—all the better.

This trust in legal doctrine is unconvincing for at least four reasons. It overvalues the Constitution, undervalues statutes, places too much faith in the judiciary, and doesn't properly contemplate bureaucratic structures and practices. I consider these issues in turn.

MAYBE CONSTITUTIONAL PROVISIONS ARE NOT SO GREAT

A constitutional right is not self-enforcing. The executive branch would primarily be in charge of interpreting and implementing a constitutional right of access to information. The president and the administrative state do not mechanically enforce constitutional rights; rather, their tendency to prioritize and emphasize different rights constitutes the kind of political decisions for which they are held accountable in subsequent electoral cycles. When rights are undefined or lack clear implementing rules, the administrative state enjoys substantial discretion over the manner and degree to which it enforces them. Courts must fill the gaps where they are seen to arise, and we should have minimal faith in courts to systematically enhance transparency for at least two reasons.

First, courts would have to balance informational access against the recognized privileges the executive branch has over certain types of information—the types most likely to be at stake in disputes that would be litigated. Examples of such conflicts abound, not only in the difficult theoretical balance between privacy and freedom of information that Emerson discussed, but also in the famous instance of the Supreme Court's decision in *Nixon v. United States* (1974), in which the Court was forced to balance the president's right to withhold information clearly within his informational privilege against the need for information in an ongoing criminal investigation. And second, courts have demonstrated limited courage in the face of executive recalcitrance, standing up to presidents at certain moments (for example, against the Nixon administration in its second term[25]) and lying down in others (for example, siding with the George W. Bush administration in the early part of its Global War on Terror[26]). FOIA has been unevenly enforced, as transparency advocates regularly complain.

It is thus not clear that the administration and enforcement of a constitutional right would prove much different from the administration and enforcement of a statutory one. The latter's imperfections are determined in part by the countercommand of alternative constitutional rights and privileges and in part by the specific facts in the case or controversy that a court would be asked to resolve when called upon to enforce an information right. Furthermore, the sprawling nature of the bureaucratic apparatus and asymmetric nature of information about what the state holds, as well as the abstract nature of defining what constitutes "information," can limit the judicial regulation of transparency just as much as the courts' legal authority—if not more so (as I argue below). Those issues do not simply disappear when the right is enshrined in something higher up the ladder of legal authorities than a statute.

MAYBE STATUTES CAN BE GREAT!

Second, statutes have status, too, and can themselves become quasi-constitutional. William Eskridge and John Ferejohn argue that when presidential administrations and administrative agencies interpret, implement, and enforce certain especially ambitious and resonant statutes over time, such laws not only fill in constitutional gaps but become "super-statutes" that prove as defining and consistent with the nation's moral character as constitutional provisions.[27] The Administrative Procedure Act, of which FOIA is a part, is one such statute. It provides, in Eskridge and Ferejohn's words, a "framework for understanding most national lawmaking" in a manner that has eclipsed the Constitution's delegation of legislative authority to Congress.[28] Tom Ginsburg has made a similar argument in a different way, by considering the constitutional/administrative law debate comparatively and finding that, across different nations, administrative law is constitution-like in its reflection of local values, in its endurance over time, and in its detailed control over administration.[29]

As a matter of substantive law, FOIA acts like a constitutional provision by providing a baseline of rights upon which individuals can rely to seek redress and a framework of procedures and obligations for the state to follow. As Frederick Schauer has noted, the impact of FOIA and its state analogs on publicly available information far outweighs that of the First Amendment.[30] Its status transcends the seemingly technical nature of the administrative procedures it has established. David Pozen has suggested that FOIA might enjoy the status of a super-statute because it "introduced a norm of open access to government documents that has commanded deep public loyalty, taken on a quasi-constitutional valence, and spawned a vast network of imitator laws at all levels of United States government and in democracies around the world." This is clearly true as a symbolic matter; as Pozen notes, the statute "entrenched a dramatic normative shift in Americans' expectations of government."[31]

Indeed, FOIA and the analogs enshrined in state statutes and constitutions (some of which are imitations of the federal model, others of which came first) *seem* constitutional. The statute's procedures to request information establish a right that is better-known and more frequently utilized by concerned members of the public than most of the rights created by or inferred from the Constitution itself. Although they may legally do so under the federal Constitution, those few U.S. states that limit the right of information access to their own citizens seem weirdly provincial (and, moreover, create a limitation that a noncitizen can easily circumvent), as if a Virginian would have lesser rights of free speech when she crossed the border into Tennessee.[32] With its procedural norms established in the language of freedoms and rights, FOIA gives a constitutional aura to what might otherwise be a pedestrian administrative statute while simultaneously creating constitutional standing for individuals that would not automatically be available under a vague constitutional right.[33] Only lawyers would view the APA as a super-statute; most concerned citizens not in government service, by contrast, view FOIA and the transparency it promises to impose as a foundational law that recognizes and protects their essential right to information.

FOIA's right of access has endured for more than fifty years, formally expanding through legislative amendment and only rarely and narrowly contracting by court decision. Indeed, its status as a statutory right, rather than a constitutional right, has allowed and even invited iterative reform by amendment.

It has created enduring norms, not least by specifying administrative rules in ways that constitutions do not. The right to request documents and attend a public meeting affects the everyday encounters of the public with the state, as well as the public's everyday imagining of how the state works and should work. Without in fact being constitutional, FOIA embodies a kind of popular constitutionalism via statute. In their administration and the public's experience, FOIA, its state analogs, and similar open government statutes may not represent the wonders of boutique, high-end constitutional litigation, but they supply an accessible right that anyone can fairly easily attempt to enjoy. In sum, FOIA might not gain anything by constitutionalization, and it's not clear whether Americans have lost anything from its status as a lowly federal statute.

MAYBE JUDICIAL REVIEW IS NOT SO GREAT

Like Harold Cross and Thomas Emerson, many current U.S transparency advocates view the judiciary as the best neutral arbiter to resolve disputes and enforce FOIA as Congress intended, reviewing agency refusals to disclose de novo.[34] But it is not clear why anyone would look upon the judiciary's five-decade record in interpreting and enforcing FOIA and declare that the answer to excessive secrecy is to marginally increase judicial scrutiny via a constitutional right. In the federal system, courts have simply not proven to be a bulwark against secrecy when an agency is willing to defend in court its refusal to disclose information under the statute.[35] The resistance of courts to efforts to constitutionalize a right to know seems to stem from more than just the lack of a clear doctrinal hook. The resistance seems ingrained, almost basic to the judicial response to challenges to the executive branch's informational authority.

We can speculate about the cause of the judiciary's reticence. No doubt courts occasionally, if not frequently, consider themselves insufficiently competent to second-guess the government regarding national security information, or about the need to protect information the disclosure of which would harm the internal workings of policy development and institutional operations. Then-professor Antonin Scalia's early complaint that Congress conscripted the judiciary in FOIA's unwise and unconstitutional overreach into the executive branch might hold an additional clue: perhaps courts view themselves as protecting the executive from FOIA's intrusion—even if the result of this deference is that FOIA ultimately requires less of the executive branch than Congress hoped and intended.[36] I am not suggesting that courts capitulated to Scalia's special pleading, but it is possible that courts have clipped FOIA enforcement at the margins because they implicitly agreed with his reasoning (though perhaps not his dismissive tone). Sometimes, and for some agencies, those margins have proved to be fairly thick.

It is therefore not clear why or how the constitutional status of a right would solve the institutional competence, risk aversion, and separation-of-powers issues that courts already face in enforcing FOIA and thereby overcome the judiciary's reluctance to force disclosure in difficult cases. The Constitution has proved effective at creating institutional tension, but not at resolving it.

OR MAYBE FREEDOM OF INFORMATION IS IMPOSSIBLE!

Perhaps the problem lies not with FOIA, or with Congress, or with the courts, or with the Constitution. Perhaps the underlying transparency project that Cross, Emerson, and current advocates have undertaken misunderstands the state and its potential for being opened. The project is a significant, consequential one, but it might not be the transformative one its proponents have hoped to call forth. FOIA might only have limited utility as a means to achieve an effective or accessible state, and as such it might work best if recognized as an administrative, essentially bureaucratic apparatus rather than as a provider of transcendent, constitutional-ish rights.

I make this argument elsewhere, but allow me to summarize it here.[37] FOIA and other transparency laws assume the potential for a direct communicative act. That is, they assume that the state, as a producer and repository of information, can control the documents it possesses and can be made to release those documents to the public; that the state's information clearly manifests government actions and motivations; and that once it enjoys access to this authoritative information, the public will act rationally upon it, establishing a virtuous circle in which the public holds the state accountable through democratic levers and the government bureaucracy responds accordingly. This information theory of governance views the state as operating through the disclosure and nondisclosure of information, whereas the public acts better or worse based on the amount of information to which it has access.

This assumption fundamentally misunderstands the contemporary state. As an organization and a geographically dispersed entity, the state sprawls. It produces an unarchivable, ever-expanding body of information that lacks a singular and coherent meaning and that is continually kept secret and leaked in a manner that the bureaucracy cannot itself control. No legal authority, of whatever type, can perfectly manage this mess. A constitutional right might provide some additional leverage against the contemporary bureaucratic state, but its enforcement cannot magically wish away the implausibility of information control. FOIA is an administrative law because the state's information is fundamentally an administrative issue, best treated in the political process of frequently amended statutes and in the bureaucratic processes of public administration.

* * *

In a brief comment in the same issue of the law review in which Thomas Emerson's 1976 article on a right to know appeared, Walter Gellhorn, a key founder of modern administrative law, dismissed Emerson's argument for its airy abstractions based on a bizarre faith in the judiciary to interpret and apply a minimally defined right. Gellhorn wrote, "We mislead ourselves by presenting every problem that confronts contemporary society as a justiciable issue to be decided by aloof judges under the rubric of constitutional principle."[38] We also mislead ourselves in thinking that every problem that FOIA has failed to solve can find its solution through the perfect statutory amendment, or the perfect institutional innovation, or if only those judges had some backbone, or if we could only get it constitutionalized. The problems that FOIA has faced for five decades—and that every effort to regulate democratic secrecy faces—are intractable features and bugs (at least in the United States) of a constitutional system that disperses authority within a vast administrative state.

NOTES

1. Sam Lebovic, *Free Speech and Unfree News* (Cambridge, Mass.: Harvard University Press, 2016).
2. Parts of what follows originally appeared in Mark Fenster, "The Transparency Fix: Advocating Legal Rights and Their Alternatives in the Pursuit of a Visible State," *University of Pittsburgh Law Review* 73 (2012): 443–503.
3. Harold Cross, *The People's Right to Know* (New York: Columbia University Press, 1953), vii–ix.
4. James Russell Wiggins, *Freedom or Secrecy* (New York: Oxford University Press, 1956).

5. Cross, *The People's Right to Know*, 12–13, xiii, 4–10, 128.
6. Cross borrowed the phrase "neglected constitutional right" from an earlier essay, but he was the most prominent early advocate. "Access to Official Information: A Neglected Constitutional Right," *Indiana Law Journal* 27 (1952): 209–30. Zechariah Chafee noted the problem of expanded secrecy in the postwar era, but he did not develop the First Amendment argument that Cross would later pursue. Zechariah Chafee Jr., *Government and Mass Communication, Vol. 1* (Chicago, Ill.: University of Chicago Press,1947), 12–13. In 1948, Alexander Meiklejohn had claimed that the democratic values inherent in the First Amendment must allow the public access to information, but he never specifically considered the relevance and problem of state information. Alexander Meiklejohn, *Free Speech and Its Relations to Self-Government* (New York: Harper & Brothers, 1948), 26, 66, 89.
7. Cross, *The People's Right to Know*, 246. On the history of the APA, especially as a political solution to the response to the administrative state's growth in the New Deal, see Ronen Shamir, *Managing Legal Uncertainty: Elite Lawyers in the New Deal* (Durham, N.C.: Duke University Press, 1995); George B. Shepherd, "Fierce Compromise: The Administrative Procedure Act Emerges from New Deal Politics," *Northwestern University Law Review* 90 (1996): 1557–1683; McNollgast, "The Political Origins of the Administrative Procedure Act," *Journal of Law, Economics, and Organization* 15 (1999): 180–217.
8. The APA's original government information provision included exceptions for information involved in "any function of the United States requiring secrecy in the public interest" and allowed information not otherwise barred from disclosure by statute to be made available by published rule "to persons properly and directly concerned except information held confidential for good cause found." Cross, *The People's Right to Know*, 226 (quoting 5 U.S.C. §§ 1002(1), 1002(c) (1946)). In addition to analyzing the APA's weaknesses, Cross's book also listed all of the existing statutory exceptions from disclosure. Cross, *The People's Right to Know*, 231–34.
9. For historical accounts of FOIA's development that begin at this point and focus on the political, and especially interparty, nature of the statute's enactment, see Michael Schudson, *The Rise of the Right to Know: Politics and the Culture of Transparency, 1945–1975* (Cambridge, Mass.: Harvard University Press, 2015), 37–62; Daniel J. Metcalfe, "The History of Government Transparency," in *Research Handbook on Transparency*, ed. Padideh Ala'i and Robert G. Vaughn (Northampton, Mass.: Edward Elgar, 2014), 247–62. My focus on the preeminent role that the press played privileges the conceptual underpinnings for that political struggle, which long predated the Moss Committee's work.

10. See Sam Archibald, "The Early Years of the Freedom of Information Act—1955 to 1974," *PS: Political Science and Politics* 26 (1993): 726–31, on the political nature of the Moss hearings (at least in their early years).

11. Robert O. Blanchard, "Present at the Creation: The Media and the Moss Committee," *Journalism and Mass Communication Quarterly* 49 (1972): 271–79.

12. Kiyul Uhm, "The Cold War Communication Crisis: The Right to Know Movement," *Journalism and Mass Communication Quarterly* 82 (2005): 131–47, at 140.

13. Gerald Wetlaufer, "Justifying Secrecy: An Objection to the General Deliberative Privilege," *Indiana Law Journal* 65 (1990): 845–926; Archibald, "The Early Years of the Freedom of Information Act," 728–30; Herbert Brucker, *Freedom of Information* (New York: Macmillan, 1949).

14. PBS, "Bill Moyers on the Freedom of Information Act," April 5, 2002, www.pbs.org/now/commentary/moyers4.html.

15. Cross, *The People's Right to Know*, 124–32, 246.

16. Thomas I. Emerson, "Legal Foundations of the Right to Know," *Washington University Law Quarterly* (1976): 1–24.

17. For an overview of Emerson's impressive academic and legal career, see Louis I. Pollak, "Thomas I. Emerson: Pillar of the Bill of Rights," *Yale Law Journal* 101 (1991): 321–30. His most influential works were an early casebook on civil rights, Thomas I. Emerson and David Haber, *Political and Civil Rights in the United States* (Buffalo, N.Y.: Dennis & Co., 1952), and his book summarizing his theory of the First Amendment, Thomas I. Emerson, *The System of Free Expression* (New York: Random House, 1970).

18. Emerson, "Legal Foundations of the Right to Know," 5–15.

19. Emerson, "Legal Foundations of the Right to Know," 14–16.

20. Emerson, "Legal Foundations of the Right to Know," 22.

21. Emerson, "Legal Foundations of the Right to Know," 17.

22. Fenster, "The Transparency Fix."

23. The contemporary scholar who most closely follows Emerson is Heidi Kitrosser, whose work invokes but does not rely solely upon the First Amendment to support her constitutional argument against an expansive executive privilege. Heidi Kitrosser, "Secrecy and Separated Powers: Executive Privilege Revisited," *Iowa Law Review* 92 (2007): 489–543, at 517–18. For more explicit Emersonian takes, see Adam Cohen, "The Media That Need Citizens: The First Amendment and the Fifth Estate," *Southern California Law Review* 95 (2011): 1–85; and Barry Sullivan, "FOIA and the First Amendment: Representative Democracy and the People's Elusive 'Right to Know,' " *Maryland Law Review* 72 (2012): 1–84. The First Amendment scholar Vincent Blasi provided a bridge between Emerson and the present. Vincent Blasi, "The Pathological Perspective and the

First Amendment," *Columbia Law Review* 85 (1985): 449–514, at 489–93. More recently, David Pozen provides a sensitive consideration of the First Amendment's applicability to government secrecy. David E. Pozen, "Deep Secrecy," *Stanford Law Review* 62 (2010): 257–339, 307–08.

24. Aziz Huq and Tom Ginsburg, "How to Lose a Constitutional Democracy," *UCLA Law Review* 65 (forthcoming, 2018).

25. United States v. Nixon, 418 U.S. 683, 706–07 (1974).

26. See, for example, Center for National Security Studies v. DOJ, 331 F.3d 918 (D.C. Cir. 2003), *cert. denied* 540 U.S. 1104 (2004).

27. William N. Eskridge Jr. and John Ferejohn, *A Republic of Statutes: The New American Constitution* (New Haven, Conn.: Yale University Press, 2010), 33. Their initial article introducing the concept was William N. Eskridge Jr. and John Ferejohn, "Super-Statutes," *Duke Law Journal* 50 (2001): 1215–76.

28. Eskridge and Ferejohn, *A Republic of Statutes*, 10–11.

29. Tom Ginsburg, "Written Constitutions and the Administrative State: On the Constitutional Character of Administrative Law," in *Comparative Administrative Law*, ed. Susan Rose-Ackerman and Peter L. Lindseth (Northampton, Mass.: Edward Elgar, 2010), 117–27.

30. Frederick Schauer, "Transparency in Three Dimensions," *University of Illinois Law Review* (2011): 1339–57, at 1355.

31. Pozen, "Deep Secrecy," 314.

32. McBurney v. Young, 133 S. Ct. 1709 (2013).

33. Akins v. Fed. Election Comm'n, 101 F.3d 731, 736 (D.C. Cir. 1996) (en banc), *vacated on other grounds*, 524 U.S. 11 (1998); David E. Pozen, "Freedom of Information Beyond the Freedom of Information Act," *University of Pennsylvania Law Review* 165 (2017): 1097–1158, at 1149.

34. 5 U.S.C. § 552(a)(4)(B) (2012).

35. For empirical studies of judicial deference under FOIA, see Robert P. Deyling, "Judicial Deference and De Novo Review in Litigation over National Security Information Under the Freedom of Information Act," *Villanova Law Review* 37 (1992): 67–112; Susan Nevelow Mart and Tom Ginsburg, "[Dis-]Informing the People's Discretion: Judicial Deference Under the National Security Exemption of the Freedom of Information Act," *Administrative Law Review* 66 (2014): 725–84; Paul R. Verkuil, "An Outcomes Analysis of Scope of Review Standards," *William and Mary Law Review* 44 (2002): 679–735. For more general complaints about the judiciary's failure to follow FOIA's statutory mandate to perform de novo review of agency decisions, especially in the national security area, see Pozen, "Freedom of Information Beyond the Freedom of Information Act," 1118–23; Margaret B. Kwoka, "Deferring to Secrecy," *Boston College Law Review* 54 (2013): 185–242.

36. Antonin Scalia, "The Freedom of Information Act Has No Clothes," *Regulation* (March/April 1982): 14–19.

37. Mark Fenster, *The Transparency Fix: Information as the Problem and Solution of Government* (Stanford, Calif.: Stanford University Press, 2017); Mark Fenster, "Seeing the State: Transparency as Metaphor," *Administrative Law Review* 62 (2010): 617–72.

38. Walter Gellhorn, "The Right to Know: First Amendment Overbreadth," *Washington University Law Quarterly* (1976): 25–28.

PART TWO

FOIA AND THE NEWS MEDIA

4

THE OTHER FOIA REQUESTERS

Margaret B. Kwoka

> The basic purpose of FOIA is to ensure an informed citizenry, vital to the functioning of a democratic society, needed to check against corruption and to hold the governors accountable to the governed.[1]

> The generation that made the nation thought secrecy in government one of the instruments of Old World tyranny and committed itself to the principle that a democracy cannot function unless the people are permitted to know what their government is up to.[2]

There is broad consensus that the objective of the Freedom of Information Act is to facilitate holding the executive branch politically accountable. President Barack Obama, on his first day in office, issued a memorandum declaring that FOIA, "which encourages accountability through transparency, is the most prominent expression of a profound national commitment to ensuring an open government."[3] One past president of the Society of Professional Journalists explained that "the federal Freedom of Information Act stands as one of the essential clauses of the working contract between a government and its citizenry."[4] The National Security Archive, an independent watchdog group, has described FOIA as a "bedrock piece of American democracy."[5] Leaders in Congress agree. Senator Charles Grassley, Chairman of the Senate Committee on the Judiciary, marked FOIA's fiftieth anniversary this way: "Put simply, FOIA was created to ensure transparency. And, as I've said many times over, transparency yields accountability."[6]

The executive branch can be held politically accountable in two principal ways, and the legislative history of FOIA evidences an intent to facilitate both mechanisms. First, direct public oversight is possible: the public can learn about government activities and use that information to pressure agencies and at the ballot box, when deciding whether to reelect a president. Speaking to the public's role in accountability, the Senate report accompanying the original legislation cited as a major concern that the executive's "hundreds of departments . . . and agencies are not directly responsible to the people."[7] Second, political accountability is enabled when Congress acts in its oversight capacity to constrain or override the executive branch's actions. When the subcommittee that laid the groundwork for FOIA investigated complaints of unwarranted secrecy, a full 44 percent of those complaints came from individual members of Congress or from congressional committees.[8] FOIA was thus designed with both direct public oversight and congressional oversight of the executive branch in mind.

Much has been said over the years about how well (or not) FOIA is working. That discussion typically has focused on how quickly agencies process requests, how much information is withheld under one of FOIA's exemptions to mandatory disclosure, or how requesters fare in litigation or in administrative appeals. Yet amidst all the sober analysis and critical complaints, one point is often cited in a more celebratory key: the astonishing frequency with which the public actually uses FOIA. At the forty-fifth anniversary of FOIA's enactment, the Department of Justice noted: "Forty-five years ago Congress enacted the FOIA as a vital means of ensuring an informed public. The Act remains vibrant to this day, with nearly 600,000 requests filed just this past fiscal year."[9] At FOIA's fiftieth anniversary, government and journalists alike heralded the now more than 700,000 requests received annually as evidence of FOIA's success in fulfilling its mission.[10]

But does this volume of requests demonstrate FOIA's success in holding government accountable? To answer that question, we need to disaggregate those 700,000 requests. FOIA allows any person to make a request and has no limitation based on the purpose of the request, so FOIA's use is hardly constrained to requests that promote accountability. One particularly important group of FOIA users is the news media. Journalists were instrumental in crafting the law and continue to be among the strongest advocates for protecting and strengthening its provisions.[11] Their central presence in FOIA discussions is natural. If FOIA is designed to ensure an informed citizenry, then to fulfill its mission reporters will presumably need to use the law to uncover important government activities and report their findings to the public. Moreover, journalists often sound the alarm bell that provokes congressional inquiry and oversight action.

But journalists do not even come close to submitting a majority of FOIA requests, or even a significant fraction thereof. Most studies have estimated that the news media is responsible for only single-digit percentages of FOIA requests received by federal agencies.[12] Even if we add to the news media the category of nonprofits—organizations that also may serve a democracy-enhancing oversight function—best estimates put the total around 15 percent of requesters government-wide.[13]

If the news media and watchdog groups are not responsible for the glut of federal FOIA requests, who is, and for what purpose are they using FOIA? It is eminently worth understanding these other FOIA requesters. What FOIA is actually used for, how FOIA resources are spent, and what information makes it into the public realm are critical questions for evaluating the success of the act. These questions are, by their nature, empirical ones. Although agencies are required to report on many other facets of their FOIA operations on an annual basis, their reporting does not illuminate these important matters. Thus examination of the agencies' raw data on their FOIA requests is required.

As I explain in this chapter, even superficial investigations of such data reveal an obvious truth: FOIA is largely used for purposes other than promoting democratic accountability. In practice, FOIA serves as a sort of fallback option for anyone looking for information about anything—and no wonder. Not only is access to FOIA in no way limited by law, but the government holds vast troves of information about nearly every aspect of our society, much of which is useful to private interests.

Requesters turn to FOIA for a wide array of reasons, including plenty of idiosyncratic ones that defy easy categorization. For example, one study of a sample of requests submitted to the National Security Agency in the late 1990s found that 12 percent concerned Unidentified Flying Objects.[14] Nonetheless, despite significant variations among agencies and requesters, two categories of requests are so pervasive in the federal government that they are worthy of special consideration: commercial requesters and first-person requesters. Commercial requesters are those seeking government information as part of their profit-making enterprises.[15] First-person requesters are individuals or their representatives requesting information about themselves.[16] These two categories of requesters are the largest cohesive groups of requesters across the federal government. I document the scope and nature of commercial and first-person requests here and argue that those requests largely fulfill purposes other than democratic oversight. I further argue that these other purposes can be better served outside of FOIA and that doing so would shrink the size of the FOIA machinery to the benefit of those requesters who seek to use the law as originally conceived.

FOIA, INC.

Examining commercial requesters and first-person requesters provides a sense of how the bulk of FOIA resources are spent. Federal agencies' own records are instructive in this regard. Each agency maintains a log of all FOIA requests received, and these logs typically contain certain fields such as the identity and affiliation of the requester, a brief description of the subject matter of the request, the date received, the date resolved, a control number assigned by the agency, and the outcome of the request in terms of records released. Given that around one hundred federal agencies separately fulfill FOIA requests and correspondingly track and monitor their own FOIA operations,[17] no comprehensive study of FOIA requesters encompassing all federal agencies has ever been conducted. However, sampling a year's worth of FOIA logs at key federal agencies paints a powerful picture of the FOIA landscape.

That picture shows commercial interests to be a dominant force in the FOIA system. At many federal agencies, including most notably at large regulatory agencies, the vast majority of FOIA requests are made by businesses. In 2013, for example, 69 percent of requests filed with the Securities and Exchange Commission (SEC), 75 percent of those filed with the Food and Drug Administration (FDA), and 79 percent of those filed with the Environmental Protection Agency (EPA) were commercial. Niche agencies can exceed even these levels. At the Defense Logistics Agency (DLA), which manages defense contracting, a full 96 percent of requests were commercial. Moreover, a small number of companies can sometimes drive these numbers. At the SEC, the largest-volume commercial requester made 2,155 FOIA requests in 2013, representing 18 percent of all SEC requests that year. In fact, just the top five requesters (four of which were deemed commercial and one of which, SECProbes.com, is plausibly characterized as commercial as well) made 70 percent of all requests at the SEC. Other agencies, including FDA, EPA, and DLA, also have numerous high-volume commercial requesters, each making more than one hundred requests a year.[18]

Although there are a variety of purposes behind commercial requesting, one theme is consistent: commercial uses of FOIA primarily fuel private profit, not the public's interest in understanding government activities. These types of private profit motives tend to take one of several forms. First, businesses often use FOIA to find out not what the government is doing but what their competitors are doing. At the SEC, one of the two largest requested categories of records are exhibits to required SEC filings, such as annual or quarterly reports, for publicly traded companies.[19] These exhibits typically contain licensing or development contracts submitted under a rule permitting confidential treatment for a particular period of time, and they are often requested the instant that time period expires. A similar phenomenon happens at the FDA. A significant number of requests to the FDA concern either the FOIA logs themselves (or chunks thereof), particularly FOIA request letters, or the records released in response to particular FOIA requests of others.[20] Merck, a large pharmaceutical company, makes dozens of requests of this nature, and a close review of a sample of them shows that Merck is trying to uncover what information its competitors are seeking about Merck itself.[21]

A second set of commercial requests serve a dual function of informing the company making the request about both competitors and the regulatory process. Again, at the FDA, the highest volume of requested records are related to FDA facilities inspections.[22] These records contain valuable information not only about the agency's inspection regime but also about the inspected company's operations. Similarly, at DLA, nearly all commercial requests (nearly all requests, for that matter) concern bid information for defense contracts.[23] This might be helpful in learning about the contract awarding process, but it is likely to be equally if not more valuable in learning about competitors' operations and pricing.

Beyond learning about competitor companies, FOIA is frequently used by businesses that provide due diligence services to clients. At the SEC, this is the most common type of commercial requester, and their requests typically seek any records pertaining to any SEC investigation of a particular company.[24] The goal of these due diligence firms is to assess any regulatory risk associated with a company targeted for a merger or other business deal by their clients. At the EPA, the same dynamic arises. The vast majority of commercial requests, estimated to have comprised around 80 percent of EPA's requests in recent years, were for any information concerning a particular property identified by address.[25] These requests are designed to help businesses comply with rules regarding due diligence of environmental risks prior to purchasing commercial property.

Finally, one group of commercial requesters deserves special treatment. These are businesses whose very business model is to request records under

FOIA and to resell those records at a profit. That is, the federal records they receive under FOIA are the commodities on which they trade. Elsewhere I have labeled these businesses as information resellers. At five of the six agencies at which I studied the commercial use of FOIA, information resellers were among the most frequent requesters. At two of those agencies, multiple resellers competed against one another. At the FDA, for instance, multiple companies use FOIA to request facilities inspections reports by the hundreds, and they sell access to whole databases of them for hundreds or thousands of dollars. At the SEC, multiple companies use FOIA to request thousands of exhibits to public filings previously submitted confidentially, and they resell access to databases of those business documents. At the DLA, one company sells access to databases of defense contracts and bids that it receives in response to FOIA requests. Another company among the top requesters at the EPA markets its consulting services as providing "comprehensive, accurate government records data" to its clients.[26]

These various business uses of FOIA have different goals, but one thread binds them together: the benefits that flow from receipt of public records are accrued privately, not publicly. Even when commercial requesters do use FOIA to learn about the government's activities, it is usually in an attempt to gain a competitive advantage, which will only be conferred if the records the requester receives are closely guarded rather than broadly publicized. If the same information were available to everyone at minimal cost, it would confer no advantage at all. Thus these uses of FOIA do not fuel the accomplishment of FOIA's primary objective of informing the citizenry and holding the executive branch politically accountable.

FIRST-PERSON FOIA

First-person uses of FOIA are very different from commercial requests in some respects, but as a class they similarly fail to advance the law's central aim of informing the public about government activities. At many agencies, particularly large benefits-conferring and law enforcement agencies, first-person requests dominate the FOIA landscape. For example, in fiscal year 2015, Immigration and Customs Enforcement (ICE) received over 100,000 requests (approximately one-seventh of the federal govenrment's total), and 98 percent of those requests were first-person requests.[27] In that same year, 76 percent of requests submitted to the Veterans Health Administration (VHA) were first-person requests,[28] and 95 percent of requests to the

Equal Employment Opportunity Commission (EEOC) were first-person requests.[29]

Reasons for first-person requesting are varied, but one common reason is a pending or anticipated administrative dispute with the agency in which the private individual has no other access to discovery. Immigration agencies provide the clearest—and most prevalent—example. The government holds an Alien File, known as an A-File, on every noncitizen, which typically contains that individual's immigration applications or forms, past statements the individual has made to an immigration officer, or information about the government's own investigative methods. For a noncitizen in removal proceedings, previous applications or forms can sometimes establish facts necessary for relief in immigration court, records relating to their past statements often go directly to credibility issues, and records relating to the government's investigation tactics could support a claim of suppression of key evidence. Even for noncitizens who are not facing removal, these documents can provide key information in determining whether individuals can apply for a different type of visa, adjust their status to become a lawful permanent resident, or qualify for citizenship.[30]

First-person FOIA requests are currently the most common use of FOIA government-wide. In fiscal year 2015, the Department of Homeland Security (DHS) received 281,138 FOIA requests, representing almost 40 percent of the federal government's total.[31] The vast majority of these requests were made to the immigration enforcement components of DHS (including ICE) and came from individuals (or their attorneys) seeking their own immigration-related files. More than 200,000 requests made to DHS components alone in 2015 were first-person FOIA requests.

First-person requesters at the EEOC are using FOIA in an analogous way, and 95 percent of FOIA requests in 2015 were for the agency's file concerning the investigation of a particular charge of employment discrimination.[32] Once a charge is filed at the EEOC, the EEOC conducts an investigation. At the conclusion of that investigation, if the EEOC decides not to move forward with a case, it sends notice of a right to sue to the charging party. The EEOC's investigative file, or "charge file," is generally not available under FOIA during the investigation, and by special statute it cannot be released even to the charging party until the period in which a lawsuit can be filed has run out. Moreover, the only time the records can be released to the responding party (the employer) is if a lawsuit is in fact filed. Thus the overwhelming majority of these requests are made by charging parties during the window of opportunity in which they can file a lawsuit after the conclusion of an investigation. FOIA is the only way for them to gain access to the EEOC's investigative materials about their own charge of discrimination.[33]

At VHA, the reasons for these first-person FOIA requests appear to be more varied than at DHS and EEOC, but they also demonstrate the private nature of the interests involved. For example, some of the highest-volume requesters at the agency include insurance underwriting firms, which are essentially making first-person requests as the representative of an individual because the individual is applying for an insurance policy. One frequent requester is a law firm that specializes in social security disability law, pre-sumably requesting its clients' medical files in support of a disability-based claim for benefits. Another group of individuals—more than five hundred in fiscal year 2015—are families of deceased veterans or the funeral homes representing them who are seeking a type of military separation documen-tation that is required to access a military funeral benefit. All in all, FOIA requests to the VHA are overwhelmingly made for veterans' medical records and deceased veterans' medical records, at 26 percent and 42 percent of total requests, respectively.[34]

To be sure, first-person FOIA requests fulfill a valuable role. Individuals who have no other right of access to their own records—their own interview transcripts, their own medical files, their own employment discrimination records—can harness FOIA's power for that purpose. Nonetheless, the ben-efits of the release of these records is largely accruing privately. For example, individuals' files are being used to help individuals secure government benefits to which they may be entitled, to secure products on the private market they want, or to settle or litigate private disputes. Although there may be public benefits as well—for example, the general public interest in fair and accurate determinations of benefits—these types of uses do not go to the heart of FOIA's imagined purpose of informing the public about government activities.

Between commercial FOIA requesting and first-person uses of FOIA, vast resources are spent fulfilling requests that do not advance FOIA's underlying mission. These two groups are the largest identifiable cohorts, but they are hardly the only nonmedia uses of the law. Even though no comprehensive government statistics are available, given the number of large agencies about which data is available, it is fair to say that most FOIA requests and cor-responding government resources spent responding to them serve interests other than educating the public about the operations of government and hold-ing government accountable.[35] The reality of FOIA does not conform to the purpose Congress envisioned in enacting the law, which belies the notion that the sheer volume of requests made each year represents an unambiguous triumph of any sort.

FOIA'S POOR FIT

Using FOIA for purposes beyond those imagined at its creation may well serve laudable goals other than informing the public about the operations of government. However, because FOIA was designed for democracy-enhancing public engagement, it is often a poor fit for these other uses to which it is being put. These other interests often are not best met by the open-to-all, request-and-response model that FOIA embodies.

Commercial entities may well make socially beneficial uses of government records in fueling innovation or promoting competition in the private marketplace, for example, and these uses may well be worth supporting in some fashion. But a close look at commercial requesting practices under FOIA reveals that such entities request the same types of records repeatedly, often apparently seeking to index or create a database of all or nearly all records in a particular category. For example, commercial requesters will ask for FDA facilities inspection reports by the hundreds. Although each report concerns a different inspection event, the type of record requested is similar each time. The same is true for requests for defense contract bids from DLA and the exhibits to public filings from the SEC.

Rather than continuing this inefficient process of retail requesting, there are easily identifiable instances in which an agency could make the entire category of records affirmatively available by publishing a database on its website for anyone to access. For example, the SEC could make confidential filings immediately available on its EDGAR database website upon the expiration of the confidential treatment period.[36] The EPA has already moved in that direction, implementing an online tool called MyProperty, which allows anyone to search for site-specific environmental records, previously the subject of thousands of FOIA requests made largely by due diligence companies.[37] These sorts of efforts could preempt the need for hundreds, sometimes thousands, of requests and would simultaneously achieve greater transparency to the public at large.

Other sorts of problems arise from first-person requesting. Oftentimes, individuals are seeking their own records as part of their effort to access a government benefit to which they believe they are entitled or to defend against an enforcement action brought by the government. Individuals obtaining the government's files related to their own administrative case is akin to individuals using the discovery process in civil litigation or criminal prosecutions. In our justice system, disclosure of relevant information is thought to lead to fairer and more accurate decision-making. As David Pozen has suggested elsewhere, these are "due process benefits" insofar as disclosure of the records serves the same purposes as due process protections,[38] even if these individuals may not formally have a due process right.

FOIA often serves these due process purposes poorly.[39] One significant problem concerns timing. Because a FOIA request goes through a completely separate process from any underlying claim to benefits or administrative proceeding, the timing of the agency's response is not tied to that underlying proceeding. Frequently, the FOIA response will not arrive in time to be of help to the individual. For example, in removal proceedings in immigration court, noncitizens may not receive a response to their FOIA request until after a disposition has been reached in their removal case. The problem is particularly acute with individuals who are detained pending the result of their proceeding because their immigration court process is expedited. Even though one of the immigration agencies, U.S. Citizenship and Immigration Services, has created a fast track for individuals who are in removal proceedings, they still often do not receive a response in time.[40] Similarly, at the VHA, families seeking discharge records to access military funeral benefits face challenges obtaining them under FOIA in time for the funeral.[41]

Moreover, the process of going through FOIA can seem wildly inefficient given the records' relationship to a pending proceeding. At the EEOC, for example, nearly all FOIA requests are made by a party who previously filed a charge of discrimination with the agency and who wants access to the agency's file of investigatory materials. Given that the charging party has been working with the EEOC over the course of the investigation and has a contact at the agency, going a separate route through the FOIA office to obtain the file hardly seems optimal. One could imagine, instead, a requirement that the EEOC officer in charge of the case release the nonexempt portions of the file to the charging party at the conclusion of the investigation. Similarly, in immigration proceedings, attorneys typically file a FOIA request at each of three or four different agencies that handle aspects of immigration enforcement.[42] Yet, at each court date, the individual in immigration court will be sitting just a few feet away from the trial attorney's file, which contains the very records the individual is seeking through an entirely collateral process under FOIA. Again, one could imagine rules of discovery that would require the trial attorney to make nonprivileged material in the file available in the immigration court proceeding itself.

Finally, if a response to a first-person FOIA request includes assertions of exemption to mandatory disclosure, allowing the government to withhold or redact certain documents, those assertions will have to be challenged, if at all, through a FOIA appeal and separate FOIA lawsuit.[43] For an individual with an underlying dispute or claim before an agency, having to engage in a second dispute resolution process over the records sought poses what is likely an undue burden. Moreover, the judge or agency official already tasked with deciding the underlying dispute is likely to be in the best position to determine the individual's right to access the records, but, under FOIA, this person will not have any role in doing so.

Even for those first-person requests that do not essentially serve as a stand-in for discovery in an underlying administrative case, FOIA often seems like a poor mechanism for accessing the relevant records. For example, the over-whelming majority of records requests at the VHA are for medical records.[44] In an age in which the federal government is encouraging and even requir-ing private industry to move toward electronic health records, using FOIA to access your own medical records or the medical records of your deceased family member seems an anachronism.

In short, for vast swaths of FOIA requests currently fueling the explosive growth in the use of FOIA, the law may be serving worthy goals, but those goals could be much better served through mechanisms tailored to them. FOIA was designed, instead, to serve the needs of the news media and certain watchdog groups, which were expected to be filing requests in response to current events, scandals, and policy debates. If it were working efficiently and cost effectively for those users, a tailored request-and-response model would likely be very practical. The routine complaints about FOIA voiced by the news media, after all, center on the reality of FOIA delay and denial, not the design of an indi-vidual right to request records.[45] The model fails, however, to fully meet the information needs of requesters who use FOIA simply because there is no alternative, a group that appears to make up a majority of FOIA requesters.

DETRACTING FROM FOIA

That FOIA is used mostly for purposes not conceived of as part of its core mis-sion detracts from FOIA's success in several ways. First, it calls into question the value of the considerable resources spent on FOIA administration across the federal government. Second, the glut of requesters using FOIA to advance private interests potentially affects its efficacy for public interest requesters such as the news media. Finally, it diverts attention away from what might be much better investments in transparency.

FOIA is notoriously costly. In fiscal year 2015, the official cost of all FOIA-related activities in the federal government reached just shy of half a billion dollars.[46] FOIA advocates like to compare this amount to what is spent on seemingly less important line items—the famous example being annual expenditures on military bands—but the amount is still more than the entire budget for the Federal Trade Commission or the National Labor Relations Board, and about six times as much as we spend on the Federal Elections Commission. Accordingly, we should question whether we are spending this money well. This is particularly true because Congress never imagined that spending would reach this level, having estimated in 1976 that FOIA compliance costs would not reach more than $100,000,[47] which is about $425,000 in today's dollars, or less than a thousandth of current spending levels.

FOIA's central mission is informing the public about government activities, and agencies voiced the concern that FOIA resources are spent for largely private, not public, benefits as early as 1980. As the Department of Justice reported at that time, "concern over costs arising from the private use of public resources" include "the use of FOIA as a substitute for discovery in litigation and the use of FOIA for commercial purposes." The department concluded that "agencies may incur heavy costs for providing information that will have primarily a direct private benefit."[48]

Indeed, FOIA spending sometimes amounts to a subsidy fueling private profit. Although requesters can be charged fees designed to cover some FOIA costs, the reality is that the federal government recoups very little in fees in comparison with its costs. This is even true for commercial requesters, the group that is subject to the highest fee categories, as these requesters tend to pay in fees less than 5 percent of the cost the agency incurred in fulfilling their requests. For all commercial requesters, but particularly for information resellers, the provision of free or low-cost federal records amounts to a giveaway that benefits the requester's bottom line.[49]

Beyond concerns about potentially ill-spent resources, the existence of resource constraints suggests that agencies that receive a deluge of requests that do not go to the heart of FOIA's principal concern may be less responsive to those requests that do implicate government accountability. That is, news media, watchdog groups, and private citizens using FOIA to uncover government activity for oversight purposes may be essentially crowded out of the process because FOIA offices are so overwhelmed with these other requesters. The potential for such crowding out is underscored by the perennial concerns about delay as a prime reason FOIA falls short of serving its intended mission.[50] If agency personnel were not tied up with voluminous private interest requests, response times and general responsiveness would likely improve for the public interest ones.

Finally, the concerns about how FOIA resources are spent and how well FOIA is achieving its core objective have led some to question the overall costs versus benefits of FOIA. Of course, as the Department of Justice has noted, the benefits of FOIA are "difficult to quantify."[51] In addition to the resources spent on requesters other than those contemplated as prime intended users of the law, other critiques of FOIA include its failure to meaningfully police national security secrecy and its potentially deleterious impact on the domestic regulatory process. This combination of the realities of FOIA led Pozen to conclude that "FOIA does the least work where it is most needed and, at least from a normative standpoint that values effective and egalitarian governance above transparency per se, does too much work everywhere else."[52] On multiple levels, then, the glut of other FOIA requesters is in part responsible for undermining the justifications for having FOIA access rights in the first place.

LESS IS MORE? SHRINKING FOIA SENSIBLY

Despite these grounds for a serious critique of FOIA, evidence shows that FOIA does, even in its current state, serve some of the news media and other oversight requesters' interests, and often serves them well. Unlike, for example, commercial requests, news media requests tend to vary widely by topic and tend to track current events or hot news items.[53] Moreover, the Transactional Records Access Clearinghouse (TRAC) recently reported that topics of FOIA lawsuits brought in 2016 "frequently read very much like the news headlines from the past year," which "underlines the important role FOIA did play in fueling public discussions."[54] TRAC uncovered a plethora of examples in which members of the news media sued under FOIA to obtain records for the very purposes FOIA was envisioned: to learn about government actions and uncover possible wrongdoing. At present, it is hard to imagine another way to provide a right of access for the idiosyncratic needs of the press as flexible or powerful as the request-and-response system created under FOIA.

Given that FOIA is still serving as a valuable mechanism for oversight, and that it would be even more successful in that arena if it were not overly used for other purposes, one promising goal is to reduce reliance on FOIA for these noncore purposes. Despite that aim, a simple ban on the use of FOIA by requesters other than the news media or nonprofits would likely be difficult to administer because it would require agencies to sort out the true or qualified requesters from sham or imposter requesters. Moreover, giving agencies yet another ground to withhold records in a world in which overwithholding is a serious risk would work at odds with transparency goals. Finally, other uses of FOIA may well be socially useful, even if they do not serve FOIA's main objective. Indeed, both the commercial and individual uses of FOIA I have described produce social benefits that we should be wary of negating.

More promising reforms seek to reduce reliance on FOIA by requiring or incentivizing agencies to meet other information needs through tailored mechanisms crafted outside of FOIA. This approach would reduce (perhaps vastly) the number of FOIA requests that are made and free up FOIA offices' resources to better serve FOIA's core mission. For other types of requesters, one-by-one requesting under FOIA makes little sense, and alternatives include targeted affirmative disclosure of entire categories of records, individual administrative discovery rights, and electronic access to personal records. Designing non-request-based systems to deliver the information people and businesses routinely need for their private affairs would remove pressure from FOIA to serve that function.

Reform efforts should focus on mandates or incentives for agencies to adopt practices that will shrink the overall work that FOIA must perform. Although the nature of private-interest FOIA requesters and the records they seek vary between agencies, Congress could require agencies to take certain steps to evaluate opportunities to preempt whole categories of FOIA requests. Legislative mandates might include a very minimum requirement that agencies publish their FOIA logs, including a variety of key fields such as the identity of the requester, the fee category of the requester (commercial, news, or other), the subject matter of the request, the fees actually charged, the date the request was made and the date it was fulfilled, and the outcome of the request. Publication of this standardized information would improve oversight of FOIA operations themselves, and it would allow the public to see how FOIA resources are being spent. This could facilitate pressure on the agency to find alternatives to FOIA that better meet the information needs at that agency.

Congress could certainly go further and could legislate a requirement that agencies evaluate their logs annually to report the most frequently requested categories of records (perhaps the top five or so such categories) as part of their annual FOIA report to the Department of Justice. Legislation could further require agencies to conduct a feasibility analysis on preempting the need for individual FOIA requests, either by engaging in categorical affirmative disclosure of frequently requested records or by other administrative policy changes, such as permitting particular kinds of administrative discovery or creating access to certain personal records by online log-in. The feasibility analysis would have to include not only the cost of the alternative but also the resources saved by reducing FOIA expenses, the potential transparency benefits of the alternatives, and any costs associated with increased screening or review necessary to implement such a system. Finally, legislation could require the agency to engage in this alternative mode of information disclosure where feasible under the agency's own analysis.[55]

Various enforcement mechanisms could complement these administrative requirements. Either by legislation or by executive order, agency feasibility analyses could be reviewed by an executive branch oversight body, such as the Department of Justice's Office of Information Policy or the Office of Government Information Services, housed at the National Archives and Records Administration.[56] A private right of action could be created to allow for quasi-private attorney general actions to enforce these mandates. At the very least, publication of the agency's thinking on the matter would prompt civil society to pressure, petition, and otherwise demand that agencies take actions to reduce their overreliance on FOIA.

With measures such as these, success in FOIA could begin to be measured not by how many requests are received but by how many requests never had to be made in the first instance. A leaner, meaner Freedom of Information Act would better serve its government oversight purpose. Alternative disclosure channels—used to preempt the need for FOIA requests but not to constrict FOIA rights—would ensure that transparency is not compromised in the process. In FOIA's next fifty years, the right goal may be to shrink FOIA.

NOTES

1. NLRB v. Robbins Tire & Rubber Co., 437 U.S. 214, 242 (1978).
2. EPA v. Mink, 410 U.S. 73, 105 (1973) (quoting Henry Steels Commager, *The Defeat of America*, New York Review of Books, October 5, 1972, at 7).

3. Memorandum from Barack Obama on Freedom of Information Act, January 21, 2009, www.whitehouse.gov/the_press_office/FreedomofInformationAct.

4. Paul McMasters, as quoted in David L. Hudson Jr., "50 Years Later, Freedom of Information Act Still Chipping Away at Government's Secretive Culture," *ABA Journal* (July 2016), www.abajournal.com/magazine/article/50th_anniversary _of_the_freedom_of_information_act.

5. National Security Archive, "FOIA@50," July 1, 2016, https://nsarchive.gwu.edu /briefing-book/foia/2016-07-01/foia50.

6. Chuck Grassley, *FOIA at Fifty: Has the Sunshine Law's Promise Been Fulfilled?*, *Hearing Before the Senate Committee on the Judiciary*, 114th Congress, July 12, 2016, www.judiciary.senate.gov/imo/media/doc/07-12-16%20Grassley%20Statement.pdf.

7. S. Rep. No. 89-813, 1st Sess. 3 (1965).

8. Michael Doyle, "The Freedom of Information Act in Theory and Practice" (master's thesis, Johns Hopkins University, Baltimore, Md., May 2001), 33 (on file with author).

9. U.S. Department of Justice, "Celebrating FOIA's Forty-Fifth Anniversary and Assessing This Past Year's Progress in Implementing Attorney General Holder's FOIA Guidelines," August 6, 2014, www.justice.gov/oip/blog/foia-post-8.

10. Hudson, "50 Years Later."

11. Mark Fenster, "The Transparency Fix: Advocating Legal Rights and Their Alternatives in the Pursuit of a Visible State," *University of Pittsburgh Law Review* 73 (2012): 443–503, at 451–66.

12. Society of Professional Journalists, "Frequent Filers: Businesses Make FOIA Their Business," July 3, 2006, www.spj.org/rrr.asp?ref=31&t=foia.

13. Max Galka, "Who Uses FOIA? An Analysis of 229,000 Requests to 85 Government Agencies," FOIA Mapper, March 13, 2017, https://foiamapper .com/who-uses-foia.

14. Doyle, "The Freedom of Information Act in Theory and Practice," 80.

15. Freedom of Information Reform Act of 1986, "Uniform Freedom of Information Act Fee Schedule and Guidelines," *Federal Register* 52 (1987): 10,012, 10,017–18.

16. U.S. Department of Justice, "FOIA Update: FOIA Counselor: Questions & Answers," January 1, 1985, www.justice.gov/oip/blog/foia-update-foia-counselor -questions-answers-15.

17. For a list of annual FOIA reports for myriad federal agencies and departments, see U.S. Department of Justice, "Annual FOIA Reports — FY 2015," June 8, 2016, www.justice.gov/oip/annual-foia-reports-fy-2015.

18. Margaret B. Kwoka, "FOIA, Inc.," *Duke Law Journal* 65 (2016): 1361–1437, at 1379–1414.

19. U.S. Securities and Exchange Commission, Freedom of Information Act responses to September 5, 2014, February 12, 2015, February 13, 2015, and April 21,

2015, requests by Margaret B. Kwoka (on file with author) [hereinafter SEC Data]; Margaret B. Kwoka, "Inside FOIA, Inc.," *Yale Law Journal Forum* 126 (2016): 265–72, at 270.

20. U.S. Department of Health and Human Services Food and Drug Administration, Freedom of Information Act responses to June 24, 2014, February 12, 2015, February 13, 2015, and April 21, 2015, requests by Margaret B. Kwoka (on file with author) [hereinafter FDA Data].

21. FDA Data at Request Letters 2013–999, 2013–1004, 2013–2329, 2013–4755, 2013– 5840, 2013–9340, 2013–2280, 2013–4178, 2013–4766, 2013–6390, 2013–7365.

22. That a request concerned inspections was ascertained by examining the subject matter of the request as summarized by FDA in its FOIA logs. For example, every entry for Eli Lilly either contained the designation of a particular "EIR," which is an abbreviation for Establishment Inspection Report, or "483," which is short for FDA Form 483, an inspection observations form used by FDA. See FDA, "Inspections, Compliance, Enforcement, and Criminal Investigations," www.fda.gov/ICECI/Inspections/ucm256377.htm; FDA Data.

23. U.S. Department of Defense, Defense Logistics Agency, Freedom of Information Act responses to October 6, 2014, February 12, 2015, February 13, 2015, and April 21, 2015, requests by Margaret B. Kwoka (on file with author).

24. SEC Data; Kwoka, "Inside FOIA, Inc.," 270–71.

25. Larry Gottesman, chief, FOIA and Privacy Act Branch, U.S. Environmental Protection Agency, Remarks at the Freedom of Information Act Advisory Committee Meeting, April 19, 2016, http://ogis.archives.gov/foia-advisory -committee/2014-2016-term/documents/04-19-2016-meeting-transcript.htm [http://perma.cc/VWZ4-HCQL].

26. Kwoka, "FOIA, Inc.," 1382–1403.

27. Immigration and Customs Enforcement, data compiled from www.ice.gov /foia/library (click on "ICE FOIA Logs").

28. 5 U.S.C. § 552a(d)(1).

29. U.S. Equal Employment Opportunity Commission, Freedom of Information Act response to April 14, 2016, request by Margaret B. Kwoka (on file with author) [hereinafter EEOC Data].

30. Geoffrey Heeren, "Shattering the One-Way Mirror: Discovery in Immigration Court," *Brooklyn Law Review* 79 (2014): 1569–1627, at 1610–12.

31. U.S. Department Homeland Security, *2015 Freedom of Information Act Report to the Attorney General of the United States*, 2016, 2,www.dhs.gov/sites/default/ files/publications/dhs-foia-annual-report-fy-2015.pdf.

32. EEOC Data.

33. Equal Employment Opportunity Commission, "Questions and Answers: FOIA Requests for Charge Files," www.eeoc.gov/eeoc/foia/qanda_foiacharge.cfm.

34. U.S. Department of Veterans Affairs, Veterans Health Administration, Freedom of Information Act response to April 14, 2016, request by Margaret B. Kwoka (on file with author) [hereinafter VHA Data].

35. Putting commercial and individual requesting together equals 66 percent of all requests. Galka, "Who Uses FOIA?"

36. Kwoka, "Inside FOIA, Inc.," 270.

37. Environmental Protection Agency, "MyProperty," www3.epa.gov/enviro/html /fii/myproperty/index.html.

38. David E. Pozen, "Freedom of Information Beyond the Freedom of Information Act," *University of Pennsylvania Law Review* 165 (2017): 1097–1158, at 1137.

39. "Where we find FOIA doing due process work, we find due process interests being served poorly." Pozen, "Freedom of Information Beyond the Freedom of Information Act," 1138.

40. Heeren, "Shattering the One-Way Mirror," 1596.

41. See, for example, Military Funeral Benefit, "DD214 and Taps, a Veteran's Final Funeral Benefit, a Tribute from a Grateful Nation," www.dd214.us/funeral.html.

42. Heeren, "Shattering the One-Way Mirror," 1593.

43. 5 U.S.C. §§ 552(a)(6), 552(a)(5)(B).

44. VHA Data.

45. See, for example, Michael Doyle, "Missed Information: The Reporting Tool That Reporters Don't Use,"*Washington Monthly*, May 2000, 38, 40.

46. U.S. Department of Justice, *Summary of Annual FOIA Reports for Fiscal Year 2015*, 2016, 21, www.justice.gov/oip/reports/fy_2015_annual_foia_report_summary /download.

47. U.S. Department of Justice, "FOIA Update: Estimating FOIA Costs," January 1, 1980, www.justice.gov/oip/blog/foia-update-estimating-foia-costs.

48. U.S. Department of Justice, "FOIA Update: Costs and Benefits—FOIA," January 1, 1980, www.justice.gov/oip/blog/foia-update-costs-and-benefits-foia.

49. Kwoka, "FOIA, Inc.," 1415–22.

50. Kwoka, "FOIA, Inc.," 1364, 1374.

51. U.S. Department of Justice, "FOIA Update: Costs and Benefits."

52. Pozen, "Freedom of Information Beyond the Freedom of Information Act," 1111.

53. Kwoka, "FOIA, Inc.," 1430.

54. FOIA Project, "FOIA Lawsuits Mirror News Headlines in FY 2016," December 9, 2016, www.foiaproject.org/2016/12/09/foia-lawsuits-make-news-headlines-in-fy -2016.

55. I testified in 2016 as to similar proposals before the U.S. Senate Committee on the Judiciary. Grassley, *FOIA at Fifty* (statement of Margaret B. Kwoka, Assistant Professor, University of Denver Sturm College of Law), www.judiciary. senate.gov/imo/media/doc/07-12-16%20Kwoka%20Testimony.pdf.

56. Kwoka, "FOIA, Inc.," 1427–37.

5

STATE FOI LAWS

More Journalist-Friendly, or Less?

Katherine Fink

JOURNALISTS IN THE UNITED STATES file more freedom of information (FOI) requests at the state level than at the national level.[1] This makes sense because more journalism is produced for local audiences[2] and American audiences pay closer attention to local news.[3] Yet almost all scholarly attention focuses on the federal Freedom of Information Act (FOIA) rather than on its state-level analogs. Responding to this imbalance in the literature, I call attention in this chapter to the importance of subnational FOI law, demonstrate the variety of FOI practices across the U.S. states, and explain why our knowledge of FOI at the state level is not likely to improve any time soon.

FOI requests at the state level have led to stories that have attracted public attention, won awards, and prompted government action. Requests under Michigan's Freedom of Information Act led to evidence that the state's Department of Environmental Quality tried to cover up lead contamination in Flint's water supply. The problem was widely reported in national and international news outlets and resulted in criminal charges against city and state officials as well as major upgrades to the water system.[4] The *Miami Herald*'s award-winning 2014 series "Innocents Lost" used records from Florida's Department of Children and Families to report on 477 children who died despite warnings the agency had received about threats to their safety. The series led to changes in Florida's child welfare laws and increased funding for child protection.[5] A request under Massachusetts Public Records Law by the Framingham-based *MetroWest Daily News* revealed possible evidence tampering in the local police department, a discovery that cast doubt on dozens of criminal prosecutions.[6]

Despite these state FOI success stories, journalists have encountered plenty of problems with FOI requests. One problem echoes a common complaint at the federal level: getting information takes so long that the information ceases to be useful. Studies of the federal FOIA have suggested that delayed responses are due, at least in part, to a preponderance of requests by businesses, which effectively crowd out requests made in the public interest, such as those from journalists. Margaret Kwoka, for example, found that businesses filed an "overwhelming majority" of FOIA requests at the four largest agencies she studied; journalists accounted for, at most, 12 percent of requests.[7]

This chapter begins with an overview of state FOI laws, highlighting some of the key differences among them and the critiques leveled by journalists and open government advocates. Next, state FOI logs are analyzed to determine whether journalists' requests are being crowded out by business requests at the state level as they are at the federal level. Gathering these data revealed some unexpected findings: many state agencies do not keep FOI request logs, retain only basic information about requesters, or do not make logs publicly available. As a result, assessing the extent to which journalists are being displaced or identifying other potential problems with state FOI practices is difficult. The chapter concludes with suggestions for improvements in state FOI administration.

STATE FOI LAWS: BACKGROUND

By the time the federal FOIA was passed in 1966, about half of the states already had their own FOI laws.[8] Wisconsin is sometimes credited as the first, passing a statute shortly after achieving statehood in 1849 requiring government records to be "open for the examination of any person."[9] Other early state laws emerged from English doctrine establishing that litigants had the right to access government documents for use as evidence.[10] Many states that lacked their own public records laws prior to FOIA still recognized a basic right to access government information under particular conditions, such as when citizens could demonstrate that they had a direct interest in that information. Later, public records laws were expanded based on an understanding that citizens should be able to access government documents for the purpose of monitoring the actions of public officials. Passage of FOIA at the federal level led to a new wave of interest among the states, and new FOI laws were passed and old laws were updated.[11]

The varied history of state FOI laws is reflected in their present-day names. Several states have a "Freedom of Information Act" or "Freedom of Information Law," which sounds similar enough to the federal version. In other states, one finds the "Public Records Act," "Government Data Practices Act," "Uniform Information Practices Act," or something else. Some states have multiple statutes addressing the availability of public records. Differences among the laws, of course, do not end there. Journalists and government accountability organizations have occasionally assembled guides outlining all fifty states' laws,[12] but requesters generally must do their own research to understand the particulars for a given state. Discrepancies in coverage and procedure can lead to an "alarming inequality among citizens of various jurisdictions in gaining access to public records."[13] For journalists, this also means inequalities in their ability to report stories on particular topics, and in particular states.

STATE FOI LAW DIFFERENCES

State FOI laws differ on a number of dimensions, including who is allowed to make a request; whether requesters must provide a reason, and if so, which reasons are deemed to be acceptable; deadlines by which agencies are required to acknowledge and fulfill requests; which information is exempt from disclosure; how long agencies are required to retain records; which types of requesters can be charged fees; and provisions for enforcing FOI laws, including appeals processes and penalties for noncompliance.

WHO MAY MAKE REQUESTS

The federal law specifies that "any person" may make a request, but some states are more restrictive. FOI laws in Alabama, Arkansas, Delaware, Georgia, Missouri, Montana, New Hampshire, New Jersey, Tennessee, and Virginia limit that right to residents of their own states. The U.S. Supreme Court has unanimously upheld Virginia's right to do so under the U.S. Constitution.[14] Not all of these states enforce those restrictions, however, and they may do so inconsistently. Attorneys general in Georgia and New Jersey have advised that, despite the wording of their states' laws, anyone may file a request there.[15] In Tennessee, agencies "are not prohibited from making records accessible to individuals who are not citizens of Tennessee,"[16] but they may choose to bar access to nonresidents.

Some states impose other types of restrictions on access as well. In Pennsylvania, requesters must be legal residents of the United States. In Louisiana, requesters must be of the "age of majority," and felony convicts cannot make requests unless the request relates to the potential for postconviction relief.[17] No one serving a prison sentence may file a public records request in Michigan.[18] In Alabama, courts have ruled that inmates may make requests, but agencies are not obligated to mail records to them.[19]

ACCEPTABLE REASONS FOR REQUESTS

The federal FOIA does not require requesters to state a reason, but some states do. Alabama agencies may deny requests that are based on a "speculative purpose or idle curiosity."[20] Some states require requesters to specify whether they plan to use the information for commercial purposes. In New York, residents' names and addresses may be withheld if the requester wants to use them for "solicitation or fund-raising purposes."[21] In Illinois, commercial requests are put on a slower time line. Public interest requests are promised a response within five days, but agencies have up to twenty-one business days to respond to commercial requests.[22]

Requesters in some states may have to prove that their reason for wanting public records outweighs the potential harm from their release. Six states allow records officers to use "balancing tests" to determine whether the benefits of public disclosure outweigh potential negative consequences for residents or businesses. Four states specifically address requests that are deemed to be nuisances due to their frequency or size, or due to the otherwise burdensome nature of fulfilling the request.[23] Illinois is one of those four states. In 2015, it added a "voluminous request" provision to its FOI law that allows agencies to add fees for requests that are sufficiently frequent or large. Voluminous requesters may be charged for documents even if they are available electronically; the maximum charge is $100. Commercial requesters also may be charged $10 for each hour that employees spend redacting information.[24]

DEADLINES FOR RESPONSES

Several states require a shorter response time than the twenty business days specified in the federal FOIA. Eight states require a response time of three days or less. Just as with the federal law, the initial response from states may be only an acknowledgment that the request was received. Finding, compiling, and releasing the requested records may take longer, and some states do not set a deadline for completion. Twelve states do not specify any deadlines for acknowledging or completing responses.

WHICH INFORMATION IS EXEMPT

The federal FOIA applies only to agencies in the executive branch of government, whereas state FOI laws may differ. Some state laws also cover records in the legislative and judicial branches, and some laws include records kept by quasi-governmental agencies. In Oregon, "public corporations," such as the state bar association, have been subject to that state's Public Records Law. Pennsylvania's Right to Know law covers "state-affiliated agencies," including the state gaming commission. Private entities that perform work for the government may or may not be covered by state FOI laws. In Tennessee, nongovernmental organizations that receive public funds may be subject to that state's Open Records Act. In Florida, emails between public employees and private entities may be available, but other states make emails available only when all parties are public employees.

State FOI laws also vary with regard to categories of information that are exempt from disclosure. The federal FOIA includes nine exemptions, many of which also can be found at the state level. Several states, including Kentucky, Louisiana, and Massachusetts, exempt trade secrets, just as Exemption 4 of the federal FOIA does. States also often have an exemption resembling FOIA's Exemption 5 for interagency communications. State versions of that exemption often refer to "deliberative" and "pre-decisional" documents, such as memos and emails between agencies; as well as "attorney work product," such as notes, research, and billing entries related to government litigation or claims. The federal FOIA's Exemption 9, related to geological and geophysical information about wells, appears in the FOI laws of California, Maryland, and Texas, among other states.

A version of FOIA's Exemption 3 also appears in many state laws. Exemption 3 effectively provides that other laws may prevent the disclosure of otherwise nonexempt information. Although the federal FOIA contains only nine exemptions, Exemption 3 means that the types of records that can be withheld are of a much greater variety. The Department of Justice's Office of Information Policy, which advises other federal agencies on FOIA compliance, has identified dozens of statutes that fall under Exemption 3.[25] Some state FOI laws refer to even more statutes. Nevada's Public Records Act cites more than four hundred other statutes that bar the release of particular records.[26] Oregon's Public Records Law identifies forty-two types of records that are always confidential and another forty that are conditionally exempt "unless the public interest requires disclosure in the particular instance."[27] However, according to transparency advocates who track the passage of new laws affecting access to information, the actual number of exemptions in Oregon is closer to four hundred fifty.[28]

State FOI laws may identify exemptions that do not appear in the federal FOIA. Some states explicitly exempt software developed or used by state government employees. California exempts records of Native American "graves, cemeteries, and sacred places."[29] Iowa, Mississippi, Oregon, South Dakota, Washington, and West Virginia exempt archaeological records or sites. (The federal government, for its part, exempts much archaeological and other sensitive historical information through the Archaeological Resources Protection Act of 1979, one of the statutes covered under FOIA Exemption 3.) Pennsylvania exempts information from disclosure if it "would result in the loss of Federal or State funds by an agency or the Commonwealth."[30] Some states, such as Delaware, exempt records related to public four-year universities. New York exempts records related to state licensing exams. Alabama and Maryland are among several states that bar the disclosure of library circulation records. Some states also exempt research that is in progress or has not been made public, such as research being conducted at universities or scientific institutions.

HOW LONG AGENCIES MUST RETAIN RECORDS

Records generally are available only if states require them to be kept. States may establish schedules for destroying records in order to dispose of documents that no longer serve any useful purpose, to reduce storage costs, and to help employees identify and preserve records that should be kept, among other reasons.[31] Rules about which records to keep, and how soon others may be destroyed, may be uniform across the state, or they may be delegated to particular officials. California's Public Records Act allows agencies to destroy records if it "will not adversely affect any interest of the district or of the public"[32] and if the agencies maintain a list of which records are destroyed. Agencies in Delaware must consult with the state archives before destroying any records. In Oklahoma, the Archives and Records Commission must determine that documents have no "administrative, legal, fiscal, research or historical value"[33] before they can be destroyed.

WHO CAN BE CHARGED FEES

Federal and state FOI laws tend to allow agencies to charge fees for finding, compiling, and duplicating requested records. The types of fees, how much agencies charge, and which fees requesters must pay all vary from state to state. The federal FOIA allows agencies to waive fees if the requested information "is likely to contribute significantly to public understanding of the operations and activities of the government,"[34] a claim often made by "noncommercial" requesters, such as journalists and researchers. Some states have similar fee waiver provisions for requests made in the public interest. In Alaska, copying fees may be waived for veterans who request records that prove their eligibility for benefits. Other states charge all requesters the same fees, regardless of who they are or why they are making the request. Wyoming's Sunshine Law provides only that fees should be "reasonable."[35]

ENFORCEMENT

FOI laws may have different means of holding records officers accountable for complying with requests. At the federal level, requesters who disagree with agency responses can file administrative appeals. If appeals are unsuccessful, requesters may file suit in court. Requesters in all fifty states may also sue in court, either immediately following a denial or after exhausting administrative appeals. In many states, the attorney general's office receives and investigates FOI complaints in the first instance. A few states have ombudspersons or commissions that act as independent mediators of FOI disputes. These entities also may offer opinions and monitor agency compliance with the law.

Such entities usually hold no enforcement power, but there are exceptions. In Connecticut, a five-member Freedom of Information Commission hears complaints from public records requesters. Complainants must attempt to resolve their cases through the commission before filing suit. Members of the commission have included journalists, government employees, and others. No more than three members can belong to the same political party. About half of cases are resolved through mediation. New Jersey has a similar panel, called the Government Records Council, modeled after the Connecticut commission. In Pennsylvania, the Office of Open Records hears appeals and issues binding decisions.[36]

Other states, such as Arizona and New York, have mediators who can offer opinions but do not have enforcement power. They operate similarly to the federal Office of Government Information Services, which was created as part of the OPEN Government Act of 2007 to try to resolve FOIA disputes outside the courts. FOI requesters in states whose mediators play only an advisory role are not necessarily worse off. According to access advocate Harry Hammitt, "the effectiveness of any given system depends largely on the political support provided by government as well as state access advocates,"[37] along with the commitment within mediation offices to support a presumption of disclosure. Even Connecticut's mediation system, which has been regarded as a national model, may not be as powerful as it would seem on paper; the office regularly has been targeted for budget cuts by state officials wary of its watchdog role.[38]

Potential sanctions for agencies found not in compliance with FOI laws depend on the state. Some states indicate that officials who knowingly violate the law can be found guilty of a misdemeanor. In Nebraska, officials can be impeached.[39] Agencies may face a flat fine, usually less than $1,000, or one that is assessed for each day they fail to comply. In Washington, the fine is up to $100 per day.[40] State laws also often allow courts to award attorneys' fees, punitive damages, or both to aggrieved requesters. Having provisions for potential punishments, however, does not necessarily mean those punishments will be implemented. One study found that allowing courts to award punitive damages did not result in greater FOI compliance.[41] Another study found that it was difficult to know which types of enforcement provisions worked best because most states "do little to keep track of how often the law is broken and what the punishment might be."[42]

COMMON CRITIQUES OF STATE FOI LAWS

Because state FOI laws may differ in so many respects, determining which ones are more or less friendly to journalists can be difficult. Still, many organizations have tried. From 2012 to 2015, the Center for Public Integrity, a nonprofit organization specializing in investigative journalism, published annual "State Integrity Investigations." The reports assigned grades to state governments based on thirteen categories related to transparency and accountability, such as Political Financing and Electoral Oversight. In the Public Access to Information category, forty-four states earned an F in 2015. Iowa scored the highest grade in that category, a C-minus.[43] It scored better than other states in part because of provisions in its law allowing access to public and private sector information and the presence of an entity to monitor and enforce FOI compliance.

The Better Government Association, a nonprofit group that focuses mostly on government accountability in Illinois, also has issued FOI report cards for all states. In partnership with insurance company Alper Services, it issued an Integrity Index, which included ratings of state FOI laws. States were rated on their response time, appeals processes, whether appeals were expedited when they reached the court system, whether plaintiffs may recover attorneys' fees, and whether agencies may be subject to civil or criminal penalties for noncompliance. The Better Government Association found that most state laws had "acceptable" response times but that officials had "little to fear" from violating the laws due to weak enforcement provisions.[44] In 2013, the last year the index was updated, Arkansas ranked highest in the FOI category with a score of 80 percent. Half of the states scored under 50 percent.

The National Freedom of Information Coalition and Better Government Association rated state FOI laws in 2007. On that report card, thirty-eight states received failing grades. Nebraska and New Jersey both earned the highest grade, a B. State laws were evaluated based on their required response time, appeals processes, the availability of expedited reviews, reimbursement of attorneys' fees, and sanctions.[45] The Better Government Association worked with Investigative Reporters and Editors on a similar report card in 2002. The rankings were based on procedural criteria (response time, appeals processes, possibility for expedited court hearings) and penalty criteria (potential reimbursement of attorneys' fees and civil or criminal punishments). Just as in 2007, Nebraska and New Jersey earned the highest grade, a B, and eight states failed.

Anecdotally, many journalists seem eager to claim that they work in one of the worst states for public records access. One *Boston Globe* story on a researcher's attempt to obtain teacher salary data labeled Massachusetts' "much-maligned" FOI law as "one of the weakest in the nation because it imposed few consequences upon violators while allowing public agencies to charge excessive fees."[46] A North Carolina newspaper named its state's law among the worst in the country because it failed to "provide an appeals process aside from expensive and time-consuming lawsuits."[47] Journalists in Pennsylvania,[48] South Carolina,[49] Michigan,[50] and Colorado[51] also have tried to claim for their states the honor of worst, or one of the worst, public records laws in the country.

The existence of so many ways to measure "worst" suggests an unclear path for potential improvements. The University of Florida's Marion Brechner Citizen Access Project observed that "access laws have too many dimensions for any state to be 'best,' or the 'most open,' on all issues."[52] In 2007, the organization created a database that broke down each state's FOI law into categories by which users could compare each state's level of openness. Each category could have several subcategories. Under the category Penalties, Appeals, Remedial Action, for instance, users could choose Civil Action or

Criminal Action. Selecting a category or subcategory then allowed for state-to-state comparisons. In each category, the organization assigned states a rating on a Sunshine Index ranging from 7 ("Sunny; completely open") to 1 ("Dark; completely closed").

A fundamental problem with all of these evaluations is that they focus on the laws on the books rather than on implementation practices or requester outcomes. Evidence on these practices and outcomes is scarce: many states do not collect such data or do not require the data to be made public. Some states do not even require agencies to keep logs of the FOI requests they receive, much less track the disposition of requests. Without consistent, visible data on how requests are processed, analyses of state FOI laws tend to be limited to legal texts, which can be selectively implemented and enforced; to appeals and lawsuits, which only represent requesters who have the requisite time and financial resources;[33] or to the complaints of journalists, which are anecdotal and can come across as personal grievances rather than issues that affect a broader public. The reality is that we do not have a good grasp on how state FOI laws are actually working—or failing to work.

ANALYSIS OF STATE FOI LOGS

To study the extent to which businesses are crowding out FOIA requests by journalists, Kwoka acquired logs from several federal agencies, including the Environmental Protection Agency (EPA), and analyzed the percentages of requests that came from each category of requesters. Federal agencies place requesters into one of three categories: (1) commercial, defined as people or organizations whose requests are based on commercial, trade, or profit interests; (2) noncommercial, such as members of the news media (regardless of whether they are for-profit or nonprofit) and educational and research institutions; and (3) other. The categories help agencies determine appropriate fees for search and review time and for duplication of records. Commercial requesters are subject to the highest fees; noncommercial requesters pay the lowest.

My research is the first to attempt a similar analysis to Kwoka's at the state level. In order to do so, I requested FOI logs from environmental agencies in each state. Examining data only from environmental agencies provides a limited, and possibly unrepresentative, look at the proportion of state FOI requests that come from journalists. However, focusing on environmental agencies allows for convenient comparisons to Kwoka's data at the federal level, as well as comparisons among states. Comparisons among other types of agencies are not so easy because the structures of state governments vary widely. However, with a few exceptions, states have an agency dedicated to environmental issues. Instead of having a separate agency, some states assign environmental issues to a division within a larger agency, such as a department of health or natural resources.

After identifying the relevant agencies or divisions in each state, I requested their FOI logs for the year 2014 using MuckRock, a website that helps facilitate and manage FOI requests. Specifically, my requests sought "the date of request, the requester's name, the requester's organizational affiliation, a description of the request, and the date the request was filled." In some cases, I used logs that another MuckRock user had already requested and made public.[54]

As logs were made available, it became clear that state practices for recording and processing FOI requests varied widely. Environmental agencies in two states, Georgia and North Dakota, tracked requests by hand. Figure 5.1 shows one page of the 2014 request log received from North Dakota. The left side of the page notes the dates requests were filed and the names, affiliations, and contact information of requesters. The right side of the page notes various other details, including the subject of the request, specific files that may contain the information requested, and dates that requests were acknowledged or completed.

Many states did not categorize requesters the way federal agencies do, so each agency's log had to be examined individually to determine which requests came from news media organizations. Organizations whose names were not immediately recognizable were searched online to determine whether they should be counted as news media—for instance, by reading how the organization described itself on an "About" page or by reading its mission, vision, or other statement of purpose. All people and organizations that identified themselves as having a journalistic purpose were counted, including freelance writers, blogs, and professional associations, such as Investigative Reporters and Editors.

FINDINGS

The logs received suggest that FOI requests by journalists are as rare at the state level as they are at the federal level. A closer examination of the logs also indicates that most news organizations were based in the states in which they filed requests, although there were exceptions when stories attracted national interest. Finally, there was no clear indication that certain types of news organizations were more likely to file FOI requests than others.

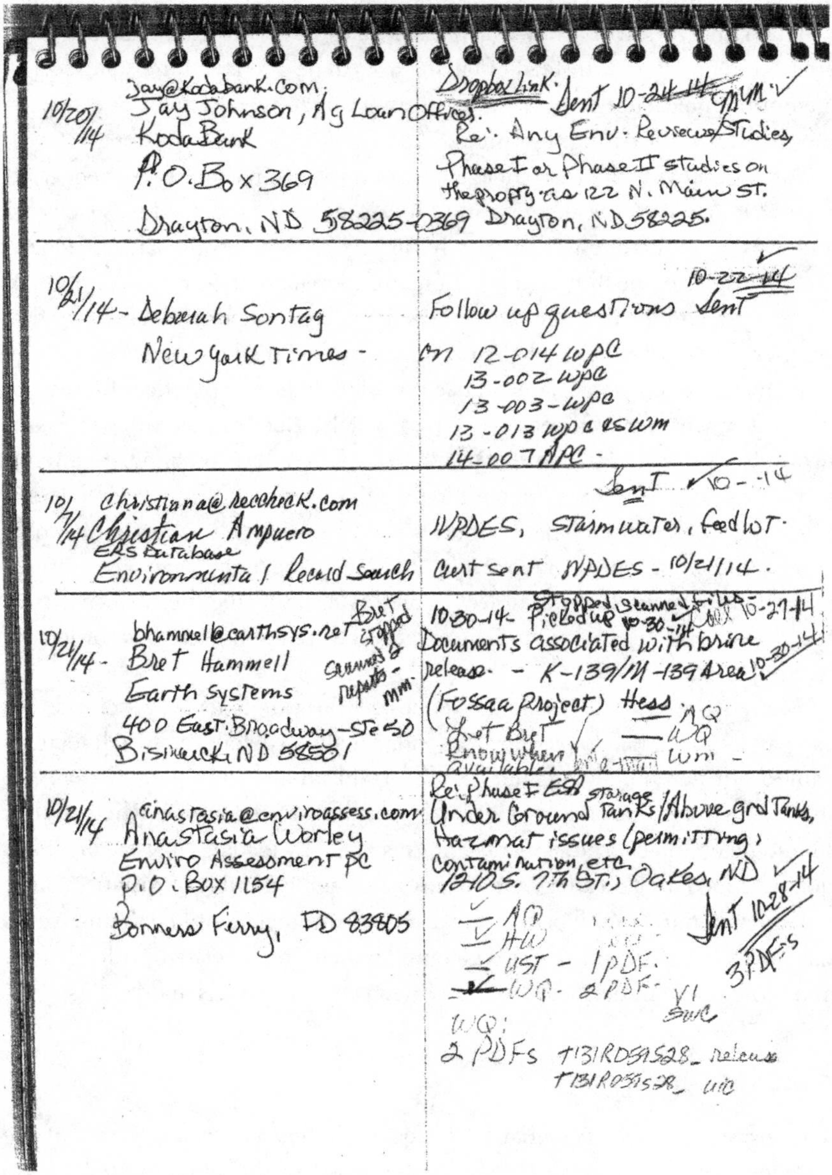

10/20/14 Jay@Kodabank.com, Jay Johnson, Ag Loan Officer, KodaBank, P.O. Box 369, Drayton, ND 58225-0369 — Dropbox Link. Sent 10-24-14 MM ✓ Re: Any Env. Reviews/Studies, Phase I or Phase II studies on the property at 122 N. Main St. Drayton, ND 58225.

10/21/14 - Deborah Sontag, New York Times - Follow up questions Sent 10-22-14 ✓ on 12-014 WPC, 13-002 WPC, 13-003-WPC, 13-013 WPC & SWM, 14-007 WPC -

10/21/14 christiana@reccheck.com, Christian Ampuero, ERS Database, Environmental Record Search — NPDES, stormwater, feedlot. Sent ✓ 10-21-14. Cert sent NPDES - 10/21/14.

10/21/14 - bhammel@earthsys.net, Bret Hammell, Earth Systems, 400 East Broadway - Ste 50, Bismarck ND 58501 — Bret stopped scanned reports - MM. 10-30-14 - Picked up 10-30-14. Stopped scanned files. 10-27-14. Documents associated with brine release - K-139/M-139 Area (Fossaa Project) Hess. AQ, WQ, WM - Let Bret know when available. 10-30-14.

10/21/14 anastasia@enviroassess.com, Anastasia Worley, Enviro Assessment PC, P.O. Box 1154, Bonners Ferry, ID 83805 — Re: Phase I ESA storage, Under Ground Tanks/Above grd Tanks, Hazmat issues (permitting), contamination, etc. 1210 S. 7th St., Oakes, ND ✓ Sent 10-28-14, 3 PDFs. ✓ AQ, ✓ HW, ✓ UST - 1 PDF, ✓ WQ - 2 PDF. WQ: 2 PDFs T131R059S28_release, T131R059S28_UIC

FIGURE 5.1 One page of the FOI request log from North Dakota (Environmental Health Division, Department of Health) in 2014.

TABLE 5.1 Percentage of FOI Requests Made by News Media to State Environmental Agencies

STATE	TOTAL REQUESTS	REQUESTS FROM NEWS MEDIA	% NEWS MEDIA
Pennsylvania	1,309	75	5.73
Wisconsin	917	34	3.71
North Dakota	251	9	3.59
Illinois	1,137	29	2.55
West Virginia	1,750	34	1.94
Texas	5,189	81	1.56
Oregon	342	5	1.46
Alaska	278	4	1.44
New York	5,127	66	1.29
Delaware	447	5	1.12
Mississippi	1,337	14	1.05
Florida	464	4	0.86
Louisiana	1,324	10	0.76
Ohio	3,492	21	0.60
Utah	1,341	8	0.60
Indiana	591	3	0.51
Washington	4,608	19	0.41
South Carolina	8,295	30	0.36
Nebraska	941	3	0.32
Colorado	812	2	0.25
Nevada	242	0	0.00
Total	40,194	456	1.13

For the twenty-one environmental agencies that provided usable data, journalists represented a small fraction of the total requests (table 5.1). Pennsylvania had the highest percentage of journalist requests, at 5.73 percent. Nevada was at the lowest end of the range: not one of the 242 FOI requests that its Division of Environmental Protection received in 2014 came from a news organization or an individual reporter.

The percentages of journalist requests at the state level are thus comparable to—although even more paltry than—what Kwoka found at the federal level. In her study, noncommercial requesters (including journalists) accounted for 3.53 percent of requests to the EPA in 2013.

TABLE 5.2 Categories of FOI Requesters for Pennsylvania's Department of Environmental Protection

CATEGORIES	NUMBER OF REQUESTS	% OF TOTAL
Consultant	642	49.05
Industry	35	2.67
Legal	221	16.88
Public	184	14.06
Government	9	0.69
Advocate	86	6.57
Inmate	12	0.92
School	20	1.53
Media	75	5.73
Not categorized	25	1.91
Total	1309	

Pennsylvania's Department of Environmental Protection was the only agency that provided data on requester categories, so it warrants a closer look (table 5.2). Media was one of nine categories the agency assigned to FOI requesters. The other categories were Consultant, Industry, Legal, Public, Government, Advocate, Inmate, and School.

Public, in this case, means "members of the public." The Advocate category includes environmental advocacy groups such as the Sierra Club and the Chesapeake Bay Foundation.

Of the nine categories, the first three correspond to what the federal FOIA would likely categorize as "commercial" requesters: consultant, industry, and legal. In addition to Media, the only other type of requester that might be considered noncommercial is School, if the requests relate to academic or scientific research. All other categories would likely fall into the federal government's Other category. Combining the categories in this way allows for a fuller comparison to Kwoka's data. The Pennsylvania data suggest a requester pattern that is still dominated by commercial interests, although to a lesser extent than at the EPA (table 5.3).

South Carolina stands out for having an unusually high number of total requests: 8,295 (table 5.4). The high number of requests in South Carolina is likely due to a quirk of its government structure. Most states have a single department, or division within a department, dedicated to environmental issues.

TABLE 5.3 Comparison of FOI Requester Types at Pennsylvania and Federal Environmental Agencies

	PENNSYLVANIA DEP (%)	EPA (%)
Commercial	68.60	79.45
Noncommercial	7.26	3.53
Other	22.23	14.72
Not categorized	1.91	2.30

TABLE 5.4 Total FOI Requests Per Capita

STATE	STATE POPULATION (2014)	TOTAL REQUESTS	TOTAL REQUESTS PER CAPITA
South Carolina	4,832,482	8,295	0.00172
West Virginia	1,850,326	1,750	0.00095
Washington	7,061,530	4,608	0.00065
Nebraska	1,881,503	941	0.00050
Delaware	935,614	447	0.00048
Utah	2,942,902	1,341	0.00046
Mississippi	2,984,926	1,337	0.00045
Alaska	737,732	278	0.00038
North Dakota	739,482	251	0.00034
Ohio	11,594,163	3,492	0.00030
Louisiana	4,649,676	1,324	0.00028
New York	19,746,227	5,127	0.00026
Texas	26,956,958	5,189	0.00019
Wisconsin	5,757,564	917	0.00016
Colorado	5,355,856	812	0.00015
Pennsylvania	12,787,209	1,309	0.00010
Illinois	12,880,580	1,137	0.00009
Indiana	6,596,855	591	0.00009
Nevada	2,839,099	242	0.00009
Oregon	3,970,239	342	0.00009
Florida	19,893,297	464	0.00002

South Carolina, however, has an agency of Health and Environmental Control, so South Carolina's logs included requests about environmental topics intermingled with requests related to health issues, such as Medicaid spending and dog bite reports.

States with larger populations did not necessarily have more FOI requests from news media (table 5.5). In fact, West Virginia's Department of Environmental Protection had the most news media requests per capita. This was likely due to an environmental story that attracted national attention in January 2014. A chemical spill in Charleston contaminated the water supply of 300,000 residents. FOI requests to the Department of Environmental Protection came not only from West Virginia news media but also from national organizations such as the *Wall Street Journal*, Al Jazeera America, Associated

TABLE 5.5 News Media FOI Requests Per Capita

STATE	STATE POPULATION (2014)	REQUESTS FROM NEWS MEDIA	TOTAL MEDIA REQUESTS PER CAPITA
West Virginia	1,850,326	34	0.0000184
North Dakota	739,482	9	0.0000122
South Carolina	4,832,482	30	0.0000062
Wisconsin	5,757,564	34	0.0000059
Pennsylvania	12,787,209	75	0.0000059
Alaska	737,732	4	0.0000054
Delaware	935,614	5	0.0000053
Mississippi	2,984,926	14	0.0000047
New York	19,746,227	66	0.0000033
Texas	26,956,958	81	0.0000030
Utah	2,942,902	8	0.0000027
Washington	7,061,530	17	0.0000024
Illinois	12,880,580	29	0.0000023
Louisiana	4,649,676	10	0.0000022
Ohio	11,594,163	21	0.0000018
Nebraska	1,881,503	3	0.0000016
Oregon	3,970,239	5	0.0000013
Indiana	6,596,855	3	0.0000005
Colorado	5,355,856	2	0.0000004
Florida	19,893,297	4	0.0000002
Nevada	2,839,099	0	0.0000000

Press, NPR, and the trade publication *E&E News* (the two E's are Energy and Environment). In total, non–West Virginia news media accounted for 47 percent of all journalist requests.

North Dakota also had more news media requests per capita than most other states. In this case, too, it was due to stories that attracted national attention. Eight of the nine news media requests received by the Environmental Health Division of North Dakota's Department of Health came from national news media. Four requests specifically came from Deborah Sontag, a *New York Times* journalist who coauthored a 2014 series on the state's lax regulation of oil companies.

In most states, national, or out-of-state, news media accounted for less than half of FOI requests for environmental information (table 5.6). Besides West

TABLE 5.6 FOI Requests by Media Type

STATE	IN-STATE MEDIA REQUESTS	ALL NEWS MEDIA REQUESTS	% OF REQUESTS BY IN-STATE MEDIA
Nevada	0	0	N/A
Colorado	2	2	100
Delaware	5	5	100
Florida	4	4	100
Indiana	3	3	100
Louisiana	10	10	100
Oregon	5	5	100
New York	63	66	95
South Carolina	27	30	90
Illinois	25	29	86
Ohio	18	21	86
Wisconsin	29	34	85
Mississippi	11	14	79
Washington	13	17	76
Pennsylvania	53	75	71
Texas	54	81	67
Utah	5	8	63
West Virginia	15	34	44
Nebraska	1	3	33
Alaska	1	4	25
North Dakota	1	9	11

Virginia and North Dakota, other exceptions included states that had few FOI requests for environmental information from news media.

FOI requesters included newspapers, magazines, wire services, television and radio stations, online organizations, and independent journalists and bloggers. Larger organizations were not necessarily more active. For instance, in Wisconsin, the most active requester was the *Lakeland Times*, a twice-weekly newspaper serving a sparsely populated region near the Canadian border. It submitted nine FOI requests to Wisconsin's Department of Natural Resources in 2014. The *Milwaukee Journal Sentinel*, a daily newspaper whose circulation is more than twenty-five times larger than the *Lakeland Times*, submitted only eight requests.

The most active media FOI requesters (table 5.7) were often, but not always, legacy news organizations. In Louisiana, seven of the ten requests

TABLE 5.7 Most Frequent Media Filers by State (States marked N/A did not receive more than one request from any media organization)

STATE	MOST FREQUENT FILER
Alaska	N/A
Colorado	*Cortez Journal*
Delaware	*News Journal*
Florida	*Tampa Bay Times*
Illinois	*Illinois Times*
Indiana	N/A
Louisiana	*The Lens*
Mississippi	*Hattiesburg Patriot*
Nebraska	*Wall Street Journal*
New York	*Newsday*
North Dakota	*New York Times*
Ohio	Associated Press, *Dayton Daily News*, WKBN-TV Youngstown
Oregon	N/A
Pennsylvania	*Pittsburgh Post Gazette*
South Carolina	WBTW—News 13
Texas	*InsideClimate News*
Utah	KSL Radio
Washington	*Seattle Times*
West Virginia	*Charleston Gazette*
Wisconsin	*Lakeland Times*

by news media to the Department of Environmental Quality came from *The Lens*, an online news organization based in New Orleans. The Pulitzer Prize-winning *InsideClimate News*, which is based in New York but reports on environmental stories around the world, took a particular interest in Texas in 2014. The organization filed twenty FOI requests to the Texas Commission on Environmental Quality, roughly a quarter of all journalist requests received by that agency in 2014.

LIMITATIONS OF THE DATA

This analysis is necessarily limited by the fact that less than half of the states provided usable data. Agencies in twenty-nine states did not provide logs or provided incomplete information.

Two states explicitly rejected the request for their logs. The Kansas Department of Health and Environment cited a provision in the state's Open Records Act that allows agencies to deny requests that place "an unreasonable burden in producing public records or if the custodian has reason to believe that repeated requests are intended to disrupt other essential functions of the public agency."[55] It was not clear which of those conditions the agency deemed to apply in this case. This was my first request addressed to the agency, although another person had made a similar request roughly a year earlier. Kansas Attorney General Derek Schmidt, in a document intended to guide agencies in their responses to public records requests, has advised citing the "unreasonable burden" provision "only in extreme circumstances."[56]

New Jersey's Department of Environmental Protection denied the request based in part on a 2005 appellate court decision on whether logs were available under the state's Open Public Records Act (OPRA). In *Gannett New Jersey Partners, LP v. County of Middlesex*, a records officer had denied a newspaper's requests for subpoenas related to an investigation into an alleged pay-for-play political scandal. The court found that OPRA "does not authorize a party to make a blanket request for every document a public agency has provided another party," nor does the act permit requests that would reveal "the nature and scope of a third party's inquiry to a government agency."[57] A New Jersey appeals court has since ruled that request logs should be made available.[58] However, the New Jersey Department of Environmental Protection also rejected my request for its FOI logs based on an exemption in OPRA for "information which, if disclosed, would give an advantage to competitors."

Agencies in seven states wrote in response to my request that they had "no responsive documents." This could mean a number of things. Agencies might not keep logs of requests they receive, or their logs might not be considered "records" for the purposes of their state's FOI law. A "no responsive documents" response also could mean that logs existed at some point but had been destroyed. Three agencies confirmed that their logs had been destroyed.

Arizona's Department of Environmental Quality agreed to provide its logs, but for a fee of at least $500. The department cited a provision in the state's Public Records Law that allows agencies to charge $500 for "commercial purpose" lists, in addition to a $120 per hour charge for custom searches of lists. The law allows reduced fees for noncommercial requests, but whether research falls into the state's noncommercial category is open to interpretation.[59] I did not agree to pay the $500 fee, so Arizona data are not included in this study.

Some states provided partial logs in response to my request. California's Department of Conservation, whose records officer cautioned that the agency was not required to keep a log and that the information it provided was "by no means comprehensive," listed a total of thirty-two requests for 2014. North Carolina and Georgia did not indicate that any entries may have been missing from their logs, but their total numbers were unusually low when compared to those of other states. North Carolina listed only forty-six requests, Georgia seventy-six. The percentages of journalists among requesters in both states also were unusually high: 39 percent in North Carolina, and 15 percent in Georgia. Neither figure seems reliable.

Environmental agencies in eight states provided logs that included names of requesters but not their organizational affiliations. Without this information, it was hard to tell whether requesters represented commercial interests, news media, other organizations, or whether they were individuals simply requesting information for themselves. Due to the arduous and perhaps impossible task of determining how those requesters should be categorized, data from states that did not provide requester affiliations were omitted from this study.

Beyond the issue of omitted states, other obvious limitations of this study include the lack of time-series data and the omission of nonenvironmental agencies. As mentioned earlier, FOI is a decentralized process at the state level, as at the federal level, with each state agency (not to mention local agencies) in charge of handling requests related only to its own records. Request patterns at environmental agencies may differ systematically from those at agencies that address other topics. Businesses, trade groups, and partisan watchdog organizations have used FOI laws to flood agencies with public records requests to impede regulation and harass political opponents.[60]

Considering how often environmental issues come up in political debates, such groups may appear more frequently in the logs of environmental agencies than in agencies that deal with less controversial topics.

Evidence also suggests, however, that news media are particularly interested in environmental agency records. One study of fourteen federal agencies found that news media filed the most FOIA requests with the EPA—almost twice as many as they filed with the second-most popular agency, the Department of Homeland Security.[61] If the same pattern exists at the state level, the percentages of journalist requests to other agencies would likely be even lower.

Due to these limitations, it is difficult to assess the overall extent to which commercial interests are crowding out journalists among state FOI requesters. It is clear that journalists account for a small percentage of requests in the states that provided data. It is not clear (except in Pennsylvania) what proportion of requests represented business interests. It also is not clear whether requests from businesses might contribute to delayed responses to journalists' requests. Unlike the federal FOIA, most state laws do not require agencies to report on their ability to respond to requests in a timely fashion. And, of course, what is considered "timely" depends on the state.

CONCLUSION AND RECOMMENDATIONS

Kwoka concluded in her analysis of federal agencies that they should release more information to the public proactively, particularly when records are likely to attract broad interest or for certain types of information that tend to be requested over and over again.[62] Increasing proactive, or affirmative, disclosure could reduce the number of FOIA requests filed with agencies that are already struggling to keep up.

More proactive disclosure would certainly help at the state level as well. In addition, states should follow the federal government's lead in tracking and reporting responses to FOI requests. The federal FOIA requires agencies on an annual basis to report, among other data:

- Number of requests received and how long it took to process them;
- Number of requests pending (backlog);
- Number of requests that were rejected and reasons they were rejected;
- Number of administrative appeals and their outcomes;
- List of all statutes cited in justifications for withholding information; and
- Number of fee waivers granted and denied

Data from each agency must be reported to the Attorney General and the Office of Government Information Services, which compile the information and publish it. Although gathering such data alone does not solve problems such as delayed responses and improper withholding of information, it can at least highlight where those problems are most extreme and help set priorities for improvement. Collecting such data at the state level could allow for more useful comparisons among states than prior report cards and rankings largely based on the text of laws rather than the implementation of those laws.

Although data on state FOI practices are limited, the logs obtained for this study suggest reason for concern. The low percentages of journalists among state FOI requesters indicate that news media requests are marginalized at the state level, perhaps even more than they are at the federal level. This is not good for the vast numbers of journalists who cover local and state news — nor for national journalists who sometimes need state-level records for their reporting. Nor is it good for the rest of us, who depend on the ability of news organizations to access and communicate information of public interest.

NOTES

1. David Cuillier, "Pressed for Time: U.S. Journalists' Use of Public Records During Economic Crisis" (paper presented at the Global Conference on Transparency Research, Newark, N.J., May 18–20, 2011).
2. John A. Hatcher and Bill Reader, "New Terrain for Research in Community Journalism," *Community Journalism* 1 (2012): 1–10.
3. Carolyn Miller, Kristen Purcell, and Tom Rosenstiel, "72 Percent of Americans Follow Local News Closely," Pew Research Center, April 12, 2012, www.pewinternet .org/2012/04/12/72-of-americans-follow-local-news-closely.
4. Monica Davey and Mitch Smith, "2 Former Flint Emergency Managers Charged Over Tainted Water," *New York Times*, December 20, 2016.
5. "Innocents Lost Wins Freedom of Information Award," *Miami Herald*, April 6, 2016.
6. Jim Haddadin, "DA: Hidden Key Granted Access to Framingham Police Evidence Room," *MetroWest Daily News*, November 4, 2016.
7. Margaret B. Kwoka, "FOIA, Inc.," *Duke Law Journal* 65 (2016): 1361–1437.
8. For information about the origins of several states' laws, see National Association of Counties, *Open Records Laws: A State by State Report*, 2010, www .naco.org/sites/default/files/documents/Open%20Records%20Laws%20A %20State%20by%20State%20Report.pdf; as well as state-specific resources such as George F. Kugler Jr., *New Jersey's Right to Know: A Report on Open*

Government (Trenton, N.J.: Attorney General's Committee on the Right to Know, 1974); and *Summary of the California Public Records Act* (Sacramento, Calif.: California Attorney General's Office, 2004).

9. Bill Lueders, *December: Early Case Sheds Light on Records*, Wisconsin Freedom of Information Coalition, 2007, www.wisfoic.org/index.php?option=com_content &view=article&id=106:december-early-case-sheds-light-on-records-&catid =44:2007-columns&Itemid=76.

10. Harold L. Cross, *The People's Right to Know: Legal Access to Public Records and Proceedings* (New York: Columbia University Press, 1953).

11. Michael Schudson, *The Rise of the Right to Know: Politics and the Culture of Transparency, 1945–1975* (Cambridge, Mass.: Harvard University Press, 2015).

12. Examples include National Freedom of Information Coalition, *State Freedom of Information Laws*, 2016, www.nfoic.org/state-freedom-of-information-laws; Public Employees for Environmental Responsibility, *Summary of State Public Records Laws*, 2014, www.peer.org/assets/images/campaigns/whistleblower/State %20Public%20Record%20Laws%20-%20All%2050%20States.pdf; and Reporters Committee for Freedom of the Press, *Open Government Guide*, 2011, www.rcfp .org/open-government-guide.

13. Society of American Archivists, "Issue Brief: State Freedom of Information Laws," September 2015, www2.archivists.org/statements/issue-brief-state-freedom -of-information-laws.

14. McBurney v. Young, 133 S. Ct. 1709 (2013).

15. Sam Olens, *A Citizen's Guide to Open Government*, Office of the Georgia Attorney General, 2014, https://law.georgia.gov/sites/law.georgia.gov/files/related _files/site_page/GeorgiasSunshineLaws2014WebEdition.pdf; State of New Jersey Government Records Council, "Frequently Asked Questions," OPRA for the Public, accessed March 29, 2017, www.nj.gov/grc/public/faqs/#4.

16. Justin P. Wilson, "Frequently Asked Questions: Tennessee Comptroller of the Treasury," Open Records Counsel, accessed March 29, 2017, www.comptroller .tn.gov/openrecords/faq.asp.

17. La. Rev. Stat. Ann. §§ 44.31–44.32.

18. Mich. Comp. Laws § 15.231(2).

19. Person v. Alabama Department of Forensic Sciences, 721 So. 2d 203 (Ala. Civ. App. 1998).

20. Charles A. Graddick, Letter to Dallas County Commissioner Cartledge W. Blackwell, October 31, 1985, Alabama Office of the Attorney General, www .ago.state.al.us/opinions/pdf/8600038.pdf.

21. N.Y. FOIL, § 89(2)(b)(iii).

22. 5 ILCS 140/2(c-10).

23. Michele Bush Kimball, "Public Records Professionals' Perceptions of Nuisance Requests for Access," *Journal of Media Law & Ethics* 5 (Winter/Spring 2016): 46–48.

24. 5 ILCS § 140 6(f).

25. U.S. Department of Justice Office of Information Policy, "Statutes Found to Qualify Under Exemption 3 of the FOIA," December 2015, www.justice.gov /oip/page/file/623931/download.

26. NRS § 239.010.

27. ORS 192.501.

28. Patrice McDermott and Roberta Richards, "The Promise of Open Government, for the Nation and for Oregon," *OLA Quarterly* 16 (2014): 33–37.

29. Ca. Gov. Code § 6254.

30. 65 Pa. Cons. Stat. Ann. § 67.708 (2010).

31. Geof Huth, "Retention and Disposition of Records: How Long to Keep Records and How to Destroy Them," New York State Archives, 2002, www.archives .nysed.gov/common/archives/files/mr_pub41.pdf.

32. Ca. Gov. Code § 60201(b).

33. OK Stat § 67–210 (2015).

34. FOIA.gov, "Frequently Asked Questions," accessed April 6, 2017, www.foia.gov /faq.html.

35. WY Stat § 16-4-202 (1997 through Reg. Sess.).

36. Pennsylvania Office of Open Records, "Citizens' Guide," revised August 2015, www.openrecords.pa.gov/RTKL/CitizensGuide.cfm.

37. Harry Hammitt, "Mediation Without Litigation," *National Freedom of Information Coalition* (2007): 21.

38. Keith M. Phaneuf, "Malloy Releases Funds Withheld from CT Watchdog Agencies," *Connecticut Mirror*, August 19, 2016.

39. Neb. Rev. Stat. § 84–712.09.

40. RCW 42.56.550(4).

41. Kate Ferguson, "Compliance Conundrum: The Use of Punitive Damage Provisions in State Freedom of Information Statutes," *Columbia Human Rights Law Review* 46 (2014): 371–412.

42. Robert Tanner, "On Sunshine Laws, Governments Talk Loudly but Stick Is Very Rarely Used," Associated Press, March 10, 2007, http://legacy.utsandiego. com/news/nation/20070310-1053-sunshineweek.html.

43. Center for Public Integrity, "How Does Your State Rank for Integrity?" November 9, 2015, www.publicintegrity.org/2015/11/03/18822/how-does-your-state -rank-integrity.

44. Better Government Association, "BGA-Alper Services Integrity Index," 2013, www.bettergov.org/sites/default/files/pdf/2013%20BGA-Alper%20Services %20Integrity%20Index.pdf.

45. National Freedom of Information Coalition, "States Failing FOI Responsiveness," October 2007, http://nfoic.org/states-failing-foi-responsiveness.

46. James Vaznis, "School Superintendents Hit the Books over Public Records Law," *Boston Globe*, July 19, 2016.

47. Bill Moss, "Davis Case Shows Weakness in NC Public Records Law," *Hendersonville Lightning*, July 29, 2012.

48. Reid R. Frazier, "Penn State Scandal May Mean Change for Open-Records Law," *PublicSource*, November 15, 2011.

49. Chelsey Dulaney, "NC, SC Flunk Public Records," *Charlotte Observer*, July 25, 2012.

50. Paul Egan, "Michigan Ranks Last in Laws on Ethics, Transparency," *Detroit Free Press*, November 9, 2015.

51. Christopher N. Osher, "Colorado Gets Grade of F for Its Open-Records Laws," *Denver Post*, November 11, 2015.

52. Bill F. Chamberlin, Cristina Popsecu, Michael F. Weigold, and Nissa Laughner, "Searching for Patterns in the Laws Governing Access to Records and Meetings in the Fifty States by Using Multiple Research Tools," *University of Florida Journal of Law & Public Policy* 18 (2007): 415–45.

53. Margaret B. Kwoka, "The Freedom of Information Act Trial," *American University Law Review* 61 (2011): 217–78.

54. Similar requests were made by MuckRock user Erik Peterson, www.muckrock.com/accounts/profile/ErikPeterson.

55. K.S.A. § 45-218(e).

56. Derek Schmidt, "Kansas Open Records Act (KORA) Guidelines," July 1, 2015, http://ag.ks.gov/docs/default-source/publications/kansas-open-records-act-(kora)-guidelines.pdf?sfvrsn=6.

57. Gannett New Jersey Partners, LP v. County of Middlesex, 379 N.J. Super. 205, 212 (App. Div. 2005).

58. See NorthJersey.com, "OPRA Requests Subject to Open Records Law, Court Rules," January 27, 2017, www.northjersey.com/story/news/2017/01/27/opra-requests-too-subject-open-records-law/97152068.

59. A.R.S. §§ 39-122(A), §39-127.

60. David E. Pozen, "Freedom of Information Beyond the Freedom of Information Act," *University of Pennsylvania Law Review* 165 (2017): 1097–1158.

61. James T. Hamilton, *Democracy's Detectives: The Economics of Investigative Journalism* (Cambridge, Mass.: Harvard University Press, 2016).

62. Kwoka, "FOIA, Inc."

6

FOIA AND INVESTIGATIVE REPORTING

Who's Asking What, Where, and When—and Why It Matters

James T. Hamilton

INVESTIGATIVE JOURNALISM involves original reporting about substantive issues in a community that someone—often someone in government—may be trying to keep secret. That generates three economic strikes against this type of accountability-promoting work. Original content can be costly, the benefits from changing laws and lives can be hard to monetize, and pulling information out of the government can entail great hassle costs imposed by public officials. Freedom of Information Act (FOIA) requests potentially offer reporters a way to lower the costs of discovering stories by making it easier to get government records.

The key word is "potentially." In this chapter, I explore how FOIAs are used in investigative reporting by analyzing two data sets I created in writing *Democracy's Detectives: The Economics of Investigative Journalism.*[1] Entries in the annual prize competitions of Investigative Reporters and Editors (IRE) show that government records requests are often a part of the investigative stories that generate public debates and changes in policies. In exploring news organizations' FOIA requests to fourteen federal departments and agencies, however, I find that journalists' use of FOIA has been declining over time. Who is doing the requesting is also changing. FOIA requests by local newspapers are down significantly, and those by other media such as niche outlets that cater to specific participants in the business of governing (such as lobbyists, interest group leaders, agency and congressional staff, and government affairs specialists in companies) are on the rise. Three policy measures would improve reporters' use of government documents and data: (1) real implementation of the FOIA reform act passed in 2016; (2) recognition by government funding bodies that journalism about public affairs is worthy of support because it is underprovided in the market; and (3) greater adoption of proactive transparency strategies.

FOIA USE IN PRIZE-WORTHY INVESTIGATIVE REPORTING

To explore the frequency of public records requests by the news media, I first assembled a data set of more than 12,500 contest entry forms submitted by U.S. media organizations from 1979 to 2010 in the annual prize competitions of IRE. The contest entry forms encouraged reporters to describe how they conducted their investigations, what was uncovered, and what impact their findings had. I did keyword searches of contest entry form PDFs to identify when reporters said they had made government records requests using the federal FOIA, state or local freedom of information (FOI) laws, or other open records laws. This is an imperfect measure of FOIA activity for many reasons: journalists might use different words than the ones I searched for to describe their records use; searches of PDFs can be flawed because of problems with document images; and references to public records can—and often do—refer to state and local requests, not simply documents obtained through the federal FOIA.

With those caveats in mind, I found that public records requests were a frequent part of investigative reporting: 14 percent of the IRE contest entry stories involved government records requests. The use varied widely by medium. Print (newspaper) investigative stories submitted to IRE contests involved records requests 17 percent of the time, compared to 12 percent for television submissions (which involved less time devoted to development of stories) and only 7 percent for magazine submissions. For newspapers, records requests were most frequent among those with medium-sized circulations, which is consistent with observations by some journalists that they used documents as a way to differentiate themselves from larger newspapers that were more likely to have direct access to policy makers.[2]

Requests for government records under FOIA or its state and local counterparts were much more likely in those investigations that had major impacts. I cannot say exactly how the records were used in the reporting, but investigations that involved records requests were also the type that generated results. For example, in the sample of more than 12,500 IRE contest entries, 40 percent of the stories that triggered review of policies involved government records requests. Government records were requested in at least 25 percent of the stories that led to people being fired, to audits, or to investigations and policy change. In IRE entries that noted that laws had been passed because of the reporting, 24 percent involved government records requests. More than one in four stories involving revelations about misconduct, sexual harassment, or waste used government records requests as part of the reporting process.

Investigative reporters put FOIA to a variety of uses: gathering documents to corroborate tips and leaks; looking for information to confirm a hypothesis or trend; broadly fishing in an area thought promising because of potential controversy or scandal; or exploring data in search of surprising patterns and outliers. Journalists may enter the FOIA process with a hypothesis to test, or with little idea about what may be going on in an agency. Documents and data provided can inform later interviews with human sources, become the basis for statistical analysis, disprove an early hunch, or even lead a reporter to an entirely new and unanticipated story.

The *Wall Street Journal*'s "Medicare Unmasked" series, which won the 2015 Pulitzer Prize for investigative reporting, shows how information obtained via FOIA can be used in multiple ways within a single investigation. In the IRE prize contest form describing the series, the *Wall Street Journal* noted that the "health-care team began digging into Medicare issues in 2009, following tips from long-time sources, and produced a series of stories at the time that led us to seek more data from the government."[3] The Centers for Medicare and Medicaid Services (CMS) initially denied the FOIA request for Medicare billing data, but after years of court battles a federal court decision forced the release of billing information on 880,000 providers. This led the *Wall Street Journal* to examine 9.2 million records on 2012 expenditures in the $600 billion Medicare program. Analyzing the data involved tips, expert guidance, and explorations of the potential stories associated with outliers found in the data.

Asked for advice to give other journalists working on similar projects, the *Wall Street Journal* noted in its prize competition entry:

It's critically important when receiving such a large data set for reporters to recognize that the limitations of this type of data can make it difficult to separate the signal from the noise. Successful stories often hinged on expert guidance that focused reporters on areas rife with waste and abuse. . . . Some outliers may be found—after extensive reporting—to have strong explanations for unusual patterns that show up in billing data. Picking areas with known controversy and using available data to drill deeper into workings of questionable treatment or billing practices can be a fruitful approach.[4]

The *Wall Street Journal* series revealed waste and abuse in the Medicare program in part by telling the stories of doctors whose billing practices were outliers in the data. Describing their approach, the reporters noted:

After analyzing the distribution of services per beneficiary performed by each doctor or provider in the 2012 data released by CMS, we used standard deviation and other statistical metrics to identify doctors and suppliers whose billing patterns were outliers among their peers in their specialties. The Journal then used the claims data and its wealth of additional details to refine our understanding of these outliers' activities.[5]

In "How a Tip About Habitat for Humanity Became a Whole Different Story," Marcelo Rochabrun of ProPublica described how documents obtained under FOIA allowed him to tell a completely different tale than the idea that initially led him to start an investigation. Rochabrun at first began to examine a Habitat for Humanity New York City affiliate because a source believed that the "nonprofit had become unwittingly involved in a massive money-laundering operation."[6] Yet when his story was published eight months later:

> it didn't focus on money laundering at all. Instead, the story detailed how the charity's management of an ambitious housing initiative had led to the displacement of low-income families in Brooklyn, families who had been forced out of their homes just days or weeks before Habitat moved to buy their former apartment buildings, which the charity described as "long vacant" structures.[7]

Rochabrun filed public records requests with New York City and used databases such as Nexis to explore the history of buildings bought by Habitat. He also noted, "Not knowing exactly what I expected to find, I also filed Freedom of Information Act requests with the federal Department of Housing and Urban Development."[8] The HUD documents ultimately proved central to Rochabrun's reporting because these "records proved to have what [he] most needed: signed documents attesting to the date Habitat had 'first visited' the properties it sought to acquire."[9]

Data on government websites can sometimes serve as the basis for investigative reports, whereas documents obtained by FOIA can serve as a way to check the information that is made public. In its series "Invisible Wounds," KARE-11 (an NBC-affiliated television station in the Minneapolis area) explored how veterans were denied adequate treatment at the Minneapolis Veterans Administration (VA) hospital by doctors who were not properly qualified. The station's reporting revealed that the "VA's own websites included false and misleading information about doctor's licenses and certifications."[10] The station based its report on "a sturdy foundation of medical records provided by individual veterans, internal VA memos provided by sources, lawsuits, Office of Inspector General reports, Congressional testimony, state medical licensing records, medical board certification records and a mountain of documents produced by multiple FOIA requests."[11]

An emerging genre of investigative reporting involves stories made possible by government emails obtained through public record requests at the federal or state level. Michael Morisy, founder of MuckRock, a website that facilitates FOIA requests, notes that the wide range of stories made possible by emails obtained through FOIA includes:

> The close connections and communications between government officials and the insurance industry they're charged with regulating . . .
>
> How the egg lobby conspired to destroy a vegan competitor, leading to the resignation of the American Egg Board's chief executive.
>
> Why the CIA spied on Senate staffers, for which CIA director John Brennan apologized . . .
>
> How Coca-Cola helped steer the CDC to push for regulations more favorable to the soda industry, after which the official in question left the agency.
>
> Details on how UC Davis attempted to erase its history of pepper-spraying protestors, which the university's chancellor apologized for.
>
> How Michigan governor Rick Snyder was warned to switch water systems well before the water poisoning became public.
>
> How officials timed releasing information related to child safety for when it was politically expedient, after which a number of officials and employees either resigned or were fired.[12]

Emails obtained through FOIA give reporters the opportunity to spot abuses of power or conflicts of interest that are otherwise hard to trace because they may not show up in formal documents such as contracts, calendars, or write-ups of regulatory actions.

PATTERNS IN MEDIA FOIA REQUESTS AT FEDERAL AGENCIES

Although the IRE contest entries and accounts by investigative journalists of how they developed their stories suggest that FOIAs can play a key role in some investigative series, the type of original reporting effort involved in requesting public records may be at risk given the financial declines experienced by news outlets. To explore how this form of scrutiny might be changing, I created a second data set designed to allow me to analyze FOIA activity over time. In 2012, I submitted FOIA requests to thirty-five federal departments and agencies, asking for FOIA request logs and/or logs of FOIAs involving fee waivers (which are often requested by media organizations) from 2000 to 2010. The response was underwhelming, and I supplemented the information I received with data on FOIA requests available on the Internet. This allowed me ultimately to assemble a data set on media FOIA requests for fourteen departments and agencies from 2005 to 2010.

This is not a random or representative sample. Rather, it is a snapshot of FOIA activity at a specific set of agencies and departments. The fourteen are Amtrak, Defense Contract Audit Agency, Department of Homeland Security, Environmental Protection Agency (EPA), Federal Highway Administration, Federal Labor Relations Authority, USDA Food Safety and Inspection Service (FSIS), Federal Trade Commission (FTC), Mine Safety and Health Administration (MSHA), Nuclear Regulatory Commission (NRC), Department of Interior Office of Surface Mining, Department of Justice Office of Violence Against Women, Department of Transportation Surface Transportation Board, and the Tennessee Valley Authority.

Patterns of media FOIA requests to such agencies offer a window into how media scrutiny of government has changed over time. Between 2005 and 2010, there were 3,331 FOIA requests from media outlets to these fourteen agencies and departments. In 2005, there were 722 media requests, and by 2010 this figure had declined by 25 percent to 543. Note that the 2010 figures were up a bit from the recession years of 2008 and 2009.

In 2005, local newspapers generated the highest number of FOIA requests (288) among all media categories at these agencies. But the number of requests by local newspapers dropped by about 50 percent by 2010. Requests by nonprofit media dropped by only 14 percent during this time period. It was a different story for the "Other Media" category, which includes the Associated Press, Bloomberg, and many niche publications aimed at those who follow the details of policy making for a living in their roles as lobbyists, company officials, or government employees. FOIAs from Other Media increased between 2005 and 2010, and by 2010 this category accounted for the most media FOIA requests.

The different economic fates of media outlets can affect scrutiny across agencies. Among the nine agencies I examined that had eighty or more media FOIA requests from 2005 to 2010, six of them had local newspapers as the top submitters. These included Amtrak, USDA FSIS, FTC, and MSHA. These requests showed that local reporters were active in scrutinizing contracts, inspections, and accidents in their areas. The Other Media requesters had the highest number of FOIAs at Homeland Security, EPA, and NRC. Their focus on the business of government led them to search out information on policy implementation, contracts, and inspections at these agencies.

The modal experience for a media outlet was sending in one FOIA request over this six-year period. Of the 575 media organizations that generated the 3,331 FOIAs, 314 sent in only one request. But there is also a set of high demanders. Thirty-three outlets sent in at least twenty FOIAs, and they accounted for over half of the media FOIAs at these agencies.

Patterns at EPA show how FOIA is geographically dispersed even as the bulk of requesting activity may be concentrated in a small number of outlets. There were 1,179 FOIA requests to EPA made by 265 media outlets from 2005 to 2010. The modal experience was a single FOIA to the EPA. There were 146 media outlets that made only one request, and those accounted for 12 percent of the total FOIAs at the agency. These included many local newspapers, magazines, and fifteen local television stations.

Nine outlets submitted twenty or more FOIAs to the EPA, and these accounted for about 40 percent of the agency's media total. These included *The Hill, Denver Post*, ProPublica, *PEC National Security News Service* (an organization that supports national security and environmental reporting), *New York Times*, Inside Washington Publishers (a news organization focused on the federal policy-making process), Associated Press, *Inside EPA*, and the Center for Public Integrity. This shows how intensive investigative scrutiny of the federal government may reside in a relatively small number of outlets with a mix of financial models: nonprofit media outlets such as the Center for Public Integrity, *PEC National Security News Service*, and ProPublica, which focus on investigative journalism; niche outlets such as *Inside EPA*, Inside Washington Publishers, and *The Hill*, which target audiences involved with the business of governing; and the *New York Times*, a national newspaper able to aggregate the attention of those around the country interested in national policies and able to derive support by selling this aggregate attention to advertisers and by selling subscriptions to readers who value the distinct coverage offered.

Across all fourteen agencies in my sample, three media outlets filed 100 or more FOIA requests overall in the latter half of the 2000s: the *New York*

Times (101 requests), Center for Public Integrity (121), and Associated Press (272). Each represents a different model to support investigative work: a daily newspaper able to spread costs across a national or international audience; a 501(c)(3) nonprofit eligible for tax-deductible donations; and a news cooperative owned by newspaper and broadcast members that can spread costs over many subscribing outlets. The combined number of FOIA requests filed by these three outlets, however, is smaller than the number filed by one non-media source, INPUT, which collects and then sells information about government contracts. INPUT submitted 500 FOIAs to these agencies. This is a reminder about how FOIAs by media outlets can be dwarfed by commercial requests.

Overall, the evidence from the IRE prize competition entries and media public records requests shows both the promise and the peril of FOIA. Government records requests are clearly part of many investigative stories that change lives and laws. Yet, for FOIA requests in particular, the scrutiny generated by local newspapers has declined significantly over time. Requests from Other Media have increased, but this often involves journalism targeted at lobbyists, company officials, and government employees rather than accountability stories told by metro newspapers aimed at the general public. A small number of news outlets generate many requests, but this should make one concerned about the future of these outlets that shoulder so much of the public-oriented FOIA load.

THE CURRENT LANDSCAPE OF MEDIA FOIAS: A PARTIAL ACCOUNTING

Investigative reporting can generate significant positive spillovers for society when the new information uncovered leads to well-founded policy changes. In *Democracy's Detectives*, I find in several case studies that a dollar invested by a newspaper in an investigative series can produce more than a hundred dollars in net policy benefits when laws and regulations are changed as a result of this type of accountability reporting.[13] Investigative reporting is underprovided in the marketplace, however, because it is hard for a news outlet to monetize the benefits spread across society when its (often expensive) series of articles leads to public debate or policy reform. These benefits can be enjoyed by people who never subscribe to the paper or view its website and ads. Seen from this perspective, the government resources devoted to providing reporters with documents and data under FOIA are a subsidy that lowers the cost of discovering important stories that otherwise might go untold in the news marketplace.

The use of FOIA by investigative reporters is only one of many applications of the law. Debates about the overall desirability of reforming or replacing FOIA should focus on a much fuller accounting of the act's likely costs and benefits. Recent research and events suggest four points to consider in a wider analysis.

FOIA *requests by journalists likely account for less than 10 percent of all FOIA requests.* Although journalists' FOIA battles are described in media coverage, the vast majority of FOIAs have nothing to do with journalism.[14] In 2017, Max Galka, the founder of FOIA Mapper, analyzed 229,000 FOIA requests at eighty-five federal agencies and estimated that queries by journalists accounted for only 7.6 percent of FOIA requests. Heavier users included businesses (39 percent of requests), law firms (16.7 percent), and individuals (20.1 percent).[15] Requesting data from federal agencies is often part of a business strategy. Galka found that five research firms focused on collecting financial information generated more than half of all FOIAs at the Securities and Exchange Commission (SEC) over an eleven-year period. During this time, the requesters paid only a fraction of the costs of processing FOIA requests. In a period when the SEC spent $52 million on FOIA compliance costs, fees charged to requesters amounted to only $608,000.[16] Although a journalist pulling revelatory documents out of a recalcitrant agency is often the image associated with the operation of FOIA, the most frequent users of the law are companies seeking commercially useful information.

FOIA *involves significant operating costs for federal agencies.* In fiscal year 2016, the federal government received close to 790,000 FOIA requests, spent an estimated $478 million to respond to FOIA queries, and employed more than 4,260 full-time FOIA employees.[17] The Associated Press estimates that in 2016 the Obama administration spent $36.2 million on defending decisions by federal agencies to refuse to hand over data and documents requested under FOIA.[18] Some of this litigation does come from media companies. Over the period 2001 to 2016, the top three news organizations involved as plaintiffs in FOIA suits are familiar names from earlier analyses in this chapter. The *New York Times* led the list of media plaintiffs, filing thirty-six suits. As *New York Times'* lawyer David McCraw put it, "we feel that using this law is an essential part of our mission."[19] Media outlets with the next largest number of suits were the Center for Public Integrity (seventeen) and the Associated Press (eight).[20]

David Pozen details how the projections of federal spending to comply with FOIA likely underestimate the amount of resources spent as agency employees search out records and determine which are responsive to requests.[21] Any calculation of the net benefits of FOIA's operation would need to include both the time and attention involved in federal efforts to comply with requests and the ability of potential lawsuit costs to discourage media requesters from going to court to fight denial of access to records under FOIA.

Born-digital media outlets are often heavy users of FOIA. Although FOIA requests by local news outlets are increasingly hampered by low staffing and constrained resources, journalists at outlets that started first as digital news sources often use FOIA as part of their reporting process. In a 2016 assessment appropriately framed as a listicle, "7 Lessons from BuzzFeed's 'FOIA-Friendly Newsroom,' " Kelly Hinchcliffe noted:

> BuzzFeed has a full-time news staff of about 200 people. The staff typically files three to five public records requests a day to federal and state agencies, and the site's data investigations team files requests for databases about every three days.[22]

BuzzFeed's Investigative Unit numbered twenty reporters in fall 2016, and when it advertised an opening (eventually filled by a Pulitzer Prize–winning reporter from the *Tampa Bay Times*), there were almost 700 applications for this investigative reporting job.[23] BuzzFeed and ProPublica were both born on the Internet, and both appear in the list of the top ten most frequent FOIA requesters among the media based on Galka's analysis.[24]

Jason Leopold of Vice News similarly relies heavily on FOIA as a reporting tool. His 2014 FOIA request to the U.S. State Department requesting the emails of Hillary Clinton set off a chain of events that eventually led to significant debate over her email use.[25] Leopold also resists having his requests denied. In the period 2001 to 2016, he was the most frequent reporter listed as a plaintiff in FOIA lawsuits. Since filing his first suit in 2012, he has initiated at least thirty-two lawsuits involving federal agencies and FOIA.[26] Overall, journalists at born-digital media outlets may use FOIA aggressively because they can share online the underlying documents and data to buttress their stories, and because the documents and data obtained can compensate in part for their relative lack of access to officials when compared to reporters from legacy media outlets who have spent more time building contacts on their beats.

Full compliance with FOIA may depend on presidential signals about the importance of transparency. In a March 2017 study for the John S. and James L. Knight Foundation, David Cuillier surveyed hundreds of FOIA experts. He concluded:

> Overwhelmingly, experts predicted that access will get worse: Nearly 9 out of 10 predicted that access to government will worsen because of the new presidential administration. "I think it's going to be a backyard brawl," said Ted Bridis, investigations editor for The Associated Press in Washington, DC.[27]

If agency officials making discretionary decisions about what information must be released under FOIA look toward the White House for signals, the early signs in the Trump administration point to less information being released. In April 2017, a new policy was announced indicating that White House visitor logs, which had been voluntarily made public in the Obama administration, would not be proactively released.[28] Although White House ethics waivers that allowed former lobbyists to work in federal agencies were made public in the Obama years, in May 2017 the Trump administration initially tried to block the Office of Government Ethics from requesting copies of these waivers from agencies.[29]

WHAT IS TO BE DONE?

A full accounting of the operation of FOIA would look at the impacts on government and society arising from many different types of requesters: businesses, law firms, news media, nonprofits, universities, and individuals. Any proposals for reform would face challenges arising from the complex distribution of costs and benefits across these groups. For FOIA requests involving the media, the ultimate benefits are spread across the public, but the costs are concentrated on federal agencies that may see the act as a drain on resources and staff time.

Despite these challenges and the incompleteness of what we know about FOIA overall, if one limits the focus to investigative reporting, there are at least three types of policy actions at the federal level that would increase the usefulness of FOIA for these journalists.

First, real implementation of the provisions of the FOIA Improvement Act of 2016 would lower the transactions costs to investigative reporters of pulling information out of federal agencies. This law contains a number of provisions that, taken together, could raise the probability that journalists would be able to use FOIA to uncover new stories, including the codification of a presumption of openness for agency records and a requirement that agencies cite specific foreseeable harms or exact legal requirements to prevent release; establishment of a sunset of twenty-five years on an agency's ability to withhold records about internal deliberations; creation of an online portal to make it possible for journalists (and others) to submit a FOIA request to multiple agencies at once; and codification of "longstanding DOJ guidance that agencies make records and documents available to requesters in an electronic format and post online records that are requested three or more times."[30] From this perspective, the fact that the 2016 law's text notes that no additional funds were authorized in the legislation to help agencies meet these new requirements is a worrisome sign that their actual implementation may depend on future congressional budget allocations, agency choices about effort, and the priorities of the Trump administration.

Second, recognition in government research and development policy that public affairs reporting involves market failures, which lead such coverage to be underprovided, could ultimately help journalists. The Defense Advanced Research Projects Agency, National Archives and Records Administration, National Endowment for the Humanities, and National Science Foundation all support the development of software and data aimed at supporting public goods such as national defense and education. Recognizing that journalism involves the generation of public goods such as education and government accountability and produces positive spillovers through minds and votes that are changed by public affairs reporting could add journalism research to the list of topics supported by government R&D.[31] Investigative reporters face myriad problems in turning documents, transcripts, and data into structured information to analyze.[32] Support for the development of reporting tools could be content-neutral and platform-agnostic — designed to avoid favoring one coverage topic over another or one distribution medium above others. When the International Consortium of Investigative Journalists mapped the relationships among offshore banking accounts in the *Panama Papers* investigative project, the software used had its origin in a digital humanities project called "Mapping the Republic of Letters," which charted the exchange of letters in the Age of Enlightenment.[33] Government support for the development of similar open-source reporting tools would help investigative journalists discover stories more readily and tell them in more engaging ways.

A third policy pathway involves strengthening alternative open government and transparency platforms. Federal, state, and local officials are often willing in open government programs to release data sets that companies can use to build businesses and to seek suggestions for public policy programs via crowd-sourcing. They have fewer incentives to publicize information that would more easily help voters hold them accountable.[34] In an aptly titled essay, "Transparency and Public Policy: Where Open Government Fails Account-ability," Sarah Cohen, a Pulitzer Prize–winning journalist, noted that even after a first term in which President Obama had made open government an early goal of his administration,

> certain records that are widely acknowledged as public in the spirit of FOIA remain locked within virtual and physical cabinets. Few public officials make their desk calendars public, despite repeated rulings at the federal level that they are open for inspection. Obtaining basic spending documents, such as contracts, grants and purchase orders, is usually a two-year effort, thanks to provisions that the recipients can review the documents and censor information they consider sensitive. Even basic records that most cities have long ago released remain almost impossible to obtain elsewhere.[35]

The need for FOIA requests would be reduced if federal agencies were willing to release data and documents routinely and proactively rather than waiting for FOIAs from reporters. Cohen has elsewhere observed that depart-ments could release "records like correspondence logs, desk calendars of cabi-net and sub-cabinet level officials, payroll records of political appointees and contracts, grants and their audits."[36] She also points out that agencies could design their information systems with possible disclosure in mind, thereby reducing the need for later redactions. This could make it easier to release to the public information from "personnel records, calendar and email systems, spending records, client records, inspection and compliance records and ben-efits records."[37]

Affirmative disclosure is also the reform favored by Pozen after extensive review of the theory and implementation of FOIA. Pozen lays out the flaws of FOIA, including that it can "be seen as reactionary in a . . . substantive, politi-cal sense insofar as it saps regulatory capacity; distributes government goods in an inegalitarian fashion; and contributes to a culture of adversarialism and derision surrounding the domestic policy bureaucracy while insulating the far more secretive national security agencies, as well as corporations, from similar scrutiny."[38] To avoid some of these problems, he outlines an alternative pathway to FOIA wherein "whole categories of records deemed appropriate for release can be posted online or otherwise published in a regular schedule."[39] Spelling out how affirmative disclosure might work, he provides design suggestions such as greater reliance on nonjudicial enforcement bodies; standardization of disclosure methods; enhanced search and navigation tools; and the use of petitions, FOIA filings, and "incident reporting" as a backstop and a spur to continual reassessment and revision.[40]

CONCLUSION

Applying the Five Ws of journalism to the use of FOIA by reporters yields a mixed story. In terms of who's asking what, when, and where, the analysis here of IRE stories and FOIA usage suggests a decline in recent years in the ability of local newspapers to file the public records requests that help hold government accountable. Economic pressures are a big reason why. Which organizations are submitting FOIAs ultimately matters because it can affect the set of investigative stories that get told. With FOIA requests having served as a frequent part of investigations that changed lives and laws, the drop in requests by local newspapers may ultimately mean fewer stories that focus on the details and impacts of government policies.

A fuller analysis of the desirability and design of FOIA would have to look beyond the use of this tool by journalists. But if one focuses narrowly on the ability of reporters to use FOIA in their investigative work, three policies seem to hold particular promise: meaningful enforcement (and congressional funding to enable enforcement) of the FOIA Improvement Act of 2016, more federal support for R&D to develop reporting tools, and greater investment in alternative open government initiatives that could take some pressure off the FOIA process.

NOTES

1. James T. Hamilton, *Democracy's Detectives: The Economics of Investigative Journalism* (Cambridge, Mass.: Harvard University Press, 2016), 136–78. Results presented here build on Chapter 5, "How Is It Produced?"
2. Hamilton, *Democracy's Detectives*, 142–44.
3. "IRE Contest Entry #26636," Investigative Reporters and Editors, 2014.
4. "IRE Contest Entry #26636."

5. "IRE Contest Entry #26636."

6. Marcelo Rochabrun, "How a Tip About Habitat for Humanity Became a Whole Different Story," *ProPublica*, October 27, 2016, www.propublica.org /article/how-a-tip-about-habitat-for-humanity-became-a-whole-different-story.

7. Rochabrun, "A Tip About Habitat for Humanity."

8. Rochabrun, "A Tip About Habitat for Humanity."

9. Rochabrun, "A Tip About Habitat for Humanity."

10. "2015 IRE Award Winners," Investigative Reporters and Editors, April 7 2016, http://ire.org/awards/ire-awards/winners/2015-ire-award-winners/#.WD4bO32 AayE.

11. "2015 IRE Award Winners."

12. Michael Morisy, "Making Government Officials' Emails Open to Scrutiny Is Key to Accountability," Nieman Lab, September 7, 2016, www.niemanlab. org/2016/09/michael-morisy-making-government-officials-emails-open-to -scrutiny-is-key-to-accountability.

13. Hamilton, *Democracy's Detectives*, 131.

14. David E. Pozen, "Freedom of Information Beyond the Freedom of Information Act," *University of Pennsylvania Law Review* 165 (2017): 1097–1158, 1131.

15. Max Galka, "Who Uses FOIA? An Analysis of 229,000 Requests to 85 Government Agencies," FOIA Mapper, March 13, 2017, https://foiamapper.com /who-uses-foia.

16. Galka, "Who Uses FOIA?"

17. Associated Press, "Obama Admin Spent $36M on Lawsuits to Keep Info Secret," *CBS News*, March 14, 2017, www.cbsnews.com/news/obama-administration-spent -36m-on-records-lawsuits-last-year.

18. Associated Press, "Obama Admin Spent $36M on Lawsuits."

19. FOIA Project Staff, "News Reporters Drive Growth in Media FOIA Litigation," FOIA Project, January 9, 2017, http://foiaproject.org/2017/01/09/news-reporters -drive-growth-in-media-foia-litigation.

20. FOIA Project Staff, "News Reporters Drive Growth."

21. Pozen, "Freedom of Information Beyond the Freedom of Information Act," 1123–31.

22. Kelly Hinchcliffe, "7 Lessons from Buzzfeed's 'FOIA-Friendly Newsroom,'" Poynter, June 14, 2016, www.poynter.org/2016/7-lessons-from-buzzfeeds-foia -friendly-newsroom/416733.

23. Peter Sterne, "Buzzfeed News Adds Pulitzer Winner, Top Pentagon Correspondent," *Politico*, December 9, 2016, www.politico.com/media/story/2016/12 /buzzfeed-news-adds-pulitzer-winner-top-pentagon-correspondent-004884.

24. Galka, "Who Uses FOIA?"

25. Jason Leopold, "How I Got Clinton's Emails," *Vice News*, November 4, 2016, https://news.vice.com/story/clinton-email-scandal-foia.

26. FOIA Project Staff, "News Reporters Drive Growth."

27. David Cuillier, "Forecasting Freedom of Information: Why It Faces Problems—And How Experts Say They Could Be Solved," John S. and James L. Knight Foundation, March 2017, https://knightfoundation.org/reports/forecasting-freedom-of-information.

28. John Wagner, "Trump Will Keep List of White House Visitors Secret," *Washington Post*, April 14, 2017.

29. Eric Lipton, "White House Moves to Block Ethics Inquiry into Ex-Lobbyists on Payroll," *New York Times*, May 22, 2017.

30. White House Office of the Press Secretary, "Fact Sheet: New Steps Toward Ensuring Openness and Transparency in Government," White House, June 30, 2016, www.whitehouse.gov/the-press-office/2016/06/30/fact-sheet-new-steps-toward-ensuring-openness-and-transparency.

31. Hamilton, *Democracy's Detectives*, 287–91.

32. Sarah Cohen, James T. Hamilton, and Fred Turner, "Computational Journalism," *Communications of the ACM* 54 (2011): 66–71.

33. Lisa Trei, "Visualization Tool Prototyped by Stanford Humanities Scholars Aids the Investigation of 'Panama Papers,' " Stanford University, June 3, 2016, http://news.stanford.edu/thedish/2016/06/03/visualization-tool-prototyped-by-stanford-humanities-scholars-aids-the-investigation-of-panama-papers.

34. Nigel Bowles, James T. Hamilton, and David A. Levy, eds., *Transparency in Politics and the Media* (New York: I. B. Tauris, 2014), xi–xxiii.

35. Sarah Cohen, "Transparency and Public Policy: Where Open Government Fails Accountability," in *Transparency in Politics and the Media*, ed. Nigel Bowles, James T. Hamilton, and David Levy (New York: I. B. Tauris, 2014), 96.

36. Hamilton, *Democracy's Detectives*, 292.

37. Hamilton, *Democracy's Detectives*, 292.

38. Pozen, "Freedom of Information Beyond the Freedom of Information Act," 1097.

39. Pozen, "Freedom of Information Beyond the Freedom of Information Act," 1149.

40. Pozen, "Freedom of Information Beyond the Freedom of Information Act," 1152–55.

PART THREE

THEORIZING TRANSPARENCY TACTICS

7

THE ECOLOGY OF TRANSPARENCY RELOADED

Seth F. Kreimer

INTRODUCTION: THE FLAWS OF FOIA?

The authors of the *Federalist Papers* disparaged a plural executive's tendency "to conceal faults, and destroy responsibility," believing that a unitary executive's actions were apt to be more "narrowly watched and readily suspected" by an informed public opinion.[1] The proposed Constitution left the task of informing the public to elements of constitutional structure. The mutual jealousy of the elective branches of national government provided one mechanism. State political structures were thought to be a second: "the executive and legislative bodies of each state will be so many sentinels over the person employed in every department of the national administration"; their "regular and effectual system of intelligence" will allow them to "communicate the same knowledge to the people."[2] But neither the Framers' Constitution nor the Bill of Rights went further. As Justice Stewart famously observed, "the Constitution itself is neither a Freedom of Information Act nor an Official Secrets Act."[3]

What the Constitution's text omits, the last two generations have embedded in "small-c" constitutional law and practice. The Freedom of Information Act, in particular, was crafted to "ensure an informed citizenry, vital to the functioning of a democratic society, needed to check against corruption and to hold the governors accountable to the governed."[4]

The late Justice Scalia argued that the Freedom of Information Act was unnecessary. While head of the Office of Legal Counsel (OLC), he coordinated the unsuccessful opposition to amendments strengthening the act. Upon his return to academia, then-professor Scalia lamented:

the obsession that gave [those amendments] birth—that the first line of defense against an arbitrary executive is do-it-yourself oversight by the public and its surrogate the press. . . . It is a romantic notion, but the facts simply do not bear them out. The major exposés of recent times, from CIA mail openings to Watergate to the FBI's COINTELPRO operation, owe virtually nothing to the FOIA but are primarily the product of the institutionalized checks and balances within our system of representative democracy.[5]

FOIA has also suffered the converse criticism—that it is necessary but ineffective. Journalists decry "a Rube Goldberg apparatus that clanks and wheezes, but rarely turns up the data."[6] Dissenting judges protest uncritical deference to the government, and commentators deplore suppression of information by an increasingly secretive security state.

A third constellation of criticism discerns a mismatch between the legal regime of transparency and the goals of good governance. FOIA is said to be the "Sistine Chapel of Cost Benefit Analysis Ignored," burdening public servants in order to benefit "corporate lawyers" and "criminal defendants."[7] Disclosure obligations, it is said, "exact financial, deliberative, and bureaucratic burdens on government, even when disclosure serves no useful purpose."[8] More recently, David Pozen has argued that the costs imposed are pathologically asymmetric. FOIA, he alleges, is "neoliberal" and "reactionary"; it "empowers opponents of regulation, distributes government goods in a regressive fashion, and contributes to a culture of contempt surrounding the domestic policy bureaucracy," while doing little to further scrutiny or control of corporate exploitation.[9]

Drawing on case studies from the Bush era "Global War on Terror" (GWOT), I argue in this chapter that critics tend to overlook important normative and practical issues. Critiques focused on denied requests and unsuccessfully litigated cases in isolation miss crucial parts of the story. Even in the heat of the GWOT, some FOIA requests produced salient information without litigation. Some litigation disclosed information without published opinions, or through accretion of low-level victories over time. And this information combined with disclosures from other sources to generate cascades of transparency and accountability that commentators focusing on FOIA case law in isolation are likely to discount.

Most centrally, FOIA does not function alone. It is part of what I refer to as an "ecology of transparency": an infrastructure of linked institutions and practices that together can generate important public benefits. What follows is a field guide to that ecology, set in a time of conflict, highlighting the interaction of elements of the ecology to disclose and lay the groundwork for repudiating government abuses. Analysts of FOIA should be alert to the elements of that ecology and the ways in which they depend on one another. Critics should acknowledge its virtues of resiliency and efficacy. Reformers should neither slight nor squander them.

THE ECOLOGY OF TRANSPARENCY: FOIA AND STRUCTURE

In claiming that the "institutionalized checks and balances" of the constitutional text render FOIA superfluous, Scalia's historical claims oversimplified matters considerably—indeed disingenuously. The "institutionalized checks and balances" Scalia praised proved efficacious during Watergate and its aftermath only with the goad and aid of extra-institutional actors: surreptitious leakers violating their institutional obligations, investigative reporters, publishers, and civilly disobedient sneak thieves. Indeed, FOIA itself helped journalists puncture the secrecy of COINTELPRO, a fact of which then–Assistant Attorney General Scalia was manifestly aware.[10] FOIA was strengthened after Watergate, along with a network of other structural checks, precisely in the hope that in future crises it could serve not as a first line of defense but a last.

In the aftermath of September 11, 2001, the second Bush administration undertook initiatives of demonstrably dubious legality and morality. But "institutionalized checks and balances" remained quiescent. Congressional opposition was largely paralyzed by the aftershocks of the attacks and, after the president's party gained control of the Senate in 2002, by party loyalty. The courts awaited justiciable controversies, delayed by secrecy and by sequestration of potential plaintiffs. When confronted with legal challenges, most judges proved unwilling to confront GWOT overreach.

One of the few arenas where efforts to constrain abuses met success lay in the mechanisms of transparency outside the tripartite constitutional structure. During the first five years of the GWOT, what Justice Scalia derided as the "romantic notion" of "do it yourself oversight" provided crucial building blocks of public resistance to abuses.

Justice Scalia's appeal to "institutionalized checks and balances" nonetheless points to an important insight. The successes of FOIA in calling the GWOT to account were predicated upon and facilitated by institutions beyond the statute itself. FOIA functioned as part of an ecology of transparency that included an infrastructure of federal civil servants, internal watchdogs, reasonably open opportunities to publish and share information, and a set of civil society actors willing to undertake prolonged campaigns for access and accountability. To grasp the significance of FOIA, it is important to examine not only disclosures of specific records but also the creation of records, requests for records, and the role disclosures can play in broader political and legal arenas.

IF A POLICY FALLS IN THE FOREST AND NO TREES ARE KILLED . . .: THE CREATION OF RECORDS

Disclosure mechanisms can have no effect in the absence of information to disclose. One could imagine a regime in which government officials seeking to conceal their actions destroy all records of them, thereby immunizing themselves from subsequent accountability. But effective bureaucracies run on records, and modern technology has exponentially enhanced the array of information recorded. It is difficult to eradicate entirely the evidence of any widespread policy.

Efforts to avoid record-keeping, or to sanitize files once kept, require unanimous consent of all participants. A secretary who declines to shred or delete his copy of a memorandum, like a computer technician who retains the prescribed backup copy, preserves information as effectively as a general or a department head. A civil service endows the federal government with a cadre of individuals whose allegiance to the current regime cannot be counted on to eliminate inconvenient information. They have been appointed by previous regimes, and they will work for subsequent ones.

Equally important, the federal bureaucracy is multivocal and professionalized. Career officials build their futures not on fealty to the current administration but on commitment to a set of departmental goals and professional norms. Some offices, indeed, such as the National Archives and Records Administration, are charged with preserving information. Such commitments generate records inconvenient to administrations bent on concealment. Further, statutes provide the State Department, Defense Department, Justice Department, Department of Homeland Security, and CIA with an independent Inspector General specifically tasked with discovering and recording malfeasance. In the Bush-era GWOT, the integrity of civil servants who committed to putting their opposition in writing was a prominent source of documentation for abuse.

A MACHINE THAT WON'T GO OF ITSELF: FOIA REQUESTERS

The existence of records does not entail their dissemination. By its terms, FOIA imposes few affirmative disclosure obligations on federal record holders. Recent initiatives have moved toward proactive disclosure, but the burden of effectuating inconvenient transparency still often rests on requesters who seek information.

From the beginning of the GWOT, efforts to obtain substantive judicial review were impeded because those most directly affected by the administration's excesses were unavailable as plaintiffs; they were hidden, absent, or exiled. Plaintiffs who objected to the abuses on principle alone were said to lack "standing." FOIA, which gives "any person" the right to seek information, provided a forum in which principled opponents of the GWOT could pass through the courthouse doors. And—a matter not to be taken for granted in international comparison—black-letter First Amendment doctrine precluded the government from retaliating against citizens who ask inconvenient questions.

Legal entitlement to seek information, however, was only the first step. To press a recalcitrant administration for disclosure under FOIA requires time, money, and expertise.

Successful efforts by the Associated Press to pry loose information regarding the Combatant Status Review Proceedings in Guantanamo began in November 2004 and extended through tenacious litigation over the course of two years. Attempts by a coalition of civil liberties organizations, librarians, and booksellers to obtain information regarding the use of the USA PATRIOT Act commenced in August 2002 and generated disclosures fitfully over the next three years as continued FOIA requests combined with litigation and political pressure. The American Civil Liberties Union's "Torture FOIA" campaign began with a request filed in October 2003; the release of more than 100,000 pages of documents required three and a half years of the legal equivalent of trench warfare.

Some requesters were members of the news media, such as the Associated Press. For the most part, only news organizations sufficiently large and solvent enough to allow speculative investigation and investment that might bring reputational gains in the medium-term future will undertake the expenditures necessary to bring FOIA effectively to bear. Constitutional structures protect an independent press. But the press is subject to the vicissitudes of public opinion, the pressure of advertisers, the need to remain on good terms with government sources, and the demands of competing priorities for their resources.

News media were not prominent at the vanguard of many successful FOIA inquiries directed at the GWOT. Well-financed nongovernmental organizations, often with assistance from the private bar, made FOIA a force to be reckoned with in this arena. The most effective requesters included the National Security Archives, the ACLU, the Electronic Privacy Information Center (EPIC), the Electronic Frontier Foundation, the Center for Constitutional Rights, Judicial Watch, and the Center for National Security Studies.[11] An independent civil society sector, protected by rights of association, backed up by the pro bono litigation muscle of private law firms, and nourished by 501(c)(3) status, proved to be the institutional matrix within which successful FOIA requests were seeded.

FOIA REQUESTS AND PREREQUISITE KNOWLEDGE

THE PROBLEM OF DEEP SECRETS Professor Alexander Bickel famously observed with regard to constitutional theory, "No answer is what the wrong question begets." The aphorism applies a fortiori to FOIA requests posed to a recalcitrant administration. For FOIA requests to generate illuminating documents, they must be framed to call forth those documents, and framing effective questions requires knowledge of the activities to be illuminated.

Some of the GWOT activities subject to FOIA requests were publicly announced. The prison camp at Guantanamo has never been a secret. The USA PATRIOT Act was enacted with great fanfare though with relatively cursory consideration. But the existence of many initiatives was shrouded in secrecy.

The use of coercive methods of interrogation was hinted at even as the administration officially denied engaging in "torture." Secret legal opinions advised officials that the president's power as commander-in-chief superseded legal limitations and that infliction of abuse short of lethal pain comported with the law. Programs of "extraordinary rendition" covertly seized suspects and ferried them to CIA "black sites" and foreign interrogators. Intelligence agencies engaged in broad, surreptitious, and often illegal surveillance of wire and Internet communications without judicial oversight while the administration disavowed any program of "warrantless wiretaps."

Veiled initiatives could not be the subject of FOIA requests unless requesters discerned their existence. Mere hints and suspicions were inadequate;

until identified with sufficient specificity that they could be the subject of reasonably precise inquiry, FOIA requests regarding such programs were likely to
be fruitless. FOIA's efficacy depended on institutions that revealed the "deep
secrets" of the existence and nature of problematic GWOT initiatives.

Prior revelations formed a prerequisite to successful FOIA requests for
statutory reasons as well. First, the stock of FOIA requests always exceeds the
available resources to process them, and an inconvenient request can rest
at the back of a long queue for processing. FOIA regulations provide that
expedited processing should be made available in cases where the requester
is "a person primarily engaged in disseminating information" who makes a
showing of "urgency to inform the public concerning actual or alleged Federal Government activity,"[12] and for matters "of widespread and exceptional
media interest in which there exist possible questions about the government's
integrity which affect public confidence."[13] These showings require that prerequisite information already be a part of public discourse.

GWOT inquiries regarding the interrogation of immigrants, data mining
for homeland security, and a covert attempt to enlist U.S. Attorneys to lobby
for funding for PATRIOT Act programs were denied expedited processing
because the requesters could not demonstrate adequate media discussion of
the requested material. Conversely, requests regarding controversial military
surveillance of political dissidents, the use of publicly disputed provisions of
the PATRIOT Act, and the revelation of illegal wiretapping programs by the
National Security Agency were held to be entitled to expedited processing on
the basis of prerequisite public contention.

Second, alongside disclosure obligations, FOIA provides a series of statutorily crafted exemptions. Exemption 6, for " files . . . the disclosure of which
would constitute a clearly unwarranted invasion of personal privacy," and
Exemption 7(c), for law enforcement files that "could reasonably be expected
to constitute an unwarranted invasion of personal privacy," were frequently
invoked without conscious irony by the second Bush regime to resist GWOT
FOIAs. In addressing these claims, courts balanced the degree of intrusion
against the degree of public interest. A requester who presses the "public
interest" side of this balance plays a stronger hand the more he or she already
knows: a deep secret or a program whose outlines are only dimly known will
not generate the requisite evidence of impropriety.

GWOT requesters were most successful in overcoming claims of these
FOIA exemptions when they adduced already-available evidence of abuse
or public contention. Public evidence of abuses at Guantanamo led to

the release of the identities of detainees who alleged mistreatment by their captors. Public controversy concerning the existence of "no-fly lists" provided the predicate for disclosing the identity of policy-makers involved. The FOIA release of pictures of the Abu Ghraib abuses was based on the active public debate engendered by the versions previously leaked to the press.

Successful FOIA requesters stood on the shoulders of prior revelation for a third and final reason. Judges in FOIA cases are called upon to make discretionary judgments regarding the reasonableness of timing, the adequacy of searches, the balance between privacy and public interests, and the plausibility of predictions of future impacts on government and private parties. Without public information regarding government abuses, courts are inclined to give the administration the benefit of the doubt. But once evidence emerges to prove an administration untrustworthy in one set of public controversies, it is likely to affect the credence granted in others. Many of the successes of requesters in GWOT FOIA cases followed initial revelations of abuses by other means and the admonition by the Supreme Court that "a state of war is not a blank check for the President when it comes to the rights of the Nation's citizens."[14]

THE STRUGGLE FOR PREREQUISITE KNOWLEDGE   Prior revelations critical to many successful FOIA requests can be impeded by a secrecy-minded executive. The second Bush administration went to great lengths to keep potential internal, as well as external, opponents ignorant of policies that would usually have fallen within their purview. These efforts at concealment, if entirely effective, could have immunized the initiatives from FOIA inquiry. They failed because of institutions and legal practices beyond FOIA itself.

Technology and the Volatility of Information GWOT concealment efforts ran aground in part on the phenomenon that, as the Internet adage puts it, "information wants to be free." Most actions leave informational spoor that can be discerned over time by sufficiently determined observers. Passers-by will notice forcible kidnaping on busy streets, family members will complain of disappearances, airport mechanics and observers will see unusual departure patterns, flight plans will be recorded in air traffic control databases. And, of course, once the subjects of initiatives are allowed to communicate with the outside world, they will tell their own tales.

The twenty-first-century information environment has brought interested private researchers and reporters the capacity to gather and sift large volumes of information seeking patterns, and to share those patterns across continents. Further, the Internet has allowed researchers to leverage a previously unavailable cadre of interested amateurs. These trends converged when covert CIA involvement in "extraordinary rendition" flights was publicly established through the combination of corporate registration statements, routine disclosures of Federal Aviation Administration flight data, and the existence of a network of "plane spotter" hobbyists who track arrivals and departures at airports, all analyzed by a loose collaboration of news reporters and European prosecutors.[15]

Partial concealment is insufficient to preserve "deep secrets," and in an open society, total concealment is a challenging task. The American legal scene is not graced with an equivalent of the "Official Secrets Act"; the law does not purport to impose criminal punishment on most who disclose, convey, or publish inconvenient information. And even leakers of classified information, who may nominally be subject to criminal liability, are rarely prosecuted.[16] In the absence of a tradition and infrastructure of suppression, retrofitting a system of public justice and administration to assure total secrecy becomes a substantial, and often insuperable, challenge. Once information is disclosed, the constitutional strictures against restraining publication of truthful information,[17] combined with the protean capacities of the Internet, foil effective suppression.

Civil Servants and Whistleblowing Free-range GWOT disclosures were supplemented by intentional releases of information by civil servants. Sometimes the releases of information followed from official action. Thus, in January 2002, as the administration struggled to suppress the dimensions of its dragnet detentions of noncitizens, the Immigration and Naturalization Service effectively revealed the identity of detainees held in Passaic and Hudson County jails when it allowed detainees to meet with advocacy groups for standard "know your rights" presentations. The Department of Justice Inspector General's critical report on the treatment of those detainees and the post–September 11 dragnet was leaked, then officially released a year later.

GWOT secrecy was breached more tellingly in unofficial disclosures by disaffected government employees. Internal disclosures first catalyzed opposition within the government, and that opposition laid the basis for leaks to the public. The arc of disclosure regarding torture is emblematic.

In late 2002, Navy investigators repelled by the recorded abuse of suspects at Guantanamo notified sympathetic superiors.[18] In December 2002, government sources provided the basis for a front-page article in the *Washington Post* providing accounts of abusive interrogation techniques. As a result of the internal opposition and the external critique, some of these techniques were temporarily suspended.[19] In April 2003, internal military dismay with the prospect of abandoning limits that had constrained abuse for two generations impelled military lawyers to confidentially approach civilian human rights advocates to spark opposition. In January 2004, after Specialist Joseph Darby submitted a complaint and a CD of Abu Ghraib pictures to a military investigator, reports of the nature of the abuse began to circulate. The administration sought to suppress the results of the ensuing investigation of that abuse, undertaken by General Antonio Taguba, which set forth both the "sadistic, blatant and wanton" prisoner abuse by guards and collusion by superiors. But information continued to leak from outraged insiders. With the broadcast of some of the Abu Ghraib photos by *60 Minutes* and the subsequent waves of disclosures, efforts at suppression continued to crumble. In May and June 2004, internal whistleblowers began to disseminate to the media and the Internet legal memoranda authorizing abusive interrogation, and the supporting documents of the Taguba report.

Leaks continued in 2005, setting the stage for FOIA requests by advocacy organizations seeking specific documents identified in the media, along with broader information on detainee abuse. By 2007, those inquiries had resulted in the release of more than 100,000 pages of documents.

As with resistance to record destruction, the crucial institutional context of these disclosures was the federal civil service. Just as the longer time horizon of civil servants encourages resistance to the destruction of records, it may support the riskier step of affirmatively disclosing abuses to outsiders. As with record-keeping, whistleblowing does not require broad participation by employees before it is effective. It takes only one individual willing to disseminate information to dispel the deep secrecy that hamstrings FOIA requesters.

Career civil servants also are more inclined than political appointees to resent violations of internal norms of departments where they have spent their careers. The Judge Advocates General who approached human rights advocates to spur them to investigate complained that the U.S. military's fifty-year history of observing the Geneva Conventions was being overturned. Mary

McCarthy, a CIA deputy inspector general who had filed reports decrying illegal interrogation techniques, was impelled to turn to the press when she "was startled to hear what she considered an outright falsehood" in CIA presentations to Congress.[20]

To be sure, not all GWOT information was leaked by principled internal critics. But the resolution of Bush regime officials to centralize dubious initiatives in the Office of Vice President Dick Cheney attests to the perceived dangers that civil servants pose to deep secrecy.

FOIA PRODUCTION AND THE RULE OF LAW ON THE SUPPLY SIDE

Even when capable requesters have the information necessary to frame incisive requests, FOIA will fail without predominantly good faith and lawful exercise of discretion by recipient officials. When administrators are required to search their files to respond to FOIA requests, what guarantee do requesters have that members of the administration will not "forget" the location of embarrassing information? When FOIA officers are required to prepare indices of documents they seek to withhold, how can we be sure that inconvenient documents are not buried in a misleading characterization?

The scope of exemptions gives wide range for administrative predictions of dire consequences from disclosure, and courts will often defer to these predictions. Satirist Tom Lehrer once observed, in the context of pornography, "when correctly viewed, everything is lewd." When viewed through the prism of the possible assembly of a "mosaic" of information by a dangerous enemy of unknown capacities, everything is a dire threat to national security. Given the availability of "national security" concerns, why would an administration ever fail to classify damaging material?

Here, again, it turns out that FOIA's efficacy depends on a law-abiding civil service. Many of the decisions regarding FOIA requests are made at a line level by career bureaucrats whose tenure will remain regardless of the political effects of disclosure or nondisclosure. They can do their jobs most easily by following regulations in good faith. Indeed, a culture of lawfulness is an asset at most levels of the federal government, and this culture is nurtured in the FOIA context by specific institutional structures.

The strengthened FOIA obligations of 1974 led to the establishment of the Office of Information and Privacy in the Department of Justice in 1981 (renamed the Office of Information Policy in 2008). That office, directed by the same attorneys for over a quarter century, took as part of its institutional mission the quest to establish a culture of lawful response to FOIA requests. The strength of this culture forms part of an explanation for the success of FOIA litigation in the context of the GWOT.

The self-interest of higher level civil servants who are expected to exercise discretion, moreover, sometimes supports disclosure. In a multivocal bureaucracy, a faction that can show itself to have opposed a problematic policy as a matter of principle or prudence may be eager to expose abuses by its rivals. The dynamic manifested itself in maneuvering over the ACLU FOIA requests for documents regarding coercive interrogation policies. The Federal Bureau of Investigation (FBI), under Robert Mueller, which had lodged objections to these tactics, affirmatively gathered a chronology of its objections, granted the ACLU's request for expedited processing, and released revelatory documents. As one account puts the matter:

> [After the initial Abu Ghraib disclosures,] the FBI general counsel's office began a more systematic effort to document the abuses that had been recorded by its agents in Iraq, Afghanistan and Guantanamo. The result was a flood of alarming reports that have now been turned over to the American Civil Liberties Union in its Freedom of Information lawsuit seeking the release of government documents on the treatment of prisoners.
>
> The release of these documents has exacerbated tensions between the FBI and the Pentagon over the issue. Defense officials have privately complained that bureau officials affirmatively decided to turn over the documents in the lawsuit in order to protect itself from charges that it was complicit in the improper treatment of prisoners.[21]

The history of the "torture files" request highlights a final structural guarantee grounded in the career civil service. FOIA's national security exemption requires that materials actually have been classified pursuant to valid executive order, and the classification process has its own career personnel and organizational dynamics. These can be resistant to efforts to overclassify in the interests of political gain, if for no other reason than the perception that political overclassification diffuses the resources necessary to protect against real threats to security. As I have described elsewhere,[22] the integrity and institutional clout of William Leonard, the director of the Information Security Oversight Office in the summer and fall of 2004, precluded the "national security" gambit and facilitated the release of more than 100,000 pages of revealing documents.

Finally, the institutional structure of the federal judiciary proved crucial in GWOT requests. As noted earlier, confrontations between requesters and a recalcitrant administration often leave substantial room for the exercise of judicial discretion. Much of the action in FOIA requests occurs in the shadow of litigation, or out of the range of effective appellate review. The efficacy of FOIA, therefore, depends in substantial measure on the rigor and skepticism with which trial judges exercise their offices.

All federal judges are, of course, life tenured; any particular FOIA request therefore has a chance of coming before a judge appointed not by the current administration but by predecessors of different ideology. Moreover, under FOIA, venue for requesters' lawsuits lies both in the location of the requested records, which is usually the District of Columbia, and in the district in which the claimant resides. For matters of national interest, an administration must potentially contend with a nationwide portfolio of litigation. That portfolio is likely to contain legal precedents and judicial opinions more diverse than the consensus in Washington, D.C., or the balance of power on the D.C. Circuit.

Strategic GWOT litigants sought judges likely to be skeptical of administration claims. Efforts to withhold documents on prisoner abuse and the details of Guantanamo detention practices were challenged by requesters in New York, outside the precedential authority of the 2–1 majority in the D.C. Circuit that gave almost unqualified deference to the administration's national security claims.[23] The challenges succeeded before Clinton appointees Alvin Hellerstein, who had served in the Judge Advocate Corps of the U.S. Army from 1959 to 1960, and Jed Rakoff, who had spent seven years in the U.S. Attorney's Office for the Southern District of New York.

In California, Judge Charles Breyer, who had served as a Watergate special prosecutor, upbraided the government for tendering "frivolous claims of exemption" regarding documents relating to the "no-fly list." Even within the District of Columbia, Clinton appointees Gladys Kessler and Ellen Segal Huvelle effected the release of documents debunking the administration's positions concerning deployment of the PATRIOT Act by forcing the administration to accelerate its processing of the relevant FOIA requests.

To be sure, many judges across the country also acquiesced to flimsy arguments resisting disclosures of information. But an administration seeking to maintain secrecy must contend with the prospect that FOIA cases will come before a bench that contains a number of reasonably skeptical judges. As with the prospect of leaks, it requires only one success on a given subject to release information into public dialogue.

THE FORCE OF FOIA: THE QUESTION OF EFFICACY

In contrast to the FOIA critics who regard the statute as unnecessary, a second group of commentators casts FOIA as a wholly ineffective check on executive overreaching in the GWOT.

The answers to these challenges come in two stages. First, as already indicated, it is important to assay successful requests and appreciate the ways in which FOIA can trigger other disclosures and discussion. FOIA's role in the ecology of transparency has been both to authenticate some prior disclosures, easing their way into public discourse, and to potentiate other subsequent disclosures in ways that the critical literature has failed to appreciate. Second, analysis requires a clear-eyed assessment of the ways in which FOIA disclosures have functioned to leverage the checking functions of other institutions, and the cumulative impact of disclosures over time.

FOIA AND THE HALF-FULL GLASS: ASSESSING CONTRIBUTIONS TO PUBLIC INFORMATION

PARTIAL DISCLOSURES   Much of the critical commentary regarding the dullness of FOIA as a weapon against abuse has focused on litigated cases. Critics highlight the degree to which GWOT cases accepted speculative, conclusory, or overreaching rationales for withholding information. There can be no dispute that courts regularly upheld administration refusals of FOIA requests related to the GWOT and in the process manifested deference bordering on abject abdication.

But some FOIA requesters also met with success. Critical commentary often fails to account for cases—predominantly in the period following the Supreme Court's rebuff of uncontrolled executive authority in prosecuting the GWOT in June 2004[24]—that rejected efforts to resist FOIA inquiries. In this period, the successful substantive challenges in the Supreme Court were part of a change in the nation's approach to the GWOT that helped FOIA requesters obtain important judgments regarding Guantanamo detainees, prisoner abuse, and surveillance. Critics often fail, moreover, to acknowledge the instances in which information has been revealed in the shadow of FOIA but without authoritative judicial mandate. As I discuss at greater length in other work, revelations emerged from FOIA requests regarding the post–September 11 dragnet, the MATRIX (Multistate Anti-TeRrorism Information eXchange) surveillance network, the Combatant Status Review Tribunals for

Guantanamo, the implementation of the PATRIOT Act, and the physical abuse of prisoners detained overseas.[25]

Judged against a benchmark of full and open discussion of problematic initiatives, FOIA falls short. But, at a time when the political branches were largely quiescent or complicit, FOIA initiatives cast important light on the "dark side" of the GWOT.

CASCADES OF TRANSPARENCY   Analysis cannot end with the documents released in response to requests or litigation. For just as leaks of prerequisite knowledge can set the stage for successful FOIA requests, information disclosed by FOIA laid the groundwork for inquiry and disclosure by other institutions. An evaluation of the efficacy of FOIA must account for the further information that cascades from initial FOIA disclosures.

As the revelations of Watergate led Congress to strengthen FOIA, they also generated a network of other institutions within the government to audit the exercise of executive authority. FOIA disclosures regarding GWOT abuses, in turn, triggered inquiries by these watchdogs within the executive branch.

The disclosure of FBI reports regarding detainee abuse in the ACLU's FOIA litigation in late 2004, for example, brought about internal investigations both by the Department of Justice Inspector General and by a specially commissioned Army investigation team. The revelation of internal reports of abuses of PATRIOT Act authority in FBI documents disclosed in the EPIC FOIA litigation in late 2005 precipitated an investigation by the Department of Justice Office of the Inspector General.

Once internal watchdogs were prodded awake, in a number of instances the process became recursive. In response to references in initial FOIA documents to reports of violations to the FBI Intelligence Oversight Board, EPIC filed a follow-on request for reports submitted by the board, which resulted in the release of more documents. The Department of Justice Inspector General, in turn, obtained an unredacted set of the reports, which fueled its own analysis.

The FOIA disclosures of FBI documentation of torture in late 2004 galvanized hearings, even in a Congress dominated by presidential allies. The weight of documents released in the Torture FOIA litigation provided leverage for further inquiry by skeptical members of Congress in confirmation hearings. Synergistically, congressional inquiry triggered by leaks and FOIA documents extracted materials that had been redacted from the initial Torture FOIA disclosures.[26]

Most important, FOIA disclosures provided a means of authenticating—and allowing mainstream media to take cognizance of—information that had emerged in bits and pieces from internal critics and targets of GWOT initiatives. Before the disclosures that began with Abu Ghraib, administration apologists shaped public discourse by touting disavowals of "torture," portraying particular leaks as "rumor, innuendo, and assertions," and denigrating critics as "either uninformed, misinformed or poorly informed."[27] Reporters, well aware that leakers can be self-interested players of varying levels of reliability, and dependent on administration sources for their flow of information on other matters, proved reluctant to openly accuse the administration of mendacity.

After the Torture FOIA releases, these ploys became less effective. FOIA provided details and substantiation for the fragmentary reports by critics that had disclosed the existence of deep secrets. FOIA disclosures provided official documents; those documents allowed the media to adopt the stance of a neutral observer reporting on the administrations' own memoranda. The patterns of abusive interrogation began to move from the realm of allegation to the realm of fact in public debate. With internal substantiation, it became less risky to report further corroborating accounts from administration critics.

THE SUBSTANTIVE IMPACT OF DISCLOSURE ON ABUSES: FOIA AND INSTITUTIONAL LEVERAGE

LITIGATION   Federal courts were not eager to confront GWOT overreaching. But the materials revealed by FOIA litigation provided building blocks for substantive litigation to challenge abuses. Most striking, advocates deployed FOIA documents before the Supreme Court in challenging the Bush administration's claim of unreviewable power over detainees. Again, it is important to appreciate the cumulative effect of transparency.

The leaks of the Abu Ghraib abuses, the Taguba report, and the legal memoranda authorizing "enhanced" interrogation set the stage for the initial rebuff of the administration's claims of unreviewable authority over detainees in 2004.[28] As documentary evidence of abuses continued to emerge from Judge Hellerstein's FOIA orders in late 2005 and 2006, the Supreme Court considered the petition for certiorari and the merits of *Hamdan v. Rumsfeld*.[29] Advocates for the detainees adduced both the Torture FOIA documents themselves and the resulting public commentary and investigation to argue that restraints on treatment of detainees were necessary to assure adherence to minimal requirements of human rights. In June 2006, the majority opinion in *Hamdan* not only granted relief to Mr. Hamdan and his compatriots in Guantanamo but was crafted to impose legal restraints on abuse by American operatives overseas.

The administration, in turn, obtained legislation to substitute Combatant Status Review Tribunals (CSRTs) for the habeas corpus remedy made available by *Hamdan*. The Supreme Court initially denied certiorari in a case upholding this substitution against constitutional challenge. But the Court reversed that denial after being confronted with the disclosure by a whistleblower of the arbitrary and cursory nature of the CSRT process, against the background of CSRT transcripts disclosed by FOIA requests and the disclosure of previously secret OLC opinions effectively authorizing the executive to ignore statutory limits on torture.[30] The ultimate resolution in *Boumediene v. United States*[31] invalidated the congressional substitution of the CSRT for habeas corpus rights.[32]

Since *Boumediene*, another development has made FOIA even more important as a foundation of litigation seeking to call government abuses to account. In *Ashcroft v. Iqbal*,[33] the Supreme Court limited the ability of plaintiffs to seek redress for government misconduct in federal court. In contrast to the prior interpretation of federal notice pleading, the *Iqbal* standard requires plaintiffs to provide details in a complaint sufficient to persuade a potentially skeptical trial judge not simply that they were injured by the government but that their account of the specific way they were injured and of those responsible is "plausible." Information about the scope of and responsibility for wrongdoing is often in the hands of government malefactors, and under the prior dispensation, plaintiffs could seek it in discovery after filing suit. But under *Iqbal* this embargoed information has itself become the ticket of admission to the courthouse. FOIA requests can dislodge information in government files and make litigation possible. Thus it has become increasingly common for civil rights attorneys to use FOIA requests to lay the groundwork for litigation campaigns.[34]

POLITICAL REDRESS AND LEGITIMACY The relief triggered by FOIA disclosures extended beyond the courts. Congress was generally timid in confronting GWOT overreaching, and internal executive watchdogs were often lax.

But the occasions where political pressure effectively goaded these institutions built on the ecology of transparency. Some programs regarding domestic surveillance were withdrawn after disclosure of their excesses; others, which relied on cooperation of state governments outside the administration's political coalition, withered because of local opposition. FOIA disclosures impeached the credibility of administration advocates who campaigned for expansion of the PATRIOT Act, and a series of disclosures of GWOT abuses immediately preceded the December 16, 2005, decision in the Senate to block the act's renewal. Evidence of abuse of National Security Letters triggered an internal FBI audit, which in turn revealed widespread abuses and generated programmatic changes to bring the bureau into line.

In April 2004, the disclosure of OLC opinions authorizing abusive interrogation techniques focused the attention of, and gave leverage to, internal critics of the opinions; the official withdrawal of a key torture opinion followed a week later. The prospect of cross-examination of Attorney General Alberto Gonzales on the basis of the ACLU's Torture FOIA materials contributed to the incentives to issue a public replacement for the withdrawn opinion on December 30, 2004. At the end of 2005, materials obtained by the Torture FOIA litigation figured prominently in the debates leading to the adoption of the McCain anti-torture amendment, as did leaks by internal critics repelled by mendacity in administration efforts to counter the initial disclosures.

Over time, all of these mutually reinforcing leaks, FOIA disclosures, and investigations altered the patterns of secrecy, and the cycle of political and civil-society acquiescence, that had enabled the Bush administration's most extreme GWOT initiatives. On one front, public confirmation of dubious tactics allowed critics both inside and outside of government to mobilize and coordinate. Within the executive branch, public disclosures pierced the mutually reinforcing groupthink that had discounted costs of extralegal tactics and had presumed their necessity and effectiveness. In Congress, revelations allowed critics to draw on the insights of skeptics within the government and to gather expertise sufficient to dispute claims of legality and efficacy. In the media, disclosures of internal evidence allowed reports of abuses without stepping outside of the frame of respectful discourse.

As a matter of practical politics, revelations forced the administration to expend political capital to defend controversial practices, from black sites to torture to unchecked surveillance, rather than simply hiding them. This—along with other military and political debacles—depleted the administration's stock of power to press forward with other less easily concealed initiatives.

Disclosures impeaching the administration's credibility and claims of lawfulness in one area generated more general skepticism. Judges, lawmakers, journalists, and the public react negatively to being deceived, and once hard evidence of deception and abuse emerged in some areas of the GWOT, these groups became less inclined to extend comity in others. As Abraham Lincoln, who made his extraconstitutional assertions of authority in public, is said to have put the matter, "If you once forfeit the confidence of your fellow-citizens, . . . you can never regain their respect and esteem. It is true that you may fool all of the people some of the time; you can even fool some of the people all the time; but you can't fool all of the people all the time."[35]

FOIA AND THE QUESTION OF PROPORTIONALITY

A final set of critics acknowledge the possibility that the disclosures mandated by FOIA and facilitated by the ecology of transparency can contribute to public accountability. These commentators express skepticism, however, that the current regime is actually well shaped to accomplish that task. Some critics maintain that FOIA contributes to private rent-seeking far more often than to public oversight and suggest that resources devoted to private requests are misdirected. Others accuse the system of an inability to match public benefits with public costs and advocate a more targeted set of institutions to provide "optimal" levels of disclosure. Although these concerns have some substance, the experience of GWOT FOIAs suggests that virtues of the current system reside precisely in the characteristics that generate critique. The breadth of the FOIA regime gives it robustness, and its situation in a resilient ecology of transparency provides a fault-tolerant mechanism adapted both to the task of bringing the popular conscience to bear against tyranny and barbarism and to the goal of limiting egregious betrayals of the public weal.

THE ROBUSTNESS OF A BROAD FOIA REGIME

Skeptics correctly observe that self-interested businesses and inquisitive private parties rather than investigative reporters or civil society organizations file most FOIA requests. A FOIA regime that responded only to requests from representatives of the "public interest" on matters of public governance could conceivably be considerably less expensive and less intrusive.

There are considerable hurdles to identifying who represents the "public interest"; one person's crank or "special interest" is another's virtuous crusader. But even properly specified, such a system would sacrifice considerable protection for transparency on politically contested issues like the GWOT.

An infrastructure of career civil servants processing FOIA requests is the sine qua non of an effectively functioning FOIA system. At a mundane level, the capital cost of establishing the bureaucracy to process "private" FOIA requests finances the same bureaucracy that processes "public" ones. More subtly, the broad availability of FOIA sets transparency as a standard operating procedure. Requests are not by definition politically charged and confrontational; they are part of the way in which civil servants normally do business. The breadth of "self-interested" requests generates the case law crucial to judicial enforcement of FOIA. A continued flow of FOIA requests into the courts, undertaken by self-interested litigants, establishes the judicial infrastructure available to public interest requesters.

A FOIA system that provides broad benefits to an array of special interests, moreover, provides robustness against political attack. Commentators have noted that transparency regimes are often established in the wake of particular scandals but prove stable only where a sufficient constituency benefits from the regime to sustain it in the face of predictable claims of overreaching or costliness.[36] The broader the constituencies that benefit from a regime of transparency, the more likely that regime is to prove sustainable. When the ACLU and the Associated Press can link arms with the Business Roundtable, information arbitrageurs, Judicial Watch, and the Competitive Enterprise Institute, legislators will be more inclined to resist predictable pressures to curtail FOIA. Plausible models of political economy suggest that Congress is most likely to establish or expand FOIA entitlements when its interests diverge from those of the executive.[37] The broader the scope of FOIA, the more such divergences are likely to appear. If one goal is to provide a hedge against egregious abuses by regimes weakly constrained by the political forces of the moment, broad inclusion of "private" requesters is not a FOIA bug but a feature.

FOIA AND OPTIMALITY

As critics allege, the structures of transparency examined here are not precisely tailored to generating optimal decisions. Some requests are denied or delayed past the time when they could allow the public to provide input into decision making. Others are granted in a fashion that could allow small public benefit but impose costs on decision makers. Optimizing decisions is not, however, the only—or the most important—goal for a system of transparency. Just as the "checking value" in First Amendment theory focuses on keeping public opinion ready to check the worst excesses of government,[38] transparency structures can serve not to achieve the best of which government is capable but to avoid the worst.

In this account, the question should not be whether decision makers balance each trade-off between "transparency" and "efficiency" optimally on the margin but whether, at a reasonable cost, the system provides both checks against tyrannical or barbaric decisions and guardrails against catastrophic government failures.

Where a sense of shame grounded in the actor's own ideals (or those the actor attributes to the electorate) would be triggered by disclosure, the possibility of disclosure itself is particularly important. Kant's publicity condition is mirrored in the Washington folk wisdom that every action must be evaluated in part by how it would eventually look on the front page of the *New York Times*.

The pathologies of the GWOT were not rooted primarily in a secret effort to maximize the interests of one private pressure group. Rather, secrecy sought to further the electoral chances of the incumbent administration by hiding the moral costs of policies adopted for public benefit as the administration conceived it. Secrecy aggrandized the unrestricted authority of the national executive. In responding to such initiatives, a static account of marginal cost-benefit optimization is likely to prove inadequate. A judge asked to balance the costs and benefits of disclosing allegedly problematic GWOT initiatives would be all too likely to succumb to the facially legitimate goals of the initiatives themselves, along with the siren song of deference to "representative institutions" endowed with both legitimacy and the mystique of knowledge of hidden threats. The messier ecology of transparency, which relies on a blanket rule of freedom of information for all, loosely joined with a chain of leakers, investigators, and advocates, is likely to be more robust in crises of fear and outrage.

The virtues of a resilient ecology of transparency extend beyond crises of national security to other egregious abuses. The linked institutions of transparency established in the 1970s—Inspectors General, disclosure of political contributions, the State Department's "Dissent Channel," the Information Security Oversight Office, the upgraded FOIA, the publication rights guaranteed by *New York Times Co. v. United States*—responded to President Nixon's domestic overreaching in the pursuit of political aggrandizement and incipient tyranny.

Commentators in early 2017 warned that the threat of creeping authoritarianism may be only weakly constrained by a federal legislature with both houses dominated by members of the president's party.[39] A minority party in Congress has neither subpoena power nor the authority to convene hearings. Minority legislators, however, like the state and local officials the Framers envisaged as "sentinels" to "communicate the same knowledge to the people," can still turn to FOIA to obtain information to begin the process of checking tyranny.[40] Civil society can do the same. So, too, in the spirit of Cass Sunstein's invocation in chapter 9 (this volume) of Amartya Sen's observations on the absence of famines in societies with free elections and a free press, FOIA stands sentinel against disastrous environmental mismanagement foisted quietly upon a federal bureaucracy and hidden from the public.[41] Although most of the GWOT examples canvassed in the articles on which this chapter is based involve national security, it seems eminently sensible to support a broadly tailored and resilient FOIA regime as insurance against other disastrous and unchecked abuses.

NEOLIBERALISM AND SELF-GOVERNMENT

David Pozen has recently argued that FOIA fosters "regressive antiregulatory ecologies" and that the cost of FOIA's disruption of governance is borne by the beneficiaries of the administrative state. In Pozen's words, "generally reasonable and well-intentioned public servants see FOIA as a serious hindrance to their statutorily assigned work."[42]

In general, public servants unconstrained by transparency obligations will tend to release only information that furthers their goals. They will no doubt experience rules requiring them to disclose information they would prefer to retain in confidence as a "hindrance to their statutorily assigned work." Some of that hindrance will effectively increase the cost of regulation, although the magnitude of the costs imposed by that hindrance seems less clear.

Not all hindered regulation, however, involves progressive efforts to control exploitative business interests. Consider, for example, the role of FOIA in "hindering" the efforts of the Department of Homeland Security under the Obama administration to induce local officials to collaborate in immigration enforcement efforts.[43] Despite potential constitutional objections, federal "public servants" tried to convince local officials that participation in the "Secure Communities" program was mandatory while simultaneously attempting to mute public opposition by maintaining to other audiences that collusion was optional.[44] As part of an ultimately successful organizing campaign to encourage local communities to assert their constitutional opposition to draconian and disruptive enforcement, a coalition of immigrant rights activists spearheaded by the National Day Laborer Organizing Network (NDLON) filed and litigated a series of FOIA requests, posted the resulting disclosures online, and used them to galvanize opposition at both state and federal levels.[45] At the same time, the results of the NDLON FOIA formed a building block for federal civil rights actions imposing limits on constitutional violations by local collaborators.[46]

In adjudicating the tenacious efforts by the administration to prevent FOIA disclosures from "hindering" the activities of DHS "public servants," the trial judge observed:

> This litigation, filed more than two years ago, has already engendered four judicial opinions—now five. I once again urge the Government to heed the now famous words of Justice Louis Brandeis: "Sunlight is said to be the best of disinfectants; electric light the most efficient policeman."[47]

Whatever epithets apply here, "regressive" is not an obvious choice. In the NDLON FOIA, an ecology of transparency led to democratic contestation and more humane self-government.

Equally important, with due respect to the many conscientious public servants in the federal government, not all public servants are assiduous, reasonable, or well intentioned.

FOIA can impose a tax on public spirited regulation, but FOIA also imposes a tax on refusals to so regulate. Temptations to shirk are subject to exposure, regulation that is slipshod or counterproductive is subject to examination, and efforts by the subjects of regulations to buy relief from public duties are subject to discovery.[48] Returning to the Sen paradigm, with FOIA available, those who suffer from public nonfeasance or misfeasance can detect it more easily and, if there is political will, the threat of political discipline makes sins of deregulation less likely to occur. It is not obvious that these deterrent effects are outweighed by the hindrance imposed when regulatory targets deploy FOIA for tactical advantage.

Neither current congressional majorities nor the president's advisors are likely to check deregulatory shirking and rent-seeking without a goad. Neoliberal forces have deployed FOIA to smear regulators in the past decade, but today's posse of civil society watchdogs is preparing to saddle up FOIA to confront efforts to "deconstruct the administrative state."[49] FOIA is well suited to help discipline the official dissemination of evidence-free "alternative facts."[50]

Finally, as Pozen reminds us, the issue is always "as compared to what?" If neoliberal forces can hijack FOIA for their purposes, it is not clear why at least two of the alternatives Pozen suggests—Congress and leakers—are not equally subject to capture and manipulation. If neoliberal interests cannot deploy FOIA, they have other tools of hindrance at their disposal. Less well-organized beneficiaries of regulation may not be equally effective in stimulating congressional oversight or internal leakers or in obtaining other leverage. Pozen has identified the direction of the effects that concern him, but their net magnitude provides an uncertain basis to condemn FOIA.

CONCLUSION

The ecology of transparency will not always prevent abuse. Advocates for human rights, civil liberties, or the public interest will often be in no position to challenge abusive policies before they take effect. Leaks may be strategic or premature, and FOIA requests may be ineffective. Useful information may be drowned out by chaff. News media, Congress, or the courts may be co-opted or intimidated. Executive actors may not worry about the future or may game the system by embedding violations in areas resistant to disclosure. The public may prove indifferent to malfeasance or inhumanity.

Still, there have been and there will be important occasions on which FOIA—as part of the ecology of transparency—proves crucial for the public weal and for public decency. In 1966, Congressman Donald Rumsfeld sponsored the original Freedom of Information Act. Four decades later, Defense Secretary Rumsfeld was one of the architects of GWOT abuses. In 2004, as he and his colleagues struggled to shield their excesses from public scrutiny, Rumsfeld proclaimed with unwitting irony, "Our great political system needs information to be self-correcting. While excesses and imbalances will inevitably exist for a time, fortunately they tend not to last. Ultimately truth prevails."[51]

Rumsfeld was wrong about many things. But he was right in observing that self-correction, like self-government, requires information. FOIA does not ensure that truth will prevail. But the absence of FOIA would make its triumph less likely.

NOTES

This chapter condenses and updates Seth F. Kreimer, "The Freedom of Information Act and the Ecology of Transparency," *University of Pennsylvania Journal of Constitutional Law* 10 (2008): 1011–80. For fuller details and scholarly apparatus, consult that work and Seth F. Kreimer, "Rays of Sunlight in a Shadow 'War': FOIA, the Abuses of Anti-Terrorism, and the Strategy of Transparency," *Lewis and Clark Law Review* 11 (2007): 1141–1220.

1. Alexander Hamilton, *Federalist Papers*, no. 70 (New York: New American Library, 1961), 424–28.
2. Alexander Hamilton, *Federalist Papers*, no. 84 (New York: New American Library, 1961), 516.
3. Potter Stewart, "Or of the Press," *Hastings Law Journal* 26 (1975): 631–37, at 636.
4. NLRB v. Robbins Tire & Rubber Co., 437 U.S. 214, 242 (1978) (quoted with approval in DOI v. Klamath Water Users Protective Ass'n, 532 U.S. 1, 16 (2001)).
5. Antonin Scalia, "The Freedom of Information Act Has No Clothes," *Regulation* (March 1982): 14–19, at 19.
6. David Carr, "Let the Sun Shine," *New York Times*, July 23, 2007.
7. Scalia, "The Freedom of Information Act Has No Clothes," 15, 16. In this volume and elsewhere, Margaret Kwoka and David Pozen echo the charge. See, for example, Margaret B. Kwoka, "FOIA, Inc.," *Duke Law Journal* 65 (2016): 1361–1437; David E. Pozen, "Freedom of Information Beyond the Freedom of Information Act," *University of Pennsylvania Law Review* 165 (2017): 1097–1158. Both observe that in FY 2015, FOIA's direct economic costs clocked in at a bit less than $.48 billion. Pozen suggests that this figure is conservative (1123–24).

   The canonical comparator is the federal expenditure on military bands, $.437 billion in 2015. Dave Philipps, "Military Is Asked to March to a Less Expensive Tune," *New York Times*, July 1, 2016. Other benchmarks are the Corporation for Public Broadcasting at $.445 billion in FY 2014, "CPB Operating Budget: Fiscal Year 2014 Operating Budget," Corporation for Public Broadcasting, www.cpb.org /aboutcpb/financials/budget; a year of Trump travel to Mar-a-Lago at $.12 billion, Drew Harwell, Amy Brittain, and Jonathan O'Connell, "Trump Family's Elaborate Lifestyle Is a 'Logistical Nightmare'—At Taxpayer Expense," *Washington Post*, February 16, 2017; and the carried interest deduction, costing between $1.8 billion and $18 billion annually in tax revenue forgone, Victor Fleischer, "How a Carried Interest Tax Could Raise $180 Billion," *New York Times*, June 5, 2015.

   Half a billion dollars is hardly inconsiderable, but as rent-seeking goes in a $4 trillion federal budget, this seems to me rather small beer. Even if a large tranche of the direct beneficiaries of FOIA are self-interested, the monetary cost is not prohibitive in context. If nothing else, similar to public broadcasting, FOIA frequently provides edifying entertainment.

8. Mark Fenster, "The Opacity of Transparency," *Iowa Law Review* 91 (2006): 885–949, at 913, 928.

9. Pozen, "Freedom of Information Beyond the Freedom of Information Act," 1100–01. See also Pozen, "Freedom of Information Beyond the Freedom of Information Act," 1146 (describing "regressive, antiregulatory ecologies [of transparency] that do meaningful damage to the administrative state and the prospects for effective governance").

10. Antonin Scalia, "FOIA Appeal from Denial of Access to FBI COINTELPRO Files Regarding Professor Morris Starsky," *Federation of American Scientists*, November 27, 1974, https://fas.org/irp/agency/doj/olc/starsky.pdf (citing Stern v. Richardson, 367 F. Supp. 1316 (D.D.C. 1973) (requiring initial FOIA release of documents disclosing COINTELPRO)). The theft of documents from the FBI office in Media, Pennsylvania, by the "Citizens' Commission to Investigate the FBI" led to exposure of examples of illicit FBI surveillance of dissidents. But it was only after a successful FOIA inquiry by journalist Carl Stern, based on a cryptic reference to COINTELPRO in the purloined documents, that COINTELPRO blossomed into public scandal and congressional remediation. James Kirkpatrick Davis, *Spying on America* (New York: Praeger, 1992), 1–9, 161–78; Betty Medsger, *The Burglary*(New York: Alfred Knopf, 2014),331–33, 497–99.

11. See Seth F. Kreimer, "Rays of Sunlight in a Shadow 'War': FOIA, the Abuses of Anti-Terrorism, and the Strategy of Transparency," *Lewis and Clark Law Review* 11 (2007): 1141–1220, at 1168–85, describing FOIA campaigns; Alasdair Roberts, *Blacked Out* (New York: Cambridge University Press, 2006), 117–20.

12. 5 U.S.C. § 552(a)(6)(E)(v)(II) (2000); see also 28 C.F.R. § 16.5(d)(1)(ii) (2006).

13. 28 C.F.R. § 16.5(d)(1)(iv) (2006).

14. Hamdi v. Rumsfeld, 542 U.S. 507, 536 (2004).

15. For example, Stephen Grey, *Ghost Plane* (New York: St. Martin's Press, 2006), 114–26; Trevor Paglen and A. C. Thompson, *Torture Taxi: On the Trail of the CIA's Rendition Flights* (Hoboken, N.J.: Melville House, 2006), 45–74, 95–121.

16. See David E. Pozen, "The Leaky Leviathan: Why the Government Condemns and Condones Unlawful Disclosures of Information," *Harvard Law Review* 127 (2013): 512–635.

17. For example, Bartnicki v. Vopper, 532 U.S. 514, 528 (2001); Smith v. Daily Mail Publ'g Co., 443 U.S. 97, 102 (1979); N.Y. Times Co. v. United States, 403 U.S. 713 (1971) (per curiam).

18. Jane Mayer, "The Memo: How an Internal Effort to Ban the Abuse and Torture of Detainees Was Thwarted," *New Yorker*, February 27, 2006. Mayer describes a report to Alberto Mora, General Counsel of the Navy, by Naval Criminal

Investigative Service (NCIS) head David Brant, relying on information obtained by NCIS psychologist Michael Gelles, who "had computer access to the Army's interrogation logs at Guantánamo."

19. See discussion of the Mora memorandum in Kreimer, "Rays of Sunlight in a Shadow 'War,' " 1163 n. 88, 1192 n. 216. A discussion of the broader array of FOIA-potentiating leaks can be found in Seth F. Kreimer, "The Freedom of Information Act and the Ecology of Transparency," *University of Pennsylvania Journal of Constitutional Law* 10 (2008): 1011–80, at 1037–42.

20. R. Jeffrey Smith, "Fired Officer Believed CIA Lied to Congress; Friends Say McCarthy Learned of Denials About Detainees' Treatment," *Washington Post*, May 14, 2006.

21. Michael Isikoff and Mark Hosenball, "Has the Government Come Clean?," *Newsweek*, January 5, 2005.

22. Kreimer, "Rays of Sunlight in a Shadow 'War,' " 1204–05.

23. Ctr. for Nat'l Sec. Studies v. U.S. Dep't of Justice, 331 F.3d 918 (D.C. Cir. 2003).

24. See Hamdi v. Rumsfeld, 542 U.S. 507, 536 (2004); Rumsfeld v. Padilla, 542 U.S. 426 (2004); Rasul v. Bush, 542 U.S. 466 (2004).

25. Kreimer, "Rays of Sunlight in a Shadow 'War,' " 1168–85.

26. See Kreimer, "Rays of Sunlight in a Shadow 'War,' " 1209 (collecting these quotations).

27. In addition to the discussions in Kreimer, "The Freedom of Information Act and the Ecology of Transparency," and "Rays of Sunlight in a Shadow 'War,' " see Jack Goldsmith, *Power and Constraint: The Accountable Presidency after 9/11* (New York: Norton, 2012), 112–21.

28. Hamdi v. Rumsfeld, 542 U.S. 507 (2004); Rasul v. Bush, 542 U.S. 466 (2004). Cf. Rumsfeld v. Padilla, 542 U.S. 426 (2004). It appears that the justices were cognizant of the mounting tide of disclosures regarding the administration's abuses as they deliberated in 2004. See, for example, Jack Goldsmith, *The Terror Presidency* (New York: Norton, 2007), 134.

29. Hamdan v. Rumsfeld, 126 S. Ct. 2749 (2006) (argued March 28, 2006, decided June 29, 2006); Hamdan v. Rumsfeld, 546 U.S. 1002 (November 7, 2005) (granting certiorari).

30. For details of the maneuvering around certiorari and the material submitted to the Court in *Boumediene*, see Kreimer, "Rays of Sunlight in a Shadow 'War,' " 1065–67.

31. 128 S. Ct. 2229 (2008).

32. In addition to the discussion in Kreimer, "Rays of Sunlight in a Shadow 'War,' " 1065–67, see David Cole, *Engines of Liberty* (New York: Basic Books, 2016), 202–08.

33. 556 U.S. 662 (2009). See, for example, Jonah Gelbach, "Material Facts in the Debate over *Twombly* and *Iqbal*," *Stanford Law Review* 68 (2016): 369–424; Jonah Gelbach, "Locking the Doors to Discovery? Assessing the Effects of *Twombly* and *Iqbal* on Access to Discovery," *Yale Law Journal* 121 (2012): 2270–2348.

34. For one recent example, see Hernandez v. Lynch EDCV 16-00620-JGB (KKx) (N.D. Calif., 2016), 7 and n. 10, www.aclu.org/sites/default/files/field_document /order_granting_pi_class_cert_and_denying_motion_to_dismiss.pdf (evaluating the range of bonds imposed on indigent immigrants challenging deportations based on responses to a FOIA request).

35. Col. Alexander K. McClure, *"Abe" Lincoln's Yarns and Stories* 184 (Chicago, Ill.: Educational Company, 1904).

36. For example, Archon Fung, Mary Graham, and David Weil, "The Political Economy of Transparency: What Makes Disclosure Policies Sustainable?," Transparency Policy, 2002, 4–5, www.transparencypolicy.net/assets/FGW Transparency1.pdf ; Archon Fung, Mary Graham, and David Weil, *Full Disclosure: The Perils and Promise of Transparency* (New York: Cambridge University Press, 2007), 110–15.

37. See also Gregory Michener's discussion on "leverage" in chapter 13 of this volume.

38. For example, Vincent Blasi, "The Pathological Perspective and the First Amendment," *Columbia Law Review* 85 (1985): 449–514, at 455; Vincent Blasi, "The Checking Value in First Amendment Theory," *American Bar Foundation Research Journal* 2 (1977): 521–649, at 523, 527.

39. For example, David Frum, "How to Build an Autocracy," *Atlantic*, March 2017, www.theatlantic.com/magazine/archive/2017/03/how-to-build-an-autocracy /513872; Masha Gessen, "Autocracy: Rules for Survival," *New York Review of Books*, November 10, 2016, www.nybooks.com/daily/2016/11/10/trump-election -autocracy-rules-for-survival; Daniel W. Drezner, "The Politics of Discomfort in the Age of Trump," *Washington Post*, March 6, 2017; Ruth Ben-Ghiat, "Trump Is Following the Authoritarian Playbook," CNN, January 17, 2017, www.cnn.com/2017/01/16/opinions/trump-following-authoritarian-playbook -ben-ghiat/?iid=EL; Jeet Heer, "Donald Trump Is Becoming an Authoritarian Leader Before Our Very Eyes," *New Republic*, January 23, 2017, https://newrepublic .com/article/140040/donald-trump-becoming-authoritarian-leader-eyes; Ezra Klein, "How to Stop an Autocracy," *Vox*, February 7, 2017, www.vox.com /policy-and-politics/2017/2/7/14454370/trump-autocracy-congress-frum.

40. For example, Nick Cahill, "California Pushes for Immigration Raid Information," *Courthouse News Service*, February 28, 2017, www.courthousenews. com/california-demands-information-immigration-raids; Edward-Isaac Dovere, "Seattle Mayor Wants to Sue Trump," *Politico*, February, 21, 2017, www.politico.

com/story/2017/02/seattle-mayor-trump-235218; Juliet Bennett Rylah, "L.A. City Attorney Files FOIA Request over LAX Detainees," *LAist*, February 15, 2017, http://laist.com/2017/02/15/feuer_foia.php; Elizabeth Warren, "Democratic Senators Ask Labor Department to Fulfill FOIA Request of Trump Nominee Labor Violations," January 13, 2017, www.warren.senate.gov/?p=press_release&id =1355; Phil McCausland, "Scott Pruitt, President Trump's EPA Nominee, Ordered to Release Thousands of Emails," *NBC News*, February 16, 2017, www.nbcnews.com/news/us-news/scott-pruitt-president-trump-s-epa-nominee -ordered-release-thousands-n722161. Rather than respond to written questions, Pruitt told senators to file an open records request eighteen times—or as Senator Ed Markey of Massachusetts said, to "go FOIA yourself."

41. Cf. "Reports of Information Removed from Government Websites," Open the Government, www.openthegovernment.org/node/5435; Matt Novak, "The EPA Just Posted a Mirror Website of the One Trump Plans to Censor," *Gizmodo*, February 16, 2017, http://gizmodo.com/the-epa-just-posted-a-mirror-website-of- the-one-trump-p-1792430343. As Novak notes, "[u]nder federal law, agencies are required to publicly post any documents that get three or more requests." The genius of this approach is that, because EPA officials were required by federal law to post the mirror site (because it's a frequently requested record), it is harder now to force the site down.

42. Pozen, "Freedom of Information Beyond the Freedom of Information Act," 1131. Pozen's thoughtful and gracious account is far longer and more nuanced than I have room to address fully in this update. I sketch a response to his concerns about the "neoliberal" tilt of FOIA.

43. FOIA has been a useful tool in the kit of immigrant rights advocates in a series of areas that I lack space to address here. It seems destined to remain so as immigration policy becomes more draconian under the Trump administration. See, for example, Mary Tuma, "Did the White House and ICE Collude? Inquiring Civil Rights Groups Want to Know," *Austin Chronicle*, February 24, 2017; "ACLU Files Demands for Documents on Implementation of Trump's Muslim Ban," ACLU, February 2, 2017, www.aclu.org/news/aclu-files-demands -documents-implementation-trumps-muslim-ban; Shirin Sinnar, "More Misleading Claims on Immigrants and Terrorism," Just Security, March 4, 2017, www.justsecurity.org/38341/misleading-claims-immigrants-terrorism.

44. "There is ample evidence that ICE and DHS have gone out of their way to mislead the public about Secure Communities." Nat'l Day Laborer Org. Network v. United States Immigration & Customs Enf't Agency, 811 F. Supp. 2d 713, 742–43 (S.D.N.Y. 2011).

45. See Erica Lynn Tokar, "Unlocking Secure Communities: The Role of the Freedom of Information Act in the Department of Homeland Security's

Secure Communities," *Legislation and Policy Brief* 5 (2013): 103–132; Hannah Weinstein, "S-Comm: Shattering Communities," *Cardozo Public Law, Policy and Ethics Journal* 10 (2012): 395–434; Rachel R. Ray, "Insecure Communities: Examining Local Government Participation in US Immigration and Customs Enforcement's 'Secure Communities' Program," *Seattle Journal for Social Justice* 10 (2011): 327–86; "National Day Laborer Organizing Network (NDLON) v. US Immigration and Customs Enforcement Agency (ICE)," Center for Constitutional Rights, February 3, 2010, https://ccrjustice.org/home/what-we -do/our-cases/national-day-laborer-organizing-network-ndlon-v-us-immigration -and-customs; Uncover the Truth: ICE and Police Collaborations, *About*, http://uncoverthetruth.org/campaign.

46. For example, Galarza v. Szalczyk, 745 F.3d 634, 642 n. 7 (3d Cir. 2014) (citing "ICE FOIA 2674.020612").

47. Nat'l Day Laborer Org. Network v. United States Immigration & Customs Enf't Agency, 877 F. Supp. 2d 87, 113 (S.D.N.Y. 2012).

48. Mr. Frum's meditation on the prospects for authoritarianism observes: "The benefit of controlling a modern state is less the power to persecute the innocent, more the power to protect the guilty." FOIA is suited to at least detect such protection. Cf. David Fahrenthold and Rosalind Helderman, "Trump Camp Says $25,000 Charity Contribution to Florida AG Was a Mistake," *Washington Post*, March 22, 2016; CREW's Most Corrupt, "CREW Files Open Records Request with Florida AG's Office Regarding Trump University," March 17, 2006, www.crewsmostcorrupt.org/legal-filings/entry/crew -files-open-records-request-with-florida-ags-office.

49. "They started by submitting 50 Freedom of Information Act requests. . . ." Edward Isaac Dovere, "Obama Lawyers Form 'Worst-Case Scenario' Group to Tackle Trump," *Politico*, February 23, 2017, www.politico.com/story/2017/02 /obama-trump-lawyers-worst-case-235280; "The post-election scramble to build a liberal version of Judicial Watch is underway. . . . Others say there's no shortage of left-leaning groups that regularly file Freedom of Information Act suits and are sure to keep it up under Trump: the American Civil Liberties Union, Electronic Frontier Foundation, the Electronic Privacy Information Center, Public Citizen and more." Josh Gerstein, "Liberals Cribbing from Conservatives' Playbook to Attack Trump," *Politico*, December, 16, 2016, www.politico .com/story/2016/12/democrats-trump-resistance-conservative-playbook-232687; Michael Morisy, "Join Our Project to FOIA the Trump Administration," *MuckRock*, January 17, 2017, www.muckrock.com/news/archives/2017/jan/17 /help-us-foia-trump-administration.

50. "The Campaign Legal Center submits this . . . request for records pertaining to the Department of Justice and Office of Management and Budget's writings

and communications regarding President Trump's allegations of widespread voter fraud." "Request Under the Freedom of Information Act," Campaign Legal Center, February 15, 2017, www.campaignlegalcenter.org/sites/default /files/02-15-17%20FOIA%20Request%20-%20Voter%20Fraud.pdf; Jason Leopold, "Here Are the Official Photos Showing Trump's Inauguration Crowds Were Smaller Than Obama's," *BuzzFeed*, March 6, 2017, www.buzzfeed.com /jasonaleopold/the-national-park-service-has-released-official-photos-of-tr?utm _term=.unRLj6wNm#.gddYqArGB (released in response to FOIA request).

51. Donald H. Rumsfeld, U.S. Secretary of Defense, "Remarks to the Newspaper Association of America / American Society of Newspaper Editors," Federation of American Scientists, April 22, 2004, https://fas.org/sgp/news/2004/04/dod042204 .html.

8

MONITORING THE U.S. EXECUTIVE BRANCH INSIDE AND OUT

The Freedom of Information Act, Inspectors General, and the Paradoxes of Transparency

Nadia Hilliard

THE FREEDOM OF INFORMATION ACT (FOIA) appeared as part of a wave of transparency and accountability reforms in the latter half of the twentieth century that included inspectors general, auditing bodies, and independent commissions. John Keane's concept of monitory democracy captures the democratic practices made possible by such reforms: monitoring tools permit citizens to hold public officials to account not only in elections but also through permanent, ongoing scrutiny of government activity.[1] Beyond their scrutinizing function, these tools are unified by their focus on transparency and the dissemination of information to the public. Together they comprise what has become a web of accountability, a set of instruments and a corresponding mode of democratic practice, with novel forms of citizen engagement, centered on information extraction and control. Political philosophers have long studied the process of "refining and enlarging" popular sentiment through the institutions of representative government, but the flow of information from state to citizen had gone undertheorized until recent decades. The process by which state-generated information is produced and transformed and the questions of who will mediate and translate it are the theoretical questions that accompany the demand for transparency.

The emergence of these monitory tools has instantiated new political roles for citizens and governing officials, redistributing authority in the public sphere. On the citizens' side, such monitory practices expand the range of democratic activities for the general public far beyond periodic voting and stimulate demand for new technologies to map and render complex government information intelligible. In government, the need for bureaucrats to manage, interpret, and narrate the voluminous output of government data has been part and parcel of the expanding postwar administrative state, leading to a burgeoning, but not yet fully developed, role as a proactive informant. These developments, however, have the potential to set in motion paradoxical dynamics that might undermine the very democratic values they are said to promote. Three paradoxes—a bureaupathology paradox, an expertise paradox, and an expectations gap paradox—have the potential to compromise the ability of transparency-directed initiatives to enhance democracy. Although my concerns about the effects of these paradoxes are primarily theoretical, they suggest caution in the design of transparency tools and the need for further empirical research into the by-products of the transparency movement.

To illustrate these paradoxes, I trace two complementary, monitory instruments: FOIA and the inspector general (IG) system. IGs are hybrid inspectors-auditors-investigators tasked with rooting out fraud, waste, and abuse in the federal bureaucracy, and they perform routine audits and special investigations at the behest of Congress and in response to internal agency requests. Their most basic duty is to send regular reports to Congress on the state of their host agency; agency heads cannot interfere with these investigations or reports except through a set of primarily national security-related exemptions. Structurally, the loyalty of IGs is divided between Congress and their agency heads in order to preserve their independence, a state of affairs that one IG described as being akin to "straddling a barbed wire fence."[2] Although they have certain law enforcement authority and can issue subpoenas and initiate proceedings in the Justice Department, IG recommendations are not legally binding and can easily go unheeded.

Before assessing the three paradoxes, it is necessary to articulate the relationship between FOIA and the IGs, and the place of each of them in the wider system of public accountability. The values of accountability and transparency have inspired a host of spatial metaphors to describe the dynamics of these relationships, such as "architecture of accountability," "ecology of transparency," and "inverse panopticon."[3] Each of these metaphors emphasizes the interrelatedness of accountability and transparency-promoting tools or arrangements, which include structural features (separation of powers, for instance), political factors (for example, partisan rivalries), and institutional or administrative tools (such as FOIA or the IGs). The spatial dimension of these metaphors matters. Those who seek information, those who disseminate it, and those who try to prevent its dissemination all come from distinct nodes in a web of actors, and their perspectives and interests have consequences for the meaning of the information that is released. This spatial dimension is precisely what pairs FOIA and the IGs as complementary tools operating from different positions vis-à-vis the executive: FOIA serves as an *external* prompt for the public release of governments records, whereas IGs ferret out information from the *inside*, as full members of their host agencies responding, in many cases, to internal requests and complaints for investigation. Both tools are directed at a very specific body of information. They both target executive branch agencies but omit the president, Congress, and the courts; FOIA also omits some components of the Executive Office of the President. Both have the capacity to influence the way government-generated information is presented to the public and which audiences will have the most ready access to it.

The relationship between FOIA and the IGs goes beyond functional similarities; they also play mutually reinforcing, or mutually corrective, roles. IGs have both a direct and an indirect effect on the way FOIA works. They can encourage agencies to make FOIA more of a priority and check that an agency is following FOIA regulations. They also can influence how documents are classified. In the 2009 Reducing Over-Classification Act, the 111th Congress instructed IGs to review the classification process and "to identify policies, procedures, rules, regulations, or management practices that may be contributing to persistent misclassification."[4] (FOIA staff themselves name overclassification as a significant barrier to timely fulfillment of requests.[5]) IG involvement in the FOIA process can thus affect not only the range of what can be effectively requested through FOIA but the very standards by which classification decisions are made in the future. Requests for full IG reports, moreover, have been made regularly through FOIA when these documents have been partially redacted. Because FOIA and the IGs operate in this shared accountability space, they are both subject to, and in turn influence, the common practices affecting all government transparency initiatives.

Despite the potential of these tools to improve democratic governance, demands for transparency can come with pitfalls. Indeed, the very tools designed to enhance transparency create dynamics and incentive structures that, in practice, might undercut the advantages of a transparent government apparatus. First, monitory instruments such as FOIA and the IGs require substantial administrative capacity to work as instruments of accountability, and the costly bureaucratic apparatus that they demand can undermine the very streamlined, democratized administration they are intended to promote. Second, despite the formal availability of government records and reports through FOIA and the IG system, accessing many such documents often requires expertise to navigate the process, allowing corporate and other private interests to benefit disproportionately from the laws. Moreover, many government documents require expertise to interpret, which privileges certain actors and skills. A final paradox revolves around expectations: if in theory a transparent, accountable government should inspire trust and confidence on the part of the citizenry, in reality the monitory tools designed to achieve that transparency can raise false hopes of what government (and grassroots activism) can realistically achieve and might ultimately lead to disappointment, dissatisfaction, and distrust. Although in some ways furthering the values of transparency and democracy, the emergence of these interconnected tools must be viewed cautiously in light of the democratic paradoxes they pose.

THE BUREAUPATHOLOGY PARADOX

One of the immediate problems posed by demands for accountability and transparency is the practical issue of how and by whom they will be implemented. The IG system and FOIA require substantial bureaucratic resources—staff, reliable funding, and expertise—to carry out their mandates, and funding has grown steadily for both tools since the 1970s. Yet material growth, which induces administrative complexity, can complicate calls for transparency and accountability, both of which are enabled by organizational simplicity and clarity. The growth of the IGs and FOIA comes, then, as a form of bureaupathology, the phenomenon of organizational dysfunction that results from excessive bureaucracy.[6] According to one version of this logic, the government expands in size (girth) and in thickness (layers), multiplying and obfuscating lines of accountability and making transparency more difficult to achieve; further reforms meant to promote accountability contribute to a vicious cycle by making the government still bigger and less intelligible.

Part of the bureaupathology paradox results from sheer bureaucratic bulk. The Inspector General Act of 1978 led to the establishment of an army of IGs at the federal level, with the initial set of twelve IGs expanding to seventy-two by 2017. Each federal department and agency now has an IG and attendant office, often with hundreds of staff; altogether, the federal IG system adds over 13,000 personnel to the ranks of the government.[7] Thousands more IG personnel exist at the state and local level. Although these offices have no doubt reduced bureaucratic waste in many instances (according to their own estimates, bringing a potential $14 return on each dollar they spend[8]), they also add to the size and complexity of a bureaucracy that they were in the first place designed to rationalize and hold to account. In theory, IGs could diminish administrative efficiency and accountability by increasing government outlays and contributing to additional regulations. Indeed, both government and academic reviews of IG work in the early 1990s found evidence of IG-induced red tape.[9] Subsequent reforms, including the Clinton-era Reinventing Government initiative, which sought to redefine IGs to have a more collaborative role, and the 2008 Inspector General Act, which strengthened their independence and broadened their investigative powers, have curbed this tendency. The IG community as a whole produces many consequential reports, but expansion of the relevant statutes has bred further strands of bureaupathology as well. The 1988 Inspector General Act reform, which added IGs at more than thirty smaller agencies, or designated federal entities (DFEs), did not provide its new cohort with the same powers of investigation as "establishment IGs" (IGs in large departments, appointed by the president and confirmed by the Senate).[10] Because DFE-IGs are selected by the department head and not subject to external scrutiny, their independence is compromised and their work often ineffective, reproducing precisely the bureaucratic redundancy they were asked to overcome.[11]

FOIA also adds a notable layer to the bureaucratic apparatus, and this apparatus continues to grow. To sketch a quick portrait of its material impact: the U.S. federal government saw the largest number of total FOIA requests then on record in 2014, with 714,231 requests made to the one hundred-odd agencies subject to the legislation; in 2015, the number was nearly as high at 713,168.[12] Moreover, 14,274 appeals were processed across the federal government, and 4,121.59 full-time FOIA staff were employed in fiscal year 2015.[13] The total estimated cost of administering the act was $480,235,967.62 that year, and less than 1 percent of this cost was recovered in FOIA fees.[14] (Beyond their merely nominal contribution to the operating costs of FOIA, processing fees were criticized by FOIA staff as "labor intensive and hard to collect" in one government-wide survey.[15]) FOIA officers at many agencies deem the current level of resources insufficient to respond to requests in a thorough and timely manner.[16] Recent efforts to improve the act's implementation and efficacy, such as the Obama administration's creation of a Chief FOIA Officer (CFO) in each agency in 2009, have arguably created new bureaucratic layers that do little to facilitate the processing of requests and that, moreover, have provoked negative reactions by agency staff.[17]

In short, bureaucratic bulk can be troubling for transparency because the greater the number of layers of government, the more difficult it is to trace decision-making processes and to pinpoint responsibility when things go wrong. But bureaupathology is not merely about bureaucratic bulk. It also can result from unintended consequences of bureaucratic structures that generate effects opposed to the original purpose of the organization. For instance, the dual reporting requirement of the original Inspector General Act, which divides IGs' loyalty between Congress and their host department in order to ensure their independence, has limited the degree to which they can engage a broader public. These statutory provisions have served to shape the norms of the profession itself, yet in some cases they may limit the ability of IGs to effect oversight. While some IGs do work closely with Congress or the media, these IGs are in the minority, and IGs who share too much information outside of their host department—either through early releases of reports to the press or through individual "tell-all" memoirs—are controversial within the community.[18] IGs who are too close to Congress find their host departments less willing and cooperative during investigations, limiting their effectiveness.

Commitment to the principles of open government, including proactive disclosure, requires administrative capacity. IG reviews, for example, must be made freely available on government websites, and all Offices of Inspectors General (OIGs) are required to maintain a substantial, proactive online presence by posting press releases and videos of congressional testimony, sending email updates, and announcing (on the Internet and by tweet) the release of each report. By making their work public—indeed, by increasingly considering the public to be a primary audience—this set of practices provides the narrative raw material with which third parties can pursue political (rather than administrative) demands for accountability. As they mature, such practices may encourage citizens and the media to participate more actively in the process of accountability and may indeed enhance American democracy. But the technological infrastructure required to make IGs' work traceable and open to both government officials and the wider public has yet to be fully constructed. In a December 2015 hearing assessing the IGs' effectiveness and transparency, Senator Heidi Heitkamp (D-ND) observed that "the current set-up right now doesn't allow Congress or the public to track outstanding recommendations or recommendations over time," prompting the creation of a database of IG recommendations to make their work (and that of their host agencies) more transparent.[19] Despite expressing support for the idea, the Council of Inspectors General on Integrity and Efficiency's Chairman and Department of Justice IG Michael Horowitz commented that "it takes a fair amount of staff to do that kind of work and information technology infrastructure. We do not think we even have the IT capacity to do that at this point."[20]

Like the IG mandate, amendments to FOIA have made the interpretation and proactive dissemination of information a government responsibility as well. Providing access to records makes it incumbent upon the government to maintain the physical and digital infrastructure with which to make this access permanent, managed, and possible. The E-FOIA Amendments of 1996, for instance, require agencies to maintain an online reading room of standard agency documents (such as rules of procedure, statements of policy, and even positions on legal matters), as well as preemptively to make available records for which they anticipate receiving multiple requests. Although Congress has ordered agencies to set up "procedures for identifying records of general interest or use to the public that are appropriate for public disclosure, and for posting such records in a publicly accessible electronic format," David Pozen notes that these novel responsibilities carry with them the possibility of inattention, lack of compliance, and information "overload" to the public.[21]

The pursuit of transparency has thus occasioned the emergence of a new, inescapably political role for government officials in both IG and FOIA offices: that of proactive informant. A proactive transparency strategy in the U.S. government is still in its infancy. Cultivation of this role might ultimately provide a corrective to the pitfalls now faced by the current, largely reactive FOIA-based transparency strategy, but it will require careful attention to how release decisions are made by bureaucrats.[22] Achieving a balance between public relations impulses and a commitment to democratic integrity will depend in part on the ability of extra-governmental actors—public intermediaries—to discipline the discretion of proactive informants and to parse the significance of the documents that emerge.

THE EXPERTISE PARADOX

FOIA is frequently hailed as a tool of citizen empowerment. Although the IG system was not intentionally designed to promote citizen involvement in bureaucratic oversight, IG reports can also provide the public with the raw information with which to mount grassroots political action in the face of bureaucratic misdeeds. However, the often-specialized information released by IGs demands interpretation and, frequently, technical and contextual knowledge to render it politically meaningful. Despite its facade as a popular tool available to any citizen, FOIA requires different kinds of expertise to be used successfully and, as a result, it has been used disproportionately by different constituencies. Expertise is not antidemocratic; democracies need expertise, both within government and outside of it, as an aid to and check on political authority.[23] But ensuring that expertise does not come into conflict with democratic principles requires an awareness of the potential for novel forms of expertise to create unintended distributional inequalities. It also requires protections for the independence of experts in government from bureaucratic or political capture. In short, the questions of how state information is framed, translated, and narrated to the public, and who is performing those tasks, are of crucial importance for understanding contemporary democratic processes.

Expertise is required at two moments in the process of seeking information through FOIA: in the access stage (the moment of filing a request for documents with an agency) and in the interpretation stage (understanding the content and significance of the records). At the access stage, FOIA is formally available to any person. All agencies have FOIA offices and websites with guidelines to facilitate making a request. But making effective FOIA requests often demands money and expertise, including the ability to pay agency fees (or the knowledge of how to have these fees waived) and the ability to appeal (and litigate, if necessary) if and when agencies prove unresponsive.[24] Corporate requesters operate in this space with the advantage of administrative acumen and, often, with the legal experience and resources to navigate a long and obstacle-ridden process. Successful FOIA requests also frequently require certain kinds of insider knowledge. Seth Kreimer observes that "for FOIA requests to generate illuminating documents, they must be precisely framed, and framing such requests requires knowledge regarding the activities to be illuminated."[25] This is certainly the case with "deep secrets" (the existence of government programs unknown to the wider public) but also, more broadly, for many government programs associated with national security.[26]

An immediate, but unintended, consequence of this premium on insider expertise is a skewed distribution of the constituencies that use FOIA. Margaret Kwoka demonstrates that commercial organizations make the bulk of FOIA requests at many agencies.[27] While corporate concerns are not necessarily at odds with the public interest, Kwoka's research suggests that their requests often focus on enhancing investor knowledge or unearthing information about competitors.[28] These requests advance the goals neither of government oversight nor of increasing public awareness of government activity.[29] In practice, FOIA's structure creates significant inequalities of access to, and benefits from, government information.

Grassroots and public interest groups have taken measures to try to reduce some of the barriers to information access that ordinary citizens experience.

The National Security Archive's guide for making effective FOIA requests, for example, includes detailed descriptions of how to read government documents, how to develop a strategy for document acquisition, and how to interpret records once they are produced.[30] Activists have developed technological innovations such as FOIA Mapper, a tool that assists citizens in crafting FOIA requests. Its inspiration arose when "years of FOIA requests taught [the designer Max] Galka that there was no easy way to determine which organization had the information he wanted," and, as a result, he tried to plot the way that government agencies store data.[31] Both the National Security Archive and the FOIA Mapper facilitate new forms of democratic practice and public mediation that target a second-order dimension of information access. Rather than making records themselves accessible, they create and disseminate explanations and "maps" to guide access. The degree to which these efforts can ultimately mitigate the structural inequalities generated by FOIA is yet to be seen.

In the second moment of information dissemination—interpretation—two types of bureaucratic peculiarities surface that affect the success of monitory tools in delivering and translating state information to citizens. First, the ability to make sense of a government document requires knowledge of how to read certain kinds of reports, as well as contextual knowledge of the agency (or event) in question. Even among people with legal and political competence, a gap exists between those who can access government data and those who can understand what the data mean. Illuminating here is Adam Candeub's insight that information is only transparent—in the sense that it helps citizens uncover influence in the public decision-making process—if it can be "computed" and translated into a set of meaningful observations.[32] If the most incriminating piece of information about a government program is embedded in an audit or technical report, citizen action will depend on having access to the relevant technical expertise as much as access to the document itself.

The advent of "big data" deepens this challenge. With the mounting reliance on advanced computational methods by government agencies for policy design, the capacity of third-party actors to trace the decision-making process increasingly demands an understanding of how to "read" and analyze large data sets. This skill can also indirectly affect the ultimate impact of IG reports. The Sunlight Foundation, a transparency advocacy organization, initiated the construction of an IG report database on the ground that "many uses of government data require first obtaining *all* the data."[33] IG reports are posted on the respective websites of individual OIGs, but there is no central repository for all such reports. Systemic analysis of government activity can thus demand more than an ability to read and parse a report; increasingly, it requires both the technological infrastructure and database-related expertise with which to conduct wide-ranging searches for information.

Big data poses challenges for IGs as well. Some OIGs have successfully used data analytics to oversee their host departments' data, but most have struggled to attract staff with the necessary skills and to build technological infrastructure. In many cases, inert bureaucratic culture and high investment costs have prevented individual OIGs from adopting these methods; in others, departmental reluctance to grant IGs access to data sets has stymied their efforts.[34] The Inspector General Act as it currently stands does not explicitly permit access to data systems and thus provides an opportunity for agencies to subvert the oversight process.

Big data itself is not *ipso facto* less transparent than ordinary data; on the contrary, Candeub argues that "big data and decentralized data processing can in fact render the government decipherable in key ways, and indeed, seems necessary given the increased government electronic surveillance of its citizens."[35] Just as big data facilitates the government's surveillance capacities, it can facilitate citizen awareness and scrutiny. Nonetheless, the use of big data in government policy making poses new challenges for the interpretation and accessibility of data, and it will lead to further inequalities between citizens with different interpretive capacities, privileging those with statistical, auditing, and computing expertise. Joshua Tauberer, a prominent transparency advocate, offers a useful illustration of the need for particular kinds of expertise in the translation and interpretation of big data. Describing the winner of the 2002 Pulitzer Prize for investigative reporting, a fourteen-part series detailing the child mortalities that resulted from inattentive social services in Washington, D.C., he writes:

> The series could not have been told without access to government records *at scale*. . . . The value of those government records came from reporters' skills in turning the records, and of course interviews, into something pointed, understandable, and actionable for their readers. Put another way, the knowledge that the [Washington] Post's readers gained from the 14-part series could not have been FOIAs from the government directly. The knowledge came from skilled synthesis by mediators who took a large quantity of raw data material and produced a completely different information product for consumers.[36]

Tauberer's narrative demonstrates both the challenges and promise of big data in furthering a transparent and accountable government. Analysis of big data enabled the force of the story, but that very analysis required a novel expertise in how to marshal and interpret information. While the press has always played a role in interpreting and narrating the significance of government documents and actions, the new skills required for this mediating role now privilege not only "traditional journalists, issue advocates, and organizers, but also app builders [including] programmers, statisticians, designers, and entrepreneurs."[37]

IGs are responsible for the production and dissemination of many internal audits and investigations, but the fruits of their labor have long been decried as being at best boring and at worst incomprehensible.[38] Often, citizens find IG reports difficult to parse, as the conflicting interpretations of the State Department IG's June 2016 review of Hillary Clinton's emails suggested.[39] Understanding these reports requires knowledge of the scope of IG investigative authority (why their investigations may go only so far), how the severity of the offense is framed and articulated in IG reviews (often as rule or policy infractions, without judgment as to their broader significance), and the kinds of evaluative statements IGs can and cannot make (they are constrained, for instance, by strong norms against speculation). IG reports need not be quite so inscrutable. Indeed, periodic innovations in how IGs frame their reports have strengthened their influence and impact. Justice Department IG Michael Bromwich, for instance, introduced the "special review" during his tenure in the 1990s to complement the statutorily mandated semi-annual reviews; these reviews permitted an extended treatment of problems that did not conform to existing IG categories of investigation. More recently, the Special Inspector General for Afghanistan Reconstruction has introduced "interactive," mobile-friendly, online reports, and managed to attract a larger readership in both Congress and the public.[40]

In sum, the disclosures made by FOIA officers and IGs are hailed as moments of publicity, but members of the public are often unable to do much of anything with these disclosures without the help of public intermediaries. Reading an IG report, or any government audit, requires knowledge and understanding of the categories developed by auditors, as well as a familiarity with the tone and scope of such reports. Mining the vast data sets that increasingly serve as the basis for policy formation requires statistical know-how and awareness of what data have been collected by government. In its current incarnation, FOIA facilitates the dissemination of event-specific information;

recognizing long-term trends and patterns requires the collection and analysis of data that transcend single events or points in time. Narratives and tools developed by public intermediaries serve as crucial bridges to render actionable the fruits of these monitory instruments. Although journalists have traditionally been best poised to play this role, the necessary skills with which to make such information intelligible to citizens have evolved to include a host of specialized technical competencies in addition to basic political judgment and narrative proficiency.

THE EXPECTATIONS GAP PARADOX

New tools generate excitement. As innovations of the postwar era, FOIA and the IG system have been promoted under the banner of transparency as correctives to the pathologies of the administrative state, and each carries with it implicit promises of better, more democratic, and more efficient government. The IG system was born alongside the Government in Ethics Act and the Civil Service Reform Act, and it came with the promise of restoring integrity to a government tarred by Watergate and a spate of bureaucratic fraud and embezzlement scandals in the preceding decade. FOIA, signed into law on Independence Day (July 4), 1966, inspired tremendous hope on the part of transparency and accountability advocates. Yet abstract promises can lead to unrealistic expectations that undermine the successes that monitory instruments do achieve. In one government-wide survey, FOIA staff at multiple agencies overwhelmingly identified the "unrealistic expectations of requesters [as] a significant problem," suggesting that some FOIA resources be directed toward hosting meetings or panels to educate requesters.[41] Managing the public's expectations of what kinds of information exist and what can be reliably collected and organized in response to a particular request for records presupposes common expectations on the part of the government and the public.

Among other expectations, more transparency should, in principle, lead to more public trust because we (as citizens) can see which actions have been taken, by whom, and why. Yet even as FOI laws have multiplied and efforts toward greater transparency have intensified worldwide, a marked decline of societal trust has been identified, in various guises, by Robert Putnam, Onora O'Neill, and a spate of polls.[42] This decline in trust has been attributed in part to the rise of demands for transparency and accountability. The results of transparency measures often show governments to be less than fully efficient or honest, giving citizens further reason to be suspicious of public officials. In her Reith lectures on trust, O'Neill observes:

> Increasing transparency can produce a flood of unsorted information and misinformation that provides little but confusion unless it can be sorted and assessed. . . . And unless the individuals and institutions who sort, process and assess information are themselves already trusted, there is little reason to think that transparency and openness are going to increase trust.[43]

Precisely because many documents released by FOIA are "unsorted" (that is, their meaning unexplained and not contextualized), their significance will depend in part on how they are released and narrated within the public sphere. O'Neill is not opposed to transparency itself. Rather, she is critical of the cultural practices that have grown in its name but that fail to bring about truly intelligible information. She condemns the rise of "audit culture," in which "increased demands for control and performance, scrutiny and audit have been imposed, and in which the performance of professionals and institutions has been more and more controlled."[44] She laments the decline of thoughtful, critical evaluation and worries that the unrealistic expectations established by the "accountability revolution" will fuel the same sense of mistrust it was designed to address.

Although O'Neill does not write of either directly, she identifies a crucial contradiction at the heart of monitory instruments such as FOIA and the IGs. Whereas both tools ostensibly bolster the government's accountability to the public, she argues that accountability reforms in practice reinforce institutions' accountability to "regulators, to [other] departments of government, to funders, and to legal standards [which] . . . impose forms of central control—quite often indeed a range of different and mutually inconsistent forms of central control," prompting the question of whose interests are primarily served by such reforms as the introduction of the CFO in FOIA offices or the centralized control of IG performance indicators by the Council of Inspectors General for Integrity and Efficiency.[45] To be sure, these alternative loci of accountability are hardly antidemocratic and, if coupled with well-developed standards of professionalization, could be true sources of public accountability. O'Neill's analysis, however, underscores the possible value conflict that arises if performance indicators are chosen that reflect, say, a bias toward efficiency in an agency in which civil rights violations occur that would not turn up on efficiency measures.

Yet even O'Neill struggles to overcome one paradox of the logic of transparency. Although critical of audit culture in general, she suggests that citizens "energetically" rely on proxy evidence of trustworthiness—such as the analysis of "auditors, examiners, regulators, evaluators, peer reviewers," and other experts—when assessing the more complex activity of public officials.[46] Paradoxically, this might imply a relocation of trust from what O'Neill calls "informed and independent evaluation" to the "performance indicators" that are symptomatic of the audit culture pathologies of which she is suspicious.[47] For instance, evaluations of IGs that focus on simple quantitative outcome measures, such as the number of criminal indictments, to the exclusion of broader political processes in which the IGs are embedded can miss the significance of IG reviews that contribute to long-lasting solutions engineered by Congress. There is a profound difference between the multidimensional standards reflective of democratic integrity relied upon by informed evaluation (which can take the form of an audit or peer review) and simple managerial benchmarks. But the difference can easily be blurred in practice when both methods are used by the experts to whom O'Neill points. Despite her enthusiasm for authoritative proxies in which to place our trust, she concedes that even their analyses can be too complex for the average citizen to comprehend and to use for meaningful political participation.

There is a further danger in delegating public judgment to the fruits of audit culture. The evaluative categories and language of auditors and regulators can be at odds with the primary democratic values that transparency is, in theory, supposed to promote. For instance, audits and investigations that evaluate the efficiency of a particular public program or institution do not always take into account the unquantifiable social and political goods associated with it. Schools serving disadvantaged communities might score low on performance assessments, but might provide community support or engender social capital in ways that national assessment and audit systems fail to measure. Similarly, the No Child Left Behind Act, in an effort to boost educational performance and hold educators to account, created incentive structures that led teachers to teach to tests and even to cheat to adhere to inflexible performance standards.[48] Unrealistic expectations about what teachers (and students) can achieve, coupled with enforcement of those expectations through accountability mechanisms such as the demands to achieve quantifiable "Adequate Yearly Progress" and to make performance measures publicly available, have arguably placed struggling schools in cycles of failure from which they cannot emerge.

Unrealistic expectations about transparency on the part of the public might hamper the democratic potential of FOIA and the IG systems, but unrealistic expectations on the part of other public officials can also limit their political effects. Both because of a lack of visibility (even within government) and a vague mandate with multiple principals, IGs operate within an ambiguous framework. They report both to Congress and to their agency head; they serve a range of different audiences, including their host agency, Congress, the president, and the public; and they are tasked with both auditing and investigation, which demand different bureaucratic cultures and expertise. This ambiguity has some benefits for IG independence. It has permitted some IGs to push the boundaries of their position, sometimes privileging certain audiences over others, or concentrating on certain types of wrongdoing at the expense of others. However, the lack of clarity about the IGs' role and their varied performance has led elected officials to expect more from IG scrutiny than is necessarily realistic given budget and time constraints. In congressional hearings, members of Congress frequently demonstrate ignorance of the scope of IG authority when questioning IGs on their investigations (for instance, about what they can and cannot investigate, and whether or not they are part of the law enforcement community). Illustrative of these false expectations is an exchange between Senator Arlen Specter and Justice Department IG Glenn Fine regarding the IG's scope of authority during a 2003 hearing on the detention of terrorist suspects. After Specter pressed Fine on why he had not pursued certain lines of investigation, Fine responded with an emphatic insistence that "litigation decisions by department attorneys are actually not subject to the Inspector General's authority."[49] Unlike other IGs, the Justice Department IG is excluded from overseeing legal matters in its host department, which are deemed the responsibility of the Office of Professional Responsibility. Although the Justice IG is the only establishment IG to have this exclusion under the Inspector General Act, many OIGs command a unique constellation of powers and responsibilities. Incorrect understanding of what each IG can do to hold the executive branch to account can serve to fuel partisan spats rather than inspire genuine administrative or political reform.

Both FOIA and the Inspector General Act feed into and suffer from the dynamics of the expectations gap paradox. The appearance of transparency is fueled by the existence of FOIA and the IGs, and in many ways these frameworks do serve the twin goals of transparency and accountability. But excessively high (and vague) expectations on the part of both the public and public officials about the kind of government these institutions might enable leads to inevitable disappointment, just as the release of incriminating records and reports further sows the seeds of citizen mistrust.

CONCLUSION: TRANSPARENCY AND PUBLIC INTERMEDIARIES

Discussing the feminist movement, Hannah Arendt once asked, "What will we lose if we win?"[50] Her question was meant to underscore the potential unintended consequences of pursuing what seemed like a primary political goal. The question can be transposed into the domain of transparency: what do we lose if we succeed in building a transparent society? Do the unintended social and political dynamics of these methods outweigh, or compromise, the benefits of transparency? The pursuit of transparency through the use of monitory mechanisms such as FOIA and the IGs may advance one vision of transparency but simultaneously undercut other democratic values.

Although analytically distinct, the bureaupathology, expertise, and expectations gap paradoxes are not separate empirically. The cost and bureaucratic bulk required to maintain a transparency regime contribute to the regime's visibility and thus to its promise of efficacy, yet they also create opportunities for privileged economic groups to dominate the process of accessing information and, to some degree, to control how that information is used. Administrative expertise in requesting records, and audit and statistical expertise in interpreting them, play a role both in creating differential access and in contributing to a transformation in the dynamics of trust. The volume of information and emerging forms of technical expertise that accompany these transparency strategies can render government practices unintelligible and further undermine basic public comprehension of the workings of government.[51] Both FOIA and the IGs fall prey to these paradoxes.

But if these tools of transparency and accountability have the capacity to undermine public trust and democratic integrity (which includes values potentially at odds with demands for administrative efficiency, such as respect for civil rights), they also may contain the seeds of rectification. O'Neill offers *narrative* as a corrective for cruder, or more quantitative, measures of accountability, and this is where the promise of both IGs and the media lies in making the relationship between FOI laws and trust a positive one. The need for legitimate narratives with which to make sense of government data will only continue to grow. IG and FOI mechanisms can, if properly structured and supported by the news media, help to overcome each other's limitations in this regard. IGs can make agency adherence to FOIA regulations a priority in their oversight and recommendations and can, moreover, bring to light the existence of documents that might be publicly unknown. We might also see a seed of promise in the ambiguity of the IG mandate: because of the gap between what Congress wants the IGs to do and what they can do, there is much scope for reform and new deployment. When IGs' work is effectively translated and narrated to the public, their professional status as impartial auditors and investigators lends legitimacy to their narratives.

The question of which democratic values are more or less served by transparency is not merely an abstract question; it is a choice that societies must continually make. Although the question itself deserves public deliberation, only a concerted effort to encourage different kinds of public intermediaries will mitigate the unintended and paradoxical consequences of transparency-enhancing practices. In discussions of transparency tools, the focus should be not only on access to information but also on the processes by which that information is translated to the public and made politically meaningful. All three paradoxes discussed in this chapter point to the need for public inter-mediaries—both governmental and nongovernmental—to make these tools truly democratic. Such intermediaries include journalists skilled in working with big data and contributors to the technical infrastructure and conceptual mapping that permit analysis of government data at scale.

The success of representative democracy depends crucially on ordinary citizens' understanding of the actions of public officials. Monitory instruments, broadly speaking and taken as a whole, have emerged as a dominant contemporary strategy to produce this knowledge. Responding to the legitimation and trust crises experienced by governments worldwide demands a web of skilled public intermediaries who can exploit these powerful new instruments for the good of the many rather than the few.

NOTES

This chapter has benefited from feedback received at the City University of London Department of International Politics' faculty research seminar and at the Rothermere American Institute's (University of Oxford) Graduate Politics seminar. In particular, detailed and thoughtful comments from Mark Erbel, Iosif Kovras, Neil Armstrong, David Pozen, and Michael Schudson were invaluable.

1. See generally John Keane, *The Life and Death of Democracy* (London: Simon & Schuster, 2009).

2. Pub. L. No. 95–452, § 2, 92 Stat. 1101 (1978). Regarding IGs' independence and their relationship with agency management, see Sherman Funk, "Dual Reporting: 'Straddling the Barbed Wire Fence,' " *Journal of Public Inquiry* (Fall 1996): 13; and Council of the Inspectors General on Integrity and Efficiency, "IG Authorities," July 14, 2011, 3.

3. See Kathleen Clark, "The Architecture of Accountability: A Case Study of the Warrantless Surveillance Program," *BYU Law Review* (2010): 357–419, at 377–81; Seth F. Kreimer, "The Freedom of Information Act and the Ecology of Transparency," *University of Pennsylvania Journal of Constitutional Law* 10 (2008): 1011–80; David Brin, *The Transparent Society* (New York: Basic Books, 1999).

4. Pub. L. No. 111–258, § 6(b); 124 Stat. 2651, quoted in Wendy Ginsberg and Michael Greene, "Federal Inspectors General: History, Characteristics, and Recent Congressional Actions," Congressional Research Service Report R43814, June 2, 2016, 11, https://fas.org/sgp/crs/misc/R43814.pdf.

5. Citizens for Responsibility and Ethics in Washington, "FOIA at the Mid-Term: Obstacles to Transparency Remain," October 1, 2010, 6, www.citizensforethics .org/files/Complete%20FOIA%20Report%209-29-10.pdf.

6. See Edward T. Giblin, "Bureaupathology and the Denigration of Competence," *Human Resource Management* 20 (1981): 22–25; "Bureaupathology," in *Oxford Dictionary of Business and Management*, 5th ed., ed. Jonathan Law (Oxford: Oxford University Press, 2009).

7. Council of the Inspectors General on Integrity and Efficiency, *Progress Report to the President, Fiscal Year 2015* (Washington, D.C.: CIGIE, 2016), 2.

8. Council of the Inspectors General on Integrity and Efficiency, *Progress Report to the President, Fiscal Year 2015*.

9. See Albert Gore and National Performance Review, *From Red Tape to Results: Creating a Government That Works Better and Costs Less* (Washington, D.C.: Government Printing Office, 1993); Paul Light, *Monitoring Government: Inspectors General and the Search for Accountability* (Washington, D.C.: Brookings Institution, 1993), 223.

10. Pub. L. No. 100–504, title I, §§ 102(a)–(d), (f), (g), 104(a), 105–107, 109, 110, 102 Stat. 2515–2529 (1988).

11. Personal interview with David C. Williams, Inspector General of the U.S. Postal Service, May 23, 2017.

12. U.S. Department of Justice, *Summary of Fiscal Year 2015 Annual FOIA Reports* (Washington, D.C.: Department of Justice, 2016), 1–2.

13. U.S. Department of Justice, *Summary of Fiscal Year 2015 Annual FOIA Reports*, 19–20.

14. U.S. Department of Justice, *Summary of Fiscal Year 2015 Annual FOIA Reports*, 20.

15. Citizens for Responsibility and Ethics in Washington, "FOIA at the Mid-Term," 6.

16. Citizens for Responsibility and Ethics in Washington, "FOIA at the Mid-Term," 3.

17. Citizens for Responsibility and Ethics in Washington, "FOIA at the Mid-Term," 3–4.

18. Personal interviews with David C. Williams, May 26, 2017, and Michael Bromwich, Department of Justice Inspector General, 1994–1999, January 3, 2013.

19. U.S. Congress, Senate Committee on Homeland Security and Governmental Affairs, Subcommittee on Regulatory Affairs and Federal Management, *Implementing Solutions: The Importance of Following Through on GAO and OIG Recommendations*, S. Rep. 114-265, 1st Sess. (2016), 3.

20. U.S. Congress, Senate Committee on Homeland Security and Governmental Affairs, Subcommittee on Regulatory Affairs and Federal Management, *Implementing Solutions*, 16.

21. FOIA Improvement Act of 2016, Pub. L. No. 114–185, § 4, 130 Stat. 538, 544 (to be codified at 44 U.S.C. § 3102(2)); David E. Pozen, "Freedom of Information Beyond the Freedom of Information Act," *University of Pennsylvania Law Review* 165 (2017): 1097–1158, at 1151–52.

22. On the fundamentally "reactionary" nature of FOIA and on alternative strategies to transparency, including proactive disclosure, see Pozen, "Freedom of Information Beyond the Freedom of Information Act."

23. See Michael Schudson, *Why Democracies Need an Unlovable Press* (Cambridge: Polity, 2013), chap. 10.

24. Kreimer, "The Freedom of Information Act and the Ecology of Transparency," 1020.

25. Kreimer, "The Freedom of Information Act and the Ecology of Transparency," 1025.

26. See David E. Pozen, "Deep Secrecy," *Stanford Law Review* 62 (2010): 257–339.

27. See Margaret Kwoka, chapter 4 in this volume; and Margaret B. Kwoka, "FOIA, Inc.," *Duke Law Journal* 65 (2016): 1361–1437.

28. Kwoka, "FOIA, Inc.," 1414.

29. Other studies over time bear out Kwoka's empirical claim. See Government Accounting Office, *Government Field Offices Should Better Implement the Freedom of Information Act*, LCD-78-120 (1978), 37; John E. Bonine, "Public-Interest Fee Waivers Under the Freedom of Information Act," *Duke Law Journal* (1981): 213–78, at 216–17; Mark Tapscott and Nicole Taylor, *Few Journalists Use the Federal Freedom of Information Act: A Study by the Center for Media and Public Policy* (Washington, D.C.: Heritage Foundation, 2001); and Coalition

of Journalists for Open Government, "Frequent Filers: Businesses Make FOIA Their Business," July 3, 2006, www.spj.org/rrr.asp?ref=31&t=FOIA.

30. See National Security Archives, *FOIA Guide*, http://nsarchive.gwu.edu/nsa /foia/foia_guide.html.

31. Kristen Hare, "What Should You FOIA? There's a New Tool to Help You Figure That Out," Poynter, March 29, 2016, www.poynter.org/2016/what-should -you-foia-this-guy-made-a-tool-to-help-you-figure-that-out/403791.

32. Adam Candeub, "Transparency in the Administrative State," *Houston Law Review* 51 (2013): 385–416, at 403.

33. Eric Mill, "Why We've Collected a Hojillion Inspector General Reports," Sunlight Foundation, May 13, 2014, https://sunlightfoundation.com/2014/05/13 /why-weve-collected-a-hojillion-inspector-general-reports.

34. Personal interview with David C. Williams, May 23, 2017.

35. Candeub, "Transparency in the Administrative State," 412–13.

36. Joshua Tauberer, "Open Government, Big Data, Mediators," 2014, https:// opengovdata.io/2014/open-government-big-data-mediators.

37. Tauberer, "Open Government, Big Data, Mediators."

38. Daniel L. Feldman and David R. Eichenthal, *The Art of the Watchdog: Fighting Fraud, Waste, Abuse, and Corruption in Government* (Albany, N.Y.: SUNY Albany Press, 2013), 115.

39. For two contrasting interpretations in the mainstream media, see Rosalind S. Helderman and Tom Hamburger, "State Dept. Inspector General Report Sharply Criticizes Clinton's Email Practices," *Washington Post*, May 25, 2016; and Jeffrey Marburg-Goodman, "Correcting the Record (Again): Hillary Clinton's Handling of State Department Emails," Huffington Post, June 7, 2016, www.huffingtonpost .com/jeffrey-marburggoodman/correcting-the-record-again_b_10323830.html.

40. Mohana Ravindranath, "One Agency Thinks IG Reports Don't Have to Be Boring," NextGov, October 17, 2016, www.nextgov.com/cio-briefing/2016/10 /one-agency-thinks-ig-reports-dont-have-be-boring/132373.

41. Citizens for Responsibility and Ethics in Washington, "FOIA at the Mid-Term," 5.

42. On the decline of public trust, see, among others, Robert D. Putnam, *Bowling Alone: The Collapse and Revival of American Community* (New York: Simon & Schuster, 2000); and Onora O'Neill, *A Question of Trust: The BBC Reith Lectures 2002* (Cambridge: Cambridge University Press, 2002).

43. O'Neill, *A Question of Trust*, 73.

44. O'Neill, *A Question of Trust*, 73.

45. O'Neill, *A Question of Trust*, 53.

46. Onora O'Neill, "Trust, Trustworthiness, and Transparency," adapted from speech at EuroPhilantopics conference, December 3, 2105, www.efc.be/human -rights-citizenship-democracy/trust-trustworthiness-transparency.

47. O'Neill, *A Question of Trust*, viii.

48. Letter of Linda M. Calborn, Government Accountability Office, to Secretary of Education Arne Duncan, May 16, 2013, "K-12 Education: States' Test Security Policies and Procedures Varied," www.gao.gov/assets/660/654721.pdf; Anya Kamenetz, "When Teachers, Not Students, Do the Cheating," NPR All Things Considered, September 29, 2014.

49. Statement of Glenn Fine, *Lessons Learned — The Inspector General's Report on the 9/11 Detainees*, Committee on the Judiciary Hearing, S. Hrg. 108-257, June 25, 2003.

50. Joanne Cutting-Gray, "Hannah Arendt, Feminism, and the Politics of Alterity: 'What Will We Lose If We Win?' " *Hypatia* 8 (Winter 1993): 35–54.

51. I thank David Pozen and Michael Schudson for making this point.

9

OUTPUT TRANSPARENCY VS. INPUT TRANSPARENCY

Cass R. Sunstein

It was . . . best for the convention for forming the Constitution to sit with closed doors, because opinions were so various and at first so crude that it was necessary they should be long debated before any uniform system of opinion could be formed. Meantime the minds of the members were changing, and much was to be gained by a yielding and accommodating spirit. Had the members committed themselves publicly at first, they would have afterwards supposed consistency required them to maintain their ground, whereas by secret discussion no man felt himself obliged to retain his opinions any longer than he was satisfied of their propriety and truth, and was open to the force of argument. . . . No Constitution would ever have been adopted by the convention if the debates had been public.

—JAMES MADISON

OUTPUTS AND INPUTS

There is a distinction between output transparency and input transparency. Suppose, for example, the Department of Transportation completes a detailed study of the kinds of policies that help reduce deaths on the highways; the Department of Labor produces an analysis of the health risks associated with exposure to silica in the workplace; or the Environmental Protection Agency produces a regulation to curtail greenhouse gas emissions from motor vehicles or adopts a policy about when it will bring enforcement actions against those who violate its water quality regulations. All of these are outputs. The government might also become aware of certain *facts*—for example, the level of inflation in European nations, the number of people who have died in federal prisons, the apparent plans of terrorist organizations, or levels of crime and air pollution in Los Angeles and Chicago. For the most part, facts should also be seen as outputs, at least if they are a product of some kind of process of information acquisition.

Now suppose that officials within the Department of Energy and the Environmental Protection Agency exchange views about what form a greenhouse gas regulation should take, or political appointees within the Department of Labor have heated debates about the risks associated with silica in the workplace and how best to handle those risks. These various views are inputs.

To be sure, there are intermediate cases. The EPA might conclude that a substance is carcinogenic, and in a sense that conclusion is an output, but it might also be an input into a subsequent regulatory judgment. The Department of Transportation might reach certain conclusions about the environmental effects of allowing a highway to be built, which seem to be an output, but those conclusions might be an input into deciding whether to allow the highway to be built. The National Environmental Policy Act can be seen as a requirement that agencies disclose outputs in the form of judgments about environmental effects, but those outputs are, by law, mere inputs into ultimate decisions about what to do. Some outputs are inputs, and in the abstract, it would be possible to characterize them as one or the other, or as both. As we shall see, the appropriate characterization depends in part on whether and how the public would benefit from disclosure.

Acknowledging the existence of hard intermediate cases, I offer two claims here. The first is that the argument on behalf of transparency is often exceptionally strong for outputs. The second is that the argument on behalf of transparency for inputs is qualitatively different and generally weaker.

If the government has information about levels of crime in Boise, about water quality in Flint, Michigan, about security lines at LaGuardia Airport, about the hazards associated with certain toys, or about the effects of driverless cars, it should usually disclose that information—certainly on request, and if people stand to gain from it, even without request. (The latter point is especially important.) In all of these cases, the benefits of transparency are significant. Sometimes members of the public can use the information in their daily lives, and such disclosures enable various forms of accountability. Most of the time, moreover, the costs of output transparency are trivial. The U.S. government should therefore offer much more in the way of output transparency. In particular, it should make outputs freely available to the public as a matter of course—at least if the public could or would benefit from them, and unless there is a particular reason that outputs need to remain confidential.

As James Madison's remarks on the Constitutional Convention make clear, input transparency is a much more complicated matter because the costs of disclosure are often high and the benefits may be low. In any case, the arguments for input transparency are qualitatively different from those that justify output transparency. There are strong reasons to protect processes of internal deliberation, above all to ensure openness, candor, and trust. In addition, it is often unclear that the public would gain much from seeing inputs, not least because of their massive volume (and usual irrelevance to anything that matters). Outside of unusual circumstances, the public would gain little or nothing, except perhaps something like gossip. Another way to put the point is that those who seek to attract eyeballs or to embarrass their political opponents often like input transparency, but the public usually does not much benefit from it.

To be sure, transparency about inputs can be informative, and certain inputs may be of keen historical interest. If the public learns that the deputy secretary of Transportation had a different view from that of the secretary on the content of a fuel economy regulation, it knows something; internal disagreement paints a different picture from internal unanimity. But how much, exactly, does the public learn, and why is it important for the public to learn it? It should be acknowledged that in some cases input transparency is a good idea, especially under circumstances of corruption (or something like it) and when relevant inputs have genuine historic importance (and when their disclosure can reduce mistakes). But the argument for input transparency is much different from the argument for output transparency, and it often stands on weaker ground.

It should be clear from these remarks that my approach to this topic is insistently and unabashedly *welfarist*: what are the benefits of transparency and what are the costs? It is true that the benefits and the costs may not be easy to quantify, but some kind of assessment of both is indispensable to an evaluation of when transparency is most and least necessary. For those who are not comfortable with talk of costs and benefits in this context, it might be useful to understand those terms not as some kind of arithmetical straitjacket but as signaling the importance of asking concrete questions about the human consequences of competing approaches. At least for difficult problems, those questions are far more productive than abstractions about "legitimacy" and "the right to know."

A clarification before we begin: I am speaking here about principle, not about the appropriate interpretation of the Freedom of Information Act or about possible amendments to the statute. One of the virtues of the developing case law, and of the most illuminating debates over amendment, is that they tend to be particularistic: they involve situations that are both specific and highly diverse, complicating broad pronouncements. Here, as elsewhere, general propositions do not decide concrete questions. It is easy to find examples that confound my categories, but categories can provide useful orientation, or at least that is my hope.

OUTPUT TRANSPARENCY

OF USABLE INFORMATION AND SUNLIGHT

1. *An instructive finding.* A remarkable finding by the economist Amartya Sen is that in the history of the world there has *never* been a famine in a system with a democratic press and free elections.[1] Sen's starting point here, which he demonstrates empirically, is that famines are a social product, not an inevitable product of scarcity of food. Whether there will be a famine, as opposed to a mere shortage, depends on people's "entitlements": that is, what they are able to obtain. Even when food is limited, entitlements can be allocated in such a way as to ensure that no one will starve.

But when will a government take the necessary steps to prevent starvation? The answer depends on that government's own incentives. When there is a democratic system with free speech and a free press, the government faces a great deal of pressure to ensure that people generally have access to food. And when officials are thus pressured, they respond. But a system without a democratic press or free elections is likely to enable government to escape public accountability and hence not to respond to famines. Government officials will not be exposed, nor will they be at risk of losing their jobs.

Here, then, is a large lesson about the relationship between a well-functioning system of free expression, disclosure of relevant information (outputs), and citizens' well-being. Free speech and freedom of information are not mere luxuries or tastes of members of the most educated classes. On the contrary, they increase the likelihood that government will actually serve people's interests.[2] This lesson suggests some of the virtues, not only for liberty but also for economic goals, of having freedom of speech and freedom of information.

2. *Obama, mostly—and navigability.* In recent years, the most prominent transparency initiatives have involved outputs. A revealing example involves the global positioning system (GPS). In 1993, President Clinton unlocked the

data that was ultimately used to make the GPS device a familiar part of everyday life. Its availability has helped countless people, often in profound ways; it has even saved lives. A GPS device makes life more *navigable* (literally). If we think about navigability as a more general idea, we can see the value of disclosure of many outputs. Information about safety seats in cars, crime rates, air and water quality, and much more can be seen as akin to GPS devices writ large: it tells people how to go in the directions they want to go.

For all of its years, the Obama administration made transparency a major priority. (I am insisting on that point while fully acknowledging, and bracketing, the many controversies during the Obama presidency over potential trade-offs between transparency and other values.) The priority was signaled by an early and defining presidential memorandum, dedicated specifically to the Freedom of Information Act. The memorandum establishes "a clear presumption: In the face of doubt, openness prevails." It adds that "agencies should take affirmative steps to make information public. They should not wait for specific requests from the public." It directs both the attorney general and the director of the Office of Management and Budget (OMB) to issue new guidance, designed to implement the governing principles.[3]

Both of the resulting documents deserve close attention, but for my purposes here, OMB's guidance is especially noteworthy. The memorandum directs agencies to publish information online. It adds that "agencies should proactively use modern technology to disseminate useful information, rather than waiting for specific requests under FOIA." Perhaps most significantly, it requires each agency to create an open government plan and an open government webpage, designed to "create and institutionalize a culture of open government." The open government plans are required to post "online in an open format at least three high-value data sets," which are in turn defined as "information that can be used to increase agency accountability and responsiveness; improve public knowledge of the agency and its operations; further the core mission of the agency; create economic opportunity; or respond to need and demand as identified through public consultation."[4]

In the abstract, it is not clear whether this initiative involves output transparency or input transparency, but in practice, the former has been primary by far.[5] The high-value data sets typically involve outputs. Since 2009, data.gov has become a principal location for posting such data sets, which amount to output transparency in action. At some point in the recent past, the site contained more than 190,000 data sets, with information on agriculture, finance, health, education, energy, and much more. With a click, you could find

Airline On-Time Performance and Causes of Flight Delays: On-Time Data; Expenditures on Children by Families (with estimates of the cost of raising children from birth through age seventeen for major budgetary components); and detailed information about product recalls. There has been much more in the same vein, focusing on the outputs of policy-making or information-gathering activity.

As a result, private sector actors have produced numerous apps that provide people with information that they can actually use. One example is AIRNow, which has up-to-the-moment information about air quality. Another is the College Affordability and Transparency Center, which provides information about college costs. Yet another is eRecall, which gives people information about recall information at the time of purchase.

The outputs released on data.gov serve two independent purposes. First, people can take advantage of them in their daily lives. Like a GPS device, most of the information makes life simpler and more navigable. The availability of this information on cell phones makes the point far from fanciful. This is no mere abstraction. If we take the idea of navigability in the large, we can see disclosure as a way of helping people get to their preferred destinations in countless domains, saving money and reducing risks in the process. To my knowledge, the benefits of data.gov have yet to be quantified, but there is little doubt that people are gaining from the disclosures in concrete ways—again, as with the benefits of GPS devices.

Second, release of the outputs can promote accountability in both the private and public sectors. Justice Louis Brandeis famously said that "sunlight is . . . the best of disinfectants." If the air quality is terrible in Los Angeles, if a particular university is unusually expensive, if students at a for-profit college do not end up with jobs, if drinking water is unsafe in San Diego, or if a company has a lot of recalled toys, transparency can serve as a spur to change. Transparency increases accountability, and when people are accountable, their performance is likely to improve.[6] The point bears on both public and private institutions. Transparency can tell citizens about the actions of public officials—for example, how long it takes for them to work on a permit application, or the levels of air pollution in San Antonio (for which officials bear some responsibility). It also informs citizens about the actions of private actors—for example, by disclosing product recalls or ratings of safety seats. In either event, it can spur improved performance.

3. *Policies: disclosure and "core missions."* One of the most interesting aspects of the OMB memorandum is that it asks agencies to consider whether

disclosure might further their "core missions." This is an exceedingly important idea that deserves far more agency use in the future, and it involves
disclosure of outputs.

Consider just a few illustrations. In environmental policy, one of the most
well-known examples is the Toxic Release Inventory (TRI), which was created
largely as a bookkeeping measure designed to ensure that the federal government would have information about toxic releases. To the surprise of many
people, the TRI has been a successful *regulatory* approach because companies
did not want to be listed as one of the "dirty dozen" in their states.[7] Accountability served as a spur toward emissions reductions. During the Obama
administration, the Occupational Safety and Health Administration followed
this lead by putting information about recent deaths in American workplaces
very visibly on osha.gov, with names of the companies where people died.[8]
The EPA did something quite similar with its Greenhouse Gas Inventory, one
of the goals of which was to spur emissions reductions.[9]

In all of these cases, the government is disclosing information that public
officials have. We can imagine, of course, a requirement of output transparency imposed by the public sector on the private sector. Requirements of that
kind are not always organized under the idea of freedom of information, but
they involve transparency and also can promote important agency missions.
Under the authority of the Affordable Care Act, for example, the Food and
Drug Administration has required chain restaurants to disclose the calories
associated with their offerings. Though the evidence is mixed, some studies
find that the early results are quite promising, with significant reductions in
body mass index among people who really do need to lose weight.[10]

I have offered just a few illustrations of disclosures intended to promote
agency missions through output transparency. An excellent collection, generally including outputs, can be found in the numerous action plans of the Open
Government Partnership, coming from dozens of nations. It is, of course, an
empirical question whether transparency will promote agency missions, but in
many cases it can.[11] (It is said that China's interest in air pollution and greenhouse gas emissions has been greatly spurred by the ready available of the Air
Quality Index on cell phones.) Because the costs of output transparency are
typically low, there is every reason to adopt a presumption in its favor.

4. *Costs and benefits, in public.* We should understand regulatory impact
analyses (RIAs) in this light. In the relevant respect, they are outputs, although
they count as inputs as well. Required by presidents from Ronald Reagan[12] to
Barack Obama,[13] and thus far unchanged by Donald Trump, these analyses

offer accounts of the expected effects of regulation, with careful attention to both costs and benefits. If a regulation would prevent two premature deaths per year, the agency must say so, and so too if it would prevent five hundred. The RIA must disclose whether the regulation would cost $25 million, $250 million, or $2.5 billion. As part of rulemaking, it must be provided to the public for scrutiny and review, accompanying proposed and final rules.[14] In its own way, the requirement of an RIA can be seen as a kind of Freedom of Information Act. It enlists sunlight as a disinfectant.

A central reason is that, by itself, cost-benefit analysis is an important safeguard against ill-considered regulations. One of its key features is that it promotes transparency about actions and alternatives and indeed about the contents of cost-benefit analyses themselves. Recent administrations have been entirely aware of this point. To promote public understanding and to ensure an "open exchange of information and perspectives," for example, regulatory preambles for lengthy or complex rules (both proposed and final) are required to include straightforward executive summaries. These summaries must describe major provisions and policy choices.[15] For one illustration of such a summary, consider table 9.1.

To be sure, a great deal must be said in order to make a table of this kind fully transparent. It is important to know what these numbers actually mean and how they are derived.[16] For example, the claim that health co-benefits are

TABLE 9.1 Benefits and Costs of EPA's Proposed Clean Power Plan Rule in 2030 (Midpoint Estimates, Billions of Dollars)

	CLIMATE CHANGE IMPACTS		HEALTH IMPACTS (CO-BENEFITS) OF CORRELATED POLLUTANTS PLUS . . .	
	DOMESTIC	GLOBAL	DOMESTIC CLIMATE IMPACTS	GLOBAL CLIMATE IMPACTS
Benefits				
Climate Change	$ 3	$ 31	$3	$31
Health Co-Benefits			$45	$45
Total Benefits	$ 3	$ 31	$48	$76
Total Compliance Costs	$ 9	$ 9	$ 9	$ 9
Net Benefits (Benefits – Costs)	–$ 6	$ 22	$ 39	$ 67

Source: Cass R. Sunstein, "Output Transparency vs. Input Transparency," August 18, 2016, http://d3i6fh83elv35t. cloudfront.net/newshour/wp-content/uploads/2014/07/EPA-cost-benefits-1024x468.jpg.

$45 billion depends on assumptions about the effects of the plan on emissions and also the effects of emissions reductions on human health. Such assumptions might be controversial. A competent RIA is transparent about those matters. If there are uncertainties and reasonable disputes, it will reveal them and promote accountability in that way as well.

COSTS AND BENEFITS OF OUTPUT TRANSPARENCY

I have been painting with a very broad brush—in principle, an unduly broad one. My suggestion has been that disclosure of outputs is justified, or presumptively justified, on welfare grounds, but this is not always the case. We can easily imagine outputs whose disclosure would produce low benefits or high costs. With respect to costs, consider the words of the OMB memorandum:

> Nothing in this Directive shall be construed to supersede existing requirements for review and clearance of pre-decisional information by the Director of the Office of Management and Budget relating to legislative, budgetary, administrative, and regulatory materials. Moreover, nothing in this Directive shall be construed to suggest that the presumption of openness precludes the legitimate protection of information whose release would threaten national security, invade personal privacy, breach confidentiality, or damage other genuinely compelling interests.[17]

In various ways, the Freedom of Information Act recognizes all of these points. No one doubts that the government has a great deal of information whose disclosure would endanger national security, and even if that information can be counted as an output, it should be kept confidential. The government also has "personally identifiable information," which receives protection under privacy laws. Although a balance must be struck between transparency and privacy, some forms of disclosure impose reduced privacy, often in an intolerable way. Some kinds of disclosure could compromise trade secrets or otherwise privileged information. If disclosure is not automatic or automated, the very act of transparency can impose costs in terms of both money and time.

On the benefit side, distinctions are also important. In principle, and if the costs of assessment were zero, it would not make sense to insist that each and every output should be disclosed. It would be better to ask, on a case-by-case basis, whether disclosing specified outputs would or could be beneficial—for example, to consumers and workers. Of the 190,000 data sets on data.gov, surely some have modest benefits or no benefits; people are not paying the slightest attention to them (and they will not in the future). A welfarist analysis would call for particularized inquiries into that question. The problem, of course, is that those inquiries may not be manageable. At the time when disclosure is being discussed, projection of benefits may be quite difficult. What people will *do* (if anything) with information may not be self-evident. The private sector is ingenious and full of alchemists. What it will find useful, or turn into gold, cannot be predicted in advance.

In view of that fact, it makes sense for agencies to make reasonable judgments about "high-value data sets," broadly understood, and to get them online *as soon as possible*—and also to announce a general presumption in favor of disclosure of outputs, armed with an intuitive understanding of the domain to which the presumption will be applied. It should be underlined that a degree of automaticity, putting relevant material online as a matter of routine, could be extremely helpful.

With respect to high-value data sets, intuitions should be disciplined by asking two questions: (1) Could people possibly benefit from this information in their daily lives? (2) Could disclosure promote accountability in a way that would improve public or private performance? In the words of the 2009 presidential memorandum:

> The Government should not keep information confidential merely because public officials might be embarrassed by disclosure, because errors and failures might be revealed, or because of speculative or abstract fears. Nondisclosure should never be based on an effort to protect the personal interests of Government officials at the expense of those they are supposed to serve.[18]

Those words are important and correct. But they have one important qualification, to which I now turn.

INPUT TRANSPARENCY

When I was clerking for Justice Thurgood Marshall in 1980, Bob Woodward and Scott Armstrong published a book on the Supreme Court called *The Brethren*. I did not speak with Woodward or Armstrong, and I am also confident that none of my three co-clerks did so. But numerous clerks (largely or perhaps entirely from previous terms) decided to open up to the authors. The portrait of Justice Marshall was highly unflattering (and, by the way, wildly inaccurate). Marshall was clearly disappointed, much less (I think) because of the unfavorable, unfair, inaccurate portrait than because of what he saw as a breach of loyalty. I do not think it is disloyal to disclose what he said to us, which was roughly this: "I am not going to change how I interact with my clerks, but if you violate my confidence, it's on your conscience."

After I left the White House in 2012, many reporters, and some people outside the world of journalism, asked me questions about internal dynamics. Who said what to the president? Who disagreed with whom? If something happened, or did not happen, who wanted it not to happen, or to happen? Who won and who lost? Of course, I did not answer any of these questions, but there was no mistaking the (astounding) persistence with which they were asked. How well I recall a conversation with a superb journalist, working for the *Washington Post*, who was much focused on the who-disagreed-with-whom questions. I finally suggested to her that she should write something on the substance of the issues that most interested her (environmental policy). She did not seem enthusiastic about the suggestion.

As I understand them in this chapter, and consistent with the standard parlance, inputs count as both predecisional and deliberative. These are independent requirements. Inputs are predecisional in the sense that they are not themselves official decisions in any respect; they antedate those decisions and are meant to inform them. If an assistant administrator in the Environmental Protection Agency advises the administrator that a new ozone regulation should set a standard of 60 rather than 65 parts per billion, the communication is predecisional. Inputs are deliberative in the sense that they are part of a process of ongoing discussion about what to do.

I have acknowledged that even with these clarifications, we can imagine difficult cases, such as when a report is compiled on (say) the risks associated with silica and this report then becomes an input into a regulation. But the core should not be obscure. If law clerks are exchanging memoranda on how to handle a dispute over affirmative action, inputs are at issue. If people in the White House are discussing the contents of an open government memorandum, we are dealing with inputs. If White House officials are speaking with the Food and Drug Administration about how to handle the risks associated with certain asthma medicines, inputs are involved.

With respect to inputs, the argument for disclosure is significantly altered, and it is also weakened in two critical respects. First, the benefits of disclosure are usually much lower (definitely not always, but usually). Second, the costs of disclosure are much higher. These are categorical statements with major qualifications, to which I will turn in due course.

INPUTS AND MORE INPUTS, AND THE AMBIGUOUS BENEFITS OF DISCLOSING THEM

From the standpoint of the public, it is often not particularly desirable to obtain inputs. To those who believe in transparency, that claim might seem controversial, implausible, or even shocking. But the sheer number and range of inputs is daunting, and it defies belief to think that the public would benefit from seeing all of them. An assistant secretary will have countless conversations in the course of a week, and in many of them, she will be receiving suggestions, venturing possible ideas, requesting more information, joking, offering doubts, and seeking out possible inclinations. Some of the inputs that she receives or offers will not be very interesting. If they are interesting, it might be for a reason that does not exactly argue for disclosure: someone might have ventured an idea, for purposes of discussion, that was or is on reflection a really bad one. The idea was (let us suppose) rejected, and so it never became an output. Is it important, or on balance desirable, for the world to see it?

Now suppose that public officials are deciding what to do about particulate matter (an air pollutant). The director of the National Economic Council urges caution, emphasizing the overriding importance of economic growth. The Domestic Policy Council urges aggressive action, emphasizing that environmental groups keenly want the U.S. government to reduce particulate matter. Invoking international relations, the Department of State does the same. The Office of Information and Regulatory Affairs calls for a middle course, with close attention to costs and benefits. The Office of the Chief of Staff is focused on political considerations. Many memoranda are exchanged, offering various alternatives and competing points of view. It is far from clear how much the public would benefit from seeing this material. What most matters is what the government actually does, not who said what to whom.

It is true that for purposes of my thesis here, this example may not be the most convincing. The problem of particulate matter is exceedingly important, which complicates my argument (for reasons to which I will turn in due course). Consider then the general area of federal regulations, the most significant of which must go through the Office of Information and Regulatory Affairs (in most administrations, about five hundred per year). Many of those regulations will never be seriously discussed in the newspapers or online. Their issuance is preceded by a great deal of internal discussion, involving paper documents, electronic documents, and email, often raising questions and doubts. This is the quintessence of a deliberative process. A number of people say a number of things. Much of the time, the benefits of disclosing the content of that process are not much higher than zero.

Within the federal government, what is true for the regulatory process is true for may discussions—but even more so. The volume of emails is extraordinarily high. As in the case of the hypothetical assistant secretary, participants in these exchanges might float ideas, offer tentative reactions, or report on what some people appear to think. In general, disclosure would serve no purpose at all, except perhaps to those interested in genuine minutiae or seeking to embarrass, injure, or ruin someone, to create a political uproar, or to uncover some kind of scandal.

TWO QUALIFICATIONS

Two principal qualifications help to explain the appeal of input transparency for many observers. It must be acknowledged that in some administrations the qualifications will have, or be perceived to have, a great deal of power.

1. *Illegitimate or illicit arguments.* Public disclosure might provide an ex ante deterrent to arguably illegitimate arguments, and it might also provide an ex post corrective. At the very least, it lets the public know how it is being governed. In the worst cases, inputs include corruption or criminality (or extreme incompetence), and We the People are certainly entitled to learn about that.

Suppose, for example, that someone opposes a decision not because it is a bad idea but because it would offend a friend, a donor, a political ally, or a powerful interest group, or because a prominent senator might object with unfortunate consequences for the administration. That sort of thing is not exactly unusual, and in some forms, it is hardly the worst imaginable input. But let us stipulate that such an argument is objectionable, or at least that the public has a right to know about it, because it might compromise the pursuit of the public interest. Disclosure could make it less likely that such opposition will be voiced, which could be a good thing, and in any case it will create accountability. In this particular respect, an appealing argument about the beneficial effects of sunlight applies to input transparency as well as to output transparency. That argument is all the stronger in cases of the most egregious inputs, entailing corruption, self-dealing, or uncomfortably close relationships with nations unfriendly to the United States. (Readers are invited to use their imaginations.)

To be sure, disclosure could have the principal effect of shifting the locus of controversial argumentation—from email and paper to telephones. Within the federal government, this already happens a great deal. If people do not want their communications to be disclosed to the public or to Congress, they will say, "Call me." (In my own experience, this was always innocent; it does not involve anything illicit, but it does involve issues that are somewhat sensitive, such as strong disagreements that are best not placed on email.) There is a substantial downside here. If internal discussions are potentially subject to disclosure, the shift from written to oral exchanges may impose losses in the form of diminished reliance on careful economic, legal, and other analyses.

Nonetheless, there is no question that a concern about illegitimate or illicit inputs animates and gives force to the argument in favor of input transparency. Suppose you believe that some process is "rigged"—that regularly or as a matter of course powerful private interests are dominating federal processes, or that officials, beholden to certain interests and groups, are pushing outcomes in the directions favored by those groups. Of course, you want that to stop. But if you cannot stop it directly, you might insist on input transparency as a way of opening it up to public view. Sunlight might be a disinfectant here as well.[19]

Again, there is a risk that you will simply drive the relevant influences underground. But in principle, that is a secondary concern if you want to open up internal processes to public scrutiny. To say the least, that is an honorable goal. For those for whom the Watergate scandal is salient, the transgressions of President Richard Nixon are a defining example here, as a degree of input transparency was necessary to ferret out those transgressions.

2. *Learning from mistakes.* The second qualification is that journalists and historians can benefit from seeing the internal give and take, if only because they could give a narrative account of what happened. This might appear to be an abstract, academic benefit, but people (including public officials) do learn from the past and that learning can provide a valuable corrective. The historical record can be absolutely indispensable for finding out what went wrong, and to understand that record, inputs are necessary. Why did the government make some colossal error in the form of an action or an omission? To answer that question, input transparency might be essential. It can create warning signs about group interactions that work poorly, about institutional blind spots, or about the need for institutional reform.

Suppose, for example, the United States government has done (too) little to prevent genocide.[20] It may be difficult or even impossible to document the failures without access to inputs. Once the failures are documented, people might take steps to reduce their likelihood in the future. In that sense, the benefits of input disclosure can be high, at least in certain domains.

But there are countervailing points. In many cases, disclosure of inputs has no benefits; it does not reduce the risk of future errors. Disclosure also imposes a risk of distortion. Suppose that people have access to an official's emails—say, the emails of an assistant administrator at the Environmental Protection Agency or of the assistant attorney general for civil rights. Suppose the email has some complaint about the EPA administrator or about the attorney general or about White House officials. The email might reflect a particular day or mood. It might be based on the author's incomplete understanding. It might be a matter of venting. It might reflect a badly distorted perspective.

Because journalists often enjoy and benefit from accusations and scandal-mongering, it might be appealing to give a great deal of publicity to this revelation of internal disagreement. Recall that it is a form of gossip. Readers might enjoy the gossip and in that sense benefit from it, but accusations and scandal-mongering are not necessarily genuine benefits for the public. A genuine scandal is another matter.

THE COSTS OF INPUT TRANSPARENCY

For input transparency, the most obvious problem, of course, is that disclosure could reduce open-mindedness and discourage candor. In a short space, James Madison captured some of the essential points. In any deliberative process, people's opinions are various and crude, and much is "to be gained by a yielding and accommodating spirit." Once people commit themselves publicly, they might not be willing to shift. Secrecy can promote openness to the force of an argument. And, of course, Madison's knockout punch: "No Constitution would ever have been adopted by the convention if the debates had been public."

What Madison did not emphasize is that input transparency can lead people not to say what they think. It can reduce candor and the free play of ideas. In that sense, it can ensure that groups will have less information than they need. In well-functioning deliberative processes, there is often a sharp separation between an idea-generating phase and a solution-finding phase. In the former phase, many things are on the table, even if they turn out, on reflection, to be absurd or intolerable. People say "yes" to getting ideas out there whether or not there is any chance that they ultimately will be adopted. If inputs are transparent, the idea-generating phase would be far more constrained than it ought to be.

Ensuring candor is, of course, the central idea behind the concept of executive privilege.[21] At best, input transparency would lead people to communicate orally rather than in writing. In fact, one of the consequences of FOIA is a reduced reliance on email and written documents. In both Republican and Democratic administrations, it is well known that whatever is put in writing might find its way into the *New York Times*, which leads people not to put things in writing. At worst, input transparency can lead to certain things not being said at all.

But reduced candor is not the only problem. In view of the incentives of the media and political opponents, disclosure of inputs can produce extremely unfortunate distractions that are destructive to self-government. Instead of focusing on outputs—on how, for example, to reduce premature deaths—a spotlight is placed on comments that seem to make some people into villains or wrongdoers, or that put any resulting decisions in the least favorable light. Of course, skeptics might respond with some passion that it is paternalistic or worse to deprive members of the public of information on the ground that they will misunderstand it or give it undue salience. One view is that the receipt of true information should be subject to the marketplace of ideas. But insofar as the problem lies not in public misunderstanding but in the incentives of those who seek to fuel fires, there is definitely a downside risk.

A BRIEF ACCOUNTING

With respect to input transparency, we seem to have incommensurable values on both sides of the ledger, not easily placed along a single metric. The benefits are often low, but not always, especially when illicit motivations, corruption, and criminality are involved and when the historical record can help to avoid massive or catastrophic mistakes. The costs can be high. But are they always?

It must be acknowledged that the costs of input transparency diminish over time, and they are certainly lower once the relevant people no longer hold public office. It is one thing to tell the director of the Office of Management and Budget that whatever she says will end up in the newspaper that night or the next day. It is quite another to say that at a future date (say, after an administration has ended) there will be a public record of internal communications, subject to safeguards for national security, personal privacy, and other values. Indeed, the Presidential Records Act[22] ventures an approach of this sort (with a five-year gap). With such an approach, the costs of disclosure are significantly reduced. They are not zero because candor will still be chilled and because people's reputations may still be wrongly maligned. But in view of the value of obtaining some kind of historical record, this approach is hardly unreasonable. My aim has not been to reach a definitive conclusion about concrete practices and proposals but to outline general concerns to help identify the appropriate trade-offs.

CONCLUSION

There is a large difference between output transparency and input transparency. For outputs, transparency can be exceedingly important. A central reason is that government often has information that people can use, perhaps to make life more navigable, perhaps to avoid serious risks. It should not keep that information to itself. Another reason is that sunlight can operate as a disinfectant. Whether the information involves the government's own performance or the performance of the private sector, disclosure can spur better performance.

One implication is the immense importance of continuing with, and amplifying, the work of data.gov. It also follows that in numerous contexts government should not be waiting for FOIA requests; it should be disclosing information on its own. This does not mean that every output should be put on the Internet. It does mean that whenever an output could or would be valuable to members of the public, it deserves to be made public. With the help of algorithmic technologies, we should expect significant developments in this direction in the future.

Inputs belong in a different category. Outside of unusual circumstances, what most matters is what government actually does, not who said what to whom. For the most part, the public is unlikely to benefit by learning that the assistant secretary disagreed with the chief of staff of the secretary on some trade agreement, or that there was an internal division on how aggressively to regulate greenhouse gases or on the valuation of statistical lives. Disclosure can have significant costs. Most obviously, it can lead people to silence themselves or to communicate in ways that cannot be recorded. More subtly, it can divert attention from the important questions involving policy and substance to less important ones that involve palace intrigue. At the same time, input transparency can put a spotlight on questionable, illicit, or corrupt practices and can provide an indispensable historical record. People learn from the past, and for current administrations, it can be essential to have a concrete sense of where past administrations went wrong.

My framework throughout has been welfarist, asking about the costs and benefits of disclosure. It should be acknowledged that the very idea of welfarism needs to be specified and that many people would start with different foundations involving, for example, the idea of political legitimacy. It should also be acknowledged that under a welfarist framework some output transparency does not make much sense and some input transparency is amply justified, even indispensable. We are speaking of categories, not individual cases. But categories provide orientation. Output transparency should be the central focus of efforts for freedom of information; we need much more of it. Input transparency can be important, especially after an administration has ended. But it should be treated far more cautiously.

NOTES

From 2009 to 2012, I served in the Obama administration as administrator of the Office of Information and Regulatory Affairs and was involved in some of the matters discussed in this chapter. I am grateful above all to Larry Summers for many valuable discussions of the topic here. I am also grateful to David Pozen, Michael Schudson, and participants in a superb symposium held in June 2016 at Columbia University in honor of the fiftieth anniversary of the Freedom of Information Act. Pozen, in particular, deserves thanks for many valuable comments and suggestions.

1. See Amartya Sen, *Poverty and Famines* (Oxford, Oxford University Press, 1981).
2. See Amartya Sen, *Development as Freedom* (New York: Random House, 1999).
3. Barack Obama, "Memorandum for the Heads of Executive Departments and Agencies, Subject: Freedom of Information Act," January 21, 2009, www.sec .gov/foia/president-memo-foia-nov2009.pdf.
4. Memorandum from Peter R. Orszag, Director, Office of Mgmt. & Budget, to the Heads of Exec. Dep'ts & Agencies, December 8, 2009, https://obama whitehouse.archives.gov/sites/default/files/omb/assets/memoranda_2010 /m10-06.pdf.
5. For a 2016 account, see Cori Zarek, "Agencies Continue to Deliver on Day-One Commitment to Open Government," White House, July 14, 2016, www .whitehouse.gov/blog/2016/07/14/agencies-continue-deliver-day-one-commitment -open-government.

6. For evidence, see Archon Fung, Mary Graham, and David Weil, *Full Disclosure: The Perils and Promise of Transparency* (New York: Cambridge University Press, 2007).

7. Archon Fung and Dana O'Rourke, "Reinventing Environmental Regulation from the Grassroots Up: Explaining and Expanding the Success of the Toxics Release Inventory," *Environmental Management* 25 (2000): 115–27.

8. See U.S. Department of Labor, Occupational Safety and Health Administration, "Worker Fatalities Reported to Federal and State OSHA," www.osha.gov/dep/fatcat/dep_fatcat.html.

9. See, for example, U.S. Environmental Protection Agency, "Inventory of U.S. Greenhouse Gas Emissions and Sinks," www.epa.gov/ghgemissions/inventory-us-greenhouse-gas-emissions-and-sinks.

10. See Partha Deb and Carmen Vargas, "Who Benefits from Calorie Labeling? An Analysis of Its Effects on Body Mass," 2016, www.nber.org/papers/w21992.

11. See Fung, Graham, and Weil, *Full Disclosure*.

12. See Executive Order 12291.

13. Executive Order 13563.

14. Executive Order 12866.

15. Cass R. Sunstein, "Output Transparency vs. Input Transparency, August 18, 2016, http://d3i6fh83elv35t.cloudfront.net/newshour/wp-content/uploads/2014/07/EPA-cost-benefits-1024x468.jpg; memorandum from Cass R. Sunstein, Adm'r, Office of Info. & Regulatory Affairs, "Clarifying Regulatory Requirements: Executive Summaries," January 4, 2012, https://obamawhitehouse.archives.gov/sites/default/files/omb/inforeg/for-agencies/clarifying-regulatory-requirements_executive-summaries.pdf.

16. See Lisa Heinzerling, "Regulatory Costs of Mythic Proportions," *Yale Law Journal* 107 (1998): 1981–2070.

17. Memorandum from Peter R. Orszag, Director, Office of Mgmt. & Budget, to the Heads of Exec. Dep'ts & Agencies.

18. Obama, "Memorandum for the Heads of Executive Departments and Agencies."

19. See Senator Elizabeth Warren, "Tilting the Scales: Corporate Capture of the Rulemaking Process," March 3, 2016, www.warren.senate.gov/files/documents/2016-3-3_Warren_ACUS_Speech.pdf.

20. Samantha Power, *A Problem from Hell* (New York: Basic Books, 2002).

21. See United States v. Nixon, 418 U.S. 683 (1974).

22. 44 U.S.C. §§ 2201–2207.

10

OPEN DATA

The Future of Transparency in the Age of Big Data

Beth Simone Noveck

INTRODUCTION: THE COLLABORATIVE POLITICAL ECONOMY OF OPEN DATA

For fifty years, the Freedom of Information Act (FOIA)[1] has been the legal bedrock of the public's right to know about the workings of the U.S. government. At the same time, FOIA's delays in responses and redactions frustrate information seekers while the volume of requests, in particular commercially and politically motivated requests, bedevil government agencies.[2] With more than 700,000 FOIA requests filed each year and a lack of funding to process them, the federal government faces the costs of a mounting backlog.[3] Arguably "flawed beyond repair,"[4] as David Pozen writes, FOIA may foster litigation without better government to show as a result.

In recent years, however, an entirely different approach to government transparency in line with the era of big data has emerged: *open government data*. Open government data—generally shortened to open data—has the potential to complement and overcome some of FOIA's worst flaws.

Open data has several definitions but is generally understood to be publicly available government information that can be universally and readily accessed, used, and redistributed free of charge in digital and machine-readable form.[5] Open data policy is a direct response to what technology makes possible. Data that are digitized and machine readable can be ingested and processed by analytics or visualization software, enabling in turn the application of new computer-aided statistical methods, often referred to as *data science*. When we can search, sort, compare, aggregate, visualize, and track a vast storehouse of public (and private) data sets, we can generate insights that help us understand more about ourselves, our communities, and our environment.

Open data represents a major governing innovation in the twenty-first century. When data are legally and technically accessible, those with know-how, whether they own the data or not, can create sophisticated and useful tools, models, and analyses across data sets to enable empirically based problem solving and advance social justice. For example, the city of Chicago is using its own data to offer the public an information-rich tool called Open Grid for exploring services and activities in one's neighborhood, while inviting private developers to collaborate on improving that tool.

Open data is not limited to statistics but also includes the text of the *Federal Register*, the daily newspaper of the U.S. government, which was released as open data in bulk form in 2010 and quickly redesigned by three independent software developers working in a café. The National Archives adopted their work, and now the *Register* is no longer a hard-to-read PDF (and the butt of legalese jokes) but a searchable and graphical online magazine.[6]

These examples show how, in enabling the co-creation by public institutions and private participants of solutions to problems, the open data policy framework could profoundly shift the relationship between citizen and state around questions of transparency from adversarial to collaborative. Because in an open data regime government must proactively publish its information with the intent that people use it, the normative essence of open data is participation rather than litigation. By catalyzing civic engagement—both scrutiny of data by the public and collaboration with the public in building new analytical tools and websites—open data is grounded in a very different conception of transparency than traditional freedom of information laws. Rather than focusing on prying secrets out of a distrusted government, open data emphasizes empirical decision making and practical problem solving, embodying a primarily utilitarian rather than a deontological theory of transparency. For example, when the start-up Panjiva.com uses open government data to help businesses find overseas suppliers and enable global trade, this reflects a new normative view of the goals of transparency—open data in service of innovation and entrepreneurship rather than accountability per se.[7]

Open data and FOIA bear many similarities, but open data places *innovation* at the center of addressing public challenges and engaging with citizens. Whereas FOIA ideally promotes reasoned and deliberative discourse about what government *did*, open data anticipates what public institutions and citizens *could do together* to create value of different kinds, especially to advance evidence-based policy making. Because open data emphasizes collaboration as the form of participation,[8] it may point the way to preserving democratic values in administrative governance.

However, open data is not a panacea for all social challenges, and not all government information is or should be shared as open data. Furthermore, and most critically, open data relies on the willingness of the data owner to publish the data. Open data policies generally do not have the "teeth" to compel disclosure when the information holders are reluctant to do so. In such situations, freedom of information laws can help citizens seek information that has not yet been made publicly available in the appropriate form.

As we shall explore, each approach offers crucial benefits that can bolster the legitimacy of public institutions. To realize robust transparency, open data's collaborative tactics will need to be blended with FOIA's adversarial right of enforcement, at least for the foreseeable future. The goal of this chapter is to chart a path toward a twenty-first-century transparency regime that takes advantage of the strengths of both FOIA and the open data model.

To that end, I begin by expanding upon the ways open data differs from FOIA. Second, I track the evolution of the open data movement and examine the hallmarks of open data policy and legislation. Third, I look at the challenges and weaknesses of each regime for advancing its respective aims. The conclusion offers additional recommendations for how to blend the best of both approaches to promote evidence-based and more effective governing.

HOW FOIA AND OPEN DATA DIFFER: TIMING, INFORMATION TYPE, AND AUDIENCE

Compared to FOIA, open data differs in three ways: open data changes the timing for disclosure, focuses on different types of information, and addresses a broader audience.

First, open data shifts the default time of disclosure. FOIA institutionalizes ex post disclosure pursuant to a specific demand by an individual requester. Open data thrives on ex ante, proactive publication of whole classes of information publicly and online, often in a centralized repository such as data.gov. Under the Obama administration's 2009 Open Government Directive, federal agencies are required to identify "high-value information" not yet available and establish a time line for publication of these data sets.

As this directive indicates, such high-value information might encompass any information that "can be used to increase agency accountability and responsiveness; improve public knowledge of the agency and its operations;

further the core mission of the agency; [or] create economic opportunity."[9] Hence, for example, under the Texas open data law, which imitates the federal regime, the state's attorney general has proactively made key criminal justice data sets available for download, such as the lists of parole absconders, attorney general opinions, child support evaders, and custodial death reports, which may then be analyzed for purposes of empirical criminal justice reform.[10]

Second, open data emphasizes different classes of information than FOIA does. Like FOIA, open data laws and policies include data *created* by the government about the workings of government—what Cass Sunstein refers to in chapter 9 of this volume as "input transparency"—but they go further than FOIA in providing greater coverage of data *collected* by the government about the economy, environment, and society.[11] Of course, FOIA requests, too, could and often do involve the latter sort of information. But FOI laws (and their many exceptions) focus on laying bare information about the way government works.

Transparency in the open data context goes well beyond the deliberations and decisions of government, the schedules of parliamentarians and ministers, the spending of treasuries, and the like. "High-value data" includes data that public institutions collect in their role as regulators (for example, workplace safety and injury records, airplane flight on-time logs, and doctors' prescriptions), as well as information gathered in their capacities as scientific research organizations (such as weather data and information about the human genome). Although a term like "high-value" data suffers from inherent ambiguity (high value to whom?), the Open Government Directive's definition has ushered in a movement toward more proactive disclosure of more kinds of information across all levels of government.

Third, open data assumes a broader audience than FOIA. FOIA was written, to a significant extent, with journalists in mind. Yet corporations—knowing what to look for, knowing where to look, and having the resources to navigate the complex process of filing requests—quickly became primary users of the act.[12] In a further departure from its journalistic origins, many current FOIA requesters attempt to hobble the machinery of the administrative state through adversarial requests of various kinds.[13]

But open data anticipates, and thus far has attracted, a diverse and less consistently corporate audience. Unlike responses to FOIA requests, open data is directed to a wider public and is published for all—not just an individual requester—to reuse. Beneficiaries of this public character include computer programmers and data scientists with the skills to draw insight from the data; academic users seeking information as the basis for original research, especially empirical social science about policy making; and commercial users looking to create new products and services. This public direction and benefit of open data can be seen in practice. For example, the New York City Mayor's Office is using municipal open data to stimulate entrepreneurship. Through its *Business Atlas*, the city provides small enterprises with the business intelligence they need to know where to open their restaurant or shop.[14]

Precisely because realizing the value from open data depends on collaboration with those willing to add value to it, the open data ecosystem is populated by actors with different incentives from those of corporate FOIA users. In some cases, for-profit companies are working side by side with nonprofits to use the data as a core asset to create data-driven products and services. One example of this is BrightScope, which worked with previously "locked up" Department of Labor Form 5500 retirement plan data to offer better decision-making tools to investors. As the founders describe it:

> While BrightScope started with DOL data, as we have grown we have gathered data and information from a variety of public sources, including the Securities and Exchange Commission (SEC), the Census Bureau, and the Financial Industry Regulatory Authority (FINRA). Through the process of identifying high-value datasets and integrating them into our databases, we have encountered all different types of public disclosure.[15]

In another departure from FOIA, one of the biggest users of open data has been government itself, including officials wishing to make use of their own data to improve how they deliver services and make policy. For example, the Centers for Medicare and Medicaid Services (CMS) uses its own billing and payment data to improve service delivery and reduce costs.[16] In addition, Chicago's city government used its data on restaurant inspections to create an algorithm to predict food-safety violations. This project increased the effectiveness of its inspections by 25 percent.[17] By giving government actors access to more and better data, and especially by giving state and local government access to the same data that federal officials have, the open data movement allows comparisons across jurisdictions and unlocks new, more innovative regulatory approaches. When the federal government ceases to have a monopoly on the data, it calls into question who is in the best and most informed position to regulate and opens opportunities for decentralized regulation.

A BRIEF HISTORY OF THE U.S. OPEN GOVERNMENT DATA MOVEMENT

On his first day in office in 2009, and fulfilling a campaign promise made in 2007, President Obama signed a Memorandum on Transparency and Open Government, declaring that "information maintained by the Federal Government is a national asset" and calling for the use of "new technologies to put information about [agency] operations and decisions online and [to make it] readily available to the public."[18]

When data.gov launched in May 2009, it made forty-seven data sets searchable, turning the principles of the memorandum into initial practice by creating a tangible and central place for agencies to list and the public to find government data.[19] Later the same year, as already noted, the Office of Management and Budget (OMB) directed federal agencies to release more than just data about the workings of government but also "high-value" information.[20] This instruction effectively broadened FOIA's understanding of and goals for government transparency, responding to what the technologies of big data and the technologies of collaboration make possible today.

The Obama White House open data policy was part of a broader set of open government mandates. These mandates called for agencies to inventory the information they have collected, and to move—although with no definitive deadlines for completion—toward the proactive publication of certain classes of information in their entirety, such as air and water quality measures, safety records, and visitor logs.[21]

In 2013, the federal government recommitted to its open data policy by issuing an Executive Order on "Making Open and Machine Readable the New Default for Government Information" to advance and accelerate open data implementation in federal agencies. The order reiterated the utilitarian and instrumentalist underpinnings of the earlier policies by stating explicitly that "openness in government strengthens our democracy, promotes the delivery of efficient and effective services, and contributes to economic growth." The order cites as examples the government's release of both weather data and geo-locational data, which enabled weather apps and GPS devices, respectively. Entrepreneurship and innovation—rather than accountability—are emphasized: "As one vital benefit of open government, making information resources easy to find, accessible, and usable can fuel entrepreneurship, innovation, and scientific discovery that improves Americans' lives and contributes significantly to job creation."[22]

Further laws have followed, broadening the scope of data covered under open data statutes and policies. The Digital Accountability and Transparency Act, signed into law in 2014, calls for publishing all federal government spending data as open data in standardized formats by 2017.[23] In late 2016, the Senate unanimously passed the Open, Public, Electronic, and Necessary Government Data Act, or the OPEN Government Data Act, which calls for inventorying and publishing all government information as open data.[24] The Congressional Budget Office scored the cost of the legislation as "negligible,"[25] and in March 2017 supporters reintroduced the bill, which passed the House in November 2017 as part of the Foundations for Evidence-Based Policymaking Act.[26]

The reintroduction of this law speaks to the persistent popularity of open data as a new tool of policy making. In addition to a supply-side push, increasing demand for data to support efficient, evidence-based practices in government has spurred the popularity of open data. The authors of *Moneyball for Government* describe this trend as follows:

> Building evidence about the practices, policies and programs that will achieve the most effective and efficient results so that policymakers can make better decisions; investing limited taxpayer dollars in practices, policies and programs that use data, evidence and evaluation to demonstrate they work; and directing funds away from practices, policies, and programs that consistently fail to achieve measurable outcomes.[27]

In the United States, this agenda appeals to both the right and center-left politically;[28] presumably, the former sees open data as a pathway to smaller, more efficient, and less wasteful government and the latter uses open data as a tool to pursue more evidence-based social programs. The bipartisan interest in data-driven approaches to governing has been fueling demand for more access to administrative information (both personally identifiable information about individuals and anonymized, population-level open data), including the data that agencies collect about companies, workplaces, the environment, and the world beyond government.[29]

In parallel with the adoption of open data policy in the United States, seventy countries have signed onto the Open Government Partnership Declaration since 2011. The declaration, which copies the U.S. framework, calls for governments to commit to "pro-actively provide high-value information, including raw data, in a timely manner, in formats that the public can easily locate, understand and use, and in formats that facilitate reuse."[30] Fifteen countries have adopted the International Open Data Charter, which goes further by calling for making government data open in digital formats by default and for investing in the creation of a culture of openness.[31] In parallel, over 436 partners from national governments and from nongovernmental, international, and private sector organizations have agreed to a joint Statement of Purpose on using open data to solve long-standing problems and to benefit farmers and the health of consumers.[32]

OPEN DATA AND FOIA: COMPETITORS OR PARTNERS?

The explosion of open data, coupled with the development of technologies to disseminate and understand it, is cause for optimism. That said, open data cannot be the sole tool for catalyzing government information-sharing. Although substantial, the current inventory of open data sets still represents only a small fraction of important government data. For instance, researchers at the World Wide Web Foundation recently found that across the globe, less than 10 percent of the data in key government data sets is fully open.[33]

Of course, open data's limitations extend beyond the slow pace of implementation (at least relative to the amount of data the government possesses). Gaps exist in both the open data regime and the FOIA regime. In the next sections, I turn to a discussion of some of open data's most pressing shortcomings before proposing practical steps to blend both regimes.

POLITICAL COMMITMENT

First, open data success depends on political commitment to transparency and collaboration. Governments of all stripes refuse to disclose data even when they should. There is a looming risk that governments will only post what is expedient and uncontroversial and seek recognition for their proactive disclosure—a practice increasingly referred to as "open-washing."[34]

Especially as presidential administrations change, there is a risk that, for example, an administration that has publicly declared itself to be hostile to the census, the long-form American Community Survey, and climate change will fail to collect and publish important data on these subjects.[35] These practices will be subject to the vagaries of politics. President Donald Trump has already revised, among other things, the Obama administration policy of disclosing who visits the White House. In the run-up to his inauguration, many groups raced to back up open data, such as environmental data, lest it be taken down.[36]

A RIGHT OF ACTION

It is important to dispel any techno-utopian strain in an open data narrative suggesting that, given enough data, all problems are solvable.[37] Without a legal right of action or other robust enforcement mechanisms, there will never be enough data in the right formats. Although newly proposed federal open data legislation would compel the inventorying and publication in machine-readable format of all government data (the legislation is silent on any exceptions), the legislation speaks to *how* data should be disclosed without adequate assurances that the data *will* in fact be disclosed.[38]

FOIA's legal right of action to sue (or threaten to sue) for information disclosure when records are withheld remains essential for ensuring access to data of public import until other mechanisms are put in place to mandate open data disclosures. For example, in 2013, transparency activist Carl Malamud had to use FOIA to request nine nonprofit tax returns from the Internal Revenue Service (IRS) because the agency would not make the returns available in digital form. Although disclosure of nonprofit returns is required by law and the filers submitted those returns electronically, the IRS wanted to send Malamud image files of the returns. The IRS typically took electronically filed returns, printed them out, scanned them back in, and sold DVDs with the image files.[39] Malamud sued for the digital originals and won.[40] The significance of the decision is that the IRS now makes all electronically filed nonprofit tax returns digitally downloadable as open data.[41] Despite considerable pressure, the IRS chose not to invest in publishing the nonprofit tax returns as downloadable data until Malamud filed suit and a judge compelled the agency. When collaboration fails, litigation can sometimes create the impetus needed to overcome resistance and support reformers inside and outside of government.

PRINCIPLES FOR OPEN DATA DESIGN

Open data, at least in theory, requires inventorying *all* data and creates an opportunity for reasoned debate between the public and the agency about what part of that corpus to publish, with what frequency, and in what formats. But because open data is often the creature of executive action, not legislation, open data is not always a systematic process with a clear definition of high-value information.

Indeed, there often seems to be no rhyme or reason behind what is defined as "high-value" information and therefore what gets published.[42] The lack of a clear or sensible publication process can frustrate and hinder the uptake of open data. Agencies post a lot of data on data.gov that no one especially wants, knows exists, or uses.[43]

As civil servants learn about the benefits of open data, a sense of priorities may emerge. Eventually, disclosure prioritization might be mandated through legislation. However, this hope is not certain to become reality.

What sorts of discourses and politics will be produced by a transparency regime that supports proactive disclosure but has no lodestar? If open data is oriented toward publication of easily understood and quantifiable information that technical people can turn into consumer tools (such as transit data that becomes a "when is my bus coming" app), will other kinds of substantive information be neglected in favor of easy disclosures that lead to headline-grabbing consumer tools such as the College Scorecard? What kind of information ecology results if complex information that forms the basis of government decision making, such as budget models, is neglected in favor of data that feeds consumer apps?

Drawing on the lessons of FOIA, which emphasizes disclosure of data by government about government, open data policy, too, should evolve to articulate normative guidance to agencies about what should be published online and when and how to make use of it. Although there is a certain appealing optimism to the early organic and ad hoc evolution of open data practices, there is a need to evolve beyond the unsystematic apps-over-substance nature of open data policy to focus on disclosures and their uses that lead to positive social change, advance democratic values, and lead to measurable progress, not in terms of the number of data sets released but in terms of the downstream impact on people's lives.

Because open data enables the publication of ever-larger data sets that can then be analyzed using algorithms, it lends itself to projects that benefit from comparisons at scale—such as macro-analyses of the efficiency, effectiveness, or disparate impact of how policies and services are delivered—rather than to insights derived from a smoking gun hidden in a single "FOIA'd" document. For example, Argentina, Lithuania, and Slovakia have launched judicial open data projects that publish average caseload and court budgets to improve equity and reduce corruption in their court systems.[44] In another example of open data being used to mitigate inequitable distribution, Transparency International and the Web Foundation have established an ongoing effort to help civil society and governments use open data to identify and fight corruption, especially in procurement.[45] Opening the entire corpus of data about food-borne illnesses, to take one final example, provides a supply of information to match the demand for better algorithms that helps Chicago allocate its restaurant inspection and enforcement resources more efficiently.[46]

Moving toward a more principled approach to open data also demands focusing on outcomes rather than on inputs. In the first generation, we celebrated the act of publishing data sets — transparency for its own sake — regardless of who (if anyone) used them and to what end. To strengthen the normative underpinnings of open data, however, it is important to start with a clear definition of the problem to be solved, be it corruption or human rights abuses or agricultural productivity, and use open data as the means to the end rather than as an end unto itself. Therefore, efforts to publicize the calendars of cabinet secretaries or the salaries of government officials may be weak candidates for open data efforts because, absent reason to suspect serious malfeasance, such disclosures will not drive changes in how government operates and may indeed sap the political will for furthering open data. Open data priorities should retain their broader orientation toward high-value problem-solving.

In addition to publishing clean, comprehensive, and timely data, an open data regime should invest in and prioritize coalition-building among those interested in using the data to tackle a well-defined problem. Open data encourages efficient outcomes in part because the proactive disclosure is often, although not always, accompanied by a plan for how to use the data and how to cultivate citizen engagement among those interested in applying the data for social good. These areas of alignment in which government and civil society or industry are prepared to collaborate to address a challenge are, obviously, excellent, although not exclusive, opportunities to realize value from open data.

HARMONIZING OPEN DATA AND FOIA: FIVE RECOMMENDATIONS

FOIA and open data both emphasize disclosure to the public of information created or collected by the government, but the normative underpinnings and the mechanics differ dramatically. As we have seen, open data is rooted in a theory about government legitimacy stemming from outcome-oriented effectiveness, in contrast to FOIA's focus on honoring the public's "right to know" what the government does. Open data substitutes a utilitarian rationale (evidence-based decision making) for transparency in place of a justification based on moral obligation.

To avoid the pitfalls of FOIA's mechanics, which can hobble some of the functioning of government, while taking advantage of the legal right of redress that FOIA affords to get at government secrets and, at the same time, to take advantage of open data's collaborative and participatory dynamics, the two approaches must self-consciously be blended. There are already developments toward harmonization, but more could and should be done.

First, the federal government should establish a single website for information requests, whether pursuant to FOIA or open data policy, and for posting information in response to those requests. All agencies should be required to participate in and use the new portal. The process should take advantage of the existing technology and infrastructure of data.gov, housed by the General Services Administration, and the transition process managed by the Office of Government Information Services (OGIS)—the so-called FOIA Ombudsperson—housed at the National Archives and Records Administration.

The FOIA Improvement Act passed in 2016 calls for setting up a single electronic portal for FOIA *requests*, and although it is silent as to where the responses to those requests will be posted, it would make sense to use data.gov (with a pointer from FOIA.gov) as a one-stop shop for requesting *and* searching for information.[47] Data.gov is already set up to act as a clearinghouse to point to data housed across the federal government, and it has an underlying information architecture that makes it a good, easy-to-remember place from which to make data searchable. There is also a well-established process for making agency information searchable via data.gov, although it is not yet a comprehensive or robust search engine for government data. A single, unified database would make it possible for more people to find and use more information quickly. Managing that transition from agency FOIA websites to using data.gov, however, requires knowledge of the FOIA process and its personnel. Hence, OGIS should play a key role in stewarding the changeover, working closely with FOIA officers and the Department of Justice's Office of Information Policy, which oversees FOIA policy within the executive branch.

Second, all information requested pursuant to FOIA or open data policy should be published in machine-readable formats.[48] Although the FOIA Improvement Act calls for releasing information electronically, it is otherwise silent as to the format. The Office of Information Policy, in collaboration with OGIS and OMB, should issue guidance defining the electronic format required under the law as the same format as open data—namely, machine-readable formats—and should post pointers back to the data published online on data.gov. By shifting to a release-to-one, release-to-all strategy and post-ing information online (perhaps with a short delay for information obtained through FOIA to maintain media incentives), requesters can search for desired information prior to filing a new request. This should cut down on FOIA requests and processing times for noncontentious information and enable greater innovation by the public, such as data analysis and visualiza-tion, using the published information. Also, releasing to all, instead of just to one, may help to cut down on the politically or economically motivated nuisance requests.

Third, bringing FOIA into the era of big data and achieving the goal of a unified database for requests and publications will be accelerated, as a practical matter, by increased dialogue between the FOIA Officers' Council, the Chief Information Officers (CIO) Council, and chief data officers.[49] The FOIA officials, under the auspices of the Department of Justice, manage the FOIA process together with the agency general counsels, whereas the CIO Council, often in collaboration with the chief technology officer or chief innovation officer or chief data scientist in an agency, has responsibility for posting open data. These communities need to collaborate and agree on data publication standards and more efficient workflow, as well as on strategies for ensuring that data publication helps to achieve the agency's core mission.

More broadly, there is a need for a more comprehensive perspective on how the government creates and uses information that cuts across the dis-ciplinary boundaries of law, technology, and policy as well as across agency silos. CIOs and FOIA officials currently convene separately as government-wide, interagency communities. They need to talk and work more closely with one another. Chief information officers, chief data officers, chief inno-vation officers, and others in charge of open data should be meeting to ask and answer how the FOIA process could embrace the collaborative nature of open data practices.

By the same token, open data managers need to understand the audiences for FOIA and their demands in order to develop more responsive approaches. The need for more internal government dialogue is mirrored by the need for more conversation between the external transparency and accountabil-ity interest groups (for example, Program on Government Oversight, Cause for Action, National Freedom of Information Coalition), which have tradi-tionally stewarded and watched over the implementation of FOIA and other "sunshine" laws, and the open data groups (for example, Omidyar Network, Center for Open Data Enterprise, Data Coalition, Open Data Institute), which often have a more technological bent and tend to focus on engendering collaboration rather than litigation. Developing a unified legal and policy framework for information collection and publication will benefit lawyers, technologists, data scientists, and policy makers as well as the public.

Fourth, federal agencies should use their own data to improve the FOIA process by using performance analytics. Whereas certain inefficiencies, such as the possibility of partially or wholly overlapping requests, are baked into the design of the FOIA process, accidental inefficiencies might be improved through scrutiny of the data. For example, comparing processing times across agencies reveals significant disparities. The FOIA Officers' Council, the Department of Justice, and the White House Counsel's Office should endeavor to implement performance improvement strategies using the reported data to reduce these variations and help agencies develop more efficient approaches.

In this world of big data, enormous quantities of information help to generate value and make it possible to search and sort and compare within and across organizations and over time. Therefore, fifth, governments should work toward creating and storing data digitally in a searchable cloud. The notion of either ferreting out a single document or posting data sets will then become increasingly outdated.

With government data in the cloud, it will be possible to run searches broadly about and across government.[50] One could, for example, anonymously search all nonprivileged memoranda to see the topics decision makers discuss over time. Furthermore, when it becomes possible to search all contracts or grant-making data across agencies and across levels of government, it should be possible to obtain a much more accurate picture of what government does and measure its impact, applying algorithms to identify effective practices or spot patterns of fraud, waste, and corruption.

Government information policy has a long way to go to realize this vision. If one wanted to conduct research today on government military spending by monitoring contract solicitations from the Department of Defense, for example, one could do so by reading solicitations and contracts published openly online. But downloading and working with that data is difficult. Analyzing these solicitations and contracts to spot trends and patterns in government spending could require going repeatedly to FBO.gov (a website where federal agencies post procurement opportunities), running a computer program to draw down a massive data file, and then comparing it to yesterday's or last year's entries.[51] To do an even more detailed analysis—such as how eventual federal outlays map onto the timing of original contract solicitations—could involve an additional layer of merging records across unconnected databases, such as joining unstructured FBO.gov data with the Federal Procurement Data System.

In such a case, we would say that the data is technically "open." However, as a practical matter, answering the question of "who the government is contracting with, when, and to what degree" is very time-consuming and requires considerable computing time, technological expertise, and data storage available only to a select few at universities or companies with the time, talent, and curiosity to do the analysis. Even those inside government, potentially with the greatest need for such analysis, may not have the necessary resources to run such painstaking manual queries. Our public institutions too often lack the infrastructure in legal, technical, and human capacity to support evidence-based policy making.

Even when available, then, supposedly open data is often not open enough to be usable. Open data, as it stands today, is only an interim step on the pathway from a paper-based FOIA world to a future in which comprehensive public information is produced and stored digitally in real-time in formats that enable agile and empirical social science. Helping open data realize its potential for collaboration requires a better approach: namely, storing clean and searchable government data in a publicly accessible cloud.

Until we get there, we need to keep both FOIA and open data in our arsenal of transparency tools, relying principally on FOIA to protect against secrecy and corruption and on open data to promote the co-creation by the government and the governed of solutions to public problems. Open data has the side effect of also strengthening active forms of citizenship and engagement.

CONCLUSION: FROM OPEN DATA TO COLLABORATIVE DEMOCRACY

The explosion of newly available data coupled with mounting evidence that data catalyzes productive, problem-solving partnerships between government and civil society suggests that open data, as a tool of governing, will continue to grow. If the trend continues, open data will lead to new empirically informed ways of holding government and others accountable, spurring consumer choice and expanding the range of approaches to tackling societal challenges. In principle, open data promotes broad-scale transparency; simplifies the disclosure process; requires publication in reusable and computable formats;

focuses on disclosure of information collected by government as regulator and researcher, not exclusively on data created by government about its own workings; and, above all, gets both more "eyeballs" and machines looking at the data to spot problems, identify patterns, devise solutions, and act.

As promising as open data may be, FOIA indispensably *complements* it by providing a legal right of action to compel disclosure, by suggesting the kinds of data to prioritize releasing, and by disclosing who is using what data and how. Open data policies still depend on the political will to publish information. They will be strengthened when, like FOIA, they can compel disclosure, especially in reusable formats.

But the most significant impact of open data in the long run may stem less from the immediate problem-solving benefits than from the way open data fosters more active citizenship and more responsive democratic institutions. It transforms transparency policy from a means to monitor government after the fact to a mechanism for getting the public to participate actively in improving societal outcomes. By eschewing the adversarial in favor of a collaborative approach to transparency, open data reflects a radically different transparency narrative and, ultimately, a different theory of democracy whereby citizen-participants collaborate in designing and building solutions to important problems together with public institutions. This collaborative model enables governments to draw directly on the collective expertise of the population in developing creative regulatory approaches and affords the public new opportunities to participate in our democracy.

NOTES

The author is grateful to David Pozen and Michael Schudson of Columbia University for organizing an excellent conference on FOIA's fiftieth anniversary at which many of the ideas in this chapter were presented.

1. 5 U.S.C. § 552 (2012).
2. David E. Pozen, "Freedom of Information Beyond the Freedom of Information Act," *University of Pennsylvania Law Review* 165 (2017): 1097–1158, at 1111–31.
3. U.S. Department of Justice, "FOIA," www.foia.gov.
4. Pozen, "Freedom of Information Beyond the Freedom of Information Act," at 1136.
5. Governance Lab, "Open Data: What's in a Name?," January 16, 2014, http://thegovlab.org/open-data-whats-in-a-name.
6. David Ferriero, "Federal Register 2.0," White House, July 26, 2010, www.whitehouse.gov/blog/2010/07/26/federal-register-20.

7. For more on the collaborative theory of participatory democracy, see Beth Simone Noveck, *Wiki Government: How Technology Can Make Government Better, Democracy Stronger, and Citizens More Powerful* (Washington, D.C.: Brookings Institution, 2010), chap. 2.

8. See, for example, Annika Wolff et al., "Removing Barriers for Citizen Participation to Urban Innovation," *Digital Cities* 9 (2015), http://oro.open.ac.uk/43854/%5Cnhttp://oro.open.ac.uk/43854/1/OU-dc9.pdf.

9. "Memorandum from Peter R. Orszag to the Heads of Exec. Dep'ts and Agencies on the Open Government Directive," White House, December 8, 2009, www.whitehouse.gov/open/documents/open-government-directive.

10. Ken Paxton, Attorney General of Texas, "High-Value Data Sets," SB 701, September 1, 2011, www.texasattorneygeneral.gov/og/high-value-data-sets.

11. In the United States alone, forty-eight cities, ten states, and the federal government had enacted open data legislation or policies by 2017. See "A Bird's Eye View of Open Data Policies," Sunlight Foundation, 2017, https://sunlightfoundation.com/policy/opendatamap.

12. Pozen, "Freedom of Information Beyond the Freedom of Information Act," 1103.

13. Pozen, "Freedom of Information Beyond the Freedom of Information Act," 1104.

14. New York City, *New York City Business Atlas*, accessed May 18, 2017, https://maps.nyc.gov/businessatlas.

15. Ryan Alfred and Mike Alfred, "From Entrepreneurs to Civic Entrepreneurs," in *Beyond Transparency*, ed. Brett Goldstein (2013), chap. 6, http://beyondtransparency.org.

16. "Building Evidence with Administrative Data," in *The President's Budget for Fiscal Year 2017: Analytical Perspectives*, 65–73, https://obamawhitehouse.archives.gov/sites/default/files/omb/budget/fy2016/assets/ap_7_evidence.pdf.

17. Beth Simone Noveck, "Five Hacks for Digital Democracy," *Nature* 544 (2017): 287–89, at 287, 288, doi:10.1038/544287a.

18. Barack Obama, "Memorandum for the Heads of Exec. Dep'ts and Agencies on Transparency and Open Government," January 21, 2009, www.presidency.ucsb.edu/ws/index.php?pid=85677; see also "Experts Praise Barack Obama's Technology and Innovation Agenda," American Presidency Project, November 14, 2007, www.presidency.ucsb.edu/ws/?pid=91809.

19. "Data.gov is primarily a federal open government data site. . . . Data.gov does not host data directly, but rather aggregates metadata about open data resources in one centralized location." Data.gov, "About," accessed May 26, 2017, www.data.gov/about.

20. See "Memorandum from Peter R. Orszag," 7–8 for definition of high-value data sets.

21. See "Memorandum from Peter R. Orszag," 3, 7–8 for a listing of several presidential open government initiatives.

22. Exec. Order No. 13,642, 3 C.F.R. § 13,642 (2013). For further reading on this topic, see Andrew Young,Christina Rogawski, and Stefaan Verhulst, "United States GPS System: Creating a Global Public Utility," *GovLab & Omidyar Network* (2016), http://odimpact.org/static/files/case-studies-gps.pdf.

23. Digital Accountability and Transparency (DATA) Act of 2014, Pub. L. No. 113-101, 128 Stat. 1146.

24. Open Government Data Act, S. 2852, 114th Cong. (2016).

25. Congressional Budget Office, Cost Estimate, S. 2852: OPEN Government Data Act, December 5, 2016, www.cbo.gov/sites/default/files/114th-congress-2015-2016/costestimate/s2852.pdf.

26. H.R. 4174, tit. II, 115th Cong. (2017).

27. Moneyball for Government, "Moneyball Principles," accessed May 18, 2017, http://moneyballforgov.com/moneyball-principles.

28. The OPEN Government Data Act was, in both the House and the Senate, jointly reintroduced by a Democrat and a Republican. See *Congressional Record* 163 (March 29, 2017), H2557; *Congressional Record* 163 (March 29, 2017), S2099.

29. The Evidence-Based Policymaking Commission Act of 2016, Pub. L. No. 114-140, 130 Stat. 317, created a commission to study the use of open government data to conduct program evaluation and was introduced by Republican Paul Ryan in the House and Democrat Patty Murray in the Senate.

30. Open Government Partnership, "Open Government Declaration," September 2011, www.opengovpartnership.org/about/open-government-declaration.

31. Open Data Charter, www.opendatacharter.net.

32. GODAN, "About GODAN," accessed April 26, 2017, www.godan.info/pages/about-godan.

33. World Wide Web Foundation, *Open Data Barometer: Global Report*, 4th ed. (2017), 12, https://opendatabarometer.org/doc/4thEdition/ODB-4thEdition-GlobalReport.pdf.

34. See, for example, Lindsay Ferris and Julia Keserü, "We Should Demand More from 'Open' Than Just Data: Thoughts on the International Open Data Conference," Sunlight Foundation, June 3, 2015, https://sunlightfoundation.com/2015/06/03/we-should-demand-more-from-open-than-just-data-thoughts-on-the-international-open-data-conference.

35. FiveThirtyEight, "Politics Podcast: Data Under Trump," January 2, 2017. See also Edward Wong, "Trump Has Called Climate Change a Chinese Hoax. Beijing Says It Is Anything But," *New York Times*, November 18, 2016.

36. See Brady Dennis, "Scientists Are Frantically Copying U.S. Climate Data, Fearing It Might Vanish Under Trump," *Washington Post*, December 13, 2016.

37. See Evgeny Morozov, "Open and Closed," *New York Times Sunday Review*, March 16, 2013.

38. See, for example, Open Government Data Act, S. 2852, 114th Cong. (2016).

39. See Beth Simone Noveck and Daniel Goroff, "Information for Impact: Liberating Non-Profit Data," Aspen Institute, 2013, https://assets.aspeninstitute.org /content/uploads/files/content/docs/psi/psi_Information-for-Impact.pdf.

40. Public.Resource.org v. U.S. Internal Revenue Serv., 78 F. Supp. 3d 1262 (N.D. Cal. 2015), *appeal dismissed* June 24, 2015, holding that the IRS must produce digital, not paper-based, copies of electronically filed nonprofit tax returns.

41. Internal Revenue Service, "IRS Makes Electronically Filed Form 990 Data Available in New Format," June 16, 2016, www.irs.gov/uac/newsroom/irs-makes -electronically-filed-form-990-data-available-in-new-format; see also Noveck and Goroff, "Information for Impact."

42. The Open Government Directive does provide a broad definition of high-value data sets. See "Memorandum from Peter R. Orszag," 7–8. However, this has not necessarily provided sufficient direction. See discussion and criticisms of the looseness of high-value data definitions in Section I.B.

43. Even when data are, in theory, posted to data.gov, there is often a lack of investment in making the data truly accessible and usable. Users frequently find just a link to a website describing data but no actual way to download that data.

44. Slovakia's judicial open data portal, https://otvorenesudy.sk/?l=sk; Lithuania's judicial open data portal, http://atvirasteismas.lt; Argentina's judicial open data portal, http://datos.jus.gob.ar, accessed July 1, 2017.

45. Transparency International, "Connecting the Dots: Building the Case for Open Data to Fight Corruption," February 23, 2017, www.transparency.org /whatwedo/publication/connecting_the_dots_building_the_case_for_open _data_to_fight_corruption.

46. Obama, "Memorandum"; Julian Spector, "Chicago Is Predicting Food Safety Violations. Why Aren't Other Cities," *CityLab*, January 7, 2016, www.citylab .com/cityfixer/2016/01/chicago-is-predicting-food-safety-violations-why-arent -other-cities/422511.

47. FOIA Improvement Act of 2016, Pub. L. No. 114-185, 130 Stat. 538.

48. Center for Open Data Enterprise, "Open Data Transition Report: An Action Plan for the Next Administration," October 24, 2016, http://opendataenterprise .org/transition-report.

49. The Chief FOIA Officers Council was created by the FOIA Improvement Act of 2016. See 5 U.S.C. § 552(k)(1). The CIO Council was created by Executive Order 13,011 on Federal Information Technology and later codified by the

E-Government Act of 2002. The new role of chief data officer has been created at various federal government agencies but has not yet been incorporated into an interagency body.

50. Of course, moving government information to the cloud will require similar attention to that paid today to publishing open data to ensure that personally identifiable information and classified information are not inadvertently disclosed.

51. For an example utilizing such data, see Michael Z. Gill, "The Economic Benefits of Conflict? Estimating Defense Firm Responses to Major Events in U.S. Foreign Policy" (working paper), 2017, http://www.michaelzgill.com /research.

11

STRIKING THE RIGHT BALANCE

Weighing the Public Interest in Access to Agency Records Under the Freedom of Information Act

Katie Townsend and Adam A. Marshall

ECHOES OF THE PAST—AN INTRODUCTION

"Improper denials occur again and again," lamented the House committee, citing what it viewed as federal agencies' "almost automatic refusal" to disclose basic information under the act.[1] The Senate committee's report was equally critical: the law is "full of loopholes which allow agencies to deny legitimate information to the public," including simply "to cover up embarrassing mistakes or irregularities."[2]

For any journalist or citizen acquainted with the federal Freedom of Information Act (FOIA), these words from members of the Ninetieth Congress undoubtedly sound familiar. Yet it was not FOIA they were talking about. These frustrations were directed toward FOIA's predecessor, the 1946 Administrative Procedure Act (APA). Nearly two decades after its enactment, that law's basic disclosure requirement had come to be regarded as a failure. Although crafted with the laudable intention of ensuring executive branch transparency, the APA's "public information" section was vague and depended on executive branch officials to "do the right thing" when deciding what information the public should have.[3]

Congress passed FOIA in 1966 to correct those deficiencies. FOIA was a "remedial"[4] statute intended to foster an "informed, intelligent electorate"[5] by creating a judicially enforceable right to request agency records. The debate over FOIA was fierce, but in the end Congress sought to strike a "workable balance"[6] between the public's right to know and the legitimate need for government secrecy by coupling a broad general mandate of access with nine specific categories of exemptions.[7]

Fifty years later, however, there is widespread concern among journalists, academics, lawyers, and the general public that FOIA's "workable balance" has tilted so far in favor of government secrecy that, like the 1946 APA provisions before it, the act is failing to serve its core purpose. In FOIA's first years, government agencies reported denying less than 1 percent of all requests in full or in part.[8] In the decades since, that percentage has exploded. According to data compiled by the Department of Justice, in 2008 almost 22 percent of all requests were denied in part or in full based on an exemption.[9] Eight years later, that number had risen to 42 percent.[10] This rise in denials, which has been enabled by judicial decisions broadly applying FOIA's exemptions, represents a worrisome trend. From legal opinions written by the Department of Justice[11] to nuclear plant safety reports[12] to evidence previously introduced in open court,[13] the list of agency records now shrouded in secrecy goes on and on. As one commenter put it, for many records, "the balance is being struck in favor of secrecy," and under FOIA's current framework "there is no practical way that this wholesale rejection practice can be challenged."[14]

Although a number of factors have contributed to the current state of FOIA, a significant limit to the law's efficacy stems from the manner in which its exemptions were crafted and have been applied. As the act stands today, courts have no discretion to order an agency to release requested records that fall within an exemption, even if the information they contain is of exceptional public interest and is not required to be withheld.[15] Indeed, even if judges believe there is no good reason for a particular exempt record to be kept secret, their hands are tied both by the language of the statute and broad precedent interpreting the scope of FOIA's exemptions.

In this chapter we submit that, as was true fifty years ago, "the needs of the electorate have outpaced the laws which guarantee public access to the facts in Government."[16] FOIA should be strengthened by the addition of a public interest "safety valve"—an override mechanism to ensure that the most important information needed by self-governing citizens will see the light of day. Although two of FOIA's privacy exemptions already incorporate a species of public interest balancing, those exemptions concern *individual* privacy interests. Public interest balancing in the context of those exemptions thus serves a somewhat distinct function and has been limited in its application by court decisions.[17] We consider the potential for a general public interest balancing test that would require the disclosure of agency records falling within the scope of one of FOIA's discretionary exemptions if the public interest in their release clearly outweighs the government's interest in withholding them. This inquiry would not replace the analysis of whether an exemption applies but would add an evaluation of the information itself to determine, even if an exemption applies, whether the public's interest should nonetheless require disclosure.

We begin by reviewing the purpose and structure of FOIA as well as relevant impediments to its effectiveness that have arisen or intensified over the past fifty years. Then we discuss the nature of a proposed public interest balancing test for FOIA's discretionary exemptions, exploring it alongside other, similar balancing tests applicable under common law and the freedom of information (FOI) laws of other nation-states. Finally, we consider how the addition of such a balancing test to FOIA could affect requesters, agencies, courts, and Congress.

THE EBB AND FLOW OF THE PUBLIC'S RIGHT TO KNOW

FOIA'S EFFORT TO PROMOTE AN INFORMED DEMOCRACY

FOIA reflects the view that access to government information plays a key role in a healthy democracy. With the rise of the federal administrative state over the course of the twentieth century, decisions affecting the everyday lives of citizens were increasingly made by the executive branch of government, not the legislative branch, and without clear mechanisms to hold executive agencies accountable. Congress made its first systematic attempt to bring transparency to these agencies in the original APA, which generally required them to make public their rules, opinions and orders, and certain records.

The APA's disclosure scheme contained significant exceptions, however, and by 1966 it was clear the act was deficient for two primary reasons. First, the standards governing what information could be kept secret were vague; access could be denied "for good cause" or if secrecy was, in the agency's view, in the "public interest."[18] In practice, this meant that agencies could almost always refuse to turn over information.[19] Second, the act's disclosure provision lacked any enforcement mechanism.[20] If a requester disagreed with an agency's refusal to disclose information, she had no recourse.

In enacting FOIA, Congress attempted to remedy these deficiencies in several ways. It limited agencies' discretion to withhold information by requiring that *all* agency records be disclosed upon request unless they fall within one of the act's nine enumerated exemptions.[21] Those exemptions, which (with a few modifications) still apply today, specify certain types of records that may be withheld based on interests Congress has determined are worthy of protection.[22] Congress also made most of FOIA's exemptions permissive rather than mandatory. As the Senate Judiciary Committee explained in 1974, if a record falls within an exemption, it *"may* be withheld where the agency makes an affirmative determination that the public interest and the specific circumstances presented dictate that the information *should* be withheld."[23] In other words, Congress originally envisioned each exemption as a balancing test, weighing potential harm against the public interest in disclosure to create "a workable balance between the right of the public to know and the need of the Government to keep information in confidence."[24]

Notwithstanding Congress's intent, since FOIA's enactment, agencies have largely viewed its exemptions not as the outer bounds of what may be withheld from the public if necessary but rather as a full authorization to withhold any and all information that, in their judgment, falls within the scope of the exemption.[25] Requested records are scrutinized not only by agency FOIA officers but often by agency superiors, who may be concerned with the political ramifications of release.[26] After records are examined within the agency of their origin, they may be sent on for additional review by other government entities, sometimes including the White House itself.[27] This multistage review process likely contributes not only to delay[28] but also to the extensive redaction of records and the frequent outright denials of requests.[29] Requesters encounter so much difficulty wrangling the release of records from agencies that the House Committee on Oversight and Government Reform recently published a report simply titled "FOIA Is Broken."[30] According to one journalist who contacted the committee, "I often describe the handling of my FOIA request as the single most disillusioning experience of my life."[31]

The instructions in the 2013 United States Citizenship and Immigration Services (USCIS) FOIA processing manual, a guide for agency employees responding to requests, provide a telling example of agency implementation of FOIA.[32] One section discusses Exemption 7(C), which permits agencies to withhold records compiled for law enforcement purposes if disclosure could reasonably be expected to constitute an unwarranted invasion of personal privacy.[33] As discussed later in the chapter, Exemption 7(C), along with Exemption 6, calls for a balancing of the public interest in the records with the privacy interest of the person they concern.[34] Thus, even if a record implicates a privacy interest, the agency is required to consider the public's interest in disclosure in determining whether the record may be withheld.[35]

The USCIS FOIA manual, however, contains no instructions on implementing the balancing test required by Exemption 7(C). In fact, the manual instructs USCIS personnel to categorically redact and deny access to certain information—including the names of all immigration officers identified in law enforcement records or conducting law enforcement activities—pursuant to that exemption.[36] According to the manual, it is irrelevant whether there is a public interest in disclosure of such information in a given case; the FOIA officer is always to withhold it. That an agency refuses to consider the public interest in connection with an exemption when Congress has explicitly required it leaves little room for hope that agencies routinely consider the public's interest when determining whether to invoke other discretionary exemptions where no such balancing is expressly required by the act.

To be sure, other avenues for providing government information to the public have been adopted since FOIA's enactment, including the publication of "open data" on the Internet.[37] These government data sets are certainly valuable, but the voluntary disclosure of such information is not a substitute for FOIA for at least two reasons. First, open data, for the most part, consists of uncontroversial factual material, such as hourly precipitation data[38] or farm program payments.[39] Although such data are important and useful for some applications, many other types of extremely consequential government information will never be voluntarily released. It is highly unlikely that the public will ever see an open data portal containing, for example, Justice Department memos analyzing whether it is legal to kill American citizens abroad without a trial.[40] Second, without an enforceable legal mandate of access, agencies may remove such data from the Internet as policies and priorities change. FOIA exists as a mandate of openness that is not subject to the whims of different administrations, and this mandate is most important when it comes to records the government would rather hide away.

JUDICIAL ENFORCEMENT AND ITS LIMITATIONS

Congress anticipated agency resistance to transparency when it devised FOIA. Indeed, the 1966 House Report notes that "no Government employee at any level believes that the 'public interest' would be served by disclosure of his failures or wrongdoings."[41] Accordingly, FOIA includes a judicial review provision to remedy the APA's lack of an enforcement mechanism. Under FOIA's framework, a dissatisfied requester may bring an action in federal court in which a judge is required to conduct a de novo review of the agency's handling of the request, meaning no deference is supposed to be given to the agency's determination as to whether the records are exempt from disclosure under the act. Courts are also authorized to conduct an in camera (nonpublic) review of the records, viewing unredacted versions in chambers to assess the validity of any claimed exemptions. FOIA also places the burden on the agency to justify its withholdings; unless an agency demonstrates that they are lawful, the requester should prevail. If a court finds that records were improperly withheld, it can order the agency to produce them.[42] Together, at least in theory, these provisions create a uniquely powerful regime of judicial oversight of agency action.

Despite Congress's desire for vigorous judicial enforcement of FOIA, courts have been unenthusiastic about conducting the type of review that the act envisions.[43] Commentators have described the judiciary's engagement with FOIA as "anemic"[44] and "a de facto system of deference."[45] Notwithstanding FOIA's requirement that courts apply the most searching, nondeferential standard of review, a study of more than 3,600 FOIA cases between 1990 and 1999 found that district courts upheld agencies' nondisclosure decisions approximately 90 percent of the time—a rate far higher than the rate of judicial approval of other types of agency actions that are reviewed under a deferential standard.[46]

A full exploration of the reasons for the judiciary's lukewarm embrace of FOIA is beyond the scope of this chapter, but two factors warrant consideration here. The first concerns the nature of the exemptions themselves. Notwithstanding Congress's intent for agencies to use FOIA's exemptions only as an outer limit of what may be withheld, the statutory language chosen by Congress, for the most part, sets up a binary test: either records fall within an exemption or they do not. In one case concerning Exemption 7, the U.S. Supreme Court relied on the act's categorical wording to reject the argument that records should be released because of the public's interest in their disclosure, stating that "Congress . . . created a scheme of categorical exclusion; it did not invite a judicial weighing of the benefits and evils of disclosure on a case-by-case basis."[47] Because courts do "not possess statutory or inherent authority to order disclosure of documents properly withheld pursuant to FOIA exemptions,"[48] the judiciary's role is generally limited to determining whether or not the exemption invoked by the agency actually applies.

The effect of the binary nature of a court's review of agency exemption claims is exacerbated by expansive judicial interpretations of the scope of FOIA's exemptions. Whether it is classification,[49] trade secrets,[50] civil discovery privileges,[51] law enforcement records,[52] or financial regulations,[53] the trend within the courts has, by and large, been to expand the reach of FOIA's exemptions. Broad interpretations of exemptions have created precedent that makes obtaining access to comparable agency records difficult, if not impossible, even under more favorable factual scenarios.

A second factor inhibiting judicial review of agency FOIA determinations concerns the nature of FOIA litigation itself—specifically, the procedural and structural advantages that agencies enjoy over plaintiffs. In most FOIA lawsuits, after a requester has exhausted her administrative remedies, she files a complaint alleging that an agency has improperly withheld records. The agency then answers, denying that it has improperly denied access. The next step in a typical civil lawsuit would be discovery, but courts almost never permit discovery in FOIA disputes.[54] Instead, the agency simply moves for summary judgment on the basis of an affidavit from an agency employee stating that the records or portions thereof that have been withheld are properly exempt. Such affidavits are generally given great weight by judges, and absent some inherent contradiction or evidence of bad faith, they are frequently all an agency needs to prevail.[55] Indeed, even when an agency fails to meet its burden to justify its withholdings, courts frequently ask for a more detailed affidavit rather than rule against the agency.[56]

The FOIA plaintiff, on the other hand, typically has little information to bolster her case. As there has been no discovery, and as the plaintiff is unable to cross-examine the agency's declarant, the only information available to the plaintiff is that which the agency may have provided in support of its motion for summary judgment or in a *Vaughn* index (an index prepared by the government setting forth a brief description of the records and an explanation of why they are exempt)[57] or what can be found in the public domain. The plaintiff can request that the court conduct an in camera review of the records at issue, but such requests are frequently rejected.[58] A FOIA plaintiff may have a powerful explanation for why access to the records would serve the public interest, but such explanations are deemed legally worthless for the vast majority of exemptions; and even for Exemptions 6 and 7(C) discussed earlier, in which the public interest must be taken into consideration, courts have significantly diminished the importance of this principle. Faced with broadly interpreted exemptions applied without consideration of the public's interest in disclosure and with substantial deference to agency determinations, it is unsurprising that FOIA requesters have found little success in the courts.

BALANCING THE PUBLIC INTEREST

For those troubled by FOIA's trajectory over the past several decades, how might the "workable balance" that Congress sought to strike be more successfully achieved, to better serve the act's core purpose of promoting an informed electorate while, at the same time, preserving the government's ability to withhold information when secrecy is necessary? One means of doing so would be an amendment to FOIA requiring agencies and courts to balance the public's interest in disclosure against the agency's interest in secrecy when determining whether requested information falls within one of the act's exemptions. The idea of incorporating a balancing test into an information access regime is not new. The laws of many nations incorporate some species of public interest balancing, and in 2014 the Senate considered but ultimately rejected a proposed public interest balancing test for Exemption 5.[59] Under that proposal, the deliberative process privilege and attorney work-product privilege would have been subjected to a straightforward public interest balancing test, and the attorney-client privilege could be overridden by a "compelling public interest in disclosure."[60] As described in more detail below, the test we propose is broader in some ways and narrower in others than other nations' laws and the previously introduced FOIA proposal. It would apply to all existing discretionary exemptions, not by supplanting them but by providing a public interest "safety valve" so that records of particularly great importance to the public could not be shielded from disclosure.

INTERNATIONAL AND COMMON LAW EXAMPLES OF PUBLIC INTEREST BALANCING

Under the common law of England, a citizen had a right to inspect public records if she could show a specific interest in the records and a court, weighing that interest against the government's interest in secrecy, determined that the records should be disclosed.[61] This common law right was, by and large, transferred to the United States, although it has primarily been limited to the context of access to judicial records.[62] U.S. courts have also broadened the type of interests that can be weighed in such balancing to include the desire of citizens and the press to keep an eye on the activities of the government.[63]

In one state—New Jersey—the American common law balancing test has persisted with respect to access to executive branch records; individuals have a right to access such records under both the state's statutory Open Public Records Act (OPRA) and the common law.[64] That dual framework can (and does) produce different outcomes when applied to certain records, primarily because the common law test considers the public interest in their release, whereas OPRA does not. In one case, for example, a newspaper sued for access to financial records related to a complex public-private arrangement involving New Jersey's largest hospital, asserting rights of access under both the common law and New Jersey's statutory open records law. The trial court held that the records were properly exempt under the statute, but it found that access should be granted under the common law.[65] The appellate court affirmed that the records should be disclosed under the common law, finding that the purported harm from their disclosure was speculative on one hand, while on the other that there was a great public interest in ensuring that "public funds . . . are being spent wisely, efficiently and consistent with the Medical Center's mission."[66]

Many nation-states around the world have incorporated public interest overrides or balancing tests into their statutory information access laws, including Australia, Belgium, India, Ireland, Japan, Mexico, New Zealand, South Africa, and the United Kingdom.[67] Although there does not appear to be a comprehensive comparative analysis of the impact of these tests (which would be complicated by differences in the nature of the underlying laws, FOI cultures, and judicial systems[68]), what is fairly clear is that they have led to the disclosure of important records and are viewed as an important structural feature of FOI laws by the international community. The Council of Europe, for example, has provided a recommendation on minimum standards for FOI laws that requires records falling within an exemption to be disclosed if "there is an overriding public interest in disclosure."[69] The Aarhus Convention, which concerns access to information on environmental matters and has forty-seven signatories, also contains a requirement to consider the public interest before claiming material is exempt.[70]

The manner in which such an override is implemented in any one country can take different forms. Mexico's Transparency and Access to Government Information Law, for example, contains a fairly specific public interest override due to the nation's history.[71] This law does not permit information to be withheld when it concerns investigations of grave violations of fundamental rights or crimes against humanity.[72] The effectiveness of Mexico's public interest override was demonstrated in 2005 when a group of lawyers was granted access to hundreds of pages of the indictment of former President

Luis Echeverría, who had been charged with genocide in connection with the killing of at least twenty-five student protesters in 1971 by paramilitary groups with whom the president allegedly had been involved.[73] Mexico's public records ombudsperson, the Instituto Federal de Acceso a la Información, noted that the information fell squarely within the crimes against humanity override in the public records law. The disclosure was the first time that such an indictment of a high-level official had been released.[74]

The United Kingdom's Freedom of Information Act takes a different approach by separating its exemptions into two categories: absolute and qualified.[75] If records fall within an absolute exemption, such as that for the parliamentary privilege, they need not be released.[76] However, if a record is subject to a qualified exemption, then the public authority may only withhold the information if "in all the circumstances of the case, the public interest in maintaining the exemption outweighs the public interest in disclosing the information."[77] Thus public authorities engage in an all-things-considered balancing of the public interest with respect to most of the act's exemptions.

Tribunals in the United Kingdom have identified several factors that should be weighed in this balancing, including the public interest in a particular issue, the suspicion of government wrongdoing, the public's need for a full understanding of the reasons for public authorities' decisions, the likelihood and severity of prejudice to the interest identified in the exemption, the age of the information, the extent to which the information will advance public knowledge on a topic, and whether the information is already in the public domain.[78] There is no set weight to be accorded these factors. After they are considered in an individual case, if the public interest in disclosure is equal to or greater than the government's interest in secrecy, then the records must be released.[79]

PUBLIC INTEREST BALANCING AND FOIA

As noted above, two of FOIA's existing exemptions—Exemptions 6 and 7(C)—already incorporate a species of public interest balancing.[80] However, those two exemptions balance the public's interest in information against an *individual's* privacy interest—not the government's interest in secrecy. In cases interpreting these exemptions, courts have generally interpreted the privacy interests of individuals broadly and the public's interest narrowly, following a 1989 decision from the Supreme Court that determined disclosure of information merely held by the government about ordinary people does not serve the act's fundamental democratic function.[81] Subsequent cases have sanctioned categorical assertions of certain privacy interests, rejecting the need for a case-by-case assessment of the public's interest in particular information held by the government.[82]

The balancing test that we propose, however, is designed to squarely address the "core purpose" of FOIA by weighing the public's interest in knowing what the government "is up to"[83] against the government's interest in withholding that information. In crafting such a test for FOIA, the statutory information access laws of other nation-states may provide some useful direction, although we do not suggest that they be adopted wholesale. For example, as with the United Kingdom's law, it is useful to think of FOIA's exemptions as either absolute or qualified for purposes of applying public interest balancing. Exemption 3, for instance, incorporates other statutes that specifically *prohibit* the release of certain records and thus can be seen as mandating that such records be withheld in an absolute fashion.[84] Because the "balance" for Exemption 3 records has already been decided by Congress in favor of total secrecy, that exemption may be viewed as absolute and not subject to an additional weighing of the public interest on a case-by-case basis. Other FOIA exemptions that Congress has made discretionary, however, would be subject to mandatory public interest balancing. Unlike the United Kingdom's approach, however, in modifying FOIA we believe there should be no executive branch "veto" of a public interest override,[85] which would present separation of powers concerns in the U.S. context and has also led to important information being withheld from the British public.[86]

With respect to developing the contours of a public interest balancing test for FOIA's discretionary exemptions, a number of factors should be kept in mind. First, the exemptions that Congress included in FOIA, although perhaps interpreted by courts more broadly than intended, reflect a recognition that the categories of records they address implicate legitimately sensitive interests. That congressional determination is itself entitled to some weight, which could be taken into account by structuring a public interest balancing test so that it requires a showing of "substantial" or "significant" public interest to overcome a discretionary exemption, in contrast to the straight balancing of public and government interests that is performed under the common law. In addition, as discussed in more detail below, a weighted balancing test also may be important to avoid overburdening courts. No matter what form the test takes, however, it is imperative that it be applied on a case-by-case basis. If a public interest test is to function effectively as a safety valve when application of a discretionary exemption would deprive citizens of vital information about their government, neither agencies nor courts should be permitted to deny requests without considering the public's interest in access to the particular records at issue.

In terms of the nature of the "public interest" that should be taken into account, there is no particular historical concern in the United States that would counsel in favor of limiting public interest balancing to situations involving, for example, serious human rights violations, as Mexico has done. Instead, agencies and courts should weigh any and all factors that seem relevant to FOIA's presumed public of an informed, intelligent electorate. Congress could, of course, specify factors that should always be considered, which might include the importance of the records to the proper functioning of the democratic process, any suspicion of government wrongdoing, the age of the records, and the public's desire to understand the reasons for government action or inaction.

Some of these factors can already be found in FOIA and its jurisprudence, at least to some extent. For example, Congress recently placed a twenty-five-year sunset on the deliberative process privilege, one of the privileges incorporated in Exemption 5 that is designed to promote robust and frank discussion within government.[87] In limiting the scope of Exemption 5, Congress recognized both that the public has an interest in understanding the reasons for officials' decisions and that the government's interest in secrecy fades with time.[88] Courts also have recognized that the deliberative process privilege is not available when records relate to government misconduct because "shielding internal government deliberations in this context does not serve the public's interest in honest, effective government."[89] A "government malfeasance" exception also has been recognized by at least one court within the context of Exemption 8.[90] Requiring consideration of the public's interest under FOIA's other exemptions would build on these decisions and nurture FOIA's core purpose: ensuring that citizens know what their government is up to.

A public interest balancing test along these lines would help to remedy both substantive and procedural weaknesses in the act that have emerged during its first fifty years. Substantively, it would ensure that in cases of great public interest a requester would not face impossible odds because of the binary nature of FOIA's exemptions. Public interest balancing would not be expected to alter the outcome in every case or even most cases, but it would allow requesters to make an argument for disclosure when extraordinary information is at stake.

Procedurally, a public interest balancing test for discretionary exemptions would help to minimize the substantial disadvantages FOIA plaintiffs currently face in litigation. Instead of being limited to arguments based on publicly available information or inconsistencies in an agency's affidavit, requesters would be able to argue—and courts obligated to consider—the value to the public of the information being sought. Journalists, news organizations, academics, civil society groups, and other members of the public who submit FOIA requests are generally well-equipped to identify and explain to agencies and courts why release of the records they have requested is important. Indeed, in some cases, FOIA plaintiffs might even elect to concede that records fall within a discretionary exemption and place all of their weight behind a public interest argument. This could be especially powerful when the application of an exemption is technically correct but the agency's rationale for withholding the requested records seems weak, such as the application of the deliberative process privilege to a decades-old "draft" of a history of the Bay of Pigs invasion.[91] Instead of being forced to argue that a FOIA exemption should be interpreted narrowly—often in the face of precedent to the contrary—a FOIA plaintiff could simply argue that the public interest in access to the requested records is paramount, focusing the court's analysis on the core purpose of the act.

PUBLIC INTEREST BALANCING IN ACTION

The addition of a public interest balancing test for FOIA's discretionary exemptions would, in all likelihood, have the most visible impact at the litigation stage. Although requesters could make, and agencies would be required to consider, public interest arguments at the administrative level, the manner in which agencies have administered FOIA suggests that such a reform would be unlikely to cut back significantly on agencies' tendency toward secrecy. That being said, where the public interest in disclosure of existing records is indisputably strong, and the government's interest in withholding them weak or nonexistent, an agency faced with the prospect of losing a lawsuit could rationally be expected to release them. The addition of a public interest balancing test for FOIA's discretionary exemptions thus has the potential to increase the amount of important information released to the public at the administrative stage without the need for litigation, at least in very clear cases. Congress could even consider incorporating administrative adjudication of such balancing into the functionality of the Office of

Government Information Services, the FOIA ombudsperson for the federal government.

Whatever its expected effects on agency behavior, public interest balancing could substantially alter FOIA litigation in the courts for certain types of requesters. Consider how a public interest balancing test could have changed the outcome in a recent D.C. Circuit case that addressed whether a manual used by the Department of Justice called the "Blue Book" was required to be released.[92] The Blue Book was created by the Justice Department in response to the botched prosecution of Senator Ted Stevens as a means to educate prosecutors on, among other things, their obligations to disclose exculpatory material to a criminal defendant.[93] Despite the enormous public interest in ensuring prosecutors comply with the Constitution, the Justice Department did not make the Blue Book public and denied a FOIA request seeking it, citing Exemption 5 and the attorney work-product privilege.[94]

A three-judge panel of the D.C. Circuit upheld that denial, citing a line of FOIA cases that expansively interprets Exemption 5 and the work-product privilege, including *Schiller v. National Labor Relations Board*, a 1992 D.C. Circuit case.[95] However, Judge Sentelle, joined by Judge Edwards, filed a separate opinion stating that he believed the court's decision was correct based on precedent but disagreed with its application to the Blue Book. According to Judge Sentelle, applying that precedent

> to the case before us is inconsistent both with the statutory purpose of FOIA and the longstanding values of justice in the United States. . . . There is no area in which it is more important for the citizens to know what their government is up to than the activity of the Department of Justice in criminally investigating and prosecuting the people. The government certainly has the power to claim a FOIA exemption to hide its internal manuals describing how it goes about that awesome undertaking. But if it chooses to exercise that power, then the people might be forgiven for cynically asking 'what is it you have to hide?' . . . I hope that we shall, in spite of *Schiller*, someday see the day when the people can see the operations of their Department of Justice. In short, I join the judgment of the majority, not because I want to, but because I have to.[96]

Given the powerful "concurrence" by two members of the three-judge panel in this case, it is hard to imagine that it would not have been decided differently if Exemption 5 was subject to a public interest balancing test.

There are, to be sure, other upstream and downstream effects that could follow from requiring public interest balancing for FOIA's discretionary exemptions, such as potentially increasing the volume of FOIA litigation and therefore increasing the burden on an already overworked federal judiciary. It should be noted, however, that even without a public interest balancing test, FOIA litigation is increasing. In fiscal year 2016 alone, more than five hundred FOIA cases were initiated by plaintiffs around the country.[97] There also are reasons to think that the addition of a public interest balancing test, as outlined in this chapter, would not dramatically increase litigation or, even if it did, would only increase litigation by individuals and entities that support FOIA's core purpose. First, as noted above, there may be discretionary exemptions that the government would choose not to assert in the face of a public interest balancing test, making litigation in those cases unnecessary. Second, use of a weighted balancing test that requires a FOIA plaintiff to demonstrate that the public interest is substantial enough to overcome the interest underlying the discretionary exemption—not merely that the government interest in secrecy is outweighed under a straight balancing test—would likely dampen any surge in litigation. Third, even if FOIA litigation did increase, such an increase is likely to come from news organizations and civil society groups that are in a position to make powerful public interest arguments. Currently, a large portion of FOIA requests come from commercial requesters seeking a competitive advantage or profit.[98] That type of request does not lend itself to the public interest balancing test outlined above. Conversely, individuals and entities acting on behalf of the public at large *will* receive a boost to their litigation prospects, which could encourage cases that more closely align with FOIA's purpose.

Even if the number of FOIA cases remained the same, the addition of a public interest balancing test for FOIA's discretionary exemptions could still result in more work for the judiciary. A judge presiding over a FOIA case would be required not only to determine whether records fall within an exemption but also to engage in a balancing analysis. Given courts' history of deference to agency arguments discussed previously, it is certainly possible that courts faced with such a task will continue to defer to agencies when weighing public interest arguments. At the same time, such arguments generally do not involve an evaluation of highly technical issues or issues for which agencies have special expertise. Indeed, courts frequently engage in weighing the public interest in other contexts, including in cases involving access to judicial records.[99] And judges are, of course, also members of the public who read the newspaper and discuss important issues of the day with family and friends. Conducting a public interest balancing analysis thus, in some ways, requires fewer judicial resources than an in camera review and draws on knowledge and experience judges already have.

Finally, for its part, Congress could face pressure from agencies to increase the number of Exemption 3 statutes that would not be subject to the public interest balancing test applicable to discretionary exemptions. Agency employees might be concerned that with the ever-present possibility of a public interest override, there is little predictability or certainty as to what may be released, chilling communications and the creation of certain records. But this seems to us like a risk well worth taking. Ultimately, being a public employee necessarily entails some understanding that one's work is for the public and may become the subject of debate. If a category of records truly needs to be protected, agencies can always appeal to Congress; from a democratic perspective, it is far preferable for those debates to occur as part of the legislative process, where public pressure can be exerted and the merits of a proposal openly debated. This back and forth already regularly occurs when new Exemption 3 statutes are proposed.[100] If Congress determines that certain records should be off-limits under FOIA, it can constrain the reach of a public interest balancing text through additional statutory reforms.

* * *

The passage of FOIA in 1966 significantly enhanced citizens' ability to obtain information about their government, but decades of application of the act's exemptions have whittled away at its effectiveness and undermined its core purpose. The addition of a public interest balancing test for FOIA's discretionary exemptions would not be a panacea. It would, however, help align FOIA with emerging international best practices, reduce the agencies' structural advantage over journalists and advocates in FOIA litigation, and ensure that the act is an effective means for the public to seek access to important agency records for many years to come.

NOTES

1. U.S. Senate, *Freedom of Information Act Source Book: Legislative Materials, Cases, Articles*, Subcommittee on Administrative Practice and Procedure of the Committee on the Judiciary (Washington, D.C.: U.S. Government Printing Office, 1974), 26–27, http://perma.cc/TFV9-JYNC.

2. U.S. Senate, *Freedom of Information Act Source Book*, 38.

3. U.S. Senate, *Freedom of Information Act Source Book*, 24–27.

4. Barry Sullivan, "FOIA and the First Amendment: Representative Democracy and the People's Elusive 'Right to Know,'" *Maryland Law Review* 72 (2012): 1–84, at 64.

5. U.S. Senate, *Freedom of Information Act Source Book*, 33.

6. U.S. Senate, *Freedom of Information Act Source Book*, 27.

7. 5 U.S.C. § 552 (2012).

8. See *Freedom of Information Act and Amendments of 1974 (P. L. 93–502). Source Book: Legislative History, Texts, and Other Documents*, Joint Committee Report (Washington, D.C.: U.S. Government Printing Office, March 1975), 104–05, http://perma.cc/HAM4-Y8A9, showing 2,195 full or partial denials of 254,637 requests between July 1967 and July 1971.

9. U.S. Department of Justice, "Data," www.foia.gov/data.html, showed 124,828 full or partial denials in FY 2008, 21.59 percent of the 578,172 requests processed that year.

10. U.S. Department of Justice, "Data," showed 322,579 full or partial denials in FY 2016, 42.46 percent of the 759,842 requests processed. It should be noted that the amount of information released in a partial denial/partial grant can, theoretically, include such extremes as only one word redacted or only one word released. Unfortunately, the government does not track or provide this information to the public. Considering only full denials as a percentage of all requests shows a more than eightfold increase since FOIA's inception, from 0.7 percent of all requests in 1971 to 1974, to 3.8 percent in FY 2008, to 5.7 percent in FY 2016.

11. Elec. Frontier Found. v. U.S. Dep't of Justice, 739 F.3d 1 (D.C. Cir. 2014).

12. Critical Mass Energy Project v. Nuclear Regulatory Comm'n, 975 F.2d 871 (D.C. Cir. 1992).

13. Prison Legal News v. Exec. Office for U.S. Attorneys, 628 F.3d 1243 (10th Cir. 2011).

14. Alan B. Morrison, "Balancing Access to Government-Controlled Information," *Journal of Law & Policy* 14 (2006): 115–136, at 119. It should be noted that amendments were made to FOIA in 2016 that, among other things, introduced a "foreseeable harm" test. FOIA Improvement Act of 2016, Pub. L. No 114-185, 130 Stat. 538. This test provides possible new avenues for challenging the assertion of exemptions, but it is too early to judge its import in either administrative or judicial proceedings. At this writing, only one judicial decision has addressed the new foreseeable harm standard. Ecological Rights Found. v. FEMA, No. 16-CV-05254-MEJ, 2017 WL 5972702 (N.D. Cal. Nov. 30, 2017).

15. Nat'l Ass'n of Criminal Def. Lawyers v. Dep't of Justice Exec. Office for United States Attorneys, 844 F.3d 246 (D.C. Cir. 2016) (Sentelle, J., dissenting).

16. U.S. Senate, *Freedom of Information Act Source Book*, 33.

17. U.S. Dep't of Justice v. Reporters Comm. for Freedom of Press, 489 U.S. 749, 780 (1989); SafeCard Servs., Inc. v. SEC, 926 F.2d 1197 (D.C. Cir. 1991).

18. U.S. Senate, *Freedom of Information Act Source Book*, 29.

19. U.S. Senate, *Freedom of Information Act Source Book*, 27–28.

20. U.S. Senate, *Freedom of Information Act Source Book*, 7.

21. U.S. Senate, *Freedom of Information Act Source Book*, 12.

22. 5 U.S.C. § 552(b).

23. U.S. Senate, *Freedom of Information Act Source Book*, 2.

24. U.S. Senate, *Freedom of Information Act Source Book*, 27.

25. See, for example., U.S. House of Representative Committee on Oversight and Government Reform, *FOIA Is Broken: A Report* (Washington, D.C.: Government Printing Office, January 2016), iii, http://perma.cc/2VST-DM6C; Ray v. Turner, 587 F.2d 1187, 1209 (D.C. Cir. 1978) (Wright, C.J., concurring); "CIA Successfully Conceals Bay of Pigs History," National Security Archive, May 21, 2014, http://perma.cc/SLF7-E64Z; Luke O'Neil, "Why Is the DEA Not Cooperating with This FOIA Request?" *Esquire*, December 2, 2015, http://perma .cc/3ABS-EKZ6; Gary Pruitt, "Government Undermining 'Right to Know' Laws," *Associated Press*, March 13, 2015, http://perma.cc/EV8S-LARH; "Justice Department Censors Nazi-Hunting History," National Security Archive, November 24, 2010, http://perma.cc/84ZY-T3ME.

26. See, for example, Dave Philipps, "Generals Sought More Positive Coverage on Head Injuries, Document Shows," *New York Times*, September 29, 2015, https:// nyti.ms/2m3MsGg.

27. United States Department of Justice, "Referrals, Consultations, and Coordination: Procedures for Processing Records When Another Agency or Entity Has an Interest in Them," August 15, 2014, http://perma.cc/4CZG-JBAZ.

28. "Delayed, Denied, Dismissed: Failures on the FOIA Front," *ProPublica*, July 21, 2016, http://perma.cc/GB52-EAD6.

29. See U.S. Department of Justice, "Data."

30. U.S. House of Representative Committee on Oversight and Government Reform, *FOIA Is Broken: A Report*.

31. U.S. House of Representative Committee on Oversight and Government Reform, *FOIA Is Broken: A Report*, 3.

32. "USCIS FOIA Manual," MuckRock, https://cdn.muckrock.com/foia_files/12-4-13 _MR6938_RES.pdf., archived at http://perma.cc/3S53-26MR.

33. 5 U.S.C. § 552(b)(7)(C).

34. 5 U.S.C. §§ 552(b)(7)(C), (b)(6).

35. 5 U.S.C. § 552(b)(6).

36. "USCIS FOIA Manual," 34.

37. See, for example, https://www.data.gov.

38. "U.S. Hourly Precipitation Data," data.gov, https://catalog.data.gov/dataset/u-s -hourly-precipitation-data.

39. "Farm Program Payments," data.gov, https://catalog.data.gov/dataset/farm-programs -payments.

40. Charlie Savage, "Court Releases Large Parts of Memo Approving Killing of American in Yemen," *New York Times*, June 23, 2014, https://nyti.ms/2k5kDgj.

41. U.S. Senate, *Freedom of Information Act Source Book*, 30.

42. 5 U.S.C. § 552(a)(4)(B).

43. See Margaret B. Kwoka, "Deferring to Secrecy," *Boston College Law Review* 54 (2013): 185–242, at 188.

44. Paul R. Verkuil, "An Outcomes Analysis of Scope of Review Standards," *William & Mary Law Review* 44 (2002): 678–735, at 718.

45. Kwoka, "Deferring to Secrecy," 185.

46. See Verkuil, "An Outcomes Analysis of Scope of Review Standards," 712–14.

47. FBI v. Abramson, 456 U.S. 615, 631 (1982).

48. Spurlock v. FBI, 69 F.3d 1010, 1018 (9th Cir. 1995).

49. See, for example, Larson v. Dep't of State, 565 F.3d 857 (D.C. Cir. 2009).

50. See, for example, Critical Mass Energy Project v. Nuclear Regulatory Comm'n, 975 F.2d 871 (D.C. Cir. 1992); Larson v. Dep't of State, 885 (Ginsburg, J. dissenting).

51. See, for example, Nat'l Sec. Archive v. CIA, 752 F.3d 460 (D.C. Cir. 2014); Elec. Frontier Found. v. U.S. Dep't of Justice, 739 F.3d 1 (D.C. Cir. 2014); Nat'l Ass'n of Criminal Def. Lawyers v. Dep't of Justice Exec. Office for United States Attorneys.

52. See, for example, U.S. Dep't of Justice v. Reporters Comm. for Freedom of Press; NLRB v. Robbins Tire & Rubber Co., 437 U.S. 214 (1978); Ctr. for Nat. Sec. Studies v. U.S. Dep't of Justice, 331 F.3d 918 (D.C. Cir. 2003).

53. See, for example, Consumers Union of U.S., Inc. v. Heimann, 589 F.2d 531 (D.C. Cir. 1978).

54. See, for example, Wheeler v. CIA, 271 F. Supp. 2d 132, 139 (D.D.C. 2003).

55. See Am. Civil Liberties Union v. U.S. Dep't of Def., 628 F.3d 612, 619 (D.C. Cir. 2011).

56. Kwoka, "Deferring to Secrecy," 232–34.

57. Vaughn v. Rosen, 484 F.2d 820 (D.C. Cir. 1973).

58. See, for example, Hayden v. NSA/Cent. Sec. Serv., 608 F.2d 1381, 1387 (D.C. Cir. 1979).

59. See S. Rep. No. 114-4, February 23, 2015, http://perma.cc/P83V-TA25.

60. S. 250, § 2, 113th Cong. (2014), http://perma.cc/3KM8-ECYF.
61. Joe Regalia, "The Common Law Right to Information," *Richmond Journal of Law and the Public Interest* 18 (2015): 89–132, at 94–95.
62. Nixon v. Warner Commc'ns, Inc., 435 U.S. 589, 598 (1978).
63. Nixon v. Warner Commc'ns, Inc., 597–98.
64. S. Jersey Pub. Co. v. New Jersey Expressway Auth., 124 N.J. 478, 489 (1991); Bergen Cty. Imp. Auth. v. N. Jersey Media Grp., Inc., 370 N.J. Super. 504, 516–17 (App. Div. 2004).
65. North Jersey Media Group, 370 N.J. Super., 509.
66. North Jersey Media Group, 370 N.J. Super., 522–23.
67. David Banisar, "Freedom of Information Around the World 2006," Privacy International, 2006, http://perma.cc/Q5ZH-JTEY: 42, 48, 85, 87, 95, 106, 113, 137, 155.
68. On the general difficulties of ranking access to information laws, see Sheila S. Coronel, "Measuring Openness: A Survey of Transparency Ratings and the Prospects for a Global Index," freedominfo.org, October 30, 2012, http://perma .cc/R5YC-LQ2E?type=image.
69. Council of Europe, "Recommendation Rec (2002) 2 of the Committee of Ministers to Member States on Access to Official Documents," Council of Europe Committee of Ministers, February 21, 2002, http://perma.cc/5WBQ -VT3R?type=image.
70. "Convention on Access to Information, Public Participation in Decision-Making and Access to Justice in Environmental Matters," United Nations, June 25, 1998, http://perma.cc/V82U-PHDH.
71. Juliet G. Pinto, "Transparency Policy Initiatives in Latin America: Understanding Policy Outcomes from an Institutional Perspective," *Communication Law and Policy* 14 (2009): 41–71.
72. "Federal Transparency and Access to Public Government Information Law," translated by Carlota McAllister, August 2004, http://perma.cc/VAX5-SVAG, Article 14.
73. Ginger Thompson, "Mexico Opens Files Related to '71 Killings," *New York Times*, February 13, 2005, https://nyti.ms/2nHtoyu.
74. Eric Heyer, "Latin American State Secrecy and Mexico's Transparency Law," *George Washington International Law Review* 38 (2006): 437–75.
75. Freedom of Information Act 2000, § 2, legsislation.gov.uk, November 30, 2000, http://perma.cc/SND8-K9W8.
76. "The Public Interest Test," Information Commissioner's Office, 2, http://perma .cc/2A56-R8HP.
77. Freedom of Information Act 2000, Part I, § 2(2)(b).
78. "The Public Interest Test," 8–26 (collecting and summarizing cases).

79. "The Public Interest Test," 5.

80. 5 U.S.C. §§ 552(b)(6), (b)(7)(C).

81. U.S. Dep't of Justice v. Reporters Comm. for Freedom of Press, 765.

82. See, for example, SafeCard Servs. v. SEC.

83. U.S. Dep't of Justice v. Reporters Comm. for Freedom of Press, 780.

84. 5 U.S.C. § 552(b)(3).

85. Freedom of Information Act 2000, § 53.

86. "Straw Vetoes Iraq Minutes Release," *BBC News*, February 25, 2009, http://perma.cc/38E5-FYQG; "Ministerial Veto on Disclosure of Cabinet Minutes Concerning Military Action Against Iraq," Information Commissioner's Office, June 10, 2009, http://perma.cc/M7TU-992Z.

87. See 5 U.S.C. § 552(b)(5); NLRB v. Sears, Roebuck & Co., 421 U.S. 132 (1975).

88. FOIA Improvement Act of 2016, Pub. L. No 114-185, 130 Stat. 538.

89. Nat'l Whistleblower Ctr. v. Dep't of Health & Human Servs., 903 F. Supp. 2d 59, 66 (D.D.C. 2012).

90. Pentagon Fed. Credit Union v. NCUA, 1996 U.S. Dist. LEXIS 22841 at *11 (E.D. VA, June 7, 1996).

91. Nat'l Sec. Archive, 752 F.3d 460.

92. Nat'l Ass'n of Criminal Def. Lawyers v. Dep't of Justice Exec. Office for United States Attorneys, 249.

93. Jimmy Hoover, "Defense Attys Press DC Circ. for Access to DOJ 'Blue Book,' " *Law 360*, January 14, 2016, http://perma.cc/J5WC-5FG6.

94. Nat'l Ass'n of Criminal Def. Lawyers v. Dep't of Justice Exec. Office for United States Attorneys, 249.

95. Nat'l Ass'n of Criminal Def. Lawyers v. Dep't of Justice Exec. Office for United States Attorneys, at 249–58 (citing, *inter alia*, Schiller v. NLRB, 964 F.2d 1205 (D.C. Cir. 1992)).

96. Nat'l Ass'n of Criminal Def. Lawyers v. Dep't of Justice Exec. Office for United States Attorneys, at 258–60 (Sentelle, J., concurring) (citations and quotations omitted).

97. "FOIA Lawsuits," The FOIA Project, http://foiaproject.org/lawsuit.

98. See Margaret B. Kwoka, "FOIA, Inc.," *Duke Law Journal* 65 (2016): 1361–1437, at 1379–1426.

99. See, for example, United States v. Hubbard, 650 F.2d 293 (D.C. Cir. 1980).

100. See Elizabeth Hempowicz, "NDAA Conferees Drop Harmful Secrecy Language from Final Bill," Project on Government Oversight, November 30, 2016, www.pogo.org/blog/2016/11/ndaa-conferees-drop-secrecy-language.html.

PART FOUR

COMPARATIVE PERSPECTIVES

12

THE GLOBAL INFLUENCE OF THE UNITED STATES ON FREEDOM OF INFORMATION

Kyu Ho Youm and Toby Mendel

THE FREEDOM OF INFORMATION ACT (FOIA) has been called a "leading legal export" of the United States to the rest of the world.[1] But this is increasingly being challenged as more myth than reality. Although there is some evidence that the U.S. FOIA provided a degree of global inspiration for the very idea of adopting an access to information or right to information (RTI) law, it is less clear to what extent other countries actually followed the substantive approach of FOIA in their own reforms.

Consider, by way of analogy, the much-discussed finding that the global impact of the U.S. Constitution has been declining in recent years.[2] In explaining the decreasing acceptance of the U.S. Constitution as a model abroad, American legal scholars David Law and Mila Versteeg offer five hypotheses, including "the advent of a superior or more attractive competitor."[3] In this connection, we should ask if the U.S. FOIA is similarly losing influence abroad. Indeed, even the initial assumption that the U.S. FOIA did provide a key template for the laws of other countries needs to be assessed critically.

Some authors have suggested that the American experience with FOIA has served as a touchstone for what is needed to ensure "minimally effective" RTI laws.[4] For example, the 1980 Basic Press Act of South Korea included an information access clause that was presumably "copied" from FOIA,[5] and the New Zealand Official Information Act of 1982 has been described as having been shaped in part by the U.S. FOIA.[6] In recent years, however, the U.S. FOIA has been criticized for various weaknesses, such as its limitation in coverage to "agencies" of the executive branch. When compared with the seemingly superior *modern* Swedish law, FOIA has a number of disadvantages, including a lack of constitutional support, lengthier processing times, and higher costs.7

Scholars have found that the U.S. FOIA, not the Swedish law, has been most influential as a source of inspiration for RTI reform—so much so that some authors have suggested that "the U.S. system is the one normally taken as a model for contemporary FOI laws."8 But what inspiration did other countries actually use when designing the substance of their laws? Even if the United States, as a powerful nation, was well positioned to promote the idea of adopting RTI laws, did other countries embrace FOIA's specific features? In this chapter, we seek to shed light on these questions, focusing mainly on the extent to which FOIA has or has not been copied in substantive legal terms rather than on how or why the basic FOI model spread.

To date, although numerous comparative and country-specific analyses have been produced,9 they contain little reference to whether foreign laws borrowed from the U.S. law in its particulars. We seek to fill this gap in the literature, relying on empirical evidence to assess the extent to which the U.S. FOIA has been influential abroad as a specific legal model.

We approach this issue through the lens of the Right to Information (RTI) Rating.10 The RTI Rating, developed by the Centre for Law and Democracy (CLD) and Access Info Europe (AIE), allocates points to the legal framework for the right to information up to a possible maximum of 150 based on sixty-one individual indicators, grouped into seven higher-order categories: Right of Access, Scope, Requesting Procedures, Exceptions and Refusals, Appeals, Sanctions and Protections, and Promotional Measures. This chapter looks at how far other countries have followed the U.S. approach over a selection of key indicators from each category. This gives us an externally verified structure and avoids the trap of looking at these laws using FOIA as the starting point, which would naturally generate a skew in favor of the argument that the U.S. approach has been emulated by other countries.

Our analysis is limited to the content of laws, to the exclusion of practice, for two main reasons. First, studying the former is far more achievable. It is extremely difficult to assess practice even in relatively simple areas such as time limits, let alone, for example, how exceptions are used (or abused). Second, we do not believe practice is a robust metric for assessing legal borrowing. For example, strong rule-of-law countries could be expected to have better track records than weak ones in implementing their laws properly. Yet this has little or nothing to do with the extent to which the United States has served as a model in this area.

For reasons of practicality, not all of the world's 110-plus FOI regimes will be examined. Instead, we identify seven notable FOI countries from different regions of the world: Canada, Hungary, India, Mexico, Nigeria, South Korea, and Tunisia. The methodology, including the reasons for choosing these countries, is elaborated in the text, but factors include geographic distribution, the strength of the legislation, and variance in terms of performance (strength) on the RTI Rating. In addition to assessing the seven chosen laws against the U.S. FOIA, we offer some normative reflections on FOIA and the ways in which we believe it to be better or worse than other approaches.

DO OTHER NATIONS FOLLOW FOIA?

RTI is more widely recognized today than ever before.[11] Sweden was the first country to grant the public a legal right to access government documents. It was not until 1966, two hundred years after Sweden, that the U.S. Congress passed the federal FOIA, becoming the third country in the world (after Sweden and Finland) to do so. As Mendel observed in 2008, over the previous fifteen years there had been "a veritable revolution" in the RTI field:

> Whereas in 1990 only 13 countries had adopted national right to information laws, upwards of 70 such laws have now been adopted globally, and they are under active consideration in another 20–30 countries. . . . In 1990, the right to information was seen predominantly as an administrative governance reform whereas today it is increasingly being seen as a fundamental human right.[12]

As of March 2017, a total of 115 countries had enacted RTI laws.[13] The strength of these laws varies substantially, although their overall quality has been increasing over time.[14] Evidence also suggests that stronger RTI laws tend to be better implemented than weaker laws.[15]

In celebrating FOIA's fiftieth anniversary in 2016, the United States could be proud of being an early RTI adopter. It does not necessarily follow, however, that the U.S. law has served as a global standard. As Mendel has written: "As an early adopter, and a country that has introduced a significant number of amendments to its law, one might assume that the United States would be a leader in this area. According to the RTI Rating . . . , that assumption is wrong."[16] This section focuses on whether the U.S. FOIA has served as a global template and, if so, in what specific ways various countries have emulated it.

METHODOLOGY

We use the RTI Rating to provide guidance for our comparative assessment because, among other things, it is a recognized external reference point for this purpose. The indicators for the RTI Rating are drawn from international standards, and they are continually applied and assessed by researchers at CLD and AIE subject to local expert review.[17] The RTI Rating is a methodology for assessing the strength of the legal framework for RTI; it does not look at how any given law is implemented in practice. It is based on sixty-one separate indicators, grouped into seven overarching categories. Each indicator measures whether or not a certain characteristic is or is not present in the legal system as a whole, not just in one specific legal instrument. As an example, Indicator 4 asks whether everyone, or only citizens of the country, has a right to make a request for information.

The RTI Rating is used in two ways in this study. First, it provides guidance regarding the particular qualities or features of an RTI law on which we focus. Due to space constraints alone, it would not be possible to canvass all sixty-one indicators here. Furthermore, some indicators are less useful in terms of tracking reliance on the U.S. approach. For example, almost all access to information laws set a maximum time limit for responding to requests. Comparing the specific time limits in different laws does not necessarily provide much illumination of the extent to which borrowing might have taken place. In contrast, a requirement to provide assistance to requesters is not a necessary or logical requirement of an access law, so a trend in that area is more suggestive that borrowing has occurred. Based on considerations such as "contribution to making an RTI system effective" and "strong ability to track borrowing," we have focused on twenty key legal features, some of which straddle more than one RTI Rating indicator.

Second, the RTI Rating provides an initial indication of whether or not a legal feature is present in the United States and the seven comparison countries. Although the information from the rating is important and useful, in most cases the study goes beyond the rating to analyze the specific nature of the feature and whether, if it is present in the comparison countries, it appears to be drawn or extrapolated from the U.S. FOIA or to have other origins.

In terms of the choice of countries, the key consideration was to ensure broad geographic distribution. Beyond that, it was deemed important to focus on countries that have a strong rule-of-law tradition because this is integral to an assessment of true legal borrowing rather than mere symbolic posturing.[18]

It was also deemed important to avoid simply looking at best-practice countries on the RTI Rating because this might generate bias in the assessment. At the same time, it would not be very useful to review very low-scoring countries insofar as they have specifically opted to adopt weak laws (that is, laws not modeled on the U.S. FOIA). The relative rankings (in parentheses) and the overall scores of the seven focus countries in March 2017 are as follows, in descending order of rank: Mexico (1) 136,[19] India (4) 128, Tunisia (10) 120, Canada (48) 90, Nigeria (52) 88, Hungary (53) 87, and South Korea (60) 82.

Finally, we sought to look at laws adopted over a period of time, starting with the relatively early 1982 Canadian law, followed by Hungary (1991), South Korea (1996), Mexico (2002), India (2005), Tunisia (2011), and Nigeria (2011).

RESULTS

RIGHT OF ACCESS   The "Right of Access" category of the RTI Rating comprises three indicators, but for this analysis we focus on what we consider to be the most important one: Indicator 1. Is RTI recognized as a "fundamental" right in a country's constitutional system?[20] Strictly speaking, this is an issue that goes beyond the formal question of the extent to which the U.S. FOIA has served as a model given that FOIA is merely a statute. However, the question of constitutional recognition is fundamentally important in its own right. Furthermore, it affects the way we should understand the text of an RTI law inasmuch as constitutional recognition has consequential implications for the way the access to information law should be interpreted.[21] For example, constitutional recognition of RTI may have crucial implications for how courts and other decision makers address conflicts between an RTI law and other laws. If the RTI law is understood as giving effect to a constitutional right, lexical superiority will tend to flow from that, at least in certain cases.

In assessing this feature, it should be noted that there has been a significant shift in approaches to this issue since the U.S. FOIA was adopted, at which time almost no one recognized RTI as a fundamental human right. Today, dozens of constitutions recognize the right and, in addition, leading courts in many countries have read it into other constitutional guarantees, most commonly the right to freedom of expression.

The United States is increasingly an outlier in this regard. The U.S. Constitution does not explicitly recognize a right to access information held by public authorities. Furthermore, the U.S. Supreme Court has held that this right cannot be read into the First Amendment right to free speech or any other constitutional guarantee as a general matter.[22]

In contrast, all seven of the comparison countries have at least some constitutional recognition of the right to information. Three of the countries—Canada, India, and South Korea—are similar to the United States in that their constitutions do not textually recognize RTI as a constitutional right. However, the Canadian Supreme Court recognized RTI relatively recently as part of freedom of expression under the Canadian Charter of Rights and Freedoms, albeit limited to cases where access to information is needed for an expressive purpose.[23] As far back as 1982, the Supreme Court of India read a right to access government-held information into the right to freedom of expression under the Constitution.[24] Similarly, in South Korea the right to information was read into the constitutional guarantee of freedom of expression in 1989.[25] In the other focus countries—Hungary, Mexico, Nigeria, and Tunisia—RTI is explicitly provided for in the constitution.

SCOPE   Two issues are considered under this category: the scope of the RTI framework in terms of persons covered (who may make a request for information) and in terms of the public authorities covered.

In terms of persons, some RTI laws are limited to citizens, whereas more expansive laws do not distinguish between citizens and foreigners. Some laws also fail to cover legal persons. The U.S. FOIA is broad in scope here, covering every individual and also legal persons. Five of the focus countries—Hungary, South Korea, Mexico, Nigeria, and Tunisia—are similarly broad in scope. The two exceptions are Canada and India. Both countries' laws cover legal entities, but the former is limited to citizens and residents and the latter is restricted to citizens.

Understood as a human right, the right to information should cover all three branches of government, and, indeed, all state actors.[26] The U.S. FOIA is in this respect an outlier because it does not apply to the legislature or the courts. In terms of the executive branch, its coverage is relatively broad, although it does not cover the president or his or her staff.

From among the seven focus countries, only Canada follows the U.S. approach by excluding both the legislature and the courts. The other six countries cover both courts and the legislature. This may be, in part, due to the fact that these countries have more robust constitutional recognition of a right to information, which then naturally applies to all branches of government.

Five of the focus countries have broad coverage of the executive branch, although Canada and India do less well here. Canada excludes the cabinet and the prime minister's office as well as some autonomous federal agencies, and India excludes a range of security and intelligence bodies as well as some research and economic bodies.

The focus countries' laws generally provide for broad coverage of state-owned enterprises and statutory and oversight bodies, although Canada has some exclusions in both categories and South Korea does not cover all state-owned enterprises.

The U.S. FOIA does not extend to private bodies that receive significant funding or that perform public functions, a position that is replicated in the Canadian law. This is despite the fact that, as a law review commentator pointed out in 2013, "a slowly accelerating trend can be identified where more recent FOI laws recognize some partial aspects of the right to access corporate information."[27] Mexico, Nigeria, and Tunisia cover both categories of bodies, India and Hungary cover private bodies that perform public functions, and South Korea covers private bodies that receive significant public funding.

REQUESTING PROCEDURES   This category is a challenge in terms of assessing borrowing behavior by countries because many of the issues measured by the RTI Rating indicators are fairly technical. Nevertheless, four issues are compared here: (1) whether public authorities are required to provide assistance to requesters, (2) whether they are required to transfer requests to other public authorities when they themselves do not hold the information, (3) whether they are required to provide information in the format sought by the requester, and (4) what fees are charged for making and processing requests.

There are two different aspects to the assistance that might be needed by requesters. First, many requesters need help simply to formulate their requests properly. The United States, Hungary, Nigeria, and South Korea do not require that such assistance be provided, whereas Canada, India, Mexico, and Tunisia do.

Assistance also may be needed due to the fact that requesters are illiterate or disabled. In this case, the U.S. FOIA fails to place any obligation on public authorities. Five of the focus countries include specific obligations in their RTI laws to assist disabled or illiterate requesters, or both, but Hungary and South Korea do not.

The second issue considered here is whether there are statutory obligations or procedures for a public authority to follow if the request is misdirected to an authority that does not hold the requested information. Specifically, is the authority required to notify the requester that it does not possess the information in question and to refer the requester to another office or to transfer the request to where it knows the record is located? Neither of these obligations exists under the U.S. FOIA or the RTI laws of Hungary and South Korea. Only India and Tunisia score full points here. Canada, Mexico, and Nigeria score partial points because they impose an obligation to transfer but the grounds for transfer are broad—making it all too easy for authorities to transfer requests even, in some cases, when they do hold the information.

The United States requires public authorities to provide information in the format preferred by requesters. It shares this obligation with all of the focus countries except Nigeria and South Korea.

In terms of fees charged, in the United States, as in all of the focus countries except Canada and India, no fee is charged simply for filing a request for information. Canada and India charge nominal fees for filing a request.

In terms of other fees, there is an important difference between the United States and all of the other countries. The U.S. FOIA explicitly envisages fees for time spent on requests for information, including the time spent searching for the information and processing the request. Needless to say, these costs tend to be far greater than those associated with photocopying or mailing information. Canada recently abolished all fees for responding to information requests. In India, Hungary, Mexico, and Nigeria, the only charges are for the costs of duplicating and sending the information. The scope of what may be charged is not entirely clear in Tunisia and South Korea, although in practice fees for time spent are rarely, if ever, charged.

There is no need for fee waivers in Canada, given that there is only the filing fee, and in India and Mexico fee waivers are available for poorer requesters. Neither the United States nor the four other focus countries—Hungary, South Korea, Nigeria, and Tunisia—provide for fee waivers based on poverty.

EXCEPTIONS AND REFUSALS   The exceptions are a key part of any RTI law. As Professor Richard Peltz-Steele has observed: "An access law is only as strong as it is lacking in exemptions. Hortatory language about the value of government transparency, a powerful presumption of access, requester-favorable mechanical processes, and strong enforcement procedures are all meaningless if important classes of records are statutorily exempt from access."[28]

We examined four key standards relating to exceptions: (1) whether the RTI law overrides other inconsistent laws, (2) the primary approach toward how exceptions are elaborated, (3) whether the exceptions are substantively legitimate under international law (that is, whether they protect interests recognized under international law and are harm-tested in the sense that they apply only where disclosure of the information would pose a risk of harm to the protected interest), and (4) whether there is a public interest override for the exceptions.

Indicator 28 of the RTI Rating, one of "the more controversial standards,"[29] states that the "standards in the RTI Law trump restrictions on information disclosure (secrecy provisions) in other legislation to the extent of any conflict." This is not the case with the U.S. FOIA, which, instead, allows certain other laws to maintain disclosure restrictions that go beyond those in the FOIA, through its third exemption, although some qualifications are placed on its reach.[30] Furthermore, this is the only FOIA exemption that is not discretionary.

India, Mexico, and Nigeria all have rules in the RTI law that provide for it to override other laws in case of conflict. This is also the presumed position in Tunisia, although it is not stated as clearly as it might be in the law. A fifth focus country, Canada, takes an interesting position on this issue, allowing only those exceptions specifically listed in a schedule to the RTI law to continue to apply over and above the rules of that law. This means that the legislature must specifically approve those exceptions, which is very different from simply preserving all secrecy provisions. Hungary and South Korea fail to provide for any overriding effect of the RTI law.

In terms of the overall approach toward exceptions, the U.S. FOIA contains nine exemptions, one of which, as noted above, refers to other laws, and seven of which describe specific categories of information. However, the remaining (first) exemption authorizes nondisclosure in situations where a record has been classified, pursuant to an executive order issued by the president, on national security or foreign policy grounds. This effectively grants the president broad powers to determine the scope of this exemption.[31] All of the other countries set out standards for exceptions that do not depend on decisions by political figures.

Many specific types of exceptions—for example, to protect interests such as national security, trade secrets and confidential commercial information, personal privacy, and law enforcement—are found in most RTI laws. Indicator 29 of the RTI Rating sets out ten categories of exceptions that are deemed to be legitimate under international law.[32] The scoring under this indicator is unique inasmuch as it allocates 10 points to countries, and then deducts 1 point for each illegitimate or decidedly overbroad exception. Indicator 30 similarly allocates 4 points for harm testing, and then deducts 1 point for each exception that is not harm-tested.

The U.S. FOIA loses 3 points on each indicator for a score of 8 out of a possible total of 14 here.[33] The exemption for geological and geophysical information relating to wells loses 1 point because it fails to identify an interest that needs the protection of secrecy (and hence is not recognized as a legitimate exception under international standards), and other exemptions are too broad or not harm-tested or both (as with the first exception, noted above).

Canada has the dubious distinction of being the only focus country that has a combined score on these exceptions below that of the United States, scoring a mere 6 points. Hungary ties the United States, also with 8 points. The problematic exceptions in these countries are, however, different from those in the U.S. FOIA. The other five focus countries do significantly better than the United States, all scoring at least 38 percent higher on these indicators, starting with Mexico (13 points); South Korea, Nigeria, and Tunisia (all 12 points); and finally India (11 points).

What has commonly been termed the "public interest override" mandates that even if the disclosure of information would pose a risk of harm to a protected interest, that information should still be disclosed if the benefits of disclosure outweigh the harm.[34] The U.S. FOIA provides for what amounts to a kind of public interest override only for two exemptions and even then primarily focuses only on individual privacy as the overriding factor.[35]

Hungary does not have a public interest override at all, and Canada and South Korea both earn 1 point out of a possible total of 4, like the United States, also due to the limited applicability of their overrides. India and Tunisia provide for broadly applicable public interest overrides, earning full points. Nigeria loses 1 point for excluding one exception from the override, and Mexico similarly loses 1 point because the override is only applied at the appeals level.

APPEALS In this category, four issues are considered, all relating to independent administrative oversight of decisions by public authorities relating to requests. The first issue is whether the law provides for an independent administrative mechanism of appeal at all. Given that the other three issues are about the powers and nature of the appeals body, if the response to the first issue is in the negative, the same will necessarily apply to the responses to the other issues.

An independent administrative appeals procedure is vitally important because it can provide applicants with a much cheaper, more rapid, and more accessible review of refusals to disclose information than the courts provide. This is particularly true in developing countries in which only a small proportion of the population has any possibility of bringing a court case. In other words, an administrative appeal is often needed to ensure that the right to information does not depend on the discretion of the public authority, given that very few requesters will ever go to court simply to gain access to information.

The U.S. FOIA allows information requesters a right to request an internal review within the agency by appealing to the head of the agency, but it does not otherwise establish an independent administrative review procedure.[36] Nigeria also fails to provide for an independent administrative system of appeals for requesters who believe that their requests for information were not dealt with in accordance with the rules in the RTI law.

All six of the other focus countries have in place a system of administrative appeals. A key issue regarding these bodies is whether or not they are independent from government, given that their function is to review decisions that have been made by a public authority. The appeals bodies in South Korea and Hungary fail to meet even the basic standards of independence and are, instead, government-controlled bodies. The other four countries, in contrast, all score at least 5 points out of a possible total of 6 on the RTI Rating for independence.

To be effective, an RTI administrative appeal or oversight body also needs the powers both to investigate claims of a breach of the law and to issue appropriate remedial orders, such as an order to disclose the information requested. In Canada and India, the oversight bodies earn the full 4 points on the RTI Rating for these two categories of powers, and the four other countries — Hungary, South Korea, Mexico, and Tunisia — earn 3 out of 4 points, indicating reasonably extensive powers.

Finally, under this category, the issue of whether the decisions of the body are binding is considered. This is the case in five of the six countries with administrative oversight bodies, with Canada being the outlier.

However, the Canadian Information Commissioner has generally benefited from a strong rate of compliance with her decisions,[37] and the government has recently made a commitment to give the office binding order-making powers.

SANCTIONS AND PROTECTIONS Two issues are considered in this category: (1) the presence and nature of sanctions for those who willfully obstruct the right to information and (2) the presence of protections for those who, in good faith, release information pursuant to the law. The U.S. FOIA provides for a sanction against agency personnel for "improperly" withholding agency records.[38] A separate law prohibits the destruction of government records.[39]

Of the seven focus countries, five—Canada, India, Mexico, Nigeria, and Tunisia—impose sanctions on RTI violators in one way or another. Canada and Nigeria are limited to criminal sanctions, which experience in different countries shows are rarely, if ever, applied.[40] However, India, Mexico, and Tunisia all provide for administrative sanctions (fines and disciplinary measures). A controversial innovation in India is that the various information commissioners are given the power to impose fines. These fines, although small, can be applied on a daily basis, providing an ongoing motivation for compliance. The experience in India, in contrast to the criminal sanction countries, is that such measures have been applied fairly regularly.[41]

The second issue here, whether immunity from sanction or prosecution is provided to officials who discharge their duties under the RTI law in good faith, is reflected in the laws of only three countries: Canada, India, and Nigeria.

PROMOTIONAL MEASURES RTI laws need a number of measures to help promote proper implementation, which can broadly be grouped together as promotional measures. Overall, the U.S. FOIA does better in the promotional measures category of the RTI Rating than in any other category.[42] Here, three promotional measures are reviewed: (1) whether public authorities are required to appoint officials with dedicated responsibilities to implement the law, often called information officers; (2) whether there is a central body with responsibility for promoting implementation, including by raising public awareness; and (3) whether a system of reporting by individual public authorities, and then by a central authority, is in place.

The U.S. FOIA and the laws in six of the seven other countries, with the exception of Hungary, require each public authority to appoint officials with dedicated responsibilities regarding implementation of the RTI law.

In the United States, since 2007, the federal Office of Government Information Services has had both a general responsibility for promoting RTI and a mandate to raise public awareness about freedom of information, so the U.S. FOIA gets the full 4 points on the RTI Rating for these two indicators. Canada is the only country from among the focus countries that receives no points here; the information commissioner's mandate is specifically limited to deciding appeals, and the office is not given a legal role for undertaking promotional tasks or raising public awareness. In Nigeria, as well, this role is not clearly provided for, although the attorney general does have a general responsibility for ensuring that government offices comply with the RTI law. The other focus countries—Hungary, India, South Korea, Mexico, and Tunisia—all score at least 3 points on these indicators.

The United States has a robust system of reporting, with both individual public authorities and a central body reporting annually on what has been done to implement the law. The same is true in six of the focus countries, the exception being South Korea where no such system of reporting is in place.

A PRELIMINARY ANALYSIS

The methodology we have applied is simply a starting point, and more qualitative as well as quantitative research is needed to reach any firm conclusions regarding the extent to which the FOIA was followed worldwide. For example, it would be interesting to see how many of the features we assessed were included in the versions of the Swedish RTI law that predated the U.S. FOIA; this might suggest either that Sweden served as a model or that these features were more or less indispensable in any RTI law. That is to say, even if some of the features we assessed were not found in the early Swedish laws, they might be of such practical importance to the success of an RTI regime that their inclusion in different laws was more or less a foregone conclusion. More research is also needed to test the correlations we have noted against direct evidence of reliance or non-reliance on the U.S. FOIA as a model.

Looking at the twenty issues we assessed, and counting cases in which five or more countries followed the U.S. FOIA approach as examples of legal "borrowing," cases in which five or more countries did not follow FOIA as examples of "diverging," and cases in which the focus countries split three one way and four the other as "inconclusive," we obtain the following results:

Borrowing	5
Diverging	10
Inconclusive	5

Cases of divergence were thus twice as common as those of borrowing, although these results still suggest that a good number of features from the U.S. FOIA were carried through to subsequent laws.

A closer analysis, however, indicates that on a number of the more important issues there were significant innovations following the U.S. FOIA. For example, in terms of the key issue of the scope of public authorities covered, only the United States and Canada exclude both the courts and the legislature, whereas fully six of the focus countries cover both. Another key issue is exceptions, which define the scope of the law in terms of the information covered. There, three of the four issues were diverging and one inconclusive, suggesting a strong move away from positions taken in the U.S. FOIA. The presence or absence of an administrative oversight body is another key feature of a strong RTI law, and here, again, the four issues divided into three diverging and one inconclusive. Having a constitutional guarantee and providing for sanctions for obstruction of access—both again arguably critical issues—were also diverging. These issues reflect fully nine of the ten examples of divergence, with only the last one, transfer of requests, being less significant.

On the other hand, many of the examples of borrowing are arguably less important. All three of the issues from the RTI Rating category of promotional measures fall into the category of borrowing, representing three of the total of five such cases. These are arguably less significant than some of the features noted in the previous paragraph. Furthermore, on one of these issues, the U.S. FOIA rules were only adopted in 2007, which precludes any possibility of borrowing for all but two of the focus countries. The two other examples of borrowing were coverage of foreigners and the right of the requester to stipulate the format in which information is provided, again arguably less significant issues than the issues for which many of the examples were diverging.

SUMMARY AND CONCLUSIONS

The U.S. Freedom of Information Act has been described as one of America's "great creations," epitomizing the country's risk-taking conception of self-governance and accountability.[43] In theory and practice, Americans have enthusiastically embraced the once radical notion that government information belongs to the public. The United States was not the first to recognize the public's right to know, however, and it has become increasingly uncertain whether the country should be seen as an international leader or a laggard in the field.

There are reasonably strong indications that the very notion of RTI was significantly popularized by the 1966 adoption by the United States of FOIA, although it should be noted that by the end of 1990 there were only fourteen such laws globally and more serious pick-up of the idea only began in earnest around 1997. Beyond popularizing the general idea of a right to access information held by public authorities, the specific approach to RTI taken by the U.S. FOIA reflects the sociopolitical, economic, cultural, and legal values of American society. Among other things, it is reactive rather than proactive in facilitating access to government records. Other countries, in contrast, especially those that have adopted RTI laws more recently, have opted for greater emphasis on proactive publication in their laws.

Our research suggests that there are a number of objectively discernible similarities between the U.S. FOIA and RTI laws from countries around the world, adopted at different times and demonstrating different levels of strength as measured against international standards. We have not assessed the question of causality regarding these similarities, but it seems reasonable to posit that at least some of the similarities must have been due to borrowing from the FOIA model. At the same time, our research indicates that in relation to many of the more important features of RTI laws, as identified through the RTI Rating, cases of divergence from the U.S. FOIA are far more prominent than those of borrowing from it. These results disprove any notion that FOIA has been transplanted abroad in its totality, and they unsettle the often unquestioned assumption that it had at least a major impact on the design of foreign RTI laws. This is hardly surprising, but our results tend to confirm the view that significant innovation and development in RTI practice have been occurring outside the United States.

One of the more important developments noted in this study since adoption of the U.S. FOIA is the trend toward constitutional protection for RTI.

This parallels international developments, whereby RTI has been recognized by authoritative international sources as a human right. Another notable development has been the extension of RTI obligations to a much wider range of state actors than under the U.S. FOIA, including not only the executive but also the courts and the legislature, which also can be seen as reflecting the human rights nature of RTI given that human rights bind all state actors. In terms of exceptions, many of the newer laws, again in contrast to the U.S. FOIA, override other inconsistent laws, either fully or at least in part, and the scope of exceptions has been narrowed in many laws to focus on a smaller range of interests and to provide for harm tests and public interest overrides for most exceptions. Finally, an important innovation has been to provide for an administrative level of appeals, with protections for the independence of the appeals body and necessary powers for this body to undertake its oversight functions.

The world owes the United States a debt for its pioneering work in the area of RTI, most especially for promoting the foundational notion that individuals have a right to access information held by public authorities. The best way for the United States to call in that debt would now be for it to take advantage of the significant developmental work that other countries have done to improve its own law, so that the United States might once again claim to be a world leader in advancing the right to know.

NOTES

1. David E. Pozen, "Freedom of Information Beyond the Freedom of Information Act," *University of Pennsylvania Law Review* 165 (2017): 1097–1158, at 1106.
2. See generally David S. Law and Mila Versteeg, "The Declining Influence of the United States Constitution," *New York University Law Review* 87 (2012): 762–858.
3. Law and Versteeg, "The Declining Influence of the United States Constitution," 851.
4. Greg Michener, "FOI Laws Around the World," *Journal of Democracy* 22 (2011): 145–59, at 148.
5. Kyu Ho Youm, "The First Amendment and the South Korean Press," *International Communication Bulletin* 28 (1992): 6.
6. K. J. Keith, "Freedom of Information and International Law," in *Freedom of Expression and Freedom of Information: Essays in Honour of Sir David Williams*, ed. Jack Beatson and Yvonne Cripps (Oxford: Oxford University Press, 2000), 349–74, at 355–56.

7. Stephen Lamble, "United States FOI Laws Are a Poor Model for Statutes in Other Nations," Freedom of Information Review 106 (2003): 50–56, at 53.

8. John M. Ackerman and Irma E. Sandoval-Ballesteros, "The Global Explosion of Freedom of Information Laws," Administrative Law Review 55 (2006): 85–130, at 111.

9. See, for example, John M. Ackerman and Irma E. Sandoval-Ballesteros; "Asia Disclosed: A Review of the Right to Information Across Asia," ARTICLE 19, 2015, www.article19.org/data/files/medialibrary/38121/FINAL-Asia-Disclosed-full.pdf; Colin J. Bennett, "Understanding Ripple Effects: The Cross-National Adoption of Policy Instruments for Bureaucratic Accountability," Governance 10 (1997): 213–33; Jamie P. Horsley, "China's FOIA Turns Eight," freedominfo.org, April 28, 2016, http://bit.ly/1rlOtgk; Toby Mendel, Freedom of Information: A Comparative Legal Survey, 2nd ed. (Paris: UNESCO, 2008); Ann Florini, ed. The Right to Know: Transparency for an Open World (New York: Columbia University Press, 2007); Michener, "FOI Laws Around the World"; Prashant Sharma, Democracy and Transparency in the Indian State: The Making of the Right to Information Act (London: Routledge, 2015); Alasdair Roberts, "India's Right to Information Act: The First Four Years," freedominfo.org, January 13, 2010, http://bit.ly/2bOoKrH.

10. See "Global Right to Information Rating," www.RTI-Rating.org, accessed February 27, 2017. For a discussion of the RTI rating, see Toby Mendel, "The Fiftieth Anniversary of the Freedom of Information Act: How It Measures Up Against International Standards and Other Laws," Communication Law & Policy 21 (2016): 468–76.

11. For a comprehensive set of resources on freedom of information in international and foreign law, see "The Global Network of Freedom of Information Advocates," freedominfo.org, accessed December 19, 2016, http://www.freedominfo.org/resources; "Good Law and Practice," Right2Info, accessed December 19, 2016, http://right2info.org.

12. Mendel, Freedom of Information, 3.

13. See "Global Right to Information Rating: Country Data," accessed March 29, 2017, http://www.rti-rating.org/country-data.

14. The "Global Right to Information Rating" provides a comparison of the scores on the RTI Rating against date of adoption and clearly shows this correlation.

15. Daniel Berliner, "Transnational Advocacy and Domestic Law: International NGOs and the Design of Freedom of Information Laws" (unpublished manuscript, n.d.), 8, citing Gregory Michener, "Assessing Freedom of Information in Latin America a Decade Later: Illuminating a Transparency Causal Mechanism," Latin American Politics and Society 57 (2015): 77–99.

16. Mendel, "The Fiftieth Anniversary of the Freedom of Information Act," 466 (citations omitted).

17. Mendel, "The Fiftieth Anniversary of the Freedom of Information Act," 468–76.

18. Where countries do not respect the rule of law, they can pass and then simply ignore or get around laws. The true implications of the content of their laws are therefore far less significant.

19. The first number represents the position or rank of the country from among the 111 countries (for example, Mexico was in first position and India in fourth), and the second number represents the total score achieved by the country's legal framework out of the possible total of 150 points allocated through the RTI Rating (for example, the Mexican legal framework achieved a score of 136 points and India earned 128 points).

20. Conceptually, as a "fundamental" right, RTI parallels what Jan Oster of Leiden University notes in arguing that media freedom should be protected as a fundamental right: "Media freedom should not be made subject to legislation, that is, to the will of temporary political majorities which may impose their values on society. Rather, legislation itself has to be justified in light of media freedom." Jan Oster, Media Freedom as a Fundamental Right (Cambridge: Cambridge University Press, 2015), 52. Oster prefers "fundamental right" to "human right" because it expresses "more adequately" that media freedom applies not only to human beings but also to legal entities such as media companies. Oster, Media Freedom as a Fundamental Right, 52 n. 170.

21. As Pnina Lahav of Boston University has observed in a related context on the value of an explicit constitutional guarantee of a free press: "the judicial awareness of the liberal justifications of a free press and the acceptability of those justifications as part of the legal argument . . . may depend on and be encouraged by the *formal* constitutional commitment to press freedom." Pnina Lahav, "Conclusion: An Outline for a General Theory of Press Law in Democracy," in Press Law in Modern Democracies: A Comparative Study, ed. Pnina Lahav (New York: Longman, 1985), 343–44 (emphasis added).

22. See, for example, Houchins v. KQED, Inc., 438 U.S. 1, 15 (1978).

23. Ontario (Public Safety and Security) v. Criminal Lawyers' Association, [2010] S.C.R. 815.

24. S.P. Gupta v. President of India [1982] 2 S.C.R. 365.

25. "Forests Survey Inspection Request" case, Constitutional Court, 88 Honma 22, Sept. 4, 1989.

26. Mendel, "The Fiftieth Anniversary of the Freedom of Information Act," 478.

27. Roy Peled, "Occupy Information: The Case for Freedom of Corporate Information," Hastings Business Law Journal 9 (2013): 260–302, at 291 (citation omitted).

28. Richard J. Peltz-Steele, The Law of Access to Government (Durham, N.C.: Carolina Academic Press, 2012), 304.

29. Mendel, "The Fiftieth Anniversary of the Freedom of Information Act," 485.

30. "This section does not apply to matters that are . . . specifically exempted from disclosure by statute (other than section 552b of this title), provided that such statute (A) requires that the matters be withheld from the public in such a manner as to leave no discretion on the issue, or (B) establishes particular criteria for withholding or refers to particular types of matters to be withheld." 5 U.S.C. § 552(b)(3) (2012).

31. A requested record needs to be "in fact properly classified" under the relevant executive order to pass muster in a legal challenge, but this does not affect the power of the president to set the scope of what is secret under Exemption 1. Furthermore, as Pozen notes in his recent study: "Courts have consistently afforded agencies great deference when classified information is at issue. In most Exemption 1 cases, courts grant the government summary judgment without allowing discovery or performing in camera inspection of the requested records, making it 'virtually impossible for individual litigants to counter the opinions of agency personnel.' " Pozen, "Freedom of Information Beyond the Freedom of Information Act," 1118 (citations omitted).

32. See also "The Public's Right to Know: Principles on Freedom of Information Legislation," ARTICLE 19, June 1999, http://bit.ly/1lYHR4n.

33. Under Indicators 29 and 30, three U.S. FOIA exceptions (for internal personnel records, geological and geophysical information and data, and foreign intelligence records) are inconsistent with the international RTI standards due to their breadth and the absence of a harm test. In addition, the harm test does not apply to the exceptions for national security information, reports by agencies in charge of regulating and supervising financial institutions, or inter-agency or intra-agency memoranda or letters.

34. See "The Public's Right to Know," 6.

35. Katie Townsend and Adam A. Marshall, chapter 11, this volume.

36. 5 U.S.C. § 552(a)(6)(A)(i) (2012). The Office of Government Information Services, created in 2007 under the OPEN Government Act, provides coordination and mediation services relating to FOIA disputes between the information requesters and the federal government agencies. See "The Office of Government Information Services," accessed February 25, 2017, https://ogis.archives.gov.

37. For example, in Canada the target set for recommendations that are complied with is 95 percent. Office of the Information Commissioner of Canada, "Report on Plans and Priorities 2016–17," accessed March 5, 2017, www.ci-oic.gc.ca/eng/rpp-2016-2017.aspx.

38. 5 U.S.C. § 552(a)(4)(F) (2012). Describing this provision, the U.S. Department of Justice states: "Sanctions may be taken against individual agency employees who are found to have acted arbitrarily or capriciously in improperly withholding records. Additionally, the court must award attorney fees and other litigation costs against the government." "Sanctions for Violating FOIA," Office of the United States Attorneys, accessed March 27, 2017, http://bit.ly/2n9tXOp.

39. 44 U.S.C. § 3106 (2012).

40. See Thomas M. Susman, Ashwini Jayaratnam, David Snowden, and Michael Vasquez, "Enforcing the Public's Right to Government Information: Can Sanctions Against Officials for Nondisclosure Work?," SSRN eLibrary, December 2012, 1, http://dx.doi.org/10.2139/ssrn.2295466.

41. See Susman, Jayaratnam, Snowden, and Vasquez, "Enforcing the Public's Right to Government Information," 18.

42. Mendel, "The Fiftieth Anniversary of the Freedom of Information Act," 489.

43. Floyd Abrams, Friend of the Court: On the Front Lines with the First Amendment (New Haven, Conn.: Yale University Press, 2013), 214.

13

TRANSPARENCY AS LEVERAGE OR TRANSPARENCY AS MONITORING?

U.S. and Nordic Paradigms in Latin America

Gregory Michener

MOMENTOUS ANNIVERSARIES merit reflection, and in 2016 this proposition held not only for the U.S. Freedom of Information Act but also for the fabled Swedish 1766 Freedom of the Press Act, the world's first freedom of information (FOI) law. Although much is made of the two-hundred-year separation in birthdates, little attention has been devoted to the distance that separates U.S. and Nordic approaches to transparency. In this chapter, I argue that these two approaches, which I label the *transparency-as-leverage paradigm* and the *transparency-as-monitoring paradigm*, provide a framework for better understanding FOI regimes around the world, and I illustrate their relevance by analyzing FOI regimes in Latin America.

Whereas many equate the U.S. approach to transparency with *holding to account*—a demand-centered system in which businesses and citizens extract advantage (that is, leverage) from and over government or political adversaries—the approach to transparency in a country such as Finland places greater emphasis on proactive publishing as a means of widespread instrumental *monitoring*, both as a mechanism for participation and accommodation and as a means of deterring and detecting deviation from norms.

These two nuanced but different approaches stem from two archetypically different political systems, in which the relationship between the executive branch and political parties adheres to divergent logics.[1] Whereas *contestation* dominates in the United States' *majoritarian*, winner-takes-all system, *inclusiveness* constitutes a primary concern in Finland's *consensus* system.[2] The U.S. transparency-as-leverage paradigm implies a much stronger politicization of transparency than does the Finnish system, which leads to the adversarial style noted by authors throughout this book.[3] Although this might suggest that consensus systems are more open, the evidence on FOI regimes does not decisively bear out that conclusion.

Contestation in majoritarian systems may render governments more combative, but it can also lead to meaningful discoveries. Concerns for inclusiveness may promote information production and sharing in consensus systems, but these practices can foster illusions of information sufficiency that instill passivity. Certain specific political and institutional configurations, especially strong oversight mechanisms, may help mitigate some of the negative externalities associated with extreme variants of each of these paradigms.

The first section of this chapter fleshes out the contours of the transparency-as-leverage and transparency-as-monitoring paradigms, drawing on the examples of the United States and Finland. Then I examine these two paradigms at work in FOI laws across Latin America. After reviewing original data on FOI compliance across Latin America, I focus on the cases of Brazil and Mexico, regional exemplars of the transparency-as-monitoring and transparency-as-leverage paradigms, respectively. The final section reviews key lessons from Latin America.

TWO MODELS OF DEMOCRACY, TWO APPROACHES TO TRANSPARENCY

This volume is representative of the dominant scholarly concerns surrounding FOI. Authors assess and reassess the value of FOI (Hamilton, Kreimer, Kwoka, Lebovic, and Schauer) and evaluate how different types of transparency or FOI designs might improve disclosure (Fenster, Fink, Noveck, Sunstein, Townsend and Marshall, Youm and Mendel). This chapter moves up the ladder of abstraction to provide a cross-national and system-based perspective on why the U.S. transparency regime, which is the focus of most chapters, is viewed by some to be so troubling.

Within the context of any democratic political system, three key factors contribute to distinguishing the transparency-as-leverage and transparency-as-monitoring paradigms. First and most obvious is the *partisan composition of government cabinets*. In consensus political systems, multiple parties are represented in the cabinet, whereas majoritarian systems tend to have only one party represented. Second, each political system places different emphases on the *type of transparency*. In consensus systems, the focus of transparency will tend more toward proactive publication (active transparency), which facilitates inclusion and monitoring as a form of participation, accommodation, and intracoalitional scrutiny of policy and behavior. For countries with majoritarian systems, in contrast, the focus of transparency has tended toward request-based demands. The *political posture of key actors*—including leaders, partisan allies and opposition, the media, and advocates—represents the third key factor to be detailed throughout the coming pages.

A PRIMER ON THE IMPORTANCE OF CABINET COMPOSITION

The United States and Finland represent ideal-typical examples of the transparency-as-leverage and transparency-as-monitoring paradigms. Whereas the executive branch of the U.S. government is controlled by a single party (Republican or Democrat) during any given electoral cycle, executive administrations in Finland tend to be governed by a coalition averaging three parties.[4] In Finland, votes are fragmented among numerous parties in the legislature, which forces leaders to cement legislative support by forming multiparty coalitions and awarding cabinet portfolios to the parties making up the coalition. Ideally, portfolios are distributed proportionally based on the number of votes each party brings to the coalition. Majoritarian and consensus systems also tend to differ based on cabinet size. Cabinets in majoritarian systems such as the United States are comparatively small, hovering between fourteen and eighteen members; cabinets in consensus democracies tend to be larger,[5] principally because a higher number of parties need accommodation. Cabinets range from eighteen members in Finland to twenty-six in India and upward of thirty in Brazil.

How do these differences produce divergent approaches to transparency?

COORDINATION, INCLUSIVENESS, AND MONITORING

Concerns regarding coordination and inclusiveness are particularly salient in consensus systems. As Indridi Indridason and Shaun Bowler argue, "coalition cabinets must be concerned with coordination both across and within parties."[6] Large, diverse coalitions tend to generate acute policy coordination dilemmas whose principal remedy is the sharing and publicity of information. Thus well-functioning consensus governments tend to produce high levels of active transparency, or what Catharina Lindstedt and Daniel Naurin refer to as "non-agent controlled transparency."[7] As David Pozen[8] and others note, the U.S. system tends toward "agent controlled transparency," which requires more intensive use of FOI laws.

As for inclusion, consensus systems tend to go hand in hand with corporatist politics, in which the state governs in collaboration with organized interest groups—rather than over them or subject to them. Transparency resolves dilemmas of inclusion by serving as a deliberative and participatory mechanism.[9] Put in terms of the politics of consensus, information is as critical to consensus as consensus is to ensuring legislative support among a broad coalition of parties and sectoral interests. Among elites, information-sharing is an expected norm, even if this sharing is not always public.[10] This practice may explain why political elites in Finland apparently "do not need media publicity to discuss issues" and, therefore, "the media do not have a similarly visible role in governing in Finland like they do, for instance, in the US."[11]

Finally, consensus systems suffer from acute principal-agent dilemmas. Setting aside voters, members of a government cabinet in consensus systems must heed the directives of dual political masters: the chief executive on one hand and their party leaders on the other. In majoritarian systems, the chief executive and the party leader tend to be one and the same. But in coalition systems, chief executives and party leaders may not share the same policy preferences, which means that cabinet members must choose between pleasing one principal more than another; hence the need for intracoalitional monitoring.[12] The larger and more diverse a cabinet is—the more members it contains, the more parties that are represented, and the more ideologically distant the parties are from one another[13]—the more useful to leaders monitoring mechanisms become. Furthermore, monitoring is useful in consensus democracies because party politics "penetrates most levels of the administration."[14] In the United States and Canada, by contrast, municipal administrations tend to be relatively insulated from party politics.

Distrust, however, may originate from other dimensions of coalition politics. Cabinet positions may be distributed in a disproportionate fashion, creating resentment among underawarded parties and resulting in intracoalition infighting. Because resentful allies may be willing to "retaliate" through policy and administrative deviance, transparency can help leaders police governing pacts.

Contrast these dynamics to those of majoritarian political systems. Here, chief executives invest high levels of trust in cabinet members precisely because they belong to the same party. In effect, the tendency of leaders should be toward maximizing cabinet confidentiality to minimize the effects of publicizing incompetence, inefficiency, unpopular plans, disagreement, or maladministration, among other unsightly realities. This dynamic sets the stage for an adversarial system, whereby opposition interests and the press attempt to pry information from the party in power. They do so to obtain political leverage and to "save" institutions against the excesses of a partisan monopoly of government. The political opposition tends to be the driving force behind transparency in majoritarian systems, in contrast to what typically occurs in consensus democracies.

Another difference between majoritarian and consensus systems is the concept of inclusiveness, which is also much less of a concern in the United States.[15] Participation in the United States occurs not through accommodation but through competitive pluralism (interest group competition). The corollary is that, claiming a majoritarian mandate, leaders often will attempt to execute their agenda regardless of demands for inclusiveness, let alone transparency, especially when they wield majority control over Congress. In part, "mandate democracy" is what drives prevailing tendencies toward contestation and adversarialism, which in turn promote executive resistance to transparency. Within this context, the mainstream press may become a partisan of excluded interests and by extension of demands for transparency. It is thus of little wonder that the U.S. press has played an instrumental role in FOI advocacy.[16]

THE UNITED STATES AND FINLAND AS ARCHETYPES

Unsurprisingly, the United States has built and reformed its FOI law on the back of two-chamber majority oppositions, when a president from one party has faced a Senate and House controlled by another:[17]

- In 1974, twin congressional opposition majorities overrode President Gerald Ford's veto, defending seminal FOIA reforms.
- In 1996, electronic FOIA amendments were approved subsequent to President Bill Clinton losing both the House and Senate in midterm elections.
- In 2007, following four years of majority government under President George W. Bush, the Democrats took back both houses and enacted the Open Government Act.
- And in 2016, the FOIA Improvement Act emerged under the administration of President Barack Obama shortly after the Democrats finally lost the Senate to Republicans.

This clear pattern should not be taken to suggest that bipartisanship has no place in improving FOIA; on the contrary, members of both parties have sponsored all major strengthening reforms. Yet bandwagoning on issues of symbolic political capital is a matter of prudence, and all parties have legislative entrepreneurs investing in the currency of openness.

This pattern likewise does not suggest that context plays no role. Transparency waxed rather than waned under President Jimmy Carter, who benefited from back-to-back unified governments (1977–1981) but also had a mandate to clean up politics after Watergate. Context also played a role following the 9/11 attacks. But the question here is whether the greatest FOIA rollback in U.S. history would have taken place had George W. Bush not benefited from four years of unified government (2003–2007). As many transparency scholars have noted and as Daniel Berliner has statistically inferred,[18] transparency does serve opposition parties—and even leaders at the end of their mandates—as a means of "binding" and even hamstringing competitors, an insurance mechanism to guard against administrative abuses and institutional capture.

The transparency-as-monitoring paradigm also encompasses concerns relating to abuses and capture, but less in the spirit of interparty competition and more in the sense of maintaining intracoalition harmony. Transparency is treated instrumentally, as a deterrent more aligned with the quiet surveillance of a "police patrol" than with the political opportunism implied by the pulling of a "fire alarm."[19] A coalition partner that strays from administrative norms or policy prerogatives threatens to damage the alliance's internal harmony and external legitimacy. For this reason, significant emphasis is placed on congressional scrutiny and "shadowing" ministers.[20] A practical example from Chile is the practice of the *cuoteo politico*, pairing ministers and vice ministers from different parties to prevent partisan "fiefdoms" from taking root.[21]

As the Brazilian example will illustrate, coalition parties often resist such "policing the bargain" arrangements. Therefore, for leaders to make good on transparency, they require strong consensus or, in its absence, formidable legislative control. They also need a powerful justifying narrative to adopt or strengthen FOI laws.[22] Finland's adoption of a new constitution in 1999, which included robust FOI rights (section 12[2]), provided just such a justifying narrative to enact a new FOI law the very same year.

In general, transparency is much less susceptible to open political disputation in countries in which consensus patterns of democracy prevail. Finland has a strong state and a strong civil society, and the government harbors a "longstanding tendency towards including civil society organizations, political opposition parties, and stakeholders in the policymaking process."[23] In contrast to majoritarian systems, consensus government often "blurs the traditional distinction between government and opposition."[24] Following the 2003

Finnish general election, for example, two historic adversaries, the Centre Party and the Social Democrats, formed a coalition with a third party, the Swedish People's Party.[25]

This spirit of consensual and moderate governance—reinforced by Finland's historically delicate geopolitical position[26]—extends to the media. As Inka Salovaara-Morring asserts, there is "a clear tendency within the political elite to try to maintain this sector [the media] within a sphere of national consensus, and the media have not done very much to challenge this consensus."[27] Notwithstanding an ostensibly staid news media, Finland ranks near the top of newspaper readership and freedom of expression rankings.[28]

A relatively depoliticized approach to transparency clearly has much to do with historical legacies and the embeddedness of transparency. Along with Sweden (of which it was then part), Finland not only enacted the world's first FOI measure but also has provided public access to government archives[29] since 1859, passed the world's first twentieth-century FOI law in 1951,[30] and is distinguished as the first country in the world to introduce electronic services into its administration.[31] As Finnish transparency scholar Tero Erkkilä astutely observes, many countries call freedom of information a civil right, which suggests a conflict of interest between the government and the general public; "in the Finnish context," Erkkilä asserts, FOI was "already understood in terms of democratic control and consensual governance."[32]

To some Nordic observers, the U.S. transparency-as-leverage paradigm seems no less than . . . foreign. This is exactly what one Swedish FOI expert, Jonas Nordin, confided after returning from a U.S. conference on FOI.[33] More specifically, Nordin expressed distressed perplexity at discussions regarding "response rates," "requester training," and the "adversarial nature of FOI." For Nordin and Erkkilä, FOI is more about routine and bureaucracy than about fire alarms and politics.

Given the routine nature of FOI in Finland, the lack of reliable statistics on the use of this country's law is not surprising. A report from 2010 divulged the improbable total of 500 requests,[34] but this number has been disavowed by Erkkilä.[35] According to Erkkilä, disclosure is so "standard" that "it is not even necessary to [invoke] your right." A large number of requests are undertaken and answered by telephone, going unrecorded.[36] In other words, most FOI requests are resolved by an informal norm rather than a formal procedure. As for appeals, approximately thirty to forty FOI cases go to court per year, and complaints about the law peaked shortly after Finland's new law took effect in 1999 (in 2002 there were seventy-eight complaints).[37]

As archetypes, the United States and Finland are ideal-types of the transparency-as-leverage and transparency-as-monitoring paradigms. The following section, on transparency and FOI in Latin America, examines how these paradigms travel to very different contexts.

TRANSPARENCY AS LEVERAGE AND MONITORING: FOI IN LATIN AMERICA

AN OVERVIEW OF FOI IN LATIN AMERICA

I have argued that the type of democracy—consensus or majoritarian—strongly influences different approaches to transparency. For most Latin American countries, however, such a distinction is often difficult to make. Over the last decade or so, countries such as Guatemala, Panama, Peru, and Colombia have alternately been governed by cabinets composed of one party or multiple parties. Fortunately, other countries are more reliable. Brazil and Mexico provide vivid examples, but as these cases will invoke comparison with other countries in Latin America, a preliminary overview of FOI regimes across the region is in order.

As of early 2017, all countries in Latin America except Bolivia, Costa Rica, and Venezuela had adopted FOI laws. Bolivia possesses a relatively ineffectual executive order on transparency and freedom of information. In contrast to other countries without FOI laws and indeed to the rest of Latin America, Costa Rica furnishes a strong de facto FOI right through administrative, constitutional, and jurisprudential means.[38]

Table 13.1 presents FOI laws across the region, dates of legislative approval, FOI constitutional provisions, institutions responsible for appeals or oversight, and scores on the Right to Information Rating (RTI Rating),[39] an evaluation created by international experts. The average Latin American RTI Rating is 91 points out of 150, which is 4 points above the global average.[40] The case studies that follow touch on other aspects of these indicators.

Table 13.2 presents the results of evaluations on government compliance with FOI laws undertaken across Latin America since 2003 by civil society organizations (CSOs), academics, and information commissioners or ombudspersons.[41] These evaluations measure both active transparency, or the extent to which agencies comply with obligations to post online information such as expenditures, personnel, and contact information, and passive transparency, or the extent to which agencies respond to FOI requests. Across Latin

TABLE 13.1 Freedom of Information in Latin America—De Jure Attributes

COUNTRY/LAW NO.*	DATE ENACTED	DE JURE STRENGTH RTI RATING (150 POINT MAXIMUM)	CONSTITUTIONAL PROVISIONS	SCOPE OF LAW	APPEAL BODY / OVERSIGHT
Argentina decree (1172/law 27275)	2003/2016	66/91	—	All branches	Courts/Recommending Commissioner
Bolivia decree 28168	2005	—	—	Executive	Ombudsman/Courts
Brazil (12.527)	2011	108	Art. 5: 14, 31	All branches	Comptroller General (CGU)/Courts
Colombia (52/1712)	1985/2014	85/102	Art. 23	All branches	Administrative Courts
Costa Rica (7202)†	—	—	Art. 30	—	Constitutional Court (4th Chamber)
Chile (20.2285)	2008	93	Art. 8	Executive	Binding Commissioner
Dominican Republic (200–04)	2004	59	—	All branches	Administrative Courts
Ecuador (24)	2004	73	Art. 91	All branches	Courts/Ombudsman
El Salvador (534)	2010	122	—	All branches	Binding Commissioner
Guatemala (57)	2008	94	Art. 30	All branches	Courts
Honduras (170)	2006	83	—	All branches	Binding Commissioner
Mexico (LFTAIPG)	2002	136	Art. 6	All branches	Binding Commissioner
Nicaragua (621)	2007	111	—	All branches	Courts/Recommending Commissioner
Panama (6)	2002/2013	74/100	Art. 44	All branches	Courts/Recommending Commissioner
Paraguay (5282)	2014	61	Art. 28	All branches	Courts
Peru (27444)	2002	93	Art. 2 (5)	All branches	Ombudsman
Venezuela	—	—	—	—	—
Uruguay (18.381)	2008	91	—	All branches	Courts/Recommending Commissioner

* Two measures, dates, or scores are listed when countries enacted new measures or their laws underwent substantial reforms.

America, 120 evaluations of FOI have been produced since 2003. Of these, 89 focus on central (or federal) levels of government, and 34 evaluations look additionally or exclusively at state and municipal levels. Results on FOI compliance show that of 12,454 requests sent to 4,634 agencies, about every other request obtains a response. Of the 4,948 agencies evaluated for compliance with active transparency, approximately 3 out of 5 are in compliance with FOI laws. Given the newness of most laws, these numbers should not be viewed as disheartening—overall, transparency is overcoming opacity in Latin America.

These evaluation results require more caveats than can be detailed in this chapter.[42] Yet dozens of interviews, reports from the Organization of American States' Rapporteurship on Freedom of Expression, and yearly qualitative accountings by the Regional Alliance for Freedom of Expression and Information, a transnational advocacy group,[43] provide appraisals that mostly confirm the numbers in table 13.2. Although it may be tempting to associate missing evaluations with a lack of civil society interest or FOI dysfunctionalities, some countries simply have not engaged in much formal evaluation. Such is the case of Uruguay, where the FOI regime is by all accounts relatively functional.[44]

TRANSPARENCY-AS-MONITORING PARADIGM: THE CASE OF BRAZIL

Three countries in Latin America stand out for their consensus forms of government—Brazil, Chile, and Uruguay. Among these Latin American consensus democracies and, indeed, among all coalition-based democracies, Brazil represents an extreme on several fronts. Brazil's Congress has the highest number of effective parties of any democratic nation. Its governments are typically formed by coalitions of a dozen or more parties, and cabinets may consist of six to eight parties, frequently exceeding thirty members. These large, diverse cabinets imply acute coordination, inclusion, and principal-agent dilemmas. Brazil therefore provides us with a particularly vivid illustration of the dynamics of the transparency-as-monitoring paradigm, transposed to a region still wrestling with legacies of authoritarianism and corruption.

Brazil's FOI law has now been in operation since 2012. From January 2013 to December 2016, the federal executive received 390,920 requests, averaging roughly 130,000 requests per year (about 0.65 requests per 1,000 citizens). Advocate and academic evaluations have shown a response rate of over 90 percent for the federal executive, although this metric says little about quality. The federal executive—Brazil's face to the world—is the least of the country's FOI worries, however; it is the remainder of the Brazilian state, particularly

TABLE 13.2 Evaluations* of De Facto Compliance with Freedom of Information in Latin America

	DATE LAW ENACTED	NUMBER OF EVALUATIONS SINCE ENACTMENT	ACTIVE (WEBSITE) TRANSPARENCY (NUMBER OF AGENCIES & % COMPLIANCE)	PASSIVE (REQUEST) TRANSPARENCY (NUMBER OF AGENCIES & REQUESTS & % COMPLIANCE)
Argentina	2016	3	—	—
Bolivia	2005	2	—	483 (1,650) / 47%
Brazil	2011	13	165 / 60%	1,870 (4,060) / 62%
Chile	2008	22	1,180 / 79%	—
Colombia	2014	3	—	—
Costa Rica	No law	No law	—	—
Dominican Republic	2004	6	220 / 64%	319 (556) / 44%
Ecuador	2004	5	113 / 26%	50 (70) / 71%
El Salvador	2011	12	356 / 76%	51 (33) / 58%
Guatemala	2008	2	41 / 54%	134 (185) / 30%
Honduras	2007	7	298 / 82%	26 (26) / 46%
Mexico	2002	17	1,714 / 76%	1,656 (5,826) / 77%
Nicaragua	2006	4	39 / 21%	45 (48) / 10%
Panama	2002/2013	1	—	—
Paraguay	2014	1	—	—
Peru	2013	17	603 / 58%	—
Uruguay	2008	3	219 / 44%	—
Venezuela	—	No law	—	—
Colombia	2014	3	—	—
Paraguay	2014	1	—	—
TOTALS		120	4,948 / 58%	4,634 (12,454) / 49%

*If the total number of institutions analyzed within a country's evaluations is not equal to or greater than 20, for either active or passive transparency, totals were excluded from the table.

Light gray cells demarcate observations under 100, whose representativeness should be questioned.

the public prosecutor (twenty-eight offices), the judiciary, and subnational governments that have demonstrated shaky implementation and compliance.[45]

PROACTIVE PUBLICATION In terms of transparency, proactive publication always has been Brazil's strong point. Less than a decade after Brazil's redemocratization and the promulgation of a new constitution in 1988, leaders began building an impressive array of transparency mechanisms, many of which I have described in greater detail elsewhere.[46] Brazil won international acclaim and awards for the participatory budgeting initiatives of municipal councils and for its online federal "transparency portal" featuring real-time expenditures.[47] Public disclosure is guaranteed constitutionally (FOI is affirmed in articles 5, 37, and 216) and serves as an integral part of Brazil's corporatist system of state-orchestrated[48] participation. Transparency mechanisms also were included in a fiscal responsibility law that arose in response to federal fiscal coordination problems.

Yet Brazil is no Finland, and as much as publicity and deliberative transparency facilitated a degree of policy coordination and inclusion, corruption and maladministration have strongly influenced concerns surrounding transparency.

CABINETS AND MOTIVATIONS FOR INSTRUMENTAL MONITORING Principal-agent and coordination dilemmas abound in the Brazilian political system. First, coalitions polarized by left-right ideological differences, such as those that supported the Workers' Party administrations (2002–2016),[49] are susceptible to conflict.[50] Second, coalitions have often lacked cohesion,[51] meaning that presidents distribute cabinet posts to coalition partners disproportionate to the votes these partners deliver in Congress. For example, in Dilma Rousseff's first term as president, the Workers' Party took 46 percent of cabinet posts (seventeen of thirty-seven), even though the party held only 27 percent of the coalition's seats in Congress.

Owing in no small part to resentments that give rise to intracoalition retaliations (denunciations, leaking), rebellions (legislative defections), and deviance (abuses of power), the Brazilian state is constantly buffeted by corruption and maladministration scandals.[52] The *Mensalão* and *Petrolão (Lava Jato)*[53] corruption scandals, for example, originated in denunciations by rancorous coalition partners and information gleaned from informants and transparency portals, respectively.

POLITICAL POSTURES OF KEY ACTORS   It is clear that first-mover support for FOI and other transparency mechanisms has come from leaders and their partisans rather than from the opposition or even coalition partners. As the passage of the FOI law under Workers' Party President Rousseff shows, coalition "allies" are the most probable resisters.[54] Not only did a senator from an allied coalition party, Fernando Collor of the Brazilian Labour Party, introduce weakening amendments to the government's bill, but a key Rousseff ally, President of the Senate José Sarney of the Brazilian Democratic Movement Party, refused to force a fast-track vote as per the president's stated desires.

This apparent disloyalty among coalition parties reflects not only intracoalition resentments but also a repudiation of the president's will to "police" her allies. To secure passage for the FOI law without weakening amendments, President Rousseff's strong legislative position likely proved essential, as did several "justifying narratives" that leveraged legal, international, and political rationales for enacting a FOI law. In the final analysis, approval of Brazil's FOI law was no simple matter, notwithstanding a clear need and several Inter-American Court decisions[55] mandating a law.

Nor was it simple in Chile or Uruguay, two other consensus democracies that enacted laws in the second half of 2008. In regional terms, Brazil, Chile, and Uruguay enacted FOI laws relatively late, especially considering their comparatively advanced levels of political development and, in the case of Brazil, its advanced active transparency initiatives (online portals).[56] One explanation is that leaders had to drag coalition allies toward the approval of FOI laws. A second explanation is the lack of pressure from the political opposition. Given Brazil's subpar FOI performance at the state and municipal level, a salient question is the extent to which leaders have failed to gain the upper hand over coalition allies to force implementation and compliance. One option is to "out" coalition resisters of transparency, but this may preclude leaders from commanding their loyalty in Congress. It also requires that the news media and citizens actually care, pay attention, and act with independence.

Brazil deviates from the Finnish model in the sense that chief executives in Brazil are the center of gravity within their political systems. In the Finnish paradigm, monitoring typically occurs in a horizontal manner—with chief executives monitoring coalition partners, and coalition partners monitoring chief executives. In Latin America, and particularly in Brazil, the deference to chief executives can mean failures in horizontal and vertical monitoring.[57]

For example, coalition partners ultimately let Rousseff lead the economy into its worst recession ever.[58]

In terms of advocacy, content analyses in Brazil, Uruguay, and, to a lesser extent, Chile make clear the comparatively minor role played by the news media in advocating FOI or projecting the demands of FOI activists. As in Finland, the news media of these countries have not traditionally questioned elite consensus. Content analyses[59] of the largest newspapers by circulation in each country confirm that news media agendas for FOI were weak at least *until* presidents declared their intentions to enact laws. For the year preceding a stated intention by presidents to pass a law, Brazil's *Folha de São Paulo* published an average of two news items per month referring to FOI. Chile's *El Mercurio* penned 3.6 news items, due largely to a precedent-setting Inter-American Court case on FOI decided against the government of Chile in September 2006. In other words, presidential commitments triggered news agendas for FOI; agendas did not originate in the news media due to endogenous concerns or pressure from opposition parties or activists (as in Mexico, to follow).

Much in the same vein as Finland, transparency in Brazil has not been the subject of opposition disputation or strong advocacy. Leaders have led the drive for transparency for practical rather than politicized reasons; the opposition has invested little in the issue; and the news media has publicized government commitments rather than driven them. In the following brief analysis of Mexico, these political postures are in many ways turned on their head.

MEXICO

Despite small setbacks and the grumbling of advocates, Mexico is undoubtedly the standard-bearer for commitments to FOI in Latin America and a reference point internationally. The Right to Information Rating places the country's FOI law at number 1 among close to 120 laws, and thanks to incremental and unprecedented reforms, its information commissioner at the National Institute for Transparency, Access to Information and Personal Data Protection (INAI) has effectively taken on the status of a fourth branch of government. Statistics on compliance also lend support to the comparative robustness of the Mexican FOI regime.

FOI AS CONTESTATION Reforms have exponentially augmented the scope and reach of the law over the years. The rights acquired through the 2002 law became national due to a 2007 constitutional reform (article 6). The difficulty of establishing "minimum standards" to guarantee FOI rights across the federation ultimately led to 2014 and 2015 constitutional reforms that established a General Law. The law brings political parties and trust funds into the orbit of FOI and gives the INAI jurisdiction over all states and branches of government. New general laws on archives and personal data have created an unprecedented National Transparency System, and requesters can use one unified portal to query any part of the federation on FOI or personal data.

The law has served as an important means of contesting government policy and practices, and transparency's emphasis has strongly fallen on the demand side. The key indicator here is the number of appeals.[60] The federal information commissioner dealt with 6,616 appeals in 2015 out of some 120,813 requests (1 in every 18 requests).[61] The number of requests per capita is comparatively large for a federal country (about 1 per 1,000 citizens)—more than Canada or the United States—and has grown at an average annual rate of approximately 12 percent since 2002. Compliance rates, based on seventeen evaluations and nearly 6,000 requests, are by far the highest in Latin America at 77 percent, as table 13.2 indicates. In the federal executive, at least, relative successes likely hinge on an information commissioner endowed with a US$48 million budget (2014) and 542 staff.[62]

THE POSTURES OF KEY ACTORS   What political dynamics are behind this extraordinary law? The 2002 law came about in what effectively amounted to a contest of one-upmanship: on one side, a small group of advocates wielding a model law,[63] supported by the country's three largest newspapers and endorsed by the principal opposition parties (PRI and PRD); on the other side, the minority government of PAN President Vicente Fox (2000–2006). Fox was in desperate need of the legitimacy enacting a law would afford; opposition parties sought to claim the FOI law for themselves and render Fox vulnerable in the process.

Since enactment, the law has grown stronger due to the constancy of political conditions: legislative majority oppositions and single-party minority presidents, both of whom court a markedly pro-FOI press. To give a sense of this press support, Mexico's largest paper of record, *Reforma*, published an average of thirteen news items per month on FOI during the year leading up to legislative approval of the FOI law. By amplifying the voice of experts and advocates, the Mexican press also has strengthened world-renowned organizations such as FUNDAR, academic evaluators such as CIDE,[64] and advocacy coalitions such as *México Informate*. These actors, in turn, have worked with the INAI and Congress (especially senators)[65] to strengthen transparency in Mexico.

A pro-transparency press and active civil society have served as an effective counterweight to executive pushback. Advocates reported resistance from within the president's office during the creation of the General Law, and subsequent resistance to the disclosure of information regarding national security (and alleged human rights abuses), mineral deposits, and state-owned enterprises.[66] Recent leaders are resisting accountability mechanisms, including the FOI law, more pervasively (Sandoval-Ballesteros, this volume).

As U.S. advocates are well aware, however, executive resistance is to be expected. A critical differentiating point between U.S. and Mexico FOI outcomes has to do with Mexico's switch from a U.S.-style winner-takes-all electoral system to a mixed electoral system[67] during the 1990s. Progressive electoral reforms have ushered in two consecutive decades in which no one party has been able to control Congress. They also have entrenched a three-bloc moderate party system, in which the median party[68] moderates polarization by alternately siding with the government or the opposition. Along with a supportive press and advocacy sector, this dynamic—moderate competition, minority governments, and one-party cabinets—appears to have done much to generate auspicious conditions for FOI.

One need only examine the persistent absence of minority governments in countries with single-party cabinets to see where FOI rights emerged weak, have crumbled, or were enacted late or not at all. Argentina is the crucial case. The country has experienced only three 2-year interludes to majority presidentialism since 1989 (1997–1999, 1999–2002, 2013–2015). Unsurprisingly, a full FOI law only emerged under minority president Mauricio Macri (2016–). Experience with presidential dominance of Congress finds equivalents in Bolivia since 2005, the Dominican Republic until 2016, Ecuador since 2008, Honduras, Nicaragua since 2007, Venezuela, and Paraguay. Unsurprisingly, these are among the most dysfunctional or weakest laws in the hemisphere. Although spirited advocates have eked out a measure of compliance in the Dominican Republic, its FOI law has the lowest RTI Rating in Latin America. It requires that applicants *justify* their requests.

Conversely, where conditions have resembled those of Mexico, outcomes show greater promise. El Salvador's FOI law ranks among the world's strongest (thanks in part to FOI evangelists from Mexico), and as table 13.2 suggests, evaluations exhibit hopeful results. In 2010, a majority of parties enacted a sweeping law shortly after the FMLN party (formerly the name of a revolutionary army) won the presidency in 2009. The sort of "insurance" motivations that drove opposition parties to support a law were also present in Guatemala and Nicaragua, where opposition majorities bound (one-party cabinet) minority presidents with strong FOI laws at the beginning of their terms.

CONCLUSION

The extent to which a country is governed by majoritarian (U.S.) or consensus (Finland) executive politics will shape general approaches to transparency, which I refer to as the transparency-as-leverage and the transparency-as-monitoring paradigms, respectively. My principal contribution here is to provide a framework for understanding different approaches toward transparency across the democratic world.

Many pathways lead to legal guarantees of transparency, although they differ significantly in form and substance. In terms of form, for instance, although the political opposition and news media tend to champion FOI in majoritarian countries, the support of these actors appears underwhelming in consensus democracies. In terms of substance, majoritarian systems tend to emphasize request-based transparency, whereas consensus systems are known for strong proactive publishing. Yet the extent to which these propositions hold across a broader population of cases obviously requires further study.

Brazil and Mexico provide strong support for the relevance of the transparency-as-leverage and transparency-as-monitoring paradigms, but they also show intermediary characteristics. The give-and-take of Mexico's minority legislatures and moderate party system has produced greater consensus and more temperate forms of contestation. In Brazil, meanwhile, suspicions and hostility among coalition partners have led to forms of contestation and adversarialism that may encourage coalition partners to resist sharing information.

Some basic lessons can be gleaned from key incongruences between the United States and Mexico and Finland and Brazil. Mexico's FOI regime has clearly avoided some of the U.S. FOIA's worst trappings, detailed throughout this volume. More moderate executive-legislative relations and minority governments may partly explain this. But in terms of de facto effectiveness, Occam's razor points to the role of Mexico's information commissioner. This institution now controls all final decisions over information handling and disclosure across all levels and branches of the Mexican state. The power of this institution—which finds its roots in a historic distrust of courts—explains the relatively efficient character of Mexico's FOI regime. It has provided a strong demonstration effect across the nation (and to other nations) as well as virtuous downstream administrative effects on compliance. The principal danger associated with this powerful institution, however, is political capture.

Oversight is key. As scholarship and reality suggest, effective oversight—including the ability to set and enforce administrative rules—reduces the negative externalities associated with excessive contestation and noncompliance. The case of Brazil leads to analogous conclusions. Where compliance is conspicuously weak, such as in many of Brazil's subnational governments, so too is oversight; where oversight is strong, such as at the federal level, transparency becomes less troubled.

NOTES

The author is grateful for the thoughtful comments of Octavio Amorim Neto and Tero Erkkilä on previous drafts.

1. This dichotomous division of democratic systems was most famously developed by Arend Lijphart, *Patterns of Democracy: Government Forms and Performance in Thirty-Six Countries*, 2nd ed. (New Haven, Conn.: Yale University Press, 2012). My focus in this chapter is solely on Lijphart's executive-parties dimension and not on the federal-unitary dimension.
2. "Contestation" and "inclusiveness" are two defining dimensions of democracy, as originally theorized by Robert Dahl, *Polyarchy: Participation and Opposition* (New Haven, Conn.: Yale University Press, 1971).
3. David Pozen highlights this aspect of the U.S. FOIA as particularly unproductive. David E. Pozen, "Freedom of Information Beyond the Freedom of Information Act," *University of Pennsylvania Law Review* 165 (2017): 1097–1158.
4. Tapio Raunio, "Polarized Pluralism in the Shadow of a Strong President," in *Delegation and Accountability in Parliamentary Democracies*, ed. Strøm Kaare, Wolfgang C. Müller, and Torbjörn Bergman (Oxford: Oxford University Press, 2006), 301–324, at 324.
5. Indridi H Indridason and Shaun Bowler, "Determinants of Cabinet Size," *European Journal of Political Research* 53 (2014): 381–403.
6. Indridason and Bowler, "Determinants of Cabinet Size," 383.
7. Catharina Lindstedt and Daniel Naurin, "Transparency Is Not Enough: Making Transparency Effective in Reducing Corruption," *International Political Science Review* 31 (2010): 301–22.
8. Pozen, "Freedom of Information Beyond the Freedom of Information Act."
9. Erna Ruijer, Stephan Grimmelikhuijsen, and Albert Meijer, "Open Data for Democracy: Developing a Theoretical Framework for Open Data Use," *Government Information Quarterly* 34 (2017): 45–52.

10. See Sartori's discussions of "visible" v. "invisible" politics. Giovanni Sartori, *Parties and Party Systems* (Essex: European Consortium for Political Research (ECPR) Press, 2005).

11. Juho Vesa, "Nordic Openness in Practice," *Nordicom Review* 36 (2006): 129–42, at 132.

12. For example, see Royce Carroll and Gary W. Cox, "Shadowing Ministers Monitoring Partners in Coalition Governments," *Comparative Political Studies* 45 (2012): 220–36.

13. On the importance of ideological heterogeneity as a mechanism that drives monitoring, see Carlos Pereira, Mariana Batista, Sérgio Praça, and Felix Lopez, "Watchdogs in Our Midst: How Presidents Monitor Coalitions in Brazil's Multiparty Presidential Regime," *Latin American Politics and Society* 59 (2017): 27–47.

14. Tapio Raunio and Matti Wiberg, "Polarized Pluralism in the Shadow of a Strong President," in *Delegation and Accountability in Parliamentary Democracies*, ed. Strøm Kaare, Wolfgang C. Müller, and Torbjörn Bergman (Oxford: Oxford University Press, 2006), 336.

15. Octavio Amorim Neto, "O Brasil, Lijphart e o modelo consensual de democracia," in *Legislativo Brasileiro Em Perspectiva Comparada*, ed. Inácio Magna and Lúcio Rennó (Belo Horizonte: Editora UFMG, 2009), 105–31, at 108.

16. Michael Schudson, *The Rise of the Right to Know: Politics and the Culture of Transparency, 1945–1975* (Cambridge, Mass.: Belknap Press, 2015), 129, 176–179; Sam Archibald, "The Early Years of the Freedom of Information Act: 1955 to 1974," *PS: Political Science and Politics* 26 (1993): 726–31.

17. From the passage of the FOIA until 2016 (fifty years), twenty-two years were spent under conditions of two-chamber majority oppositions.

18. Daniel Berliner, "The Political Origins of Transparency," *Journal of Politics* 76 (2014): 479–91; Daniel Berliner and Aaron Erlich, "Competing for Transparency: Political Competition and Institutional Reform in Mexican States," *American Political Science Review* 109 (2015): 110–28.

19. Matthew D. McCubbins and Thomas Schwartz, "Congressional Oversight Overlooked: Police Patrols Versus Fire Alarms," *American Journal of Political Science* 28 (1984): 165–79.

20. Royce Carroll and Gary W. Cox, "Shadowing Ministers Monitoring Partners in Coalition Governments," *Comparative Political Studies* 45 (2012): 220–36.

21. Ferraro, Agustín, "Friends in High Places: Congressional Influence on the Bureaucracy in Chile," *Latin American Politics and Society* 50 (2008): 101–29.

22. Gregory Michener, "How Cabinet Size and Legislative Control Shape the Strength of Transparency Laws," *Governance* 28 (2015): 77–94.

23. Norbert Gôtz and Carl Marklund, "Introduction," in *The Paradox of Openness: Transparency and Participation in Nordic Cultures of Consensus* (Leiden: Brill, 2014), 3.

24. Miko Mattila and Tapio Raunio, "Government Formation in the Nordic Countries: The Electoral Connection," *Scandinavian Political Studies* 25 (2002): 259–80, at 267.

25. David Arter, "Parliamentary Democracy in Scandinavia," *Parliamentary Affairs* 57 (2004): 581–600, at 583.

26. Finland's size and proximity to Russia have shaped the country's informational and political culture in many ways. See Inka Salovaara-Morring, "Mind the Gap? Press Freedom and Pluralism in Finland," in *Press Freedom and Pluralism in Europe*, ed. Andrea Czepek, Melanie Hellwig, and Eva Nowak (Chicago, Ill.: University of Chicago Press, 2009), 213–27.

27. Salovaara-Morring, "Mind the Gap? Press Freedom and Pluralism in Finland," 217.

28. Refer to the 2015 report, "Finland," Freedom of the Press, Freedom House, 2015, https://freedomhouse.org/report/freedom-press/2015/finland.

29. Anne Thurston, *Managing Records and Information for Transparent, Accountable, and Inclusive Governance in the Digital Environment: Lessons from Nordic Countries* (Washington, D.C.: World Bank, 2015).

30. The Laki yleisten asiakirjain julkisuudesta 9.2.1951/83 (Act on the Openness of Public Documents of 1951).

31. Darren C. Zook, "The Curious Case of Finland's Clean Politics," *Journal of Democracy* 20 (2009): 157–68.

32. Tero Erkkilä, *Government Transparency: Impacts and Unintended Consequences* (Houndmills, Basingstoke, UK: Palgrave Macmillan, 2012), 14.

33. Discussion by author with Jonas Nordin, December 2016.

34. Roger Vleugels, "Overview of All FOI Law Around the World," *Fringe Special*, 2010, www.right2info.org/resources/publications/laws-1/ati-laws_fringe-special _roger-vleugels_2011-oct.

35. Discussion by author with Tero Erkkilä, December 2016.

36. The Constitution Unit, "Finland: International Focus," Freedom of Information and Data Protection, 2017, www.ucl.ac.uk/constitution-unit/research/foi /countries/finland.

37. Erkkilä, *Government Transparency*, 12–14.

38. See Jorge Córdoba Ortega, "La legislación costarricense y el derecho de acceso a la información pública," 2009, www.archivonacional.go.cr/pdf/legislacion _cost_derecho_acceso_infor.pdf ; and Alejandro Delgado and Gerardo Bolaños, "Legislación y Mejores Prácticas sobre Acceso a la Información Pública," 2007, www.oas.org/dil/esp/acceso_a_la_informacion_mejores_practicas_respuestas _costa_rica.pdf.

39. http://www.rti-rating.org.

40. The standard deviation for Latin American laws is 20 points, and for all 111 laws on the RTI Rating it is 22.6 points.

41. The database of all evaluations, including links to individual reports, is available at www.transparencyevaluation.net, which is a joint research project of the Open Society Foundations and the Getulio Vargas Foundation (FGV).

42. For an overview, see Gregory Michener, "Assessing Freedom of Information in Latin America a Decade Later: Illuminating a Transparency Causal Mechanism," *Latin American Politics and Society* 57 (2015): 77–99.

43. The Regional Alliance for Freedom of Expression and Information (Alianza Regional) has been issuing annual copies of a report titled *Saber Más* (Know More) since 2009.

44. Fabrizio Scrollini Mendez, "Right to Information Arenas: Exploring the Right to Information in Chile, New Zealand and Uruguay" (PhD diss., London School of Economics and Political Science, September 2015).

45. Gregory Michener, Irene Niskier, and Evelyn Contreras, "From Opacity to Transparency? Evaluating Access to Information in Brazil Five Years Later," *Revista de Administração Pública* 47 (2018, forthcoming).

46. Michener, "How Cabinet Size and Legislative Control Shape the Strength of Transparency Laws."

47. Pedro Cavalcante and Marizaura Camões, "Do the Brazilian Innovations in Public Management Constitute a New Model?" *RAI Revista de Administração E Inovação* 14 (2017): 90–96.

48. Alketa Peci, Juliana Figale, and Filipe Sobral, "The 'Invasion' of Manufactured Civil Society: Government–Nonprofit Partnerships in a Brazilian State," *Public Administration and Development* 31 (2011): 377–89.

49. Cesar Zucco Jr., "Ideology or What? Legislative Behavior in Multiparty Presidential Settings," *Journal of Politics* 71 (2009): 1076–92.

50. Carlos Pereira, Frederico Bertholini, and Eric D. Raile, "All the President's Men and Women: Coalition Management Strategies and Governing Costs in a Multiparty Presidency," *Presidential Studies Quarterly* 46 (2016): 550–68.

51. Ocatavio Amorim Neto, "Presidential Cabinets, Electoral Cycles, and Coalition Discipline in Brazil," *Dados* 43 (2000): 479–519.

52. Manuel Balán, "Competition by Denunciation: The Political Dynamics of Corruption Scandals in Argentina and Chile," *Comparative Politics* 43 (2011): 459–78.

53. The Petrolão Scandal subsumes the "Car Wash Investigation" (*Lava Jato*). See Gregory Michener and Carlos Pereira, "A Great Leap Forward for Democracy and the Rule of Law? Brazil's Mensalão Trial," *Journal of Latin American Studies* 48 (2016): 477–507.

54. Michener, "How Cabinet Size and Legislative Control Shape the Strength of Transparency Laws."

55. See, for example, Reyes v. Chile, Inter-Am. Ct. H.R. (ser. C) No. 151 (Sept. 19, 2006).

56. Eight of the region's eighteen countries had already enacted laws by this time.

57. David Heald, "Varieties of Transparency," in *Transparency: The Key to Better Governance? Proceedings of the British Academy*, ed. Christopher Hood and David Heald (Oxford: Oxford University Press, 2006), 25–43.

58. Octavio Amorim Neto, "A Crise Política Brasileira de 2015–2016: Diagnóstico, Sequelas E Profilaxia," *Relações Internacionais* 52 (2016): 43–54.

59. Research assistants conducted content analyses for the entire year on newspaper websites and qualifying news items that mentioned or focused on FOI "as a legal right or legislation." Alternative ways of phrasing FOI were queried in the relevant language. Results have not yet been double-coded.

60. It is important to note that the institutional design of the law renders it easier for requesters to launch appeals than in other countries, which may account for the high number of appeals.

61. "Informes anuales de labores," INAI, accessed March 3, 2018, http://inicio.ifai .org.mx/SitePages/Informes-2016.aspx.

62. Organization of American States, *Annual Report of the Inter-American Commission on Human Rights 2014: Report of the Office of the Special Rapporteur for Freedom of Expression* (Washington. D.C.: OAS, 2011), 399–400.

63. Referred to as "the Grupo Oaxaca."

64. Mexico's leading public administration university.

65. "Alianza Regional para la Libertad de la Expresión e Información," *Saber Más VIIII: Una Década de Acceso a La Información En Las Américas* (2016), 109–11, accessed December 2016, www.alianzaregional.net/wp-content/uploads /INFORME_SABER_MAS_VIII_.pdf.

66. "Alianza Regional para la Libertad de la Expresión e Información," 104–11.

67. Referred to as Mixed-Member Majoritarian.

68. See, for example, Gabriel Negretto, "Minority Presidents and Types of Government in Latin America," *Latin American Politics and Society* 48 (2006): 63–92.

14

STRUCTURAL CORRUPTION AND THE DEMOCRATIC-EXPANSIVE MODEL OF TRANSPARENCY IN MEXICO

Irma Eréndira Sandoval-Ballesteros

MANY PEOPLE HOPED THAT the emergence of vigorous political competition over the last two decades in Mexico would have a transformative impact on the struggle against corruption and for transparency. But this has not been the case. Competition between political parties has not translated into better oversight or real accountability. An improved equilibrium between social interests and government institutions is still missing.

In this chapter, I explore the Mexican case to learn how to understand, define, and practice transparency in a way that prevents the "freezing" of democratization processes in the developing world. I argue that corruption and opacity can be satisfactorily addressed only in a broad, coordinated manner that takes into account both political-economic considerations and fundamental power disparities. Until this type of strategy is implemented, corruption will remain one of the key features of Mexican politics and society.

Only ten years ago, Mexico's emerging democracy was the poster child of transparency reform. In February of 2007, an important reform in the area of access to information gave constitutional backing to Mexico's 2002 freedom of information law and received unanimous support from all political parties. Its aim was to improve compliance with the law, bringing state and municipal governments up to federal standards. Since then, at least on paper, Mexico stands out as one of the best designed access to information regimes in the world. For instance, no fewer than three chapters in the present volume identify the Mexican regime as a global leader.[1]

Nevertheless, compliance has been highly problematic. It has been particularly difficult to open up the judiciary and the legislature to public scrutiny, and there is little evidence that access to information has actually transformed the authoritarian ways of exercising power in Mexico. Difficulties with implementation and compliance arose very early, calling into question the long-term impact of what is—on paper—an impressive law.

In the first part of this chapter, I summarize my proposed *structural approach* to corruption and a *democratic-expansive approach* to transparency. In the second part, I discuss the gap between Mexico's advanced legal transparency regime and the persistence of vast corruption. In the final section, I explore the linkages between privatization and corruption and the consequent need to extend oversight and transparency beyond the public sector.

A DEMOCRATIC-EXPANSIVE UNDERSTANDING OF TRANSPARENCY

Mexico's recent history suggests that the struggle to give transparency meaning ultimately depends just as much on political will and social mobilization as it does on legal reforms or technical formulas. I begin by outlining what I call a democratic-expansive vision of transparency—one that imagines transparency not as a brake on bureaucracy but as a means to genuinely expand democratic governance—and explaining why it must guide a new understanding of accountability in Mexico.

The typical approach to transparency reform proposes a basic dose of bureaucratic hygiene to improve internal control and perhaps also to establish a so-called culture of legality among citizens and public employees. This approach envisions opacity as largely a technical or administrative problem. It focuses on bureaucratic fixes rather than on the generation of tools and conditions through which citizens can defend their fundamental rights.

Armed with this bureaucratic perspective, large teams of experts and advisors in law, political science, and public administration travel throughout the world issuing reports and recommendations on how to improve access to information. Academics, commissioners, and other officials continually organize high-level forums, conferences, and costly meetings to analyze proposals and government responses. Some of them offer suggestions to improve the treatment of government information: facilitating electronic records requests, modernizing Internet procurement procedures, or decreasing the time it takes to respond to citizen inquiries, for example.

This work is not without value, but unfortunately it is not powerful enough to overcome the enormous resistance to transparency and accountability in Mexico and similar countries.[2] The problem these countries face is not merely technical but political and structural at its root. In principle, it is not in the immediate interest of top public servants, judges, and elected officials to reveal detailed information about many of their actions, decisions, budgets, and expenditures. Transparency can lead to scandal, and this type of public attention can inflict significant damage on political careers.

The tendency in Mexico has therefore been to defend transparency rhetorically, without following up with concrete steps to realize its transformative potential. Thus emerges what we might call a "public relations" approach, the other side of the coin of bureaucratic or technical myopia. The public relations approach is a *discursive facade* that uses the rhetoric of transparency to procure legitimacy and stability for governments[3] and trust for investors[4] in the face of growing demands for accountability on the part of citizens.

A satisfactory response to those demands requires a democratic-expansive understanding of transparency. This approach views transparency as a matter of political rights and citizenship rather than bureaucratic hygiene.[5] The principal goal of transparency, in this view, is to assist in a collective project of invigorating democracy and accountability. Civil society organizations play a critical role in this project: monitoring government compliance with access to information laws, ensuring that the transparency agenda is not co-opted by politicians or bureaucrats, and connecting transparency efforts to the concerns of the common citizen.[6]

Just as transparency needs to be understood in broader and more political terms, so too must corruption. For decades, the concept of corruption often has been reduced to a mere synonym for low-level public officials receiving bribes. Mexico's anticorruption efforts have focused on such bribes and related behaviors. They have largely disregarded "structural corruption," a specific form of social domination that is characterized by the misappropriation of resources and enabled by a pronounced inequality of power. Structural corruption encompasses both illegal acts and perfectly lawful but morally questionable acts. In general, it focuses less on the discrete pecuniary maneuvers of individual officials and more on the accumulation of power and privilege by illegitimate means. It sees corruption not only as a cause but also as a symptom of democratic failure.

If corruption is not just a question of low-level public servants filling their pockets at the expense of common citizens, then combating it will not principally be an issue of disciplining or reeducating rogue actors.[7] The real corruption problems lie, on one hand, in the capture of the state by powerful economic interests and, on the other hand, in the pyramidal structure of institutionalized rent-seeking in which bureaucrats are forced to extort citizens by orders of their superiors. Structural corruption also is reflected in what might be called, following Alvaro Delgado,[8] a "pact of impunity" between Mexico's two main political parties—the Revolutionary Institutional Party (PRI) and the right-wing National Action Party (PAN)—that has marked the transition to democracy in recent years. This informal agreement enabled the PAN to rule vast zones of the country while the PRI remained the dominant party throughout the transition period when PAN occupied the presidency. The most important effect of this arrangement is that it effectively insulated political and economic elites from society and allowed practices such as closed-door deals, money laundering, collusion between businesses and politicians, illicit finance in electoral processes, and opaque privatization to flourish. Real regime change never occurred.

In moving beyond the bribery model of corruption, a structural perspective on corruption also moves beyond the public sector. It worries about abuses of power and zones of opacity wherever they occur, including when private entities capture government regulators or when they take over functions normally reserved for government.[9] Following the same logic, the democratic-expansive approach to transparency that I advocate would extend disclosure and accountability controls normally reserved for the public sector into the private sphere.

THE DISCONNECT BETWEEN TRANSPARENCY AND CORRUPTION

There is a stark contrast between Mexico's highly developed transparency regime and its high levels of corruption. Whereas Mexico is consistently evaluated as having one of the most sophisticated legal frameworks for transparency in the world (table 14.1), its rankings on the international scoreboards for corruption are consistently poor.

Mexico's transparency law has particularly strong procedural guarantees.[10] For instance, it provides for total access when the requested information is necessary for investigating grave violations of human rights or crimes against humanity. This, in theory, establishes a blanket public interest override for all information related to critical issues such as political assassinations, the persecution of ethnic or political minorities, or government censorship of the press. In practice, there have been serious problems with the interpretation and implementation of this clause. Nevertheless, its mere existence was a major achievement for the pro-access community and distinguished Mexico

TABLE 14.1 Global Right to Information Rating

RANKING POSITION	COUNTRY	DATE	RIGHT OF ACCESS	SCOPE	REQUESTING PROCEDURES	EXCEPTIONS & REFUSALS	APPEALS	SANCTIONS & PROTECTIONS	PROMOTIONAL MEASURES	TOTAL
						COUNTRY DATA				
1	Mexico	2002	6	30	28	28	26	4	14	136
2	Serbia	2003	5	30	22	26	29	7	16	135
3	Sri Lanka	2016	5	28	26	23	29	4	16	131
4	Slovenia	2003	3	30	26	25	28	4	13	129
5	India	2005	5	25	25	26	29	5	13	128
6	Albania	1999	6	29	26	27	23	6	10	127
7	Croatia	2003	5	30	22	26	29	5	9	126
8	Liberia	2010	5	30	19	27	20	7	16	124
9	El Salvador	2011	6	30	24	22	23	1	16	122
10	Sierra Leone	2013	0	29	25	18	28	7	15	122
102	Uzbekistan	1997	3	25	10	13	7	1	0	59
103	Taiwan	2005	2	21	9	17	6	1	2	58
104	Kazakhstan	2015	1	26	21	1	7	0	1	57
105	Germany	2005	0	19	7	11	15	0	2	54
106	Jordan	2007	0	25	6	10	9	0	5	55
107	Iran	2009	0	23	5	10	3	2	7	50
108	Tajikistan	2002	4	8	17	16	2	0	2	49
109	Philippines	2016	5	13	17	4	4	1	2	46
110	Liechtenstein	1999	0	17	10	5	1	2	4	39
111	Austria	1987	2	14	8	2	4	2	0	32

Source: "Global Right to Information Rating," Centre for Law and Democracy, http://www.rti-rating.org/year-2017.

in the global context, although other nations have incorporated similar provisions in their access laws over the past decade.[11]

Another innovation is that the law requires every government office to set up a liaison office (*oficina de enlace*) to handle access to information requests and to respond to such requests within twenty working days. If the office fails to respond in time, the answer is automatically considered to be positive and the information must be handed over in the following ten working days. The existence of such an "*afirmativa ficta*" clause is crucial because it puts considerable pressure on government agencies to respond expeditiously to citizen requests.

This contrasts with the U.S. Freedom of Information Act (FOIA). A recent report by a congressional committee confirmed that "mute refusals" are common responses to access to information requests in the United States. This seriously undermines the effectiveness of one of the most developed freedom of information legal frameworks in the world.[12]

Furthermore, the agency in charge of enforcing transparency, Mexico's National Institute for Transparency, Access to Information and Personal Data Protection (INAI), stands out as a particularly powerful oversight organization. The INAI functions simultaneously as an administrative court in charge of reviewing the government's negative responses to information requests and as an ombudsperson responsible for strengthening the "culture of transparency" in both government and society.

The U.S. framework now includes a modest ombudsperson's office, but this Office of Government Information Services does not have the powers of an administrative court, and U.S. policy makers could learn from the Mexican example. For instance, the congressional report cited above suggests that, in general, U.S. government agencies do little to proactively sponsor a culture of transparency or to promote a friendly environment for users of FOIA. The United States also has no equivalent to the mandate included in Article 6 of the Mexican Constitution that dictates "maximum disclosure of public information" as the overriding principle in the interpretation and implementation of freedom of information guarantees.

Notwithstanding its admirable institutional design of transparency, Mexico remains one of the most corrupt countries in the world. In 2016, it received a failing score of 34 out of 100 on the Transparency International Corruption Perceptions Index, tied with Moldova, Sierra Leone, and Honduras (table 14.2).[13] Mexico is ranked at the same level as Laos, Azerbaijan, and Paraguay and at a lower level than Bolivia, Panama, Sri Lanka, Niger, Zambia, Rwanda, and

TABLE 14.2 Corruption Perception Index, 2016

RANK	COUNTRY	SCORE	RANK	COUNTRY	SCORE
1	Denmark	90	113	Vietnam	33
1	New Zealand	90	116	Mali	32
3	Finland	89	116	Pakistan	32
4	Sweden	88	116	Tanzania	32
5	Switzerland	86	116	Togo	32
6	Norway	85	120	Dominican Republic	31
7	Singapore	84	120	Ecuador	31
8	Netherlands	83	120	Malawi	31
9	Canada	82	123	Azerbaijan	30
10	Germany	81	123	Djibouti	30
10	Luxembourg	81	123	Honduras	30
10	United Kingdom	81	123	Laos	30
13	Australia	79	123	Mexico	30
14	Iceland	78	123	Moldova	30
15	Belgium	77	123	Paraguay	30
15	Hong Kong	77	123	Sierra Leone	30
17	Austria	75	131	Iran	29
18	United States	74	131	Kazakhstan	29
19	Ireland	73	131	Nepal	29
20	Japan	72	131	Russia	29
101	Gabon	35	131	Ukraine	29
101	Niger	35	136	Guatemala	28
101	Peru	35	136	Kyrgyzstan	28
101	Philippines	35	136	Lebanon	28
101	Thailand	35	136	Papua New Guinea	28
101	Timor-Leste	35	142	Guinea	27
101	Trinidad and Tobago	35	142	Mauritania	27
108	Algeria	34	142	Mozambique	27
108	Côte d'Ivoire	34	145	Bangladesh	26
108	Egypt	34	145	Cameroon	26
108	Ethiopia	34	145	Gambia	26
108	Guyana	34	145	Kenya	26
113	Armenia	33	145	Madagascar	26
113	Bolivia	33	145	Nicaragua	26

(continued)

TABLE 14.2 Corruption Perception Index, 2016 (*continued*)

RANK	COUNTRY	SCORE	RANK	COUNTRY	SCORE
151	Tajikistan	25	164	Angola	18
151	Uganda	25	164	Eritrea	18
153	Comoros	24	166	Iraq	17
154	Turkmenistan	22	166	Venezuela	17
154	Zimbabwe	22	168	Guinea-Bissau	16
156	Cambodia	21	169	Afghanistan	15
156	Democratic Republic of Congo	21	170	Libya	14
156	Uzbekistan	21	170	Sudan	14
159	Burundi	20	170	Yemen	14
159	Central African Republic	20	173	Syria	13
159	Chad	20	174	Korea (North)	12
159	Haiti	20	175	South Sudan	11
159	Republic of Congo	20	176	Somalia	10

Source: Transparency International, "Corruption Perception Index," 2016, www.transparency.org/cpi.

Trinidad and Tobago. Mexico is the most corrupt country in the OECD[14] and even more corrupt than most of the emerging powers, equally or more corrupt than monarchies and dictatorships, and just as corrupt as countries that in recent years have experienced wars, genocides, humanitarian crises, and famines.

The Siamese twin of corruption is *impunity*, and this may be the key to explaining the disconnect between transparency and corruption in the country. According to the Center for Studies on Impunity and Justice at the University of the Americas Puebla, Mexico ranks first on the 2017 "Global Impunity Index" out of all Latin American nations (figure 14.1).[15]

Mexico's transparency control bodies are hesitant to follow up and enforce their decisions, and often they do not apply any sanctions to public servants who have intentionally hidden or altered public information.[16] During the time that the Mexican FOIA has been in force, there have been only a few cases in which a public official has been sanctioned in any way for obstructing the law's implementation.[17] To be sure, sanctions against government officials for lackluster efforts to respond fully and promptly to requests for access to information are rare to nonexistent elsewhere in the world too. But in Mexico,

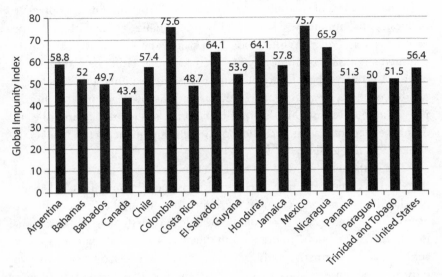

FIGURE 14.1 Global Impunity Index
Source: Center for Studies on Impunity and Justice at the University of the Americas, Puebla.

the absence of sanctions both reflects and contributes to a much larger pattern of impunity.

Under Mexico's new General Act of Transparency and Access to Public Information, the INAI has broad authority to initiate a "penalty procedure" and sanction officials who hide or alter public information. The law provides a long list of particular circumstances—at least fifteen instances—under which sanctions might apply, and it further provides that economic penalties may not be paid with public funds. As in other areas of Mexican life where impunity for wrongdoing is the norm, the problem is not the law itself but rather its enforcement.

In addition, instead of pushing for reforms that would expand and guarantee the effectiveness of transparency, President Enrique Peña Nieto has decided to roll back protections for accountability. For instance, the most recent reforms to the Mexican FOIA grant impunity to the executive in two ways. First, the legal advisor of the president has been given the authority to bring challenges to the Supreme Court of Justice against final resolutions taken by the INAI, at least when national security is at stake. Second, the law now includes a prohibition against bringing the president of the republic to justice for cases of corruption—effectively codifying the informal practice of presidential impunity. This is highly problematic, particularly after the case known as "Peña's White House," in which the president and his wife acquired a mansion built for them by Juan Armando Hinojosa Cantú, CEO of HIGA Group, a beneficiary of major contracts for public infrastructure.[18] More recently, a new corruption scandal has raised allegations that Brazilian construction giant Odebrecht paid about ten million dollars in bribes in exchange for contracts and that the money ended up financing President Peña Nieto's 2012 electoral run.[19]

Thus, although the Mexican FOIA has been cast as the cornerstone of the effort to achieve open and accountable public administration, it has not generated an honest government committed to the public interest. Public oversight may under certain conditions be able to keep those in power scrupulous in managing public resources. But the "first world" transparency regime achieved at the normative and institutional levels in Mexico has not, for the most part, empowered citizens to oversee the internal operation of government institutions.

For decades, the Mexican government has functioned as a sophisticated mechanism for consolidating economic and political privilege and defending the elite from the social and economic demands of popular groups inspired by the revolutionary agenda reflected in the Mexican Constitution. For more than seventy years, Mexico's authoritarian state-party regime ruled the country through the PRI. This regime came to an end in 2000, and a new political party, PAN, that supposedly was different both in ideology and social base took over and governed for twelve years. But the alternation in office of PRI and PAN did not transform the basic way power and authority are managed in Mexico. Opacity, corporatism, patronage, and capture—features that PAN systematically denounced when in opposition—were adopted by the party when it won power.

Indeed, in some respects, the situation has become even worse. For instance, as a result of the fragmentation of the monolithic state-party edifice, the governors of the thirty-one states and the mayor of Mexico City have increased their relative power over their respective territories. This entrenchment of federalism has not necessarily led to greater accountability or better service provision. Provincial governors in Mexico are infamous for their heavy-handed attempts to control politics, economics, and society. Previously they were at least held accountable by the president, but today they have more freedom to abuse their power. The weakened standing of the presidency has made some of these governors into the modern-day equivalent of feudal lords.[20]

Moreover, under the administration of President Peña Nieto, the freedoms of expression and protest have come under heavy fire. Marches are systematically repressed, social and political leaders are jailed or assassinated, and journalists are censored, forced out of their jobs, or murdered without an effective government response. On May 15, 2017, Mexican journalist Jesús Valdez, director and founder of the weekly newspaper *Ríodoce* and correspondent for the newspaper *La Jornada*, was murdered. He was one of the most renowned journalists in the country and spent much of his career reporting on organized crime, drug trafficking, and the collusion between crime and government (*narco-gobiernos*) and its impact on society.[21] His death brings the total number of journalists murdered in Mexico between 2000 and 2017 to 127.[22] More than thirty journalists have been assassinated during the Peña Nieto administration. In the first five months of 2017 alone, a handful of journalists were murdered and many more were attacked all over the country. In 2016, 99.75 percent of attacks against journalists went unpunished.

Mexico, in short, is the home of impunity. Freedom of expression and the right to access information are supposedly the oxygen of democracy. Both elements are fundamental rights, and both are being severely undermined by organized violence and other repressive forces that operate with effective insulation from, or even the acquiescence of, the state.

The traditional exclusion of society is even more prominent in the economic realm. In fact, transparency and accountability of financial and economic policies are two of the major challenges in contemporary Mexico. Financial authorities have systematically closed the door to access to information about these policies.

In other work, I have tried to demonstrate the opacity still predominant in the economic arena. For example, the large-scale corruption present in the 1994 bailout of Mexico's banking sector took place against a growing chorus of celebratory rhetoric about transparency in the country. Using the language of "banking secrets," the financial authorities held back investigations of extensive irregularities and kept the details of the bailout hidden.[23] Mexico's transparency laws have come a long way since 1994, but they continue to fall short with regard to economic, financial, and monetary issues—with likely negative effects not only on freedom of information but also on economic development.

Mexico is one of the most unequal countries on the planet. It is home to one of the richest men in the world, Carlos Slim, as well as to more than 65 million poor people.[24] Although Mexico is the fourteenth largest economy in the world and a member of the OECD, its scandalous 48.1 Gini Coefficient[25] reveals serious problems with the distribution of income.

In addition, government spending is still highly ineffective, and the civil service remains in its infancy.[26] Abuses of human rights are widespread,[27] and poverty and inequality have not significantly declined in recent years. In other words, neither transparency law nor regime change in Mexico seems to have led to a major modification in the way government does business. Even though some authors have described the transition to democracy as closely connected with broader liberalizing reforms, this has not been the case in Mexico. A large literature assumes a basic synergy between markets and democracies. Much of this literature pays little attention to the underlying power relations, which may tend to centralize processes of private sector decision making rather than stimulate socially beneficial competition.

In sum, extreme economic inequality and the political capture of the state by powerful economic elites have undermined many of the goals associated with the transition to democracy in Mexico—and have reduced the effective meaning of transparency.

BREAKING THE ANTI-PUBLIC SECTOR BIAS

Around the world, "public" responsibilities and governance functions of the highest importance, such as education, health, public safety, pensions, prisons, financial services, and a wide variety of urban infrastructure and development programs, have been absorbed by private corporations, associations, nongovernmental organizations, independent contractors, or quasi-government entities. This transformation presents enormous challenges for transparency. It opens up a wide range of emergency exits for actors who are unwilling to submit to the new forms of accountability that have been applied to government institutions in recent years. Very few national laws on access to information provide for strong, effective mechanisms of transparency applicable to private companies that carry out public functions. This situation is the Achilles' heel for the contemporary legal practice of transparency.[28]

According to Mexican law, in particular Article 142 of the Mexican FOIA, individual and corporate entities that receive public resources or perform acts of public authority should be subject to transparency requirements. This is a good start, but it is clearly insufficient. The rule in the private sector is not transparency but opacity. Mexican corporate law is packed with provisions for bank secrecy, tax secrecy, trade secrets, and other secrecy privileges that are said to protect competition and the privacy of investors. This secrecy carves out a niche of impunity and opacity for the benefit of economic powers and interest groups outside the formal channels of the state.

Effective oversight by society and public opinion depends on the Mexican FOIA having the capacity to render transparent not only traditional formal powers but also the new "powers that be" such as business organizations, transnational corporations, financial giants, and the media. This is what is really at stake in breaking the *anti–public sector bias* that takes the state to be the source of all opacity and corruption that a FOI law must confront. Implicitly, markets and private spheres are treated as clean arenas free of corruption and waste.

In reality, in Mexico as in the rest of Latin America, corruption is intimately linked to privatization and neoliberalism.[29] The dominant perspective depicts the wave of economic reforms that took place during the 1990s in Latin America as the imposition of a cold economic orthodoxy on a wasteful bureaucracy and a corrupt political class.[30] Yet, as my research on the changes in the Mexican banking sector reveals, these supposedly "liberalizing" economic reforms have led to more instead of less corruption and waste.[31] In general, neoliberalism should not be conceptualized as an economic project with political implications but as a political project with economic consequences. The reforms did not reduce the state and empower technocracy; rather, the reforms reshaped the state and political power in accord with the interests of new distribution coalitions. Throughout this process, opacity has prevailed.

Today Mexico's political regime seems not to have learned its lesson regarding the mutually reinforcing character of opacity, unconstitutionality, and impunity. With the enactment by President Felipe Calderón of the Law of Public-Private Associations in 2011, the country has opened the door to private ownership and control of a wide range of public services, including highways, hospitals, jails, and schools. This legal transformation, of doubtful constitutionality according to leading Mexican legal scholars,[32] has meant private takeover of existing government services and has created incentives for private corporations to propose new construction projects to the government to serve profit-making rather than the public interest.

Both the administration of past president Calderón and that of President Peña Nieto have justified the Law of Public-Private Associations as necessary in order to compensate for the fiscal crisis that limited public investment in crucial social sectors. This transfer of public services to private hands has dramatically reduced the reach of basic transparency and anticorruption oversight because private projects are not required to subject themselves to the same accountability controls as normal government projects. This trend is already reviving the failed experience of privatization of the 1990s.[33]

PRI and PAN governments have been united in empowering corporations over people. They have demonstrated a lack of respect for the Mexican Constitution and its social legacy. Under President Peña Nieto, Mexico has privatized its oil and electricity industries,[34] rolled back protections for labor, aggressively imposed neoliberal education reforms,[35] increased covert surveillance of its citizens,[36] and consolidated the militarization of law enforcement. This "privatization solution" or "public-privatization answer" to the fiscal crisis of the state rewards the very actors responsible for the original problem. Tax revenues are so low in Mexico precisely because powerful economic elites dodge taxes by hiding their money in offshore accounts or simply intimidating treasury authorities.[37]

One recent example of how the opacity of the private sector can lead to impunity for government corruption is the global scandal in which the Mexican government stands out again for its participation in the Brazilian construction company Odebrecht's efforts at money laundering and bribery. Odebrecht, whose founder is now in jail, paid enormous sums in bribes for contracts to the highest levels of twelve Latin American governments.[38] In Mexico, it is accused of having bribed government institutions with over US$11 million during the administrations of presidents Calderón and Peña Nieto.

In 2016, the Panama Papers revealed that a Panamanian law firm helped set up thousands of secret shell companies for notorious Mexican oligarchs and drug lords in a variety of tax havens. The CEO of the state oil company PEMEX, Emilio Lozoya, was revealed to be one of the firm's principal clients. In 2017, the Odebrecht settlement—which was made publicly known thanks to investigations by the U.S. Department of Justice—shed light on a private company spending millions of dollars bribing politicians and political parties across Latin America. Once this hemispheric network of corruption was made known by the international press, the agency in charge of combating corruption in Mexico, the Public Function Ministry, had to acknowledge the existence of contracts between corporations (such as Odebrecht) known to have bribed politicians across Latin America and Mexican state entities such as the Federal Commission of Electricity and PEMEX. The details of these contracts, however, continue to be withheld from the public.[39]

Again and again, a combination of personal impunity and selective disclosure, especially when it involves powerful economic interests, demonstrates both the depths of structural corruption and the inadequacy of transparency strategies that target government entities exclusively.

CONCLUSION

Mexico's democratic transition has failed to empower society or settle accounts with the past. Instead, as in many Latin American transitions, democratization in Mexico often has meant no more than the diversification of the power bases for the same moguls and oligarchs as before. This is the underlying reason the Mexican FOIA has not lived up to its promise or its global hype.

I have made two key arguments in this chapter. First, we need a new framework for understanding transparency and combating corruption that takes into account the failings of old accountability strategies. Second, we should go beyond both the anti–public sector bias and the bureaucratic obsessions that undergird most studies of corruption and transparency in the developing and the developed world alike.

Democratic theorists have long agreed that citizens need reliable information about how the system works in order to exercise their rights as full participants in a democracy. Mexico is not fulfilling this basic condition. In countries like Mexico, reformers should adopt a structural understanding of corruption and tie the protection of transparency to a vision of strengthening citizen participation in democracy. The former defines corruption as the abuse of power plus impunity in the absence of citizen participation. The latter insists on the extension of transparency and accountability controls normally reserved for the public sector into the private sphere. Anything less fails to take into account broader realities of social and political power and thereby fails to establish concrete links between transparency, accountability, democracy, and justice.

NOTES

Assistance provided by Isabel Salat and Ma. Fernanda Soto was instrumental in organizing the data used in this chapter.

1. Katie Townsend and Adam A. Marshall, chapter 11; Kyu Ho Youm and Toby Mendel, chapter 12; and Gregory Michener, chapter 13.
2. A set of proposed amendments to Bosnia and Herzegovina's law on freedom of access to information, which aim to withhold large volumes of information about the functioning of public bodies, is a recent example of such resistance. For more on this case, see "OSCE Media Freedom Representative Expresses Concern About Access to information Law Amendments in Bosnia and Herzegovina," June 4, 2013, www.osce.org/fom/102269.
3. See Secretaría de la Función Pública, *Transparencia, Buen Gobierno y Combate a la Corrupción en la Función Pública* (Mexico City: Fondo de Cultura Económica, 2005).

4. See Brad Rawlins, "Measuring the Relationship Between Organizational Transparency and Employee Trust," *Public Relations Journal* 2 (Spring 2008): 1–21.

5. See Irma Eréndira Sandoval, "Transparency Under Dispute: Public Relations, Bureaucracy, and Democracy in Mexico," in *Research Handbook on Transparency*, ed. Padideh Ala'i and Robert G. Vaughn (Northampton, Mass.: Edward Elgar, 2014), 157–84.

6. See Irma E. Sandoval-Ballesteros, "Hacia un proyecto democrático-expansivo de transparencia," *Revista Mexicana de Ciencias Políticas y Sociales*, Facultad de Ciencias Políticas y Sociales, National Autonomous University of Mexico, Mexico City, 2013.

7. Another implication of the structural perspective is that it is time to put behind us both "modernizationist" approaches that frame corruption as principally an issue of economic underdevelopment and moralistic approaches that focus on the cultural roots of the problem. Recent work has demonstrated that economic growth and a wide variety of cultures can coexist with corrupt practices. For more on these themes, see Ernesto Garzón Valdés, "Derecho, Ética y Política," Center of Constitutional Rights, 1993; Irma E. Sandoval, "From Institutional to Structural Corruption: Rethinking Accountability in a World of Public-Private Partnerships," Edmond J. Safra Research Lab Working Papers, No. 2, 2013. See also Susan Rose-Ackerman and Bonnie J. Palifka, *Corruption and Government: Causes, Consequences, and Reform* (New York: Cambridge University Press, 2016); and Susan Rose-Ackerman, "The Law and Economics of Bribery and Extortion," *Annual Review of Law and Social Science* 6 (2010): 217–38.

8. See Alvaro Delgado, *El Amasiato, el pacto secreto Peña-Calderón* (Mexico City: Ediciones Proceso, 2016).

9. See Irma E. Sandoval-Ballesteros, "Enfoque de la corrupción estructural: poder, impunidad y voz ciudadana," Universidad Nacional Autónoma de México-Instituto de Investigaciones Sociales, *Revista Mexicana de Sociología* 78, no. 1 (enero-marzo, 2016): 119–52. México, D.F. ISSN: 0188-2503/16/07801-05.

10. See Katie Townsend and Adam A. Marshall, chapter 11, this volume.

11. See John M. Ackerman and Irma E. Sandoval, "The Global Explosion of Freedom of Information Laws," *Administrative Law Review* 58 (2006): 85–130.

12. U.S. House of Representatives Committee on Oversight and Government Reform, *FOIA Is Broken: A Report*, 114th Congress, January 2016, https://oversight. house.gov/wp-content/uploads/2016/01/FINAL-FOIA-Report-January-2016.pdf.

13. See Transparency International Corruption Perceptions Index 2016, www .transparency.org/news/feature/corruption_perceptions_index_2016.

14. See OECD Foreign Bribery Report, December 2, 2014, www.oecd.org/daf /oecd-foreign-bribery-report-9789264226616-en.htm.

15. See UDLAP, "Index of Global Impunity—Mexico," August 2017, www.udlap .mx/cesij/files/IGI-2017_eng.pdf. For an interesting analysis that also finds impunity to be one of the key elements explaining the lack of progress in fighting corruption despite Mexico's model of access to information law, see Eduardo Bohórquez, Irasema Guzman, and Germán Petersen, "Control de corrupción en México; ¿la impunidad neutraliza el efecto de los avances en la transparencia?" *Este País* 297: (January 2016).

16. The INAI itself has been experiencing severe internal turmoil. Several years ago, there was an open dispute among commissioners regarding violations of the guarantee of anonymity of citizen requests. In 2013, INAI's Internal Audit Unit began an investigation of a commissioner who was accused by an INAI colleague of a conflict of interest. The commissioner allegedly had made requests for information from her own computer, under a pseudonym, and then presented and defended those same requests.

    At the same time, Mexico's investments in transparency have proved highly costly for society. In some states, there is more public money for information commissioners' salaries than for public education in indigenous communities. On average, commissioners receive more than forty-three times the minimum wage, versus the multiple of three that an average teacher receives in Mexico. See Cristina Gómez, "ITAIT destaca por sueldos según estudio del CIDE," accessed March 3, 2018, http://m.milenio.com/region/CIDE-ITAIT-estudio_sueldos_Tamaulipas _0_467953246.html.

17. See Anexo 3.1, "Denuncias de hechos por persistir el incumplimiento de las resoluciones emitidas por el pleno del INAI en 14vo. Informe de Labores al H. Congreso de la Unión," 2016, http://inicio.inai.org.mx/SitePages/Informes-2016. aspx. See also John Ackerman, *El Instituto Federal de Acceso a la Información Pública: Diseño, Desempeño y Sociedad Civil*, Centro de Investigaciones y Estudios Superiores de Antropología Social-Instituto de Investigaciones Histórico-Sociales, Universidad Veracruzana, 2007.

18. See Juan Montes, "Mexico Finance Minister Bought House from Government Contractor," *Wall Street Journal*, December 11, 2014. See also *Redacción AN*, "La casa blanca de Enrique Peña Nieto," *Aristegui Noticias*, 2014, http:// aristeguinoticias.com/0911/mexico/la-casa-blanca-de-enrique-pena-nieto; Joshua Partlow, "Mexico's President Apologized for a Corruption Scandal. But the Nightmare Goes on for the Reporter Who Uncovered It," *Washington Post*, July 22, 2016.

19. See Parker Asmann, "Was Mexico President's 2012 Campaign Funded by Odercrecht?," *InSight Crime*, October 27, 2017.

20. For general background on the topic, see Wayne Cornelius, Todd A. Eisenstadt, and Jane Hindley, eds., *Subnational Politics and Democratization in Mexico*

(La Jolla, Calif.: Center for U.S.-Mexico Studies, UC San Diego, 1999); Austin Bay, "Mexico Versus Mexico: The Battle over Impunity," *Times Record News,* May 3, 2017. As an example, consider the case of the ex-governor of the state of Tabasco, Andres Granier, who has been accused of plunging the state into debt by squandering and embezzling millions of dollars before fleeing to Miami. State prosecutors have found 88.5 million pesos, about $7 million in cash, in an office used by his former treasurer, Jose Saiz. Granier himself was secretly recorded bragging about owning hundreds of suits and pairs of shoes and about shopping exclusively at Beverly Hills luxury stores. See Richard Fausset and Cecilia Sanchez, "Former Mexican Official's Boasts Add Fire to Corruption Probes," *Los Angeles Times,* June 12, 2013.

21. Editorial Board, "In Mexico, Journalism Is Literally Being Killed Off," *Washington Post,* May 21, 2017.

22. See Azam Ahmed, "In Mexico 'It's Easy to Kill a Journalist,'" *New York Times,* April 29, 2017. See also Amnesty International, "5to homicidio de periodista en el año. La libertad de expresión bajo amenaza en México," https://amnistia.org .mx/contenido/mexico-quinto-homicidio-de-un-periodista-en-el-ano-la-libertad -de-expresion-bajo-amenaza.

23. For a comparative analysis of Zedillo's and Obama's bailouts, see Irma E. Sandoval, "Financial Crisis and Bailout: Legal Challenges and International Lessons from Mexico, Korea and the United States," in *Comparative Administrative Law,* ed. Susan Rose-Ackerman and Peter L. Lindseth (London: Edward Elgar, 2010), 543–68.

24. Gerardo Esquivel Hernández, "Desigualdad extrema en México. Concentración del poder económico y político," OXFAM 2016, www.cambialasreglas .org/pdf/desigualdadextrema_informe.pdf. Some independent calculations suggest that there are 100 million poor people in the country. See Julio Bolvitnik, "Evolución de la pobreza y la estratificación social en México, 2012–2014," www .julioboltvinik.org/images/stories/pobreza%20presentacin%20de%20resultados %202014%20conferencia%20de%20prensa.pdf.

25. "Trends in Income Inequality in Mexico," OECD, May 21, 2015, www.oecd.org /mexico/OECD2015-In-It-Together-Highlights-Mexico.pdf.

26. "Estudio de la OECD sobre el proceso presupuestario en México," OECD, 2009, www.oecd.org/dataoecd/11/30/48190152.pdf.

27. Amnistía Internacional, "Informe de 2016–2017: El estado de los Derechos Humanos en el Mundo," 307–12, www.amnesty.org/download/Documents /POL1048002017SPANISH.PDF.

28. Irma E. Sandoval, "Enfoque de la corrupción estructural: poder, impunidad y voz ciudadana," *Revista Mexicana de Sociología* 78 (2016): 119–52.

29. Luigi Manzetti, "Political Opportunism and Privatization Failures," in *Contemporary Debates on Corruption and Transparency: Rethinking State, Market and Society*, ed. Irma Eréndira Sandoval (Washington, D.C.: World Bank and National Autonomous University of Mexico, 2011), 95–116.

30. Ezra Suleiman and John Waterbury, eds., *The Political Economy of Public Sector Reform and Privatization* (Boulder, Colo.: Westview Press, 1990); Marc E. Williams, *Market Reforms in Mexico: Coalitions, Institutions and the Politics of Policy Changes* (Lanham, Md.: Rowan & Littlefield, 2001). See also Anne O. Krueger, "Government Failures in Development," NBER Working Paper No. 3340, www.nber.org/papers/w3340.

31. Irma E. Sandoval-Ballesteros, *Crisis, Rentismo e Intervencionismo Neoliberal en la Banca: México (1982–1999)* (Mexico City: Centro de Estudios Espinosa Yglesias, 2011). See also Sandoval, "Financial Crisis and Bailout."

32. Asa C. Laurell and Joel Herrera, "Claves para entender los contratos de asociación público-privada," in *Interés Público, Asociaciones Público-Privadas y Poderes Fácticos*, ed. Irma E. Sandoval (Mexico City: National Autonomous University of Mexico, 2015), 123–44.

33. Héctor E. Schamis, "Avoiding Collusion, Averting Collision: What Do We Know About the Political Economy of Privatization?," in *Contemporary Debates on Corruption and Transparency: Rethinking State, Market and Society*, 35–76.

34. See Irma Erendira Sandoval, "Mexico on the Verge of Political Meltdown," *Al Jazeera America*, January 9, 2015, http://america.aljazeera.com/opinions/2015/1/mexico-pena-nietocorruptionstudentsayotzinapa.html#.

35. See Azam Ahmed and Kirk Semple, "Clashes Draw Support for Teachers' Protest in Mexico," *New York Times*, June 26, 2016.

36. See Julio Sánchez Onofre, "Espionaje gubernamental quiebra Alianza por el Gobierno Abierto," *El Economista*, May 23, 2017. See also "Por espionaje, Sociedad Civil concluye participación del Secretariado Técnico Tripartita," *Fundar*, May 23, 2017, http://fundar.org.mx/por-espionaje-sociedad-civil-concluye-participacion-del-secretariado-tecnico-tripartita.

37. Christopher Woody, "Leaked Documents Show the Mexican President's Close Friend Moved $100 Million Offshore After Corruption Probe," *Business Insider*, April 4, 2016.

38. David Segal, "Petrobras Oil Scandal Leaves Brazilians Lamenting a Lost Dream," *New York Times*, August 7, 2015.

39. For instance, during President Calderon's term, PEMEX signed a contract with an Odebrecht's subsidiary, Braskem, to administer sixty-six thousand daily ethanol barrels under "preferential prices." This costly material would be destined

for a polyethylene factory, which was envisioned to be built in the south of Mexico in Coatzacoalcos, Veracruz. This contract has been declared under reserve for twenty-five years. Odebrecht also received lucrative contracts from the public electricity company. See Raúl Olmos, "Pemex publica contratos con Odebrecht pero censura los datos centrales," *Animal Político*, April 6, 2016.

CONTRIBUTORS

MARK FENSTER is a professor of law at the University of Florida. He is the author of *The Transparency Fix: Secrets, Leaks, and Uncontrollable Government Information* (Stanford University Press, 2017) and *Conspiracy Theories: Secrecy and Power in American Culture*, 2nd edition (University of Minnesota Press, 2008).

KATHERINE FINK is an assistant professor in the Department of Media, Communications, and Visual Arts at Pace University. She is also an affiliated fellow of the Information Society Project at Yale Law School, a former fellow of the Brown Institute for Media Innovation at Columbia Journalism School, and a former radio journalist.

JAMES T. HAMILTON is the Hearst Professor of Communication and director of the journalism program at Stanford. His books, *Democracy's Detectives: The Economics of Investigative Journalism* (Harvard, 2016) and *All the News That's Fit to Sell: How the Market Transforms Information into News* (Princeton, 2006), examine the market for accountability journalism. As cofounder of the Stanford Computational Journalism Lab, he studies story discovery methods.

NADIA HILLIARD is a junior research fellow at Balliol College, Oxford University, and a postdoctoral research associate at City, University of London. She is the author of *The Accountability State: US Federal Inspectors General and the Pursuit of Democratic Integrity* (University Press of Kansas, 2017).

SETH F. KREIMER is the Kenneth W. Gemmill Professor of Law at the University of Pennsylvania Law School. He has studied, written, and taught in the fields of constitutional law, privacy, and transparency for three and a half decades. He has regularly consulted with the ACLU and other organizations on constitutional litigation.

MARGARET B. KWOKA is an associate professor of law at the University of Denver. Her research focuses on government secrecy and the Freedom of Information Act. She has litigated numerous FOIA cases, has testified about FOIA before Congress, and sits on the FOIA Advisory Committee. Her recent research on FOIA requesters appears in the *Yale Law Journal* and *Duke Law Journal*.

SAM LEBOVIC is an assistant professor of history at George Mason University and the author of *Free Speech and Unfree News: The Paradox of Press Freedom in America* (Harvard, 2016).

ADAM A. MARSHALL is the Knight Foundation Litigation Attorney at the Reporters Committee for Freedom of the Press, where his work focuses on federal and state public records litigation. Adam also provides training, advocacy, and information on a wide array of open government issues.

TOBY MENDEL is the executive director of the Centre for Law and Democracy, a Canadian-based international human rights NGO that provides legal and capacity building expertise, including on the rights to information and freedom of expression. He has published widely on these rights and collaborated extensively with IGOs, governments, and NGOs in countries around the world to promote them.

GREGORY MICHENER is an assistant professor of government at the Getulio Vargas Foundation (FGV-EBAPE), Rio de Janeiro. Founder of FGV's Public Transparency Program and the Open Society Foundation–supported Transparency Evaluation Network, Michener studies the conceptualization, measurement, evaluation, and politics (especially in Latin America) of transparency and freedom of information policies.

BETH SIMONE NOVECK is the Jerry Hultin Global Network Professor at New York University, where she directs the Governance Lab. She served in the White House as first U.S. deputy chief technology officer and director of the Open Government Initiative. Her most recent book is *Smart Citizens, Smarter State: The Technologies of Expertise and the Future of Governing* (Harvard, 2015). She tweets @bethnoveck.

DAVID E. POZEN is a professor of law at Columbia Law School. He teaches and writes about constitutional law, nonprofit law, and information law, among other topics. During the 2017–2018 academic year, Pozen served as the Knight First Amendment Institute's inaugural visiting scholar.

IRMA ERÉNDIRA SANDOVAL-BALLESTEROS is a professor at the Institute for Social Research and director of the Laboratory for Documentation and Analysis of Corruption and Transparency at the National Autonomous University of Mexico. She recently served as deputy to the Mexico City Constitutional Convention and was previously a fellow at Harvard's Edmond J. Safra Center for Ethics and a visiting professor at Sciences Po.

FREDERICK SCHAUER is the David and Mary Harrison Distinguished Professor of Law at the University of Virginia and was previously, for nineteen years, the Frank Stanton Professor of the First Amendment at Harvard University. Among his six books are *Free Speech: A Philosophical Enquiry* (Cambridge, 1982), *Profiles, Probabilities, and Stereotypes* (Harvard, 2003), *Thinking Like a Lawyer* (Harvard, 2009), and *The Force of Law* (Harvard, 2015).

MICHAEL SCHUDSON is a professor of journalism at Columbia Journalism School and a sociologist and historian of the news media and American political culture. He is the author of eight books as well as coauthor or coeditor of several more, touching on journalism, the media and democracy, cultural memory, and, in 2015, *The Rise of the Right to Know* (Harvard).

CASS R. SUNSTEIN is the Robert Walmsley University Professor at Harvard Law School. He is the author of many books, including *Impeachment* (Harvard, 2017) and *The Ethics of Influence* (Cambridge University Press, 2016). He served as administrator of the White House Office of Information and Regulatory Affairs during the first term of the Obama administration.

KATIE TOWNSEND is the litigation director at the Reporters Committee for Freedom of the Press. She oversees the litigation work of Reporters Committee attorneys and represents the Reporters Committee, news organizations, and individual journalists in court access, freedom of information, and other First Amendment and press freedom matters in state and federal courts throughout the United States.

KYU HO YOUM is the Jonathan Marshall First Amendment Chair at the University of Oregon School of Journalism and Communication. He has published extensively about global free speech issues, and his research has been cited by U.S. and foreign courts, including the UK Supreme Court and the High Court of Australia. Youm is currently writing a book on international and comparative media law.

INDEX

FOIA refers to the federal Freedom of Information Act throughout. Page numbers in italics indicate tables or figures.

"7 Lessons from BuzzFeed's 'FOIA-Friendly Newsroom'" (Hinchcliffe), 125

60 Minutes, 144

Aarhus Convention, 234
Abu Ghraib abuses, 142, 144, 146, 147, 149
Access Info Europe (AIE), 250, 252
accountability. See government accountability
ACLU. See American Civil Liberties Union
Administrative Procedure Act (1946), 55, 228; amendment advocated by Cross, 57; deficiencies of, 226, 228; FOIA as amendment to, 14, 48n48, 52; quasi-constitutionality of, 62–64; secrecy exemptions, 67n8. See also FOIA
adversarial nature of FOIA, 209, 269, 275, 286n3
Affordable Care Act, 193

Agriculture, Department of, 16, 24, 121–22
AIE (Access Info Europe), 250, 252
air quality, 192, 193, 198. See also climate change
Alabama, 93, 94, 96
Alaska, 97, 103, 105, 106, 107, 108
Alper Services, 98–99
amendments to FOIA, 42, 63; 1974 amendments, 22, 59, 145–46; after Watergate, 137, 149, 274; E-FOIA Amendments (1996), 172, 273; FOIA Improvement Act (2016), 26, 127–28, 217, 225n49, 273; interpretation and proactive dissemination of information required, 172; party politics and, 273. See also reforming FOIA
American Civil Liberties Union (ACLU), 139, 140, 146, 152, 164n49
American Society of Newspaper Editors (ASNE), 53, 54, 55–57
Amtrak, 121–22

APA. *See* Administrative Procedure Act
appeals following FOI denial:
internationally, 258–60, 264, 267n37,
277, 283, 290n60, 295; under U.S.
FOIA (*see* courts; litigation)
archaeological information, 96
Archibald, Sam, 13
Argentina, 215, 277, 279, 284, 299
Arizona, 97, 110
Arkansas, 93, 99
Armstrong, Scott, 196–97
Ashcroft v. Iqbal, 151
ASNE, 53, 54, 55–57
Associated Press, 106–7, 122–23, 124, 125,
139
audit culture, 178–79
Australia, 234, 297
authoritarianism, prospect for, 156,
164n48
Azerbaijan, 296, 297

Bartnicki v. Vopper, 47n36
Belgium, 234, 297
benefits of FOIA: under the current
administration, 156, 162–63n40,
163n41; investigative reporting's
benefits, 123–24; positive impacts on
regulatory state, 156–58, 163nn43–44,
164nn48–49, 164–65n50; private
vs. public benefits, 80–81, 154 (*see
also* commercial FOIA requests;
first-person FOIA requests); in
Schudson's view, 5–6
Better Government Association, 98–99
Bickel, Alexander, 140
big data. *See* data; information access
Bilz, Kenworthey, 50n55
Blasi, Vincent, 68–69n23
Bolivia, 275, 277, 279, 284, 296, 297
Boumediene v. United States, 151

Bowler, Shaun, 271
Brandeis, Louis, Justice, 157, 192
Brazil, 271, 277, 278–82, 279, 285, 286,
289n53. *See also* Odebrecht
The Brethren (Woodward and
Armstrong), 196–97
Breyer, Charles, Judge, 147
BrightScope, 210
Bromwich, Michael, 176
Brooker, Herbert, 57
bureaucracy, federal. *See* civil servants;
federal agencies; *and specific
departments and agencies*
bureaucratic approach to transparency
reform, 292–93
bureaupathology paradox, 167, 168,
169–72, 181
Burger, Warren E., Chief Justice, 38, 38
Bush administration (George W.), 62,
142–45, 152–53, 273. *See also* Global
War on Terror; OPEN Government
Act (2007)
BuzzFeed, 125

cabinet composition, 270, 271, 272, 280
Calderón, Felipe, 303
California, 96, 110
Campaign Legal Center, 164–65n50
Canada: Corruption Perception Index
score, 297; FOI (RTI) law adopted,
253; Global Impunity Index score,
299; municipal administrations,
272; RTI Rating evaluation, 253–62,
267n37
Candeub, Adam, 174–75
Center for Constitutional Rights, 140
Center for National Security Studies,
140
Center for Open Data Enterprise,
218–19

Center for Public Integrity, 98, 122–23, 125

Centers for Medicare and Medicaid Services (CMS), 118–19, 210

Central Intelligence Agency, 138

Centre for Law and Democracy (CLD), 250, 252

Chafee, Zechariah, 67n6

Chicago, 207, 210, 216

Chief FOIA Officers (CFOs), 170

Chief Information Officers (CIO) Council, 218, 225n49

Chile, 274, 277, 279, 281, 282, 299

China, 193

Church of the Lukumi Babalu Aye, Inc. v. City of Hialeah, 44n8

CIA, 138

citizens: benefits of open data for, 192, 195–96; and the expertise paradox, 172–73, 176 (*see also* expertise paradox); FOIA as tool of citizen empowerment, 172; and monitory tools/practices, 166; open data and civic engagement, 207 (*see also* open data); success of democracy dependent on understanding of, 182. *See also* first-person FOIA requests; noncitizens; privacy; public interest; public trust in government

Citizens Divided: Campaign Finance Reform and the Constitution (Post), 45n16

Citizens United v. Federal Election Commission, 45n16

Civilian Aeronautics Board, 17

civil servants: bureaupathology paradox, 167, 168, 169–72, 181; FOIA effectiveness dependent on, 142–46, 154, 169; in the IG system, 169 (*see also* Inspectors General); and

monitory tools/practices, 166–67; and secrecy, 138, 143–45. *See also* federal agencies; *and specific agencies*

Clark, Ramsey (Atty. Gen.), 27; memorandum, 17–18, 21, 23

classification system, 21–23, 146, 168. *See also* national security; national security agencies

CLD (Centre for Law and Democracy), 250, 252

climate change, 194–95, *194*

Clinton, Bill, 190–91, 273

Clinton, Hillary, 125, 176

Clinton administration, 170, 190–91

CMS (Centers for Medicare and Medicaid Services), 118–19, 210

Cohen, Sarah, 128

COINTELPRO, 136, 137, 160n10

college costs, 192

Collor, Fernando, 281

Colombia, 275, 277, 279, 299

Colorado: environmental FOI logs analyzed, *103*, *105*, *106*, *107*, *108*; journalists and FOI law, 99, *103*

Combatant Status Review Tribunals, 139, 148–49, 151. *See also* Guantanamo prison

commercial FOIA requests, 173; as bulk of FOIA requests, 6, 50n59, 51n69, 92, 173, 209, 240; and corporate competition, 77; and FOIA costs, 84; FOIA's mission not advanced, 80–81, 173; high-volume requesters, 76; news media use outweighed by, 4, 8, 18–19, 75, 76, 84–85, 92, 123, 124; to Pennsylvania vs. federal environmental agencies, *104*, *105*; proposed alternatives, 81, 86; purpose of, 76–78, 173; reselling of

commercial FOIA requests (*continued*)
FOIA'd information, 19, 78–79, 123;
unintended due process function
served, 50n59, 51n69. *See also*
private entities and the private
sector; *and under* state FOI laws
common law right to information,
233–34
conceptual foundations of FOIA. *See*
foundations of FOIA
Congress: on agency withholding of
information, 226; FOIA amended
(2016), 26 (*see also* amendments
to FOIA); FOIA enacted, 2, 13–14,
56–57, 226, 228, 251; and FOIA
exemptions, 228–29, 231, 236, 237, 241
(*see also* exemptions to FOIA); and
FOIA expenditures, 84; and FOIA
reform, 87, 237 (*see also* reforming
FOIA); on FOIA's "brokenness," 4,
229; and the Global War on Terror,
137, 149, 151–53 (*see also* Global War
on Terror); House Report on FOIA,
14, 17, 23 (*see also* Clark, Ramsey:
memorandum); information access
and disclosure, 38; Inspectors
General and, 167, 171, 180 (*see also*
Inspectors General); and judicial
enforcement of FOIA, 230; and the
national security exemption, 22;
not covered by FOIA, 7, 168, 254;
open data acts, 212 (*see also* open
data); and proactive disclosure, 172;
resource allocation, 41, 50n59; and
the scope of FOIA, 154; single-party
control of, and FOIA's role, 156;
subject to capture/manipulation, 158.
See also Administrative Procedure
Act; FOIA; *and specific individuals
and acts*

Connecticut, 97, 98
consensus systems, 269–76. *See also*
Brazil; Finland; political systems
and transparency
Constitution, U.S., 35–36; amendment
difficult, 40; constitutional vs.
statutory approach to the right to
information, 39–43, 48n47, 50n57,
53–66; declining global impact,
249; enforcement of constitutional
rights, 61–62; Madison on the
need for closed-door debate re,
187, 201; negative and positive
rights under, 35–37, 44nn6, 8,
10, 44–45n12, 45nn16, 18; and
political accountability, 74; right
to information absent in, 8, 37–39,
48nn43, 46, 253–54, 296; Seventh
and Eighth Amendments, 44n6; and
states' right to restrict FOI requests
to residents, 93; Stewart on, 34; and
transparency, 34, 135. *See also* First
Amendment; freedom of speech;
freedom of the press
contestation systems, 269–76, 282–83.
See also Mexico's FOI (RTI) law;
political systems and transparency
corporations: FOIA requests (*see*
commercial FOIA requests); open
data used by, 209–10 (*see also* open
data). *See also* private entities and
the private sector
corruption: in Brazil, 280, 289n53;
Corruption Perceptions Index,
296–98, 297–98t; disconnect
between transparency and, 294–302;
FOIA as protection against, 73,
135, 220; input transparency and,
189, 199, 202, 204; open data and,
215, 216, 219; public impression of,

19; structural corruption, 293–94, 306n7; and transparency in Mexico, 9–10, 291, 293–94, 296–305. *See also* government accountability

Costa Rica, 275, 277, 279, 299

cost of regulations, 193–95

costs of FOIA: in 2015, 84, 170; in 2016, 124–25; agency concerns about, 23–24; comparable line items, 84, 159n7; cost-benefit ratio questioned, 85, 136; costs of implementing reforms, 128; fees, 23–24, 84, 96–97, 100, 124, 170, 173, 256; journalists' requests and, 123–25, 126; outweighed by benefits, 6, 123–24; and resource allocation, 41, 50n59; and the robustness of FOIA infrastructure, 154. *See also* drawbacks of FOIA

Council of Europe, 234

counsel, right to, 35

courts: authority lacking re FOIA exemptions, 227; and the constitutional vs. statutory approach to information access, 41–42, 60; deference to executive withholding, 4, 64–65, 142, 145, 148, 155, 231–32, 240, 267n31; enforcement of a theoretical constitutional right to information, 61–62; Gellhorn on judicial review, 66; and GWOT-related FOIA requests, 137, 141, 142, 147, 155; and GWOT-related litigation, 161n28; and immigration policy-related FOIA litigation, 157; institutional structure of the federal judiciary, 147; judicial enforcement of FOIA, and its limitations, 14, 230–32; judicial infrastructure required for FOIA, 154; lawmaking

by litigation, 42, 51n61, 60; and the national security exemption, 21–22; not covered by FOIA, 7, 168, 254; open data projects, 215; procedure for FOIA litigation, 232. *See also* litigation; Supreme Court

criminal trials, access to, 38, 47n41

Cross, Harold, 54–58, 60–61, 67n6

Cuillier, David, 126

data: big data, 118, 174–77, 215; covered by FOIA vs. open data policies, 209; data science, 206; high-value data sets, 191–93, 196, 209–10, 214–15, 224n42–43. *See also* data.gov; open data

data.gov (website), 191–92, 195–96, 211, 217, 222–23n19, 224n43. *See also* data

Davis, Kenneth Culp, 22

Dawson, William, 56

Defense, Department of. *See* Department of Defense

Defense Advanced Research Projects Agency, 127

Defense Contract Audit Agency, 121

Defense Logistics Agency (DLA), 19, 76, 77, 81

Delaware: environmental FOI logs analyzed, *103, 105, 106, 107, 108;* FOI law, 93, 96

Delgado, Alvaro, 294

deliberative discussion: exempted under some state FOI laws, 95; on federal regulations, 198–99; and FOIA's Exemption 5, 25–26, 95, 237, 239, 267n33; FOIA's feared impact on, 15, 23–26 (*see also* exemptions to FOIA: Exemption 5); illegitimate/objectionable arguments, 199–200; input transparency and, 188, 189,

deliberative discussion (*continued*)
197–204; need for closed-door
discussions, 187; some secrecy
beneficial, 5
democracy: audit culture and, 178–79;
and expertise, 172–73; and famine,
156, 190; monitory tools, 166 (*see
also* FOIA; foreign FOI laws;
Inspectors General; state FOI laws);
necessity of information access for,
57, 58; negative impacts of FOIA
on (*see* deliberative discussion;
drawbacks of FOIA); transparency
and democratic values, 182 (*see also*
transparency). *See also* expertise
paradox; political systems and
transparency
*Democracy's Detectives: the Economics
of Investigative Journalism*
(Hamilton), 116, 123. *See also*
Hamilton, James T.
Democratic Party, and FOIA's passage,
56–57
denial of FOIA requests: agency
review process and, 229–30;
appeals, 259, 267n36; courts'
deference to withholding agencies,
4, 64–65, 142, 145, 148, 155, 231–32,
240, 267n31; courts empowered
to force disclosure, 14; denials
increasing, 227, 242nn8–10; judicial
enforcement, and its limitations,
230–32 (*see also* courts); limited
to specific instances/exemptions,
14 (*see also* exemptions to FOIA);
public-interest balancing test
needed to counteract, 227–28, 233,
235–41; sanctions for improper
denial, 260, 268n38. *See also* courts;
litigation

Denver Post, 122
Department of Agriculture, 16, 24,
121–22
Department of Defense (DOD), 16, 18,
20–21, 24, 138, 146. *See also* national
security; national security agencies;
torture
Department of Homeland Security
(DHS), 79, 121–23, 138, 156–57,
163n44. *See also* Immigration and
Customs Enforcement
Department of Justice (DOJ): annual
FOIA reports to, 87, 111–12; benefits
of FOIA "difficult to quantify,"
85; Blue Book withheld, 239;
FOIA limited by DOJ report, 14;
FOIA officials under auspices
of, 218; and FOIA performance
improvement, 219; *Guide to the
Freedom of Information Act* (2015),
25; and GWOT accountability,
149; independent Inspector
General, 138, 143, 149, 176, 180;
Office of Information and Privacy
(Information Policy), 145–46; Office
of Violence Against Women, 121;
and the Panama papers, 304; report
on post–September 11 dragnet
detentions, 143; sanctions authorized
for improperly withholding records,
268n38; statutes covered under
Exemption 3 identified, 95; voter
fraud allegations, FOIA request re,
164–65n50
DHS. *See* Department of Homeland
Security
Digital Accountability and
Transparency Act (2014), 212
disclosure, proactive. *See* proactive
disclosure

DLA. *See* Defense Logistics Agency
DOD. *See* Department of Defense
DOJ. *See* Department of Justice
Dominican Republic, 277, 279, 284, 297
drawbacks of FOIA: antiregulatory effects, 19–20, 156, 163n42 (*see also* regulatory state); cost-benefit ratio questioned, 85, 136 (*see also* costs of FOIA); denials increasing, 227; described as ineffective, 136; "FOIA Is Broken" (2016 report), 4, 229; foreign counterparts stronger/more effective, 7, 249–50 (*see also* foreign FOI laws; Right to Information (RTI) Rating); government secrecy legitimated, 5 (*see also* secrecy); impact on deliberative discussion, 15, 23–26 (*see also* deliberative discussion); mission not advanced by commercial and individual use, 80–81, 173; national security state overly deferred to, 22–23 (*see also* national security; national security agencies); overclassification of documents, 22, 146, 168; a poor fit for commercial and individual uses, 81–83; Pozen on FOIA's flaws, 128–29, 160n9, 206 (*see also* Pozen, David E.); Scalia on FOIA as superfluous, 135–36, 137; written documents avoided, 202. *See also* transparency: drawbacks
due diligence firms, 77
due process, 50n59, 51n69, 82

Echeverría, Luis, 235
economy, FOIA and regulation of, 15–20
Ecuador, 277, 279, 284, 297

education, public, 179
EEOC, 78–80, 82
effectiveness of FOIA, 3–4; claims of ineffectiveness, 136, 148; contributions to public information, 148–50; dependent on civil servants, 142–46, 154; expansion of state secrecy despite FOIA, 52–53; FOIA a poor fit for commercial and individual uses, 81–83; FOIA's mission not advanced by commercial and individual use, 80–81, 83–85, 173; and GWOT accountability, 136, 137–38, 148–53 (*see also* Global War on Terror); institutional leverage, 150–53; news media interests well served, 85; optimality, 154–56; partial disclosures, 148–49; popularity of FOIA, 263; potential for state communication of information assumed, 65–66; proposed alternatives for commercial/individual use, 81–83, 86; response times, 19, 82, 85, 92, 206, 229; robustness of a broad regime, 153–54; "uneven" effectiveness, 8. *See also* benefits of FOIA; use of FOIA
E-FOIA Amendments (1996), 172, 273
Eisenhower, Dwight D., 25, 56
Electronic Frontier Foundation, 140, 164n49
Electronic Privacy Information Center (EPIC), 140, 149, 164n49
El Salvador, 277, 279, 284–85, 295, 299
email, 120, 199, 200, 201; Clinton emails, 125, 176
Emerson, Thomas I., 58–61, 66, 68n17
enforcement: of federal FOIA, 52–53, 97; of state FOI laws, 97–98

enforcement of FOIA. *See also* courts; litigation; Supreme Court

environmental agencies, state. *See* state environmental agency FOI logs

environmental policy, 193

Environmental Protection Agency (EPA): commercial FOIA requests, 19, 76; cost-benefit analysis of proposed Clean Power Plan Rule, 194–95, *194*; Greenhouse Gas Inventory, 193; Kwoka's analysis of FOIA logs from, 100, 103 (*see also* Kwoka, Margaret B.); media FOIA requests, 103, *105*, 111, 121–23; MyProperty online tool, 81; output vs. input transparency, 187–88; Pennsylvania FOI logs compared with EPA logs, 104, *104*, *105*; website mirrored, 163n41. *See also* Pruitt, Scott

EPIC, 140, 149, 164n49

Equal Employment Opportunity Commission (EEOC), 78–80, 82

Erkkilä, Tero, 275

Eskridge, William, 62

executive branch: agency opposition to FOIA based on faith in executive branch rationality/authority, 26–27; cabinet, 271; and the enforcement of constitutional rights, 61; executive privilege and FOIA, 24–26, 58, 62; FOIA compliance dependent on presidential signals, 126; FOIA coverage limited, 7 (*see also* exemptions to FOIA); monitoring from the inside (*see* Inspectors General); political accountability, 73–74; president's ability to withhold information on national defense and foreign policy, 22; president's

administrative prerogative over executive branch secrets, 56; veto of public interest override, 236. *See also* federal agencies; president, U.S.; *and specific presidents and administrations*

Executive Order 10501, 21. *See also* national security

exemptions to FOIA, 14, 226, 228–29; agency review process and, 229–30; binary test and judicial review, 231–32; courts lacking authority re, 227; Exemption 1 (classified/national security information), 20–23, 25, 146, 195, 257, 267nn31, 33 (*see also* national security); Exemption 2 (material related to agencies' internal personnel rules and practices), 17; Exemption 3 (material withheld under other statutes), 17, 95, 96, 236, 241, 257, 267n30; Exemption 4 (information provided in confidence), 18; Exemption 5 (deliberative discussions), 25–26, 95, 237, 239, 267n33 (*see also* deliberative discussion; executive branch: executive privilege and FOIA); Exemption 6 (private personal information), 141, 195, 229–30, 232, 235, 267n33; Exemption 7 (investigatory material for law enforcement purposes), 17–18, 141, 229–30, 232, 235; Exemption 8 (information related to regulation/supervision of financial institutions), 18, 237, 267n33; Exemption 9 (geological information; oil wells), 18, 95, 258, 267n33; first-person FOIA requests and, 83; government malfeasance exception, 237; invoked for GWOT-related requests, 141; national security exemptions, 20–23; public-interest balancing test needed, 227–28, 235–38 (*see also under* reforming FOIA); RTI Rating and, 257–58; types of exemptions, 17–18. *See also* denial of FOIA requests

exemptions to state FOI laws, 95–96

expectations gap paradox, 167, 169, 177–81, 182

expertise paradox, 167, 168–69, 172–77

extraordinary rendition, 140, 142–43. *See also* Global War on Terror

FBI, 136, 137, 146, 149–50, 152, 160n10

FDA. *See* Food and Drug Administration

Federal Advisory Committee Act (1972), 51n63

federal agencies: annual FOIA reports, 87, 111–12; chief data officers, 225n49; civil servants and secrecy, 138, 143–45; courts' deference to withholding by, 4, 64–65, 142, 145, 148, 155, 231–32, 240, 267n31; distrust of the public and FOIA opposition, 27–28; executive privilege and FOIA opposition, 24–26; faith in executive branch's judgement revealed by FOIA opposition, 26–27; FOIA compliance dependent on law-abiding civil service, 145–46; FOIA compliance dependent on presidential signals, 126; FOIA logs, 76, 86–87, 100, 121; FOIA opposed on grounds of cost, 23–24; FOIA review process, 229–30; and GWOT initiatives (*see* Global War on Terror); and the IG system,

169 (*see also* Inspectors General); importance of record-keeping, 138; improving FOIA process through performance analytics, 219; material related to internal personnel rules and practices exempted from FOIA, 17; meaning of FOIA shaped by opposition of, 14–15, 28 (*see also* Clark, Ramsey: memorandum); and misdirected FOIA requests, 256; and open data policies, 191–93, 210 (*see also* open data); opposition to FOIA generally, 13–15, 23, 28; patterns in media FOIA requests at, 120–23 (*see also* news media and FOIA); proactive (affirmative) disclosure suggested, 128–29; public scrutiny deemed detrimental to operations of, 24; regulation of the economy and FOIA, 15–20; request types categorized, 100; response times for FOIA requests, 19, 82, 85, 92, 206, 229; withholding of information by, 4, 226, 229–31, 260 (*see also* denial of FOIA requests). *See also* civil servants; executive branch; national security agencies; use of FOIA; *and specific agencies and departments*

Federal Bureau of Investigation. *See* FBI

Federal Communications Commission, 17

Federal Highway Administration, 121

Federalist Papers, 135

Federal Labor Relations Authority, 121

Federal Register, 207

Federal Reserve Board, 16

Federal Trade Commission (FTC), 84, 121–22

fees: for federal FOIA use, 23–24, 84, 96–97, 100, 124, 170, 173, 256; for foreign RTI requests, 256; for state FOI law use, 94, 96–97, 110

Fenster, Mark, 311; chapter by, 6, 8, 52–70

Ferejohn, John, 62

Fine, Glenn, 180

Fink, Katherine, 311; chapter by, 7, 8, 9, 91–115

Finland: Brazil compared with, 281–82; cabinet, 271; Corruption Perception Index score, 297; geopolitical position, 275, 288n26; history of FOI measures in, 251, 274, 275; media in, 271, 275; transparency-as-monitoring paradigm in, 269, 274–75

First Amendment: campaign to establish Press Clause as shield, 54; corporate rights under, 36, 45n16; Cross on the right to know and, 55 (see also Cross, Harold); Emerson on the right to know and, 58–60 (see also Emerson, Thomas I.); Meiklejohn on the right to information and, 67n6; as negative right, 35, 37, 44nn6, 8, 10; positive right to information not guaranteed, 34, 37–39, 48nn43, 46, 253–54. See also freedom of religion; freedom of speech; freedom of the press

first-person FOIA requests, 8, 75, 78–81; assistance not provided, 255–56; equal right of access, 27; immigration-related requests, 78, 79, 82; need for records poorly served by FOIA, 81–83; as percentage of overall requests, 124; proposed alternatives, 81–82, 86. See also state

FOI laws: first-person requests; and specific agencies

"fishbowl" concerns, 23–26. See also deliberative discussion

Flint, Michigan, water supply, 91

Florida, 95, 103, 105, 106, 107, 108

FOIA: adversarial nature of, 269, 275, 286n3; amendments (see amendments to FOIA); appeals (see courts; litigation; and specific cases); basic features/terms, 2, 3, 14, 52; benefits and positive impacts (see benefits of FOIA); canonicity, 2; costs (see costs of FOIA); and democracy (see democracy); denial of requests (see denial of FOIA requests); drawbacks and negative impacts (see drawbacks of FOIA); effectiveness (see effectiveness of FOIA); enacted, 2, 13–14, 177, 226, 228, 251; exemptions to (see exemptions to FOIA); federal agencies and (see federal agencies); fiftieth anniversary, 3, 73; foundations of (see foundations of FOIA); and the Global War on Terror (see Global War on Terror); Inspectors General and (see Inspectors General); interpreting FOIA's past and present, 3–4; as model for FOI measures elsewhere, 2–3, 249–52, 261–64 (see also foreign FOI laws; state FOI laws; and specific states and countries); news media and (see news media and FOIA); objective of, 73, 135, 226, 228; Officers, 170, 218, 219, 225n49; and open data policies (see open data); partisanship and, 273–74; as part of an "ecology of transparency," 136–47; quasi-constitutional status, 3–4, 6, 62–64; reforms (*see* amendments to FOIA; reforming FOIA); as "remedy" for absence of constitutional right to information, 39–42; requests and use of (*see* commercial FOIA requests; first-person FOIA requests; use of FOIA); respecting without romanticizing, 5–8; scope, 7, 254–55 (*see also specific areas of coverage or noncoverage*); stability and entrenchment of, 41; sustainability, 153–54; and transparency paradoxes (*see* transparency); U.S. RTI Rating and, 251, 254, 255–56, 257–58 (*see also* Right to Information Rating). *See also* government accountability; right to information; transparency

"FOIA, Inc." (Kwoka), 48n48, 51n69. *See also* Kwoka, Margaret B.

FOIA Improvement Act (2016), 26, 127–28, 217, 225n49, 273

"FOIA Is Broken" (2016 report), 4, 229

FOIA Mapper, 124, 174

FOIA Officers, 170, 218; FOIA Officers' Council, 219, 225n49

FOI laws, U.S.-style. *See* foreign FOI laws; state FOI laws

Food and Drug Administration (FDA): chain restaurants required to disclose calorie counts, 193; commercial FOIA requests, 19, 76, 77, 81, 89n22; FOIA costs, 24

Ford, Gerald, 22, 273

foreign FOI laws, 4, 249–64; appeals, 258–60, 264; exceptions and refusals, 256–58, 262, 264; fees, 256; FOIA as model, 2–3, 249–52, 261–64; growth of, 251; in Latin America,

9, 276–86, 277, 279, 289nn40–41, 290n56 (*see also specific countries*); promotional measures, 260–61, 262; public interest balancing tests, 234–35; requesting procedures, 255–56; response time limits, 252; right of access (constitutional or statutory), 253–54, 262, 263–64; RTI as fundamental right, 253–54, 264, 266n20; sanctions and protections, 260, 262; scope, 254–55, 262, 264. *See also* Right to Information Rating; *and specific countries*

Foundations for Evidence-Based Policymaking Act (2017), 212, 223n29

foundations of FOIA (historical and conceptual): Administrative Procedure Act (1946), 14, 48n48, 52, 55, 226, 228; agency and White House opposition generally, 13–14 (*see also* federal agencies); agency distrust of the public, 26–27; campaign to establish a FOI law, 6, 53–58, 67nn6, 9; Clark memorandum, 17–18, 21, 23; Emerson's views on the right to know, 58–60; FOIA as administrative act, 52–66; FOIA as part of group of transparency and accountability reforms, 166; FOIA enacted, 2, 13–14, 177, 226, 251; key elements/terms of FOIA, 2, 3, 14, 52; meaning of FOIA shaped by agencies' opposition, 14–15, 28 (*see also* exemptions to FOIA; federal agencies); national security and, 8, 20–23 (*see also* national security); negative and positive rights (generally), 34–37, 42–43, 44nn6, 8, 10, 44–45n12, 45nn16, 18;

foundations of FOIA (historical and conceptual) (*continued*)
objective of FOIA, 73, 135, 226, 228; presumption of disclosure created, 14; regulation of the economy and FOIA, 8, 15–20; right to information not constitutionally guaranteed, 37–39, 48nn43, 46, 253–54, 296; Rumsfeld as sponsor, 158; statutory vs. constitutional approach to access to information, 39–43, 48n47, 50n57, 53–66; title, 57–58; transparency as impediment to policymaking, 8, 23–26

Fox, Vicente, 283

freedom of information. *See* FOIA; foreign FOI laws; right to information; Right to Information Rating; state FOI laws; transparency; *and headings related to FOIA, such as* costs of FOIA

Freedom of Information Act. *See* FOIA; *and headings related to FOIA, such as* use of FOIA

"Freedom of Information Beyond the Freedom of Information Act" (Pozen), 50n59, 159n7, 160n9, 163n42. *See also* Pozen, David E.

freedom of religion, 35, 36, 39–40, 44nn6, 8, 45n16. *See also* First Amendment

freedom of speech, 35, 36, 44n10, 45n16, 46n22, 190. *See also* First Amendment

freedom of the press: and famine, 156, 190; as fundamental right, 266n20; and leaked/stolen information, 37, 47n36; Liebling on, 46n28; right to information not constitutionally guaranteed, 37–39, 48nn43, 46 (*see*

also right to information); value of constitutional guarantee, 266n21. *See also* First Amendment; news media; news media and FOIA

Freedom of the Press Act (1766; Sweden), 251, 269. *See also* Sweden

Freedom or Secrecy (Wiggins), 54

Free Speech and Unfree News (Lebovic), 54. *See also* Lebovic, Sam

Frum, David, 164n48

FTC, 84, 121–22

Galka, Max, 124, 125, 174

Gannett Co. v. DePasquale, 47n41

Gannett New Jersey Partners, LP v. County of Middlesex, 109

Gellhorn, Walter, 66

General Services Administration (GSA), 16, 27–28, 217. *See also* data.gov

Georgia, 93, 101, 110

Gerstein, Josh, 164n49

Gideon v. Wainwright, 35, 37

Ginsberg, Tom, 62–63

Global Impunity Index, 298, 299

global positioning system (GPS), 190–91

Global War on Terror (GWOT), 135–56; failure of concealment efforts, 142–45; FOIA and institutional leverage, 150–53; FOIA disclosures crucial to public understanding of, 6; FOIA exemptions invoked, 141; FOIA requests related to, 139–40; FOIA's role in GWOT accountability, 136, 137–38, 148–53; institutional checks and balances and, 137–38; internal investigations, 149–50, 160–61n18; pathologies of,

155; prerequisite knowledge for
FOIA requests, 140–45; record-
keeping crucial for accountability,
138. *See also* Rumsfeld, Donald
government. *See* civil servants;
Congress; courts; deliberative
discussion; executive branch;
federal agencies; government
accountability; president, U.S.;
regulatory state; *and specific
departments and agencies*
government accountability: agency
opposition to FOIA and, 17;
bureaupathology paradox and,
167, 168, 169–72, 181; and the
expectations gap paradox,
167, 169, 177–81, 182; and the
expertise paradox, 167, 168–69,
172–77, 181; FOIA's role in GWOT
accountability, 136, 137–38, 148–53
(*see also* Global War on Terror);
interrelatedness of transparency and,
167; monitory tools, 166 (*see also*
FOIA; Inspectors General (IGs);
state FOI laws); output transparency
and, 192 (*see also* output
transparency); oversight interests
well served by FOIA, 85; public vs.
nonpublic loci of accountability,
178–79. *See also* corruption; federal
agencies; FOIA; foreign FOI laws;
state FOI laws; transparency
GPS system, 190–91, 211
Granier, Andres, 308n20
Grassley, Charles, 73
GSA. *See* General Services
Administration
Guantanamo prison, 139–42, 144–51,
160–61n18. *See also* torture and
torture documents

Guatemala, 275, 277, 279, 285, 297
*Guide to the Freedom of Information
Act* (DOJ, 2015), 25
GWOT. *See* Global War on Terror

Habitat for Humanity, 119
Hamdan v. Rumsfeld, 150
Hamilton, James T., 311; chapter by, 6,
8–9, 116–31
Hammitt, Harry, 97–98
harm test, 94, 252n14, 267n33
Health, Education, and Welfare,
Department of (HEW), 15–16, 23
Heitkamp, Heidi, 171
Hellerstein, Alvin, Judge, 147, 150
The Hill (newspaper and website), 122
Hilliard, Nadia, 311; chapter by, 5, 9,
166–86
Hinchcliffe, Kelly, 125
historical foundations of FOIA. *See*
foundations of FOIA
historical record, learning from,
200–201
Hohfeld, Wesley, 34–35
*The Hollow Hope: Can Courts Bring
About Social Change?* (Rosenberg),
49n55
Honduras, 277, 279, 284, 296, 297,
299
Horowitz, Michael, 171
Houchins v. KQED, 38, 42
House Report on FOIA, 14, 17, 23. *See
also* Clark, Ramsey: memorandum
Housing and Urban Development,
Department of (HUD), 119
"How a Tip About Habitat for
Humanity Became a Whole
Different Story" (Rochabrun), 119
Hungary, 253, 254–59, 261
Huvelle, Ellen Segal, 147

ICE. *See* Immigration and Customs
Enforcement
IGs. *See* Inspectors General
illegal wiretapping, 140, 141
Illinois, 94, *103, 105, 106, 107, 108*
immigration: detainees' identities
revealed by INS, 143; enforcement
policies, 156–57, 163nn43–44; FOIA
as tool for rights advocates, 157,
163n43; FOIA requests related to,
78, 79, 82
Immigration and Customs
Enforcement (ICE), 78, 79, 157,
163n44
Immigration and Naturalization
Service (INS), 143
impunity, 294, 298–302, 299, 308n20
INAI (Mexico's information
commissioner), 282, 283, 284, 285–
86, 296, 299, 307n16
inclusion, 271–72, 273
India, 234, 253–61, 271, 295
Indiana, *103, 105, 106, 107, 108*
individuals, use of FOIA by. *See* first-
person FOIA requests
Indridason, Indridi, 271
information, interpretation of, 174–76.
See also expertise paradox
information, right to. *See* right to
information
information access: big data, 118,
174–77, 215; in consensus systems,
271–72; desirability of, 39, 48–49n49;
expertise needed for access/
interpretation, 172–77, 181 (*see also*
expertise paradox). *See also* open
data; proactive disclosure
information collection, FOIA
exemptions related to, 17–18
information resellers, 19, 78–79, 123

Information Security Oversight Office,
146, 155
information volatility, 142–43
INPUT (information reseller), 123
input transparency, 188, 189, 196–204
INS, 143
InsideClimate News, 109
Inside EPA, 122
Inside Washington Publishers, 122
Inspectors General (IGs):
bureaupathology paradox and,
169–72, 181; costs, 169–70;
departments/agencies with, 138;
DOJ IG's investigations/reports
on GWOT practices, 143, 149;
and the expectations gap paradox,
177–81, 182; expertise paradox and,
172–77, 181; IG system established,
155–56, 169, 177; Inspector General
Act(s) and reforms, 169, 170, 180;
publishing of reports/reviews by,
171, 174–75; relationship between
FOIA and, 167–68; role, duties,
authority, and independence, 138,
167, 171, 180
insurance underwriting firms, 80
intelligence agencies. *See* CIA; FBI;
Global War on Terror; illegal
wiretapping; National Security
Agency; torture and torture
documents
Interior Department, 18, 121
Internal Revenue Service (IRS), 214,
224n40
International Open Data Charter, 213
Internet, 142–43. *See also* data.gov
interrogation techniques, 144–45, 146,
160–61n18. *See also* Abu Ghraib
abuses; Guantanamo prison; torture
and torture documents

investigative journalism and FOIA, 116–31; benefits and costs, 123–25; FOIA use in prize-worthy investigative reporting, 117–20; frequency of FOI requests, 6, 116, 121, 123, 129; local vs. other/niche media, 116, 121–22, 123; patterns in FOIA requests at federal agencies, 120–23; working with large data sets, 118, 175–77. *See also* news media and FOIA

Investigative Reporters and Editors (IRE), 99, 116, 117–20, 129. *See also* investigative journalism and FOIA

"Invisible Wounds" (KARE-11 story), 119–20

Iowa, 96

IRE. *See* Investigative Reporters and Editors

Ireland, 234, 297

IRS, 214, 224n40

Japan, 234, 297

Johnson, Lyndon B., 14, 25, 57. *See also* Johnson administration

Johnson administration, 13–15. *See also* federal agencies

journalism. *See* investigative journalism and FOIA; news media; news media and FOIA; news media and state FOI laws

Judicial Watch, 140, 164n49

judiciary. *See* courts; litigation; Supreme Court

Justice Department. *See* Department of Justice

Kansas, 109

KARE-11 (NBC affiliate), 119–20

Keane, John, 166

Kessler, Gladys, Judge, 147

Kitrosser, Heidi, 68n23

Kreimer, Seth F., 311; chapter by, 5, 6, 9, 135–65; on the "ecology of transparency," 3; on framing FOIA requests, 140, 173

Kwoka, Margaret B., 311; chapter by, 9, 73–90; commercial FOIA requests analyzed, 19, 51n69, 100; commercial sector found to be primary FOIA users, 6, 8, 50n59, 51n69, 92, 173; concerns over private-interest requesters, 7; noncommercial requester statistics, 103; proactive release of information suggested, 111

Labor Department, 16, 27, 187, 188, 210

Lahav, Pnina, 266n21

Lakeland Times (Wisconsin newspaper), 108

Landmark Communications, Inc. v. Virginia, 47n36

Latin America: FOI (RTI) laws, 9, 276–86, 277, 279, 289nn40–41, 43, 290n56; news media, 282, 283–84, 290n59, 301; Panama Papers scandal, 304; Right to Information (RTI) Ratings, 275, 277, 284, 289n40, 295. *See also specific countries*

Law, David, 249

Law of Public-Private Associations (Mexico, 2011), 303–4

leaks, 37, 47n36, 143–45, 158

learning from mistakes, 200–201

Lebovic, Sam, 312; on the campaign for FOI legislation, 54; chapter by, 5, 8, 13–33

Lehrer, Tom, 145

Leonard, William, 146

Leopold, Jason, 125

Liebling, A. J., 46n28
Lincoln, Abraham, 153
Lindstedt, Catharina, 271
Lithuania, 215
litigation: FOIA statistics, 240; GWOT-related litigation, 146, 150–51, 152, 161n28; immigration policy-related FOIA lawsuits, 157; judicial enforcement of FOIA, and its limitations, 230–32; under New Jersey's OPRA and common law, 234; news media FOIA lawsuits, 124–25; over DOJ Blue Book, 239; over nonprofit tax returns, 214, 224n40; procedure for FOIA litigation, 232; public interest balancing and, 237–41; Shell Oil lawsuit, 18. *See also* courts; Supreme Court; *and specific cases*
Long, Edward, 13
Louisiana: environmental FOI logs analyzed, *103, 105, 106, 107, 108–9, 108*; FOI law, 93–94
loyalty, 196–97
Lozoya, Emilio, 304

Madison, James, 187, 201
majoritarian political systems. *See* contestation systems
"Making Open and Machine Readable the New Default for Government Information" (Executive Order, 2013), 211
Malamud, Carl, 214, 224n40
Markey, Ed, 163n40
Marshall, Adam A., 312; chapter by, 6, 9, 226–46
Marshall, Thurgood, Justice, 196–97
Maryland, 96
Massachusetts, 99

Mayer, Jane, 160–61n18
McCarthy, Joseph ("Joe"), 25, 56
McCarthy, Mary, 144–45
McCraw, David, 124
medical records, 80, 83, 120
"Medicare Unmasked" series (*Wall Street Journal*), 118–19
Meiklejohn, Alexander, 67n6
Mendel, Tony, 312; chapter by, 7, 9, 249–68; on the growth of RTI laws, 251; on the U.S.'s RTI Rating, 251
Merck, 77
Mexico: anti-corruption efforts, 293–94; Corruption Perception Index score, 296–98, 297; disconnect between transparency and corruption in, 293–305, 309–10n39; Global Impunity Index score, 298, 299; inequality in, 301–2, 308n24; news media, 283–84, 301; political system, 284, 285; public vs. private sector in, 302–4. *See also* Mexico's FOI (RTI) laws
Mexico's FOI (RTI) laws: adoption date, 253, 283; appeals, 258–59, 277, 283, 290n60, 295; breaking the anti-public sector bias, 302–4; compliance, 279, 283, 291–92; constitutional reforms, 283, 291; corruption and, 9–10, 293–305; costs, 283, 307n16; de jure attributes, 277; and a democratic-expansive understanding of transparency, 293–94; exceptions and refusals, 257–58, 295; executive/presidential impunity, 299–301, 308n20; FOI as contestation, 282–83; INAI and, 282, 283, 284, 285–86, 296, 299, 307n16; as international gold standard, 7; national, unified portal, 283; party

politics and, 283, 284, 294, 300, 304; political dynamics behind, 283–84; as poster child of transparency reform, 291; and the private sector, 302–4; promotional measures, 261, 295, 296; public interest balancing, 234–35, 294; requesting procedures and fees, 255–56, 295; request statistics, 283; response times, 296; right of access, 254, 277, 295, 296; RTI Rating, 253, 266n19, 277, 282, 295; sanctions and protections, 260, 295, 298–302; scope of RTI framework, 254–55, 277, 282–83, 295, 302–4; Transparency and Access to Government Information Law, 234–35; U.S. FOIA contrasted with, 285–86, 295, 296. *See also* Mexico

Michener, Gregory, 312; chapter by, 5, 7, 9, 269–90

Michigan, 92, 94, 99

Milwaukee Journal Sentinel, 108

Mine Safety and Health Administration (MSHA), 121–22

Mississippi, 96, *103*, *105*, *106*, *107*, *108*

Missouri, 93

Moldova, 296, 297

Moneyball for Government (Nussle and Orszag, eds.), 212

Montana, 93

Morisy, Michael, 120. *See also* MuckRock

Moss, John, 14–15, 21, 25, 55–56

Moyers, Bill, 57

MuckRock (website), 101, 120

Nadler, Janice, 50n55

NASA (National Aeronautics and Space Administration), 17, 23

National Action Party (PAN; Mexico), 294, 300, 304

National Archives and Records Administration, 127, 138, 217. See also *Federal Register*

National Day Laborer Organizing Network (NDLON), 157

National Endowment for the Humanities, 127

National Environmental Policy Act, 188

National Freedom of Information Coalition, 99, 218

National Institute for Transparency, Access to Information and Personal Data Protection (INAI; Mexico). *See* INAI

National Labor Relations Board, 16–17, 18, 84

National Science Foundation, 127

national security: abuses of National Security Letters, 152; difficulty of maintaining deep secrets, 142–45; Emerson on exempting from right to know, 58; FOIA critiqued for failure to meaningfully police, 85; FOIA exemption covering, 20–23, 25, 146, 195, 257, 267nn31, 33; leaks of classified information, 143; open data and, 225n50. *See also* Global War on Terror; national security agencies; secrecy

national security agencies, 4, 20–21. *See also* CIA; Department of Defense; FBI; NSA

National Security Agency (NSA), 75, 141

National Security Archive (independent watchdog group), 73, 140, 174

Naurin, David, 271

navigability: of FOIA process, 52, 209 (*see also* expertise paradox); output transparency and, 191, 192, 203

Nebraska: environmental FOI logs analyzed, *103, 105, 106, 107, 108;* FOI law, 98, 99

negative impacts of FOIA. *See* drawbacks of FOIA

negative rights (liberties), 35–37, 44nn6, 8, 10, 44–45n12, 45nn16, 18. *See also* First Amendment; *and specific rights*

neoliberalism: and corruption, 303; and self-government, 156–58, 163nn43–44, 164n48–49, 164–65n50

Nevada, 95, *103, 103, 105, 106, 107*

New Hampshire, 93

New Jersey, 93, 97, 99, 109, 233–34

news media: campaign to establish Press Clause as shield, 54; in Finland, 271, 275; First Amendment rights, 35; FOI advocacy by, 273; free press and famine, 156, 190; government support for reporting tools and data, 127; and input transparency, 196–97, 200, 201; in Latin America, 282, 283–84, 290n59, 301; and the public interest, 123–24, 127; and public trust, 182. *See also* freedom of the press; news media and state FOI laws

news media and FOIA, 116–31; benefits and costs of FOIA, 123–25, 126; COINTELPRO exposed, 160n10; declining use of FOIA, 8, 116, 121, 123, 129; digital-first outlets' use of FOIA, 125; EPA vs. DHS request filings, 111; FOIA requests by local vs. other media, 116, 121–22, 123; FOIA's ineffectiveness lamented by journalists, 136; and the Global

War on Terror, 139–40, 141 (*see also* Global War on Terror); journalists expected to be main users of FOIA, 8, 83, 209; journalists' use of FOIA important, 74; lawsuits, 124–25; media support for FOIA, 6, 41; media use as percentage of FOIA requests, 75; news media interests well served by FOIA, 85; patterns in FOIA requests at federal agencies, 120–23; press campaign and the establishment of FOIA, 53–57, 67n19; purpose of FOIA requests, 116, 118; reform proposals to improve FOIA usefulness for journalists, 116, 126–29 (*see also* freedom of the press); response times and, 19; use outweighed by commercial sector requests, 4, 18–19, 84–85, 92, 123, 124; working with large data sets, 118, 174–77. *See also* investigative journalism and FOIA; news media and state FOI laws

news media and state FOI laws: journalists' use of state FOI laws, 91, *101–9, 102, 103, 104, 106, 107, 108,* 111–12; media use of FOI laws declining, 8; own state's FOI laws often deemed worst by local journalists, 99; press guides to state FOI laws, 93; shield laws and press access to information, 49n49; state FOI requests vs. FOIA requests, 91

New York (state): environmental FOI logs analyzed, *103, 105, 106, 107, 108;* FOI law, 94, 96, 97

New York City, 119, 210

New York Times, 102, 107, 122–23, 124

New York Times Co. v. United States (Pentagon Papers case), 47n36, 156

New Zealand, 234, 249, 297

NGOs. *See* nongovernmental organizations

Nicaragua, 277, 279, 284, 285, 297, 299

Nigeria, 253–61

Nixon, Richard, 25, 56, 62, 155, 200

Nixon v. United States, 62

No Child Left Behind Act, 179

no-fly lists, 142

noncitizens: FOIA requests by, 78, 79, 143–45; post–September 11 dragnet detentions of, 143, 148. *See also* immigration

nongovernmental organizations (NGOs), 95, 140. *See also specific organizations*

nonprofit groups, 75

Nordic countries, FOI laws in. *See* Finland; Sweden

Nordin, Jonas, 275

North Carolina, 99, 110

North Dakota, 101, 102, 103, 105, 106, 107, 107, 108

Novak, Matt, 163n41

Noveck, Beth Simone, 6–7, 312; chapter by, 5, 9, 206–25

NSA, 75, 141

Nuclear Regulatory Commission, 121

Obama, Barack, 3–4, 73, 211, 273

Obama administration: Chief FOIA Officers (CFOs) created, 170; FOIA costs (2016), 124–25; and the FOIA Improvement Act, 273 [*see also* FOIA Improvement Act (2016)]; and immigration enforcement, 156–57; open government policy, 191–93, 196, 208, 211–12; RIAs under, 193–94

Occupational Safety and Health Administration (OSHA), 193

Odebrecht, 300, 304, 309–10n39

Office of Government Information Services (OGIS), 97, 112, 217–18, 261, 267n36, 296

Office of Information and Regulatory Affairs, 198

Office of Information Policy, 217–18

Office of Legal Counsel, 26–27

Office of Management and Budget (OMB): Open Government Directive (2009), 191, 192–93, 195, 196, 208, 209, 211 (*see also* open data); voter fraud allegations, FOIA request re, 164–65n50

Offices of Inspectors General. *See* Inspectors General (IGs)

OGIS. *See* Office of Government Information Services

Ohio, 103, 105, 106, 107, 108

oil wells, 18, 95, 258, 267n33

Oklahoma, 96

O'Neill, Onora, 177–79, 181

open data, 6–7, 206–25; appeal and usefulness to government, 210, 212; challenges of using, 219–20; data.gov (website), 191–92, 195–96, 211, 217, 222–23n19, 224n43; defined, 206–7; and FOIA, 208–10, 213–20, 221, 230; high-value data, 191–93, 196, 209–10, 214–15, 224n42–43; history of the U.S. open government data movement, 211–13; internationally, 193, 212–13, 215; open data organizations, 218–19; as policy-making tool, 212, 223n28; political commitment to, 213; principles for design, 214–16, 224n42–43; promise of, 206–8, 220–21; recommendations, 216–20, 225n50; right of action, 214; state and local open data policies/

open data (*continued*)
   projects, 207, 209, 210, 216, 222n11;
   users/beneficiaries, 209–10. *See also*
   data
OPEN Government Act (2007), 97,
   273. *See also* Office of Government
   Information Services
OPEN Government Data Act (2016),
   212, 223n28
Open Government Directive (OMB
   memorandum, 2009), 191, 192–93,
   195, 196, 208, 209, 211. *See also* open
   data
Open Government Partnership
   Declaration, 193, 212–13
open government policies, 191–93,
   195–96, 208. *See also* open
   data; OPEN Government Act;
   OPEN Government Data Act;
   Open Government Directive;
   Open Government Partnership
   Declaration
opposition to FOIA. *See* federal
   agencies
Oregon, 95–96, 103, 105, 106, 107, 108
Organization of American States'
   Rapporteurship on Freedom of
   Expression, 278
OSHA, 193
Oster, Jan, 266n20
output transparency, 187–96, 203, 204

PAN (Mexico), 294, 300, 304
Panama, 275, 277, 279, 296, 299
Panama Papers, 304
Paraguay, 277, 279, 284, 296, 297, 299
party politics: and Brazil's FOI system,
   280–82; and Mexico's FOI system,
   283, 284, 294, 300, 304; and U.S.
   FOIA, 273–74, 287n17

PATRIOT Act, 139, 140, 141, 147, 149, 152
PEC National Security News Service,
   122
Peltz-Steele, Richard, 256–57
PEMEX, 304, 309–10n39
Peña Nieto, Enrique, 299–300, 301, 303
Pennsylvania: environmental FOI logs
   analyzed, 103–4, 103, 104, 105, 106,
   107, 108; FOI enforcement, 97; FOI
   law, 93, 95, 96, 99
Pentagon Papers case, 47n36
The People's Right to Know (Cross),
   54–55, 57–58, 60, 67n6. *See also*
   Cross, Harold
personal data. *See* first-person FOIA
   requests; privacy
Peru, 275, 277, 279, 297
political systems and transparency, 269–
   90; cabinet composition, 270, 271;
   contestation systems vs. consensus
   systems, 269–76, 284–85, 286nn1–2;
   at the local level, 272; transparency-
   as-leverage paradigm, 269–71,
   272–74, 276, 278–86; transparency-
   as-monitoring paradigm, 269–72,
   274–76, 278–82, 285–86
Pope, James S., 21, 22, 54, 56
popularity of FOIA, 263
positive impacts of FOIA. *See* benefits
   of FOIA; government accountability
positive rights, 35–36, 42–43. *See also*
   right to information
Post, Robert C., 45n16
Pozen, David E., 312; on the adversarial
   aspect of FOIA, 286n3; and
   affirmative (proactive) disclosure,
   128, 172; on the arbitrariness of
   FOIA application, 50n59; Congress
   and leakers as alternatives to FOIA,
   158; on "due process" benefits of

FOIA use, 82; on the flaws of FOIA, 128–29, 160n9, 206; on FOIA as "reactionary," 128–29, 136; on FOIA as super-statute, 63; on FOIA costs, 125, 136, 159n7; on FOIA's (in) efficiency, 85; on judicial deference, 267n31; on the negative impacts of FOIA, 5, 163n42; on secrecy and the First Amendment, 69n23; on U.S. system as "agent controlled transparency," 271

president, U.S.: administrative prerogative over executive branch secrets, 56, 267n31; Emerson on president's privilege, 58; and FOIA compliance broadly, 126; not covered by FOIA, 168, 254. See also executive branch; and specific presidents and administrations

Presidential Records Act, 203

press, freedom of. See freedom of the press

PRI (Mexico), 283, 294, 304

prisoner abuse. See Abu Ghraib abuses; Guantanamo prison

privacy: balancing public interest with personal privacy interest, 229–30, 232, 235–36; Cross skeptical re privacy rights/interests, 54; FOIA Exemption 6 covering personal information, 141, 195, 229–30, 232, 235, 267n33; free citizens' need for, 5; open data and personally identified information, 225n50; right to information vs. privacy rights, 48–49n49, 58–59

private entities and the private sector: constitutional liberties not guaranteed against restriction by, 35, 44–45n10; corporate speech and

religious freedom rights, 36, 45n16; in Mexico, 302–4; not subject to FOIA requests, 7, 20, 255; requiring output transparency from, 193. See also commercial FOIA requests

privileges, law of, 49n49

proactive disclosure: as active transparency, 270 (see also transparency: active vs. request-based); benefits of, 188, 191–95; in Brazil, 280; of IG reviews, 171; open data policies (see open data); physical/digital infrastructure required for, 172; as regulatory approach, 193; required by FOIA amendments, 172; suggested as alternative/addition to FOIA, 81–83, 86, 111–12, 128–29. See also information access

product recalls, 192

ProPublica, 119, 122, 125

Pruitt, Scott, 163n40

public disclosure, fear of, 155

public interest: agency understanding/distrust of the public, 27–28; audit culture and, 179; balancing personal privacy interest with, 229–30, 232, 235–36; discretionary FOIA exemptions and, 229–30; and the global war on terror, 6 (see also Global War on Terror); journalism's role, 123–24, 127; output transparency and, 188; and political accountability, 73–74. See also citizens; public interest override; public trust in government

public interest override (balancing test): examples, 233–35; foreign RTI/FOI laws and, 258; needed for FOIA, 227–28, 233; revising FOIA

public interest override (balancing test) (*continued*)
to provide, 6, 233, 235–41. *See also* public interest
public relations approach to transparency reform, 293
Public.Resource.org v. U.S. Internal Revenue Serv., 214, 224n40
public sector, bias against, 7, 302–4
public trust in government, 20, 177–78, 179, 181–82
Putnam, Robert, 177

Rakoff, Jed, Judge, 147
records: federal FOIA logs, 76, 86–87, 100, 121; importance of record-keeping, 138; requested under FOIA (*see* commercial FOIA requests; first-person FOIA requests; Global War on Terror; news media and FOIA); state FOI request logs, 92, 96, 100–111. *See also* federal agencies
red tape, 170
Reducing Over-Classification Act (2009), 168
Reforma (Mexican newspaper), 283
reforming FOIA: costs of implementing reforms, 128; government output, increasing disclosure of, 6 (*see also* output transparency); proactive (affirmative) disclosure suggested, 81–83, 86, 111–12, 128 (*see also* proactive disclosure); proposals to improve FOIA usefulness for journalists, 116, 126–29; public-interest balancing test needed, 6, 227–28, 235–38; in relation to open data, 216–20; shrinking FOIA sensibly, 85–87. *See also* amendments to FOIA

Regional Alliance for Freedom of Expression and Information, 278, 289n43
regulatory impact analyses (RIAs), 193–95, 194
regulatory state: agency concerns re FOIA impact on, 15–18 (*see also* federal agencies); cost-benefit analysis of regulations, 193–95, 194; information disclosure as regulatory approach, 193; input transparency and, 197–204; negative impacts of FOIA on, 19–20, 85, 156, 163n42; positive impacts of FOIA on, 156–58, 163nn43–44, 164n48–49, 164–65n50
Reinventing Government initiative, 170
religion, freedom of. *See* freedom of religion
Republican Party, and FOIA, 13
requests under FOIA. *See* commercial FOIA requests; first-person FOIA requests; Global War on Terror; news media and FOIA; use of FOIA
reselling of FOIA'D information. *See* information resellers
response times, 229–30; for federal FOIA requests, 19, 82, 85, 92, 206, 229; for state FOI requests, 94, 111
Revolutionary Institutional Party (PRI; Mexico), 283, 294, 304
Richmond Newspapers, Inc. v. Virginia, 47n41
rights (generally), 34–37, 42–43, 44n6, 44–45n12, 45n20. *See also* Constitution, U.S.; freedom of religion; freedom of speech; freedom of the press; negative rights (liberties); positive rights; right to information

Right to Information (RTI) Rating, 9, 250, 252–53; appeals, 258–60, 264, 295; exceptions and refusals, 257–58, 262, 264, 295; of Latin American countries, 275, 277, 284, 289n40, 295; promotional measures, 260–61, 262, 295; requesting procedures, 255–56, 295; right of access, 253–54, 262, 263–64, 266nn20–21, 295; sanctions and protections, 260, 262, 295; scope, 254–55, 262, 264, 295; of specific countries, 253, 266n19, 295 (*see also specific countries*); U.S. FOIA law and, 251, 254, 255–56, 257–58, 259, 260–61. *See also* right to information

right to information (RTI; right to know), 34–51; common law right, 233–34; Cross's campaign for, 54–58, 67n6; desirability of, 39, 49n51; Emerson on, 58–60; established through FOIA, 63, 228–29; exceptions key to RTI laws, 256–58; feasibility of state transparency, 65–66; FOIA's global influence, 2–3, 249–52, 261–64 (*see also* foreign FOI laws; *and specific countries*); as fundamental right, 253–54, 264, 266n20; and government action in the public interest, 190; limited to FOIA's statutory terms, 52; not guaranteed in U.S. Constitution, 8, 37–39, 48nn43, 46, 253–54, 296; Pope on, 56; vs. privacy rights, 48–49n49; statutory vs. constitutional approach, 39–43, 48n47, 50n57, 53–66. *See also* FOIA; foreign FOI laws; Right to Information (RTI) Rating; transparency; *and headings related to FOIA; and in specific countries*

Rochabrun, Marcelo, 119
Rosenberg, Gerald N., 49–50n55
Rousseff, Dilma, 280, 281, 282
rule of law, 252, 266n18
Rumsfeld, Donald, 13, 158

sale of FOIA'd information, 19, 78–79, 123
Salovaara-Morring, Inka, 275
Sandoval-Ballesteros, Irma Eréndira, 312; chapter by, 7, 9–10, 291–310
Sarney, José, 281
Scalia, Antonin, Justice, 64–65, 135–36, 137, 160n10
Schauer, Frederick, 312; chapter by, 6, 8, 34–51; on FOIA's impact/status, 63
Schlei, Norman, 27
Schmidt, Derek, 109
Schudson, Michael, 5–6, 313
SEC. *See* Securities and Exchange Commission
secrecy: APA exemptions, 67n8; courts not historically a bulwark against, 64–65; difficulty of maintaining deep secrets, 142–45; expansion of state secrecy despite FOIA, 52–53; FOIA exemptions and (*see* exemptions to FOIA); government tendency documented by Cross, 54–55; GWOT initiatives shrouded in, 140–42, 152, 155 (*see also* Global War on Terror); knowledge of secrets a prerequisite for FOIA requests, 140–45, 173; legitimated by FOIA, 5; national security need for secrecy acknowledge by transparency advocates, 21; and political negotiation/decisionmaking, 5; president's

secrecy (*continued*)
administrative prerogative over
executive branch secrets, 56; and
the rise in FOIA denials, 227. *See
also* national security; national
security agencies; *and specific
agencies*
Securities and Exchange Commission
(SEC): BrightScope and, 210;
commercial FOIA requests, 19, 76,
77, 81, 124; concerns about FOIA,
16; EDGAR database website, 81;
FOIA costs and fees, 124
Sen, Amartya, 156, 190
Sentelle, David B., Judge, 239
separation of powers, 24–25. *See
also* executive branch: executive
privilege and FOIA
Shell Oil, 18
Sierra Leone, 295, 296, 297
Slovakia, 215
social (welfare) rights, 36–37, 46n31
Society of Professional Journalists, 73
Sontag, Deborah, 102, 107
South Carolina: environmental agency
FOI logs analyzed, 103, 104–6, 105,
106, 107, 108; journalists and FOI
law, 99, 103
South Dakota, 96
South Korea, 249, 253–59, 261
Specter, Arlen, 180
speech, freedom of. *See* freedom of
speech
State Department: "Dissent
Channel," 155; and FOIA costs,
23; and hypothetical discussions
on air quality regulations, 198;
independent Inspector General,
138; initial concerns re FOIA, 20–21;
review of H. Clinton emails, 176;

Vice News request for Clinton
emails, 125
state environmental agency FOI logs,
100–111, 102, 103, 104, 105
state FOI laws, 3–4, 91–115;
background, 92–93; commercial
requests, 94, 104, 104; common
critiques (ratings and effectiveness),
98–100; differences between, 93–98;
enforcement, 97–98; exemptions,
95–96; fees, 94, 96–97, 110;
first-person requests, 63, 93–94;
journalists' perception of, 99;
media use of, 91, 101–9, 102, 103,
104, 106, 107, 108, 111–12 (*see also*
news media and FOI laws); open
data policies/projects, 209, 222n11;
proactive release of information
suggested, 111–12; record retention
requirements, 96; request logs, 92,
100–111; response times, 92, 94,
99, 111; success stories, 91; used for
political purposes, 110–11
statutory approach to FOI, 39–42, 43,
62–64. *See also* right to information:
statutory vs. constitutional approach
statutory exemptions to FOIA. *See*
exemptions to FOIA: Exemption 3
Stern, Carl, 160n10
Stewart, Potter, Justice, 34, 38
Sunlight Foundation, 174
Sunstein, Cass R., 313; chapter by, 6, 9,
187–205; on FOIA reforms, 26; Sen
invoked, 156
Supreme Court: and access to criminal
trials, 38, 47n41; and the balancing
of public and personal privacy
interests, 235–36; book about, 196–
97; and the consideration of non-
state entities' actions as state actions,

45n12; and executive privilege, 62;
on the First Amendment and the
right to information, 38, 253–54;
and GWOT-related cases, 142, 148,
150–51, 161n28; on the judiciary's
role in FOIA cases, 231; lawmaking
by litigation, 42, 51n61; and the
national security exemption, 22;
rulings' effect on public attitudes,
40, 49–50n55; and states' right to
restrict FOI requests to residents, 93.
See also specific cases
Sweden, 249–50, 251, 261, 269, 297

Taguba, Antonio, Gen., 144, 150
Tauberer, Joshua, 175
Tennessee, 93, 95
Tennessee Valley Authority (TVA), 121
Texas: environmental agency FOI logs
analyzed, 103, 105, 106, 107, 108,
109; open data law, 209
torture and torture documents, 139, 140,
143–45, 146, 149–51, 152, 160–61n18
Townsend, Katie, 313; chapter by, 6, 9,
226–46
Toxic Release Inventory (TRI), 193
trade secrets, 95. *See also* exemptions
to FOIA
Transactional Records Access
Clearinghouse (TRAC), 85
transparency: 20th-century wave of
reforms, 166; abuse not always
prevented by, 158; and accountability,
192 (*see also* government
accountability); active vs. request-
based, 270–71 (*see also* use of FOIA);
benefits, 188–89, 190–93, 195–96,
197–201, 202, 203–4; bureaupathology
paradox and, 167, 168, 169–72, 181;
constitutional vs. statutory approach,
39–43, 48n47, 50n57, 53–66;
Constitution and, 34, 135 (*see also*
Constitution, U.S.); costs, 189, 194,
197, 200–204 (*see also* costs of FOIA);
democratic-expansive understanding
of, 292–94; and democratic values,
182 (*see also* democracy); disconnect
between corruption and, 294–302
(*see also* corruption); drawbacks
(deleterious impacts), 5, 168–69
(*see also* drawbacks of FOIA; *and
specific areas of impact*); expectations
gap paradox and, 167, 169, 177–81,
182; expertise paradox and, 167,
168–69, 172–77, 181; feasibility
of, 65–66; FOIA and optimality,
154–56; FOIA as part of an "ecology
of transparency," 136–37, 148,
152, 153–58 (*see also* Global War
on Terror); FOIA compliance
dependent on presidential signals
re, 126; input transparency, 188, 189,
196–204; internal watchdogs, 149,
168 (*see also* Inspectors General);
interrelatedness of accountability
and, 167; in Latin America (*see*
Latin America); monitory tools, 166
(*see also* FOIA; foreign FOI laws;
Inspectors General (IGs); state FOI
laws); negative impacts of, 48–49n49;
Obama administration and, 191–93
(*see also* Obama administration);
output transparency, 187–96,
203, 204; oversight key to, 286;
proactive release of information
suggested, 128–29; and regulation
of the economy, 15–20; resistance
to, 305, 305n2 (*see also* denial
of FOIA requests); respecting
without romanticizing, 5–8;

transparency (*continued*)
  robustness of a broad FOIA regime,
  153–54; transparency-as-leverage
  paradigm, 5, 269–71, 272–74, 276,
  278–86; transparency-as-monitoring
  paradigm, 269–72, 274–76, 278–82,
  285–86; transparency skepticism, 1
  (*see also* Pozen, David E.); Trump
  administration and, 126. *See also*
  FOIA; foreign FOI laws; government
  accountability; open data; open
  government policies; political
  systems and transparency; proactive
  disclosure; right to information;
  secrecy; state FOI laws; transparency
  advocates; *and headings related to*
  FOIA
transparency advocates, 21, 52–54.
  See also news media and FOI
  laws; transparency; *and specific*
  organizations and individuals
"Transparency and Public Policy:
  Where Open Government Fails
  Accountability" (Cohen), 128
Transparency International, 215, 296,
  297–98t
Transportation, Department of, 121,
  187, 188
Treasury Department, 20–21, 23, 27
Trinidad and Tobago, 296, 297, 299
Trump, Donald, 159n7, 165n50, 213
Trump administration, 126, 193–94, 213
trust, public. *See* public trust in
  government
Tunisia, 253–61

United Kingdom, 234, 235, 297
United States Citizenship and
  Immigration Services (USCIS),
  229–30

United States v. Alvarez, 44n10
University of Florida, Marion Brechner
  Citizen Access Project, 99–100
Uruguay, 277, 279, 281
USA PATRIOT Act. *See* PATRIOT
  Act
U.S. Citizenship and Immigration
  Services, 82. *See also* immigration
USDA Food Safety and Inspection
  Service (FSIS), 121–22
use of FOIA: adversarial requests,
  209 (*see also* transparency:
  transparency-as-leverage paradigm);
  anyone empowered to use,
  regardless of standing, 14, 139,
  173, 254; assistance not provided,
  255–56; bureaupathology paradox
  and, 169, 170, 172, 181; expectations
  gap paradox, 177–78, 180–81;
  expedited processing requirements,
  141; expertise required, 172–77, 181;
  fees, 23–24, 84, 96–97, 100, 124, 170,
  173, 256; FOIA request logs, 76,
  86–87, 100, 121; during the GWOT
  (*see* Global War on Terror);
  information withheld (*see* denial
  of FOIA requests); journalists
  expected to be main requesters, 8
  (*see also* news media and FOIA);
  making effective FOIA requests,
  140, 141, 173–74; by the news
  media, 74–75; by NGOs, 140; by
  noncitizens, 27, 78, 79; prerequisite
  knowledge and, 140–45, 173; private
  vs. public benefits, 80–81; proposed
  alternatives, 81–82; reasons for
  FOIA requests, 75–76 (*see also*
  commercial FOIA requests; first-
  person FOIA requests); request
  statistics (2014–15), 170; single

electronic portal called for, 217; usage rates, 3, 10n2, 74, 170, 206. *See also* news media and FOIA; *and specific agencies*

U.S. House of Representatives Committee on Oversight and Government Reform. *See* "FOIA Is Broken" (2016 report)

Utah, 105, 106, 107, 108

Valdez, Jesús, 301

Venezuela, 275, 277, 279, 284, 298

Versteeg, Mila, 249

Veterans Health Administration (VHA): first-person FOIA requests, 78, 80, 82, 83; Minneapolis VA hospital troubles, 119–20

Vice News, 125

Virginia, 93

voter fraud allegations, 164–65n50

Wall Street Journal, 106, 118–19

Washington (state), 96, 103, 105, 106, 107, 108

Washington Post, 144, 175–76

Watergate: IG system born in wake of, 155–56, 177; "institutionalized checks and balances" and, 136, 137; Nixon's abuse of executive privilege, 136, 156, 200; transparency increased after, 137, 149, 274

weather data, 211

West Virginia: environmental FOI logs analyzed, 103, 105, 106–7, 106, 107, 108; FOI law, 96

whistleblowing, 143–45

White, Lee, 13

White House Counsel's Office, 219

Wiggins, James Russell, 54

wiretapping, illegal, 140, 141

Wisconsin, 103, 105, 106, 108, 108

Woodward, Bob, 196–97

Worker's Party (Brazil), 280. *See also* Rousseff, Dilma

workplace safety, 193

World Wide Web Foundation, 213, 215

Wyoming, 97

Youm, Kyu Ho, 313; chapter by, 7, 9, 249–68